Praise for *The Tyranny of Clichés*

"Whether you love or hate what he has to say, you've got to love the way Jonah Goldberg says it."
—Senator Marco Rubio

"In *The Tyranny of Clichés*, Jonah Goldberg draws on both the Great Books and popular culture to rip apart the commandments of the modern therapeutic society. Behind all the feel-good, come-together mush, Goldberg finds the age-old driving forces—power, profit, and plain old ignorance. The dissection of these feel-good assumptions is informal and light, but the conclusions are deadly serious—and chilling."
—Victor Davis Hanson, senior fellow, Hoover Institution, Stanford University

"What can one say to the self-proclaimed 'independent' who never has nor ever will vote other than Democratic; or to the wise soul suggesting, of any conflict at all, 'the truth must lie somewhere in between'? Mr. Goldberg reminds us that one must stand up and demand of the muddled and supine either an absolute declaration of their principles and acknowledgment of the results of actions having flowed therefrom or a straightforward admission of their intransigence in refusing a concise reply." —David Mamet, bestselling author of *The Secret Knowledge*

"Everyone says 'think for yourself' but very few people do. In *The Tyranny of Clichés*, Jonah Goldberg reveals how we've become trapped by ideas we think we understand but don't. A must read."
—Vince Vaughn, actor and producer

"Straw man down! In the PC prison yard of accepted political thought, Jonah Goldberg has just shivved progressivism. Bold, brilliant, and bursting with humor, every page of *The Tyranny of Clichés* is right on the money. If you thought *Liberal Fascism* was good, wait till you read *The Tyranny of Clichés*—it is fantastic!"
—Brad Thor, bestselling author of *Full Black*

SENTINEL

THE TYRANNY OF CLICHÉS

Jonah Goldberg's first book, *Liberal Fascism*, was a number one *New York Times* bestseller. A fellow at the American Enterprise Institute, he is the founding editor of the *National Review Online*. He is also a *Los Angeles Times* columnist, a Fox News contributor, and a member of the board of contributors at *USA Today*. *The Atlantic* named him one of America's fifty most influential commentators. He lives with his family in Washington, D.C.

The Tyranny of Clichés

How Liberals Cheat in the War of Ideas

JONAH GOLDBERG

Sentinel

SENTINEL
Published by the Penguin Group
Penguin Group (USA) Inc., 375 Hudson Street,
New York, New York 10014, USA

USA / Canada / UK / Ireland / Australia / New Zealand / India / South Africa / China
Penguin Books Ltd, Registered Offices: 80 Strand, London WC2R 0RL, England
For more information about the Penguin Group visit penguin.com

First published in the United States of America by Sentinel, a member of Penguin Group (USA) Inc., 2012
This paperback edition with a new afterword published 2013

THE LIBRARY OF CONGRESS HAS CATALOGED THE HARDCOVER EDITION AS FOLLOWS:
Goldberg, Jonah.
The tyranny of clichés : How liberals cheat in the war of ideas / Jonah Goldberg.
pages cm
Includes bibliographical references and index.
ISBN 978-1-59523-086-7 (hc.)
ISBN 978-1-59523-102-4 (pbk.)
1. Liberalism-United States. 2. Cliches—United States. I. Title.
JC574.2.U6G64 2012
320.51'30973—dc23
2012000535

Printed in the United States of America
1 3 5 7 9 10 8 6 4 2

Set in Bell MT Std
Designed by Spring Hoteling

To the memory of my big brother, Josh

CONTENTS

Introduction . . . 1

1: Ideology . . . 19

2: Pragmatism . . . 39

3: No Labels . . . 59

4: Dogma . . . 66

5: Separation of Church and State . . . 76

6: Power Corrupts . . . 84

7: Diversity . . . 89

8: Social Darwinism . . . 100

9: Slippery Slope . . . 114

10: Dissent . . . 122

11: Social Justice . . . 131

12: Community . . . 147

13: Ten Guilty Men . . . 153

14: Living Constitution . . . 159

15: Let Them Eat Cake . . . 171

16: Violence Never Solves Anything . . . 180

17: Middle Class . . . 190

18: Science . . . 204

19: Youth ... 220

20: Ounce of Prevention ... 228

21: The Catholic Church ... 234

22: Spiritual but Not Religious ... 256

23: Understanding ... 261

24: Democracy and Unity ... 268

Afterword ... 279

Acknowledgments ... 289

Notes ... 291

Index ... 315

INTRODUCTION

[W]e have now sunk to a depth at which the restatement of the obvious is the first duty of intelligent men.

—George Orwell, *The Collected Essays, Journalism and Letters of George Orwell*

The Cowardice of Clichés

According to legend, when George Will signed up to become a syndicated columnist in the 1970s, he asked his friend William F. Buckley, Jr.—the founder of *National Review* and a columnist himself—"How will I ever write two columns a week?" Buckley responded (I'm paraphrasing), "Oh it will be easy. At least two things a week will annoy you, and you'll write about them."

Buckley was right. Annoyance is an inspiration, aggravation a muse. That which gets your blood up, also gets the ink—or these days, pixels—flowing. Show me an author without passion for what he holds to be the truth and I will show you either a boring writer or someone who misses a lot of deadlines, or both. Nothing writes itself, and what gets the writer to push that boulder uphill is more often than not irritation with those saying wrong things righteously.

Which brings me to this book. There's a kind of argument-that-isn't-an-argument that vexes me. I first started to notice it on university campuses. I've spoken to a lot of college audiences. Often, I will encounter an earnest student, much more serious looking than the typical hippie with open-toed shoes and a closed mind. During the Q&A session after my speech he will say something like "Mr. Goldberg, I may disagree with what you have to say, but I will defend to the death your right to say it."

Then he will sit down, and the audience will applaud. Faculty will nod proudly at this wiser-than-his-years hatchling under their wings. What a glorious moment for everybody. Blessed are the bridge builders.

My response? Who gives a rat's ass?

First of all, my right to speak never was in doubt. Indeed, I'm usually *paid* to speak. Besides, I've given my speech already and we're in Q&A time: Shouldn't you have told me this beforehand? Second, the kid is almost surely lying. He'll take a bullet for me? *Really?*

Clichés like these are a way to earn bravery on the cheap, defending principles you haven't thought through or perhaps only vaguely support. Or, heck, maybe he really would leap on a grenade so I could finish talking about how stupid high-speed rail is. But it still doesn't matter, because mouthing these sorts of clichés is *a way to avoid arguments, not make them.* Imagine a defendant is on the stand. The prosecutor peppers the accused murderer with questions: "Is this your chain saw?" "Where were you on the night of the fourteenth?" "How can you explain the victim's foot being in your freezer?"

Now imagine the defendant responds, "Sir, I may disagree with your line of questioning, but I will defend to the death your right to ask me these things."

The prosecutor, if he's not a complete idiot, will say, "Stop trying to change the subject and answer my questions."

One last point about "I may disagree with you but I'll defend to the death your right to say it": The implication is not only that the person saying this is brave but also that we live in a society where such bravery might be required. It suggests that speech is so imperiled that bloodshed may be called for. Many people think that's how the phrase was born, that they're echoing the heroism of some forgotten general or martyr willing to sacrifice himself for the liberty of others. But they're wrong.

The phrase is usually attributed to Voltaire, though he didn't say it. It was a historian's paraphrasing of Voltaire's attitude, written more than a century after Voltaire's death. And even his attitude wasn't all that sincere. According to S. G. Tallentyre's *The Friends of Voltaire,* the quote traces itself back to a hullaballoo over a book by the French utilitarian philosopher Claude Adrien Helvétius. The book, *De l'Espirit*, argued that people behave the way they do out of a desire to avoid pain or feel pleasure. Or something. Regardless, everyone hated the book, including Voltaire (who took offense at what he considered to be the author's insufficient praise of him). *De l'Espirit* was essentially ignored until the dauphin, the king's son, read it. He *really* hated it. Parliament ended up banning it. The tome was even publicly burned. Like a 1920s book that could catapult its sales by being BANNED IN BOSTON!, *De l'Espirit* became a sensation, translated into every language imaginable, precisely because it had been censored. And, just as suddenly, Helvétius became a celebrity, his salon instantly fashionable.

"What the book could never have done for itself, or for its author, persecution did for them both," writes Tallentyre.

> The men who had hated it, and had not particularly loved Helvétius, flocked round him now. Voltaire forgave him all injuries, intentional or unintentional. "What a fuss about an omelette!" [Voltaire] had exclaimed when he heard of the burning. How abominably unjust to persecute a man for such an airy trifle as that! "I disapprove of what you say, but I will defend to the death your right to say it," was his attitude now.[1]

So it is an expression born in glibness—defined by vanity, not courage—and it remains so to this day.

This is only one example of the problem. I started to notice that the same thing happens in writing, on TV, in books; people invoke these clichés as placeholders for arguments not won, ideas not fully understood. At the same time, the same sorts of people cavalierly denounce far more thought-out positions because they're too "ideological." Indeed, in America, we train people to be skeptical of ideology. College students in particular are quick to object with a certain gotcha tone: "That sounds like an ideological statement."

Such skepticism doesn't bother me. Indeed, I encourage it. The problem is that while our radar is great at spotting in-bound ideological statements, clichés sail right through. People will say "It is better that ten men go free than one innocent man go to jail" and *then stop talking*, as if they've made an argument simply by saying that. They will take the slippery slope at face value. They'll say "Diversity is strength," as if it means something, and "Violence never solved anything," as if that were not only plausible but so true that no further explication is required.

"We are only as free as the least free among us" they'll proclaim, misquoting Martin Luther King, Jr., or Elie Wiesel, or was it Captain Jean-Luc Picard? But of course, this isn't even remotely true. It is a very nice thing to say. It's a noble thing to try to live by. But it's in no meaningful sense true. Rather, it is the sort of thing people assert in the hopes that it will win them uncontested ground in an argument.

Sometimes the problem is simply lazy thinking. But in other cases the lazy thinking merely creates the vulnerability for radical thinking. Some incredibly ideological ideas simply ride into your head like the dream spelunkers in the movie *Inception*—setting up, working their way through your programming—all because they're wrapped in the protective coating of clichés.

One Man's Terrorist Is Another Man's Freedom Fighter

Consider "One man's terrorist is another man's freedom fighter." This is surely true if the other man is a terrorist sympathizer—or an idiot. Otherwise the expression is simply pithy hogwash.

It's difficult to think of a cliché that more baldly disqualifies ostensibly intelligent people from the pretense of moral or intellectual seriousness. It is simply absurd to contend that because people may argue over who is or is not a terrorist that it is therefore impossible to make meaningful distinctions between terrorists and freedom fighters. The reasoning behind the expression, which entered the discourse in the late 1970s and was inadvertently popularized by Ronald Reagan in 1986 (he rejected it completely, of course) is the sort of thing that would make any good Jesuit weep. It steamrolls through a fallacious comparison, confusing ends and means on its way, in order to celebrate both relativism and nihilism and elevate moral cowardice as an intellectual principle.

First of all, one could certainly argue that terrorists and freedom fighters need not be opposites. Freedom fighters can also be terrorists and vice versa (the abolitionist John Brown comes to mind as someone who may have been both). Certainly, fighting for freedom does not absolve you from the crime of terrorism, anymore than blowing up a pizza parlor automatically means you're fighting *for* freedom. To suggest otherwise is to say that a freedom fighter is morally immune to condemnation for his actions. Surely there are freedom fighters who reject terrorism and hence deserve our praise. Shall we say George Washington, Martin Luther King, and Mohandas Gandhi are indistinguishable from Osama bin Laden or Timothy McVeigh? Most reasonable and decent people would recoil at the suggestion that Martin Luther King was a terrorist (some liberals might interject at this point and say, "Aha, but some Southern racists said exactly that about King!," to which a sane person would respond, "Yes, and they were wrong to do so").

If one man pushes an old lady in front of an oncoming bus and another man pushes an old lady out of the way of an oncoming bus, to borrow Bill Buckley's famous puncturing of moral equivalence arguments, it will not suffice to say that they are both the sorts of men who push old ladies around. But this is precisely the sort of thing some people are up to when they say "one man's terrorist is another man's freedom fighter." Their notion of freedom fighter hinges on a slew of deeply ideological and dangerous positions that have been hidden away. What freedom is al Qaeda fighting for exactly? Hamas? The freedom to lock women away in burlap sacks, crush homosexuals, and throw acid in the faces of children?

Calling these murderers freedom fighters reminds me of G. K. Chesterton's line about how "the word 'good' has many meanings: For example, if a man were to shoot his grandmother at a range of five hundred yards, I should call him a good shot, but not necessarily a good man.'"[2]

The other people who use the phrase are simply frightened, either intellectually or physically. The news editor for the BBC says, "It is the style of the BBC World Service to call no one a terrorist, aware as we are that one man's terrorist is another one's freedom fighter." The global news editor for Reuters: "We all know that one man's terrorist is another man's freedom fighter, and that Reuters upholds the principle that we do not use the word terrorist."

Some news organizations justify such policies on the grounds that they need to keep their reporters safe in parts of the world where, er, terrorists/freedom fighters hold sway. And so they refuse to call the men who slit the throats of children, blow up their local kebab stands, and the like "terrorists." That might sound, if not exactly brave (no "defending to the death" reporters' rights to tell the truth here, you will notice), then at least reasonable. But when terrorists attacked the London subway, suddenly these same organizations saw nothing wrong with calling terrorists what they are.

Again, if you want to call members of Hamas freedom fighters, be my guest. We'll have an argument about it. What really offends is a morally obtuse, radically ideological phrase being bandied around as a way not to start an argument but to close one off. "Oh, let's not argue about Israel. Besides, we all know one man's terrorist is another man's freedom fighter." It's a way of getting in your cheap shot just before the bell.

The Center

Other clichés aren't so much pithy phrases used in everyday debate. They're shorthand concepts, clichéd ways of thinking massaged into the way we see the world. Ideological marketers, such as Republican focus group maven Frank Luntz or Berkeley linguist George Lakoff, are paid huge sums of money to invent new buzzwords and phrases that are a fraction as successful as some of these ancient clichés. People at least understand that Luntz's phrase "death tax" has some political and ideological salesmanship to it. I'm writing about many of the clichés and concepts that are more central to how we think about politics, in part because we take them as apolitical and mainstream.

How central are they to our thinking? Well, how about the word "center"? First of all, you do realize that whenever we talk about "the center" in politics it's entirely metaphorical, right? There is no way to actually take the geographic concept of centrality and apply it literally to, say, abortion, or gay rights, or gun control. There's a certain Goldilocks bias to discussions of politics: If Papa Bear's porridge is too hot and Mama Bear's is too cold, then Baby Bear's is always just right. It must work the same way in politics, right? Centrists, moderates, middle-of-the-roaders, independents: They all suffer from variants of this confusion. The "extreme" Republicans argue ten. The "extreme" Democrats argue for zero. Therefore the smart, sensible, reasonable position must be five.

Well, the Wahhabis want to kill all the gays and Jews. The Sufis don't want to kill any gays or Jews. So the moderate, sensible position must be to kill just the gays, but not the Jews. Or maybe the other way around? Or half of all the gays and Jews? Or maybe all the gay Jews? Or maybe we can have a very complicated compromise along the lines of last year's debt-ceiling negotiations, where a small percentage of Jews are killed now and we kill a larger number of gays in the out years?

The point is that sometimes the extreme is 100 percent correct while the centrist position is 100 percent wrong. But there's something about being not as wrong as one of the other extremes that some people just find so enticing and seductive. I just don't get it.

If I say we need one hundred feet of bridge to cross a one-hundred-foot chasm that makes me an extremist. Somebody else says we don't need to build a bridge at all because we don't need to cross the chasm in the first place. That makes him an extremist. The third guy is the centrist because he insists that we compromise by building a fifty-foot bridge that ends in the middle of thin air? As an extremist I'll tell you that the other extremist has a much better grasp on reality than the centrist does. The extremists have a serious disagreement about what to do. The independent who splits the difference has no idea what to do and doesn't want to bother with figuring it out.

And yet we hear constantly how independents who borrow a little from this side and borrow a little from that side are somehow more politically sophisticated and mature than the straight-line thinkers of the left and the right. But here's the thing: The straight-line thinkers tend to think in a straight line not because they are hidebound and close-minded and clinging to an ideological agenda. They tend to think in a reasonably straight line because they've worked out a reasonably consistent way of seeing the world. The independents and moderates who just grab stuff from this shelf, then from that shelf, like a panicked survivor of the dawn of the dead grabbing what he or she can from the supermarket before the zombies spot her, do not value consistency at all.

The self-appointed guardians of this notion that the center is also the high ground can mostly be found in the press corps, because it validates their own self-conception. They honestly believe they are neither left nor right, and so they value the politicians and voters who share this political ambivalence.

More critical, this nonsense survives because our politics are arranged so as to ensure it. When a country is evenly divided ideologically, it's unavoidable that those who split the differences will get outsized power, because they are the ones who will ultimately decide elections. That's why every general election that begins with "securing the base" ends with the presidential candidates begging for support from centrists, independents, moderates, and the folks who really put the *asses* in masses: the Undecideds. Every four years after each presidential debate we are forced to listen to interviews with undecided voters who not only can't see major differences between the political candidates (which, by that point in the campaign, means they've not been paying attention), but who also think the reason we have presidential debates is to give tutorials on policy minutiae: "I didn't hear enough about what they would do about education." "I wanted more specifics about what [So-and-so] would do for someone like me." Meanwhile, back in their election headquarters the anchors nod along as if this reaction is damning of the candidates' performances.

After an eighteen-month campaign, all of the informed, conscious, and ideologically consistent voters have already made up their minds. All that's left are the undecided centrists, who actually think they have the more sophisticated and serious position; their indecision comes, actually, by virtue of the fact they've either not paid much attention until way too late in the game, or more simply, they're a**holes who think they must be at the center of the universe.

Now, hold on, I mean that in a fairly literal way. Let me explain.

The notion that the center is a place of privilege and esteem has a very long pedigree, with a somewhat anti-Catholic bias. For instance, you may have heard that Galileo dealt the Western, Christian mind a devastating blow when he confirmed that Copernicus was right. The Earth revolves around the Sun and the Sun is at the center of the solar system (i.e., heliocentrism). John Bargh, a scientist at Yale, says in David Brooks's *The Social Animal* that Galileo "removed the Earth from its privileged position at the center of the universe." The *Britannica Concise Encyclopedia* tells us that the "[d]ethronement of Earth from the center of the universe caused profound shock." The less reliable but more relied upon Wikipedia agrees: "[T]he transition between these two theories met much resistance, not only from the Catholic Church, which was reluctant to accept a theory not placing God's creation at the center of the universe, but also from those who saw geocentrism as a fact that could not be subverted by a new, weakly justified theory." Get that? The Church opposed heliocentrism because it couldn't handle man's "dethronement" from the center of the universe; meanwhile, other, more sensible, opponents objected because they thought the science was weak. Inconceivable that the Church might have thought the science was weak, too.

This history has it exactly backward. The Church did not consider the "center of the universe" to be a place of privilege. That is a modern conceit. Before Copernicus the consensus among Western scientists and theologians was, in accordance with Aristotle, that the Earth was either at, or was, the anal aperture of the universe, literally.

In 1486, Giovanni Pico, a leading philosopher of the Italian Renaissance, penned his *Oration on the Dignity of Man*, commonly referred to as the manifesto of the Italian Renaissance. In it he observed that the Earth resided in "the excremetary and filthy parts of the lower world." Two centuries earlier, Thomas Aquinas concluded that "in the universe, the earth—that all the spheres encircle and that, as for place, lies in the center—is the most material and coarsest of all bodies." In Dante's *Inferno*, the lowest pit of Hell is at the exact center of the planet, which historian Dennis R. Danielson describes as the "dead center of the whole universe."[3]

Pre-Copernican cosmology, in short, didn't see the center of the universe as a place of privilege and esteem but as a lowly, dirty, filthy place. Think of it this way: The modern mind thinks in latitudes, left and right, forward and backward. The medieval mind saw things in terms of up and down. Aristotle observed that the heavier and coarser things tended to accumulate at the bottom, or center. As in the human body, the bowels and viscera are at the center. As you move up you reach the noble organ, the heart. And the mind resides at the top. The celestial heavens and stars were *above*. Humanity was *below*, in the coarse center. This was not simply or solely a Christian view. Moses Maimonides, the greatest of medieval Jewish philosophers, insisted that "in the case of the Universe . . . the nearer the parts are to the center, the greater is their turbidness, their solidity, their inertness, their dimness and darkness, because they are further away from the loftiest element, from the source of light and brightness."

Dennis R. Danielson, who has tracked the history of this myth, suggests that it begins with the seventeenth-century dramatist Cyrano de Bergerac. He claimed that pre-Copernican geocentrism was a testament to "the insupportable arrogance of Mankinde, which fancies, [*sic*] that Nature was only created to serve it." In 1686, the French writer Bernard le Bouvier de Fontenelle hailed Copernicus for taking the Earth and throwing it "out of the center of the World." According to de Fontenelle, Copernicus sought to "abate the Vanity of men who had thrust themselves into the chief place of the Universe."[4]

It took a long time to make a scientifically persuasive case that the Earth isn't the center of the universe and that it revolves around the Sun. If you can't sympathize with that, please stop referring to the rising and setting of the sun across our sky, since we are the ones moving, not it. The theological reason men stuck with the old scientific paradigm had nothing to do with arrogance and everything to do with humility.

And there's the rub. The real arrogance here is on the part of those who see the past as populated with unsophisticated bumpkins, as if ignorance of scientific truth is the same thing as stupidity. But if in fifty years it's discovered that there's life on Mars, does that mean future generations can look at us today and legitimately say, "Look at those idiots, they didn't even know there was life on Mars"?

We find the same sort of bias in glib assertions about "flat-earthism." We've all heard about how Columbus proved to the skeptics that the world was round (the basis for one of my favorite Bugs Bunny cartoons). It's not true, as we will see in a moment. But first of all, is it really so crazy that people five hundred or a thousand years ago might have thought the world was flat? Really? Cut some slack for the people who lived without powerful telescopes, satellites, and the rest for at least considering this a somewhat open question. Anyway, it's simply not true that medieval Christianity taught that the world is flat. This myth, like many others discussed later in this book, stems from the biases of Protestant historians in the nineteenth century, who were eager to paint the Catholic Church as a giant wet blanket on scientific and human progress (see Chapter 21, The Catholic Church). Hence the myth that the Church tortured and imprisoned Galileo for his confirmation of Copernicus's findings. There's a legitimate question of whether he was in a jail cell for three days—or not at all. But he certainly wasn't tortured. More important, the people who most ardently clamored for the Church to silence and punish Galileo were his jealous, lesser, scientific colleagues, not the theologians. When Galileo's heretical *Starry Messenger* was released, the Vatican threw a huge book party for him.[5]

"The principal truth to be drawn from the Galileo story is less dramatic than is the myth," Robert Nisbet wrote in his 1983 masterpiece *Prejudices: A Philosophical Dictionary*,

> but far more in accord with the emotions and institutional conditions that prevail today much as they did in the sixteenth century. Rivalry, jealousy, and vindictiveness from other scientists and philosophers were Galileo's lot, and they are not infrequently the lot of unorthodox minds in modern times. Anyone who believes that inquisitions went out with the triumph of secularism over religion has not paid attention to the records of foundations, federal research agencies, professional societies, and academic institutions and departments.[6]

In a similar vein, the legend that Giordorno Bruno was the "first martyr to science" is a myth as well. Bruno met with quite an ugly end, but it was not because of his scientific work; it was because he was an unrepentant theological heretic who denied the virgin birth and thought Jesus was a clever magician. Neither Galileo nor Bruno nor any scientists were punished for what they believed about astronomy.[7]

Often, what we think are the facts of the past are in reality simply reflections of what we want to believe about the present.

Hindsight Is 20/20

How often do we hear people say we must "get on the right side of history," as if they know their own history? "When they say it, what do people mean?" asks my *National Review* colleague Jay Nordlinger.

They may mean "my side," or "the good side," or "the side that posterity will smile on." People may be alluding to the ultimate triumph of liberal democracy. Or they may be alluding to the ultimate triumph of socialism, or a stricter form of collectivism. For generations, the Left has assumed that history marches with them: Get out of the way, or be crushed.

The phrase has what British historian Robert Conquest calls a "Marxist twang." The Marxists believed that history was predictable and unidirectional, so of course there must be a right side and a wrong side to it. The candle makers were on the wrong side, the lightbulb makers the right side. But history doesn't work like that. There were times when it was obvious that technology aided tyrants and there have been times—much like our own—when it seemed equally obvious that technology must liberate the individual. The truth is, it must do neither. As Richard Pipes tells Nordlinger, "The whole notion is nonsensical." To which Nordlinger adds, "History does not have sides, although historians do."[8]

Marxism surely contributed to the idea that there's a right side to history, but the chief culprit is the arrogance of the present (Marxism, one could say, is a subspecies of this arrogance). We look back on the past and see it as prologue to our moment in time. History becomes a movie for which we know the ending and we think the characters of yesteryear are fools for not seeing it, too. Like the idiot teenager who declares, "I'll search the attic" in a horror movie, we marvel at the stupidity of earlier generations.

This assumption that the past is stupid and the present is wise too often binds the modern mind. It is a form of "Whiggish" history that assumes time proceeds in a steady, recognizable forward progression. Hence the nonsensical phrase "hindsight is 20/20." No it's not. Indeed, it's hard to think of a more untrue phrase casually flung about in intelligent conversation. If hindsight is 20/20, why do historians disagree about, well, just about everything after the date and place of an event? If we could see the past with perfect clarity, married couples wouldn't argue about who started the argument. Shi'a and Sunni would never have split. Jews would all be Christians or Christians would all be something else. Everyone would agree on who was the greatest boxer who ever lived and that Yoko Ono broke up the Beatles. Economists would stop saying "on the other hand."

The Whiggish assumption in contemporary politics that today must be better than yesterday, this year more advanced than last year, this century wiser than the one that preceded it is held most dogmatically by so-called progressives. For them history is a vehicle with no reverse gear, and the engine that powers it is nothing more or less than the State. This is the hardened, metaphysical, dogmatic cliché that makes it possible for journalists to glibly describe any expansion of the government into our lives as a "step forward" or an "advancement" and any retrenchment of government as a step "backward." A Republican proposal of market-based reform always amounts to "turning back the clock." As discussed at length in a subsequent chapter, this is the core assumption behind the idea of the "living Constitution"—an idea that assumes with Hegelian orthodoxy that expansions of the State are the sine qua non of progress (see Chapter 14, Living Constitution).

One small example: During the recent debate over reforming Medicare, many liberals insisted that any backsliding amounted to a sacrilegious violation of a fundamental "covenant." Writing in *The New Republic*, Jonathan Cohn, a leading health care expert, quotes LBJ's Medicare law signing statement:

> "No longer will older Americans be denied the healing miracle of modern medicine," Johnson said at the signing ceremony. "No longer will illness crush and destroy the savings that they have so carefully put away over a lifetime so that they might enjoy dignity in their later years."

"Read those quotes carefully," Cohn advises us, "because they spell out the covenant that Johnson made with the American people on that day: A promise that the elderly and (certain groups) of the poor would get comprehensive medical insurance, no matter what."[9] Now I cannot and will not criticize Cohn for believing that the government should ensure that the truly needy and elderly receive medical care. That is an honorable, intellectually defensible position. Though I should at least mention that wanting the needy to receive health care does not necessarily require a vast expansion of the federal government. But my point isn't to debate the means to a desirable end.

No, the reason why I find Cohn's argument so useful is that it illustrates the progressive mind-set so perfectly. Cohn argues that LBJ made a covenant with the American people—a covenant is a sacred contract—

to ensure that the poor would henceforth and forever get comprehensive medical insurance. Here's the problem: Presidents cannot bind future presidents, never mind future Congresses. Any law can be revisited, any presidential decree may be rescinded. One would hope that Cohn would recognize this fact given that his magazine routinely argues that not even the Constitution itself should be considered permanently binding and restrictive (which is to say it shouldn't permanently bind or constrict progressives in ways they find inconvenient). What offends Cohn and his fellow progressives is the suggestion that any liberal victory once pocketed can ever be reversed. Laws and words have no binding power on future generations, but once Team Progressive puts points on the scoreboard, they can never come off. That is what is sacred, because *their* conception of history only goes in one direction.

This is the living, breathing heart of the progressive worldview. It is as ideological as any conviction can be. And that is fine. There is nothing wrong and a great deal that is right with having ideological convictions. What is offensive to logic, culturally pernicious, and, yes, infuriating to me is the claim that it is not an ideological tenet. Progressives lie to themselves and the world about this fact. They hide their ideological agenda within Trojan Horse clichés and smug assertions that they are simply pragmatists, fact finders, and empiricists who are clearheaded slaves to "what works."

Consider one largely bipartisan example of what I am talking about: competitiveness. For decades American presidents, Republican and Democrat, have invoked competitiveness as an excuse to intervene in the private sector. Often competitiveness means the exact opposite: protecting industries or firms that cannot compete. In the name of competitiveness we subsidize car companies or solar power companies—or shield them through tariffs—while claiming it is vital to do so to stay competitive.

But President Obama has lifted the rhetoric to new heights with all of his talk about "winning the future" (a phrase Newt Gingrich tried to corner some years earlier, so it must poll well). According to President Obama—and pop gurus like Thomas Friedman—the State must pick new industries and new products that will create the jobs of the twenty-first century. Like the ideological pilgrims who went to the Soviet Union and found "the future—and it works" (in Lincoln Steffens's memorable phrase), journalists like Friedman are feted in China and ride high-speed rail systems and come back saying we must adopt similar authoritarian or statist policies if we want to compete with China.

The vast majority of economists, on the left and the right, consider competitiveness—that is, economic competitiveness between nations—to be at least a deeply flawed if not completely worthless concept. Businesses compete, nations don't. If China was the victim of a horrendous plague or ravaged by a destructive civil war, America might benefit in terms of geopolitical status, force projection, etc., but it would be dealt a massive economic blow as well, having lost income from a vital trading partner. Or as Paul Krugman put it in his famous 1994 *Foreign Affairs* essay, "Competitiveness: A Dangerous Obsession" (these were the days when Krugman cared more about academic and intellectual rigor than journalistic bombast):

> [T]he moral is clear: while competitive problems could arise in principle, as a practical, empirical matter the major nations of the world are not to any significant degree in economic competition with each other. Of course, there is always a rivalry for status and power—countries that grow faster will see their political rank rise. So it is always interesting to *compare* countries. But asserting that Japanese growth diminishes U.S. status is very different from saying that it reduces the U.S. standard of living—and it is the latter that the rhetoric of competitiveness asserts.[10]

The appeal of competitiveness lies in its power as a buzzword, not as a serious concept. Business audiences like it, because they think in those terms and think governments should be run like businesses. More problematic, the public likes it because it is ultimately a base appeal to nationalism disguised as technocratic expertise. We can beat the Chinese by throwing money at certain industries! Implicit in this line of argumentation is the assumption that government officials are smarter than investors. It was this logic that empowered the Obama administration to throw billions into green energy white elephants like Solyndra.

There are policies that one could lump under the rubric of competitiveness that would actually help the United States of America become more affluent vis-à-vis other nations, but such policies aren't nearly as exciting for policy makers, because it is very difficult to take credit for their successes. A flatter, more progrowth tax policy, for example, would attract more investment and entrepreneurship. Spending on basic scientific research and education can be defended on grounds of competitiveness; so could more intelligent immigration policies. But such policies are defensible on more basic grounds: They're good for our economy and for our productivity.

But that's not the appeal of competitiveness. Industrial planners like competitiveness because they like industrial planning. They like spending money on dams and roads and windmills because there's a photo op at the ribbon cutting. They like to believe they are smarter and wiser than the free market economy, and if only we could put them in charge, they could impose a more rational, planned economic system. That is why Thomas Friedman wishes we could be "China for a Day," because in China planners are given command over the economy (why not "Nazis for a Day"?). Before there was Friedman and his man crush on Chinese communism there was the cabal of industrial planners—Kevin Phillips, James Fallows, Lester Thurow, et al.—of the 1980s and early 1990s, who were convinced that Japan's MITI—the Ministry of International Trade and Industry (renamed in 2001)—was needed to replace our outdated system. Phillips wrote in his *Staying on Top: The Business Case for a National Industrial Strategy*: "[B]usinessmen . . . must set aside old concepts of laissez-faire. . . . It is time for the United States of America to begin plotting its economic future."[11] Before then, in the 1960s it was the Whiz Kids who held that modern economics was too complicated to leave to voters and consumers. They inherited the argument from the New Dealers, who pushed for an "economic dictatorship" in the words of Stuart Chase. They, in turn, were standing on the shoulders of the progressive technocrats, who took their cues from the Soviet Union (and Woodrow Wilson), who insisted, in the words of Walter Lippmann, that we must abandon the "drift" of nineteenth-century laissez capitalism and adopt the "mastery" of economic planners. You can keep going, but the story is the same: arrogant intellectuals trying to win czarlike power over the economy with fake arguments that sound reasonable.

So that is what this book is about. It is about the clichés that have a tyrannical hold on our minds and the phrases that serve to advance ideological agendas that would expand and enhance the State's mastery over our lives. By no means are all expansions of the State tyrannical, but for all intents and purposes, all advances of tyranny are statist. These are the themes and convictions that inform the coming chapters. They informed my decision to include some clichés while ignoring others. The first few chapters are an attempt to flesh out this fundamental point, by coming to the defense of ideology properly understood.

I do not claim that the conservative mind isn't bound by clichés from time to time, or that my collection exhausts the subjects covered, never mind those not covered. But I would and do argue that conservatives are more honest about their indebtedness to ideology. We declare our principles and make our arguments more openly. My only humble hope is that what I write here helps people, conservatives and liberals alike, rethink the way they understand the world around them, and maybe enjoy themselves a bit in the process.

1
IDEOLOGY

Our blight is ideologies—they are the long-expected Anti-Christ!

—Carl Jung, *The Tibetan Book of the Great Liberation: Or the Method of Realizing Nirvana through Knowing the Mind*

I think President Obama is a committed, practicing nonideologue. He's consumed by neither tactics nor ideology. He is more concerned about outcomes than he is about process and categorizations.

—David Axelrod, *Politico*, April 24, 2009

On the way to his inauguration as the forty-fourth president of the United States of America, Barack Obama stopped in Baltimore to deliver a speech to tens of thousands of well-wishers.

"What is required," declared the president-elect, "is a new declaration of independence, not just in our nation, but in our own lives—from ideology and small thinking, prejudice and bigotry—an appeal not to our easy instincts but to our better angels."[1]

Far more revealing than anything he said in his inaugural address, Obama's comments in Baltimore capture not just the tone of his presidency—self-serving verbiage passing itself off as statesmanlike wisdom—but also reveal a great deal about the essence of American liberalism.

Let us look at, in reverse order, the four things from which the president says we must declare our independence. First there is bigotry. Fair enough. No reasonable person disputes that it would be nice if we could put bigotry behind us. And yet, it's worth noting that traditional bigotry was at its lowest point in American history, as evidenced not least by the fact that it had just elected the first black president, and by a significant margin.

Then there is prejudice. This is a word we all have been taught to despise as a lesser form of bigotry, if not a lazy synonym for it. But let us assume Obama means prejudice as a stepbrother of bigotry rather than as an identical twin. For if there's no difference between the words, his speechwriter should be flogged for wasting Obama's breath with pointless redundancy. Surely what the president-elect meant here—if he meant anything at all—is uninformed opinion, irrational bias, *prejudgment.* I have no doubt that the president and I could argue at great length about what constitutes prejudice in the particulars. And, more to the point, it's a good guess that the prejudice he has in mind is defined almost entirely as a shortcoming of his political opponents. But yes, fine, let us be done with prejudice, too.

And what about small thinking? This is a tougher one than it appears. Web searching and dictionary thumbing don't get you too far. But I gather that small thinking is pettiness, selfishness, seeking trifling advantages and niggling victories over your fellow man. It is another way of saying small-minded, which means unimaginative, capricious, and petty.

So far, other than the fact that it is boring, gassy rhetoric, I don't really have a problem. If Obama wants to call for a declaration of independence from prejudice, bigotry, and small thinking, who am I to complain? And if, in his second term (should he get one), he opts to launch a new war of liberation against stinginess, grumpiness, and mopery, that's fine by me, too.

But it should be said again that the man's opinion of America on the eve of his presidency is awfully low. Are these the traits that best describe America in 2008 (or now, for that matter)? Or even best describe its chief shortcomings? Small-minded thinking, prejudiced, and bigoted? How odd that a black man with the name Barack Hussein Obama is elected president and then turns on the country that elected him with a wagging finger and an exhortation to abandon precisely the qualities the American people lacked sufficiently in order to elect him in the first place. Perhaps if he received 100 percent of the vote he would have felt less compelled to chastise Americans for their remaining shortcomings. Of course, the actual people attending the massive rally didn't mind such scolding because they knew it was aimed at *other Americans*, the ones who didn't vote for him.

But wait, there were four traits the American people needed to free themselves from. The last one (which was really the first one, since we are dealing with his small parade of horribles in reverse order) was *ideology*.

And it is here where the president-elect truly showed his hand. For Obama, ideology is part of the same motley tribe as bigotry, prejudice, and small thinking. Ideological thinking is surely not a trait he associates with himself. Indeed, it is something he hopes to lead his fellow Americans away from, to help them transcend this regrettable vestige of our "easy instincts."

But there's a problem: While small thinking, prejudice, and bigotry are indeed fruits of our easy instincts, ideology—as Obama means it—is not. To be sure, there are evil, cruel, or simply wrongheaded ideologies that are little more than elaborate rationalizations of tribal instincts (and as I have argued in another book, they go by names such as fascism, communism, jihadism, and socialism). But such ideologies do not define *ideology* per se. If Nazis are ideologues, so are peace activists. If lovers of the free market are driven by ideological imperatives, so are those who wish to spread the wealth around.

What Works

There is a presumption, however, that liberals are not ideological. No, it's more than a presumption, it is a flat-out assertion. You would be hard-pressed to find a prominent liberal intellectual, politician, or journalist who hasn't baldly stated at one point or another that liberals only care about "what works." They contrast this with their political opponents, always on the right, who are all ideologues— "extremists," "dogmatists," and the like.

President Obama, for instance, is deeply, profoundly, habitually committed to the notion that he's a pragmatist boldly standing athwart ideology. He's interested in results, not mere labels. "My interest is finding something that works," he told *60 Minutes* at the beginning of his administration. "And whether it's coming from FDR or it's coming from Ronald Reagan, if the idea is right for the times then we're gonna [*sic*] apply it. And things that don't work, we're gonna get rid of." One finds in *The Audacity of Hope* numerous assaults on the evils of ideology—indeed "any tyrannical consistency"—that drives people away from the humility of pragmatism. And, of course, here he is in his inaugural address:

> What the cynics fail to understand is that the ground has shifted beneath them, that the stale political arguments that have consumed us for so long no longer apply.
>
> The question we ask today is not whether our government is too big or too small, but whether it works.[2]

This is Obama's standard refrain, and his biggest defenders routinely repeat it back, almost as if they think it's actually true. During the intense debt-ceiling negotiations in July and August 2011, Obama would claim incessantly that Republicans were "constantly being locked into ideologically rigid positions," while he was a compromiser and a pragmatist. This dichotomy of ideology versus pragmatism in which he casts himself as the disciple of cool reason and common sense and his opponents as blinkered ideologues is a fiction. It is part lie he tells us and part lie he tells himself.

Remember Barack Obama's famous explanation for why voters in western Pennsylvania wouldn't support him in the Democratic primary? These "bitter" Americans "cling to guns or religion or antipathy to people who aren't like them or anti-immigrant sentiment or anti-trade sentiment as a way to explain their frustrations."[3] That is how Barack Obama sees ideology (indeed, that is what he thinks of *Hillary Clinton*'s supporters). It is those bitter savages with their white-knuckled grips on their boomsticks and their sky god whom Barack Obama seeks to emancipate through a "new declaration of independence."

How much such statements stem from ideological preconceptions and how much they stem from simple arrogance or political spin is always hard to glean. President Obama thinks very highly of himself, and there's a natural tendency—call it an easy instinct—to assume that other people disagree with you for small-minded, prejudicial, bigoted, or ideological reasons. After all, if you not only believe you understand the facts better than your opponents, but you're also convinced that the facts themselves are obvious and transparent, it's only human to think that maybe your opponents disagree because there's something wrong with how they think. If you see a duck standing in front of you and somebody comes along and says it's a cat, it's hardly unreasonable for you to conclude that he's crazy, or lying, or that he just sees the world very, very differently than normal people do.

It's a different matter altogether when you're looking at something a good deal more complicated than a duck, and the other person isn't saying something that is objectively nuts. Imagine I say to a liberal friend: "Let's have Mexican food for lunch today." He replies that he wants to get Chinese instead. We simply have different opinions. We can both invoke facts and arguments for why our preference should win: I might argue that we had Chinese last time, they're having a special two-for-one deal at the Mexican place, I have a crush on the waitress at the Mexican joint, whatever. At the end of the day the disagreement will boil down to competing preferences. Unlike the situation with the duck, there is no right answer independent of your preferences. But the liberal cannot leave it there. He insists that his preferences are pragmatic, empirical, and based on what works, while my determination to have Mexican food is ideological.

Look again at what he told *60 Minutes*: "And whether it's coming from FDR or it's coming from Ronald Reagan, if the idea is right for the times then we're gonna [*sic*] apply it." The process of deciding whether something is "right for the times" is an inescapably ideological one.

This is the game liberals and centrists play. Sure, you will find pockets on the right doing the same thing, particularly in foreign policy (the best working definition of a foreign policy realist is an ideologue who lost an argument). But on the whole conservatives and libertarians differ from liberals in that we are *honest about our ideologies.* We debate and modify them from time to time to be sure, opening us up to the charge of hypocrisy by liberals who insist that not only are conservatives inflexible ideologues, but that we are also hypocrites whenever we show signs of flexibility.

Meanwhile, liberals and other progressives hold it as a bedrock article of ideological faith that they are not ideological. In short: *Pragmatism is the disguise progressive and other ideologues don when they want to demonize competing ideologies.*

Claiming that you are for what works is nothing like the get-out-of-ideological-jail–free card those who flash it around think it is. To date I am aware of no ideological school—be it Nazism, communism, Fabianism, progressivism, Toryism, Trostkyism, neoconservatism, paleoconservatism, libertarianism, Gandhism, futurism, Ludditism, anarchism, Lovestonism, Chavism, Castroism, Kemalism, Maoism, Stalinism, Uribism, Reaganism, Thatcherism, Thisism, or Thatism, just to name a few—that claims it does not work. And ideology without a claim on reality is little different than a game of Dungeons and Dragons or a Civil War reenactment club.

Now, obviously, just because all ideologues claim their ideology works doesn't mean they're all right. Every form of hard socialism promised to deliver prosperity for all. They all failed. Why socialism manages to survive one failure after another can be at least partially explained by the simple fact that the relevant question isn't about what works but about what works for *whom*? Mexican food works for my lunch because I want Mexican food. Similarly, an intrusive welfare state works for the people who make a living thinking up what an intrusive welfare state should do next.

How much the welfare state works for its supposed beneficiaries is a different question altogether. The debate is skewed a bit because we live in a democracy, and as history shows, once the government starts writing checks to people, the people getting the checks want to keep getting checks (particularly given that the majority of them get more from government than they ever pay in). This has been the aim of liberalism since at least the New Deal, to turn Americans into clients of the state.

Regardless, in that debate liberals insist they are empiricists and fact finders, pragmatists and realists going where the data take them, pitting them against crazy ideologues who insist that a duck is a cat, as it were.

Because, again, pragmatism is the disguise progressives and other ideologues don when they want to demonize competing ideologies.

In 2005, then *New Republic* senior editor Jonathan Chait penned a now famous essay, "Fact Finders: The Anti-Dogma Dogma,"[4] stating boldly that liberals go where the facts take them and conservatives go where their ideology commands, heedless of the facts. It's worth quoting at some length:

> Imagine that God were to appear on Earth for the unlikely purpose of settling, once and for all, our disputes over economic policy. And suppose that, to my enormous surprise, he announced that every empirical claim advanced by conservatives was correct. Cutting taxes produces such great economic growth that even the poor benefit. Privatizing or eliminating social programs like Medicare and Social Security will cause the elderly to save more money and enjoy higher living standards. Slashing regulations, by eliminating unintended side effects, actually does a better job helping those whom the regulations were intended to help than the regulations themselves. Suppose that God presented these conclusions so convincingly—if his stature alone did not suffice—that everybody immediately accepted them as truth.
>
> How would liberals respond? No doubt by rethinking and abandoning nearly all their long-held positions. Liberalism, after all, claims to produce certain outcomes: more prosperity and security, especially for the poor and middle classes; a cleaner environment; safer foods and drugs; and so on. If it were proved beyond a doubt that liberal policies fail to produce those outcomes—or even, as conservatives often claim, that such policies hurt their intended beneficiaries—then their rationale would disappear.

Meanwhile, if God told economic conservatives they were wrong, conservatives, or at least most of them, would keep chug-chugging along, because they are dogmatically immune to facts. According to Chait, "Economic conservatism, unlike liberalism, would survive having all its empirical underpinnings knocked out from beneath it." He continues:

> We're accustomed to thinking of liberalism and conservatism as parallel ideologies, with conservatives preferring less government and liberals preferring more. The equivalency breaks down, though, when you consider that liberals never claim that increasing the size of government is an end in itself. Liberals only support larger government if they have some reason to believe that it will lead to material improvement in people's lives. Conservatives also want material improvement in people's lives, of course, but proving that their policies can produce such an outcome is a luxury, not a necessity.

And so on. Chait moves on to his empirical linchpin to prove his point that "empirical reasoning simply does not drive [conservative] thinking. What appears to be conservative economic reasoning is actually a kind of backward reasoning. It begins with the conclusion and marches back through the premises." He goes on:

> Consider the conservative view of health care. Conservatives repeat the mantra that the United States has "the best health care system in the world"—a formulation used endlessly by President Bush. That isn't true by almost any objective measure. The United States devotes a far higher share of its economy to health care than any other country. Yet, according to the most recent World Health Organization study, the United States ranks just 37th in overall health care performance.

It's an illustrative choice of facts. I want to be careful here not to sound hyperbolic, so I am relying on the work of Scott W. Atlas, a senior fellow at the Hoover Institution and professor of radiology and chief of neuroradiology at Stanford Medical Center when I say that the lengthy WHO study Chait uses to prove the empiricism of liberals might be the worst study ever. This is what Atlas concludes, or at least that's what I take him to be saying, in his article titled "The Worst Study Ever?" He calls it "an intellectual fraud of historic consequence—a profoundly deceptive document that is only marginally a measure of health-care performance at all. The report's true achievement was to rank countries according to their alignment with a specific political and economic ideal—socialized medicine—and then claim it was an objective measure of 'quality.'"[5]

To take one small example: A full 25 percent of a health-care system's final score in the WHO study is derived from what it calls a health-care system's "Financial Fairness." Essentially, the more socialized a system is—with the wealthy paying more through taxation—the better it is. Indeed, Atlas shows that "almost two-thirds of the study was an assessment of *equality*. The actual health outcomes of a nation, which logic dictates should be of greatest importance in any health-care index, accounted for only 25 percent of the weighting. In other words, the WHO study was dominated by concerns outside the realm of health care."

Oh, and the data behind these rankings weren't even empirical. Rather than collect hard numbers about health outcomes or anything else, these rankings were weighted by polling the *impressions* of "key informants" in the health-care profession, half of whom were WHO staff and had a bias toward state-run health-care systems. At least that's my reasonable guess (if the World Health Organization bureaucracy is a hotbed of free-marketers, I'll be glad to retract).

As Atlas suggests, a reasonable person, even an avowed empiricist, might think a ranking of health-care systems would score the quality of the health care those systems provide and not how successful they are at redistributing costs. A government-run soup kitchen might do wonderful and vital work, but only an ideologue would declare one a contender for the best restaurant in the world simply because they give away free food to the poor that is paid for by the wealthy.

Or, here's a better example. Most surveys find that Harvard, Princeton, Yale, MIT, Stanford, and a handful of other schools are the best universities in the country or the world. And while all of them have generous financial aid packages, nobody would count the generosity of financial aid as two thirds of a school's score. If we did, then the top twenty schools in the country would be community colleges and public universities.

Conversely, it *is* true that America has the best health-care system in the world in some ways and not in others. For example, if you are very ill and/or very rich things look better here than pretty much anywhere else.

Saudi kings and Chinese billionaires come to the United States when they are sick because they know this. If you have a bad heart or a scary cancer diagnosis, America is where you go to seek treatment. And if you're already in America, you have a better chance of surviving such a diagnosis than you do elsewhere. Our overall cancer survival rates beat every industrialized country in the world.[6] We beat Canada—glorious Canada!—when it comes to preventative care.[7] In other words, what you think of our health-care system depends at least to a significant degree on how you define best. And that depends to a great extent on your ideological preferences.

The empirical measures most frequently cited as proof not just of American health care's inferiority but as evidence that liberals care about the facts are similarly loaded. For instance, Chait and others are very fond of pointing to our allegedly low life expectancy as an indictment of our health-care system. "Americans tend to believe that we have the best health care system in the world," writes Nobel Prize–winning economist Paul Krugman in the *New York Times*. "But it isn't true. We spend far more per person on health care . . . yet rank near the bottom among industrial countries in indicators from life expectancy to infant mortality."[8]

Again, this is just a reiteration of the logic behind the WHO study. Saying we spend too much on health care—which we do—is not really an argument against the *quality* of our health-care system but against its cost (and I very much doubt liberals would complain about costs nearly so much under socialized medicine). If you read Krugman, Chait, and others closely, they often seem to conflate bad health-care outcomes with high costs, as if lowering the costs will improve the outcomes. Lower costs are nice and desirable (and in my opinion achievable with market reforms), but paying less for ineffective health care isn't as desirable as paying more for effective health care. I'd like to pay ten dollars for a cure that works. But I'll pay one hundred dollars, if that's what it costs, rather than "save" ninety dollars on a cure that doesn't. At times it seems as if any argument is a good argument if it justifies (or seems to justify) inserting government into health care.

And on that point, comparing infant mortality and life expectancy rates aren't great arguments either. A lot of the claims that America lags behind in infant mortality hinge on, not to be indelicate, how different countries count dead babies and how they treat sick ones. In America, if a mother gives birth to a very low birth weight or otherwise gravely ill baby, doctors will spend time and resources trying to resuscitate it. When these nonviable babies die, it counts toward the infant mortality rate. In France or Japan, they're more likely to record it as a stillbirth, which doesn't count toward such rates.[9] Meanwhile, just to twist the ideological knife for a moment: The government policy with a near 100 percent mortality rate for babies? Abortion.

As for our life expectancy, by any measure it's not really low. You always hear these phrases like "at the bottom" or "near the bottom" or "dead last" when talking about life expectancy, but the caveat is that we're talking about rates among advanced industrialized countries. Our life expectancy is just three years and four months lower than number one–ranked Japan's. Moreover, if you factor out things like murder, car crashes and other fatal accidents, etc.—problems that have little to nothing to do with our health-care system—guess what happens? America has the highest life expectancy in the world. Indeed, in America, the longer you live, the longer you're likely to live (at least until you die).

Moreover there's a deep statist bias to the whole discussion. Who says life expectancy is the government's business? Don't get me wrong: It is the government's business if people are dying at a young age from murder or epidemic diseases or outbreaks of zombism. But many things that influence life expectancy are personal choices, from drinking alcohol and eating red meat to riding motorcycles and BASE jumping.

Cultural choices and genetic nonchoices play a role, too. Here are some interesting statistics: According to the 2006 study *Eight Americas,* Asian American women have a life expectancy of 87 years (in Bergen County, New Jersey, Asian American women live on average to 91 years). Asian Americans as a group—i.e., men and women—have a life expectancy of 84.9 years. This isn't because they're rich. Their per capita income according to the study: $21,556. Second-generation Asian American women live three years longer than women in Japan—the longest-living national group in the world. Meanwhile, American Indians in South Dakota have an average life expectancy of only 58 years (and they already have access to the federal government–run Indian Health Service). Black inner-city men do almost as badly, living to only 66.7 years. White folks in the Northern Plains live longer than most other whites, especially whites from Appalachia and the Mississippi Valley.[10]

Are you really going to tell me that implementing ObamaCare will smooth all that out? If we really want to improve life expectancy for black men, we could put them all in jail, because their life expectancy in prison is higher than it is outside of it (which, for the record, is just a monumentally depressing statistic).[11] The point here isn't to relitigate the debate over our health-care system or to claim that our system was great before Obama got his mitts on it. Rather, it is simply to note that saying you're being empirical, and wielding numbers like so many stage props, doesn't make you empirical, any more than me wielding a giant hammer and speaking Norwegian makes me Thor. More important, even if all of the numbers and statistics being thrown around were accurate and compiled in good faith, the weight we give these numbers is ultimately a question of ideology or, if you prefer, principle.

And that raises the core problem with arguments like Chait's. It's not just that he denies his own ideological biases; he makes it sound like there's something wrong, dangerously wrong, with *having* ideological biases. Chait mocks Milton Friedman for saying, "[F]reedom in economic arrangements is itself a component of freedom broadly understood, so economic freedom is an end in itself." That crazy bastard! (And we all know that the Nobel Prize–winning economist never concerned himself with things like data and facts!)

The upshot is that Chait believes that economic freedom is *not* an end in itself. And of course he's hardly alone. As we'll see, this is a core tenet of progressives like Chait going back a century. And countless liberal intellectuals and politicians think it is just crazy that conservatives oppose the individual mandate under ObamaCare because they think the government can't force people to buy things they don't want to buy. But surely progressives would agree that it's wrong (we'll leave out whether they think it's constitutional for another time) for the government to force Americans to buy copies of Sarah Palin's latest book or a gun or a subscription to *National Review*. In other words, they too agree that at some point economic freedom is a real freedom, albeit maybe not all that important. They surely believe that freedom of speech is an "end in itself," right? I mean, if Congress passed a law saying that people may only say things that have empirical value—as determined by a government board or commission—they'd have a problem with that, at least in principle. (Let's leave aside their fondness for reimposing the Fairness Doctrine.) Certainly prochoice feminists believe that reproductive freedom is an end in itself. Surely feminists don't want the government empirically deciding which babies should be allowed to live and which shouldn't (though this too is a surprisingly recent liberal principle).

Liberal commitment to these principles may be weaker than I would like or they would claim, but we should all be willing to concede that they're in liberalism's philosophy somewhere. We can even witness them popping up from time to time. During the 2008 Democratic presidential primaries ABC's Charlie Gibson asked Obama if he would continue to favor raising capital gains taxes even if he knew—not believed, but knew—that lowering them would raise more revenues. He said he'd still consider raising them out of "fairness." How, exactly, is that not an ideological position?

Ideology Misunderstood

What is ideology? Academics have an infinite capacity to make this a profoundly complicated question. How could it be otherwise for a profession that has managed to make the films of Keanu Reeves into a realm of serious inquiry? But there's really no need for that. As we'll see in a bit, the word ideology is a relatively recent immigrant to the English language, and it brought an enormous amount of baggage with it. For the moment, consider instead the German synonym *Weltanschauung*, which means a "worldview" or "an orientation to how you see the world." Erik von Kuehnelt-Leddihn (to whom I am indebted) once remarked: "I know conservatives who say yes to *Weltanschauung* and no to ideology, but they seem incapable of distinguishing between them (not surprisingly, because there is no distinction)."[12] Look up ideology and *Weltanschauung* in various dictionaries and often the most pronounced difference is in the spelling.

In the past, demonizing ideology was a bipartisan sport. For decades conservative intellectuals treated ideology as if it was some kind of mental zombie virus that escaped a German lab, mutated in France, and then came to the United States, where it incubates on college campuses.

Others, including many liberals and self-proclaimed moderates, have treated ideology as simply a clever rationalization for prejudice, bigotry and small-mindedness (where have we heard that before?).

These criticisms have been entirely accurate when aimed at specific ideologies (I'm looking at you Klansmen and Frankfurt School Marxists), but it's silly to confuse the substance with the category. Knives fall under the category of lethal weapons, but we don't automatically treat all knives as murder weapons. Or take the various clichéd indictments of hate. Hate is not a family value, we're often told. But my guess is that the bulk of people who say hate is not a family value also teach their kids to hate Nazis and other bigots.

An ideology, at the most fundamental level, is simply a checklist of ideas you have about the world. Having an ideology doesn't mean you've been brainwashed, it means you've come to conclusions about how the world works at some basic level. Just as there are good ideologies and bad ideologies, there can be good ideas and bad ideas, but no one would simply say that ideas in and of themselves are bad. Jesus had the idea that we should all love each other. Hitler had the idea of a thousand-year *reich.* Steven Bochco had the idea that *Cop Rock* would be a hit. Clearly we can distinguish between the good, the bad, and the ugly.

Kuehnelt-Leddihn argues that the confused antipathy to ideology is an Anglo-American phenomenon stemming from the Protestant revolution, whereas on the European continent the idea that ideology is simply a fact of life has long been a given. As Friedrich Hayek said: "every social order rests on an ideology." Ludwig von Mises concurred, arguing that the choice isn't between ideology and no ideology but between good ideology and bad: "If they prefer bad doctrines, nothing can prevent disaster." Like "the air we breathe," observed the German writer Eugen Lemberg, ideologies "are indispensible presuppositions for the preservation of our life and our species as well as for the functioning of our society."[13]

In Defense of Conservative Ideology, or How I Learned to Love Book Learning

Given that modern conservatism was born as a reaction to various utopian ideologies, starting with the French Revolution, it's not surprising that the first opponents of ideology were on the political right.

Edmund Burke, the founding father of modern conservatism, was a famous anti-ideologue who derided the Jacobin madness that was sweeping the continent.

But it's vital to understand that what the original conservatives denounced as ideology was in fact only a certain kind of ideology, one that was both utopian and characterized by what Friedrich Hayek called "intellectual hubris." What Burke objected to was the effort of radicals to denounce the past, to deride the "wisdom of the ancients," to believe that a small clique of visionary experts could impose a whole new system of living on society without taking into account the gravity of culture or the immutability of human nature. Burke saw the French revolutionaries as overcome with a Rousseauian madness that says we are all born noble, pure, and free, and it is only through the corruptness of society that we become enslaved. "Man is born free," Rousseau famously wrote, "but everywhere he is in chains." All that was required to solve this sorry state of affairs was to come up with a better system, a more rational plan, a blueprint for creating the Kingdom of Heaven on Earth. It was this kind of utopian madness that Edmund Burke and his heirs stood athwart, yelling, "Stop."

He saw the bloody excesses of the French Revolution as confirmation of his hostility toward too much abstraction. Meanwhile, he sympathized with, and ultimately supported, the American revolutionaries on the grounds that they were British subjects who were merely pressing their rights under British law. Indeed, he did not see them as revolutionaries at all but as combatants in a civil war within the British Empire, and the Americans were "purely on the defensive."

But to say Burke was opposed to certain ideologies does not mean that Burkeanism is not an ideology all its own. Although it took roughly two centuries for the Burkean conservative worldview—i.e. traditional conservative ideology—to become the recognizable system of thought we have today. Burke's successors and champions, Russell Kirk chief among them, subscribed to the notion that "conservatism is the negation of ideology."[14] He defined ideology very narrowly, as "political fanaticism, a body of beliefs alleged to point the way to a perfect society." Other philosophers of the right have long offered similar critiques, led by Michael Oakeshott and Eric Voegelin. All of these thinkers share an understanding of ideology as a utopian "political religion," a fallacious faith in the perfectibility of man and the possibility of creating a heaven on earth. And they were all correct if by ideology you mean the various utopian totalitarianisms that sprung forth from the Pandora's box of the French Revolution. But they were all wrong if by ideology you simply mean your worldview, your set of principles, your checklist by which you measure and judge events and actions. The latter is how I define ideology.

Anti-ideology polemics enjoyed a comeback during the roughest years of the Bush administration. The argument took various forms, but the core indictment was that conservatism had become a kind of ideological madness. Liberal sociologist Alan Wolfe took to the pages of *The New Republic* to revive the discredited pseudoscience of Marxist psychologist Theodor Adorno in an effort to cast conservatives as nuts. Samuel Tanenhaus, the editor of *The New York Times Book Review* and author of a valuable biography of Whitaker Chambers, wrote an essay for *The New Republic*, "The Death of Conservatism," which eventually became a book by the same name. Unfortunately, when the book came out in the fall of 2009, it was already clear that the rumors of conservatism's death had been greatly exaggerated. "Today's conservatives" proclaimed Tanenhaus, "resemble the exhumed figures of Pompeii, trapped in postures of frozen flight, clenched in the rigor mortis of a defunct ideology."[15] Moments later those figures came to life for the tea parties and delivered the Republicans a historic midterm election victory.

This defunct ideology business was taken to absurd extremes by Andrew Sullivan, a blogger and author who at times seemed driven to a kind of nonclinical dementia by his irrational hatred for George W. Bush and conservatism generally. A self-proclaimed disciple of the philosopher Michael Oakeshott, Sullivan testified for a gnawing need for a new or renewed "conservatism of doubt." "As a politics," Sullivan writes in his *The Conservative Soul*,

> its essence is an acceptance of the unknowability of ultimate truth, an acknowledgment of the distinction between what is true forever and what is true for the here and now, and an embrace of the discrepancy between theoretical and practical knowledge. It

> is an anti-ideology, a non-program, a way of looking at the world whose most perfect expression might be called inactivism.[16]

I find the words enticing and admirable. But as anyone who has read Sullivan's work knows well, the sermon has no relationship to the man preaching it. It's all very well and good to decry certainty and extol empiricism, but it's quite another to live by such values. The reality is that Sullivan is using the Trojan Horse of conservative empiricism to deliver an army of theoretical, theological, and ideological certainties fighting under the banner of humility and doubt. Boiled down, Sullivan's crusade amounts to the exact same shtick I've been describing: Defend your own "way of looking at the world"—i.e., your *Weltanschauung*—as coolly pragmatic and empirical while describing your opponents' as blindly and dangerously ideological. Those who disagree with the excitable Sullivan are immediately cast as ideologues, "Christianists," fundamentalists, bigots, and fools.

Make no mistake, Sullivan's approach is more moralistic than empirical, more preachy than skeptical. While he's not a complete stranger to facts and data, his real aim is to elevate the conscience—specifically, his own—above any external source of authority. To make his case, he invokes a famous ancient Chinese tale from a footnote in Oakeshott's essay "Rationalism in Politics":

> Duke Huan of Ch'i was reading a book at the upper end of the hall; the wheelwright was making a wheel at the lower end. Putting aside his mallet and chisel, he called to the Duke and asked him what book he was reading. "One that records the words of the Sages," answered the Duke. "Are those Sages alive?" asked the wheelwright. "Oh, no," said the Duke, "they are dead." "In that case," said the wheelwright, "what you are reading can be nothing but the lees and scum of bygone men." "How dare you, a wheelwright, find fault with the book I am reading. If you can explain your statement, I will let it pass. If not, you shall die." "Speaking as a wheelwright," he replied, "I look at the matter in this way; when I am making a wheel, if my stroke is too slow,

> then it bites deep but is not steady; if my stroke is too fast, then it is steady, but it does not go deep. The right pace, neither slow nor fast, cannot get into the hand unless it comes from the heart. It is a thing that cannot be put into words [rules]; there is an art in it that I cannot explain to my son. That is why it is impossible for me to let him take over my work, and here I am at the age of seventy, still making wheels. In my opinion it must have been the same with the men of old. All that was worth handing on, died with them; the rest, they put into their books. That is why I said that what you were reading was the lees and scum of bygone men."

The lesson here, according to Sullivan, is one that "fundamentalists" of all sorts fail to understand. We learn by doing. And, he adds, what is true of wheel making is true of all practical activity, and what is true of all practical activity must also be "true of moral life, because moral life is about the way we act, not the way we think."[17]

Think about it for a moment. Here we have a book by Andrew Sullivan, in which he cites a book by Michael Oakeshott, written before Sullivan was born, in which Oakeshott recounts a tale written down in a book—a scroll, actually—some six hundred years before Jesus was born, and according to Sullivan, the moral of the story is that books are essentially worthless!

Imagine you are a young intellectual on the make. Like the Jacobins, Bolsheviks, Progressives, and National Socialists before you, you have really exciting ideas about how to start the world over from scratch. Ensconced in your basement apartment, Diet Coke cans and pizza boxes littering the floor, you're convinced that if only the world would accept the oracular wisdom of your blog posts, everything would be so much better. Then one day you pick up a copy of *Rationalism in Politics* at a used-book store. "This ought to be fun to mock," you say to yourself. But then you read it. And, slowly at first, you discover that Oakeshott is right. Social planners cannot straighten the crooked timber of humanity simply by applying some algorithms or imposing really clever taxes. It is folly to think you know all you need to know about life as long as you have a computer with a good Wi-Fi connection. You truly take to heart Oakeshott's lovely epigram, "The conjunction of ruling and dreaming generates tyranny."[18]

But wait a second; that'd be impossible because—at least according to Sullivan—you can't learn such important lessons from a book. So let the Revolution Commence!

We learn an enormous number of important things from books, and not just the "technical knowledge" Oakeshott concedes is valuable. To believe the wheelwright's indictment of book learning (and who wouldn't look to the seventy-year-old manual laborer as the genius here?), everything worth knowing dies with the person who knew it. That's crazy talk. It is surely not true of great novels that can connect us to the fabric and mystery of the human condition. But it's also not true of nonfiction books. When Edmund Burke says the "example is the school of mankind, and they will learn at no other,"[19] he does not mean literally that each person must make each mistake in order to learn from it. If I see a kid fuse his tongue to a frozen flagpole, I don't need to replicate the error myself to learn from the example. Similarly, we don't all need to fight a land war in Asia or go against a Sicilian when death is on the line to avoid someone else's blunder.

In other words, if someone recounts these blunders in a book or captures them on film, we can learn from such examples without personally experiencing them. Over time these lessons are incorporated into other books, including textbooks. Knowledge is cumulative. It's an imperfect process, to be sure, and forgetting history can lead to repeating it (as the roughly accurate cliché goes). But over time smart people gather all of these important ideas and boil them down into general principles. The result: an ideology. What on earth is so scary about that?

It's true that sometimes words get hijacked by events and it's not worth trying to salvage them. For example, almost everyone believes in censorship at some extreme (snuff films? hard-core porn on Nickelodeon?). But we've come to call the censorship we don't like censorship and the censorship we do like reasonable regulations. The term "ideology" may have a bad odor in some quarters, but I don't think its reputation is irretrievably tarnished, either. But let's say it were for a moment. We would still need a word to describe the systemic way we order and prioritize our core values. If you want to use creed or value system or even just priorities, that's fine. But you can be sure that if conservatives switched to "creed," it would take at most months before columnists on the *New York Times* op-ed page were caterwauling about the dangers posed by right-wing creedism.

It's a bad idea to run away from labels. Liberals bristle at being called liberals because, well, for a lot of reasons, I think. But they say they don't like to be labeled because it's too confining and simplistic. We'll tackle the "substance" of those claims later. But for now, as a tactical matter, all this does is give the impression that you're embarrassed to admit what you are. That might be why, despite a half century of slander from the news media, academia, and Hollywood, Americans continue to define themselves as conservative over liberal by more than a 2 to 1 margin.

Regardless, whatever word you choose, humans need limiting principles, bright lines, ideals, dogma. Bundle them together and you've got a field guide to life that helps you sift your way through new facts and data. The opponents will tell you that such field guides are a burden as we hew our way through the wilderness of life, causing us to underappreciate nature in all her glory. Maybe there's some truth to that. But field guides also help the traveler distinguish the edible from the inedible, make-do toilet paper from poison ivy, and grizzly bear scat from vegan granola. Some might even say that having such a field guide allows one to get through life more easily, by allowing the traveler to more immediately recognize what is important; to appreciate what is valuable; and simply, to survive.

2

PRAGMATISM

> I react pragmatically. Where the market works, I'm for that. Where the government is necessary, I'm for that. I'm deeply suspicious of somebody who says, "I'm in favor of privatization," or, "I'm deeply in favor of public ownership." I'm in favor of whatever works in the particular case.
>
> —John Kenneth Galbraith, C-SPAN, November 13, 1994

How We Got Here: From *Ideologie* to "Pragmatism"

> We must lay the blame for the ills that our fair France has suffered on ideology, that shadowy metaphysics which subtly searches for first causes on which to base the legislation of peoples, rather than making use of laws known to the human heart and of the lessons of history. These errors must inevitably and did in fact lead to the rule of bloodthirsty men. . . . When someone is summoned to revitalize a state, he must follow exactly the opposite principles.
>
> —Napoleon Bonaparte, 1812[1]

We are indebted to Napoleon for many things. My personal favorite is canned goods. Among Napoleon's less appreciated accomplishments is our modern understanding of the word "ideology." Napoleon's success at turning the word into a term of abuse in certain respects spells the end of the Enlightenment and the dawn of the Pragmatic Age.

Now when it comes to enlightenments I've long followed the rule of the dad in *So I Married an Axe Murderer*: "If it's not Scottish, it's crap." By this I mean that a conservative in the Anglo-American tradition tends to revere folks like Adam Smith and John Locke and, of course, Edmund Burke (only one of whom was in fact Scottish) while looking askance at events on the continent because of the whole French Revolution, the birth of totalitarianism, the debut of socialism, the Terror, and all of that unpleasantness.

But this is not really fair. The French Enlightenment was a lot like the *Star Wars* franchise: It started great; it just evolved into disaster over time, as the characters became more and more unbelievable. Montesquieu, after all, influenced the Founding Fathers as much as anyone, and was the author of the whole idea of the separation of powers. Before the Reign of Terror kicked in, many of the French *philosophes* had done a great deal of the legwork on free-market economics, the benefits of limited, democratic, and representative government, the rule of law. Jean-Baptiste Say—known for the often misunderstood Say's Law and as the inventor of the word "entrepreneur"—was Adam Smith's greatest popularizer and champion in Europe.

In 1794, Say became the founding editor of *La Décade philosophique, littéraire, et politique*, a hugely influential journal that championed laissez-faire economics, the rights of man, limited government, and what we would today call either libertarianism or classical liberalism. The intellectuals around this journal and their allies came to be called the *Idéologistes*, chiefly because of their association with another guy with an absurdly French name, Antoine Louis Claude Destutt, comte de Tracy—the man credited with coining the word "ideology" (or *idéologie*, in the French) in 1796.

Tracy, a man of noble birth and privilege, nonetheless himself favored American-style government and opposed both monarchy and the totalitarianism of the terrorist faction of the French Revolution (the Robespierrists threw Tracy in prison for about a year). While more secular than most American Founders (much like his friend Thomas Jefferson), he was in every way a classical liberal, passionately supporting property rights ("We have seen that *property* exists in nature: for it is impossible that every one should not be the proprietor of his individuality and of his faculties") and laissez-faire economics:

> For it is very certain that in general the most powerful encouragement that can be given to industry of every kind, is to let it alone, and not to meddle with it. The human mind would advance very rapidly if only not restrained; and it would be led, by the force of things to do always what is most essential on every occurrence. To direct it artificially on one side rather than on another, is commonly to lead it astray instead of guiding it.[2]

Tracy wasn't as influential as Say or Smith, but he was recognized as one of the major intellectuals of his day. He was, for instance, one of Thomas Jefferson's favorite thinkers. Jefferson paid for one of the translations of Tracy's work into English and its publication in the United States, because it was Jefferson's "hearty prayers" that Tracy's *Treatise on Political Economy* would become the standard economic text in America.[3] Former president John Adams—an ally of Jefferson's—said it was the best book yet written on economics, and that Tracy's chapter on money expressed "the sentiments that I have entertained all my lifetime."[4]

Originally, Tracy conceived of *idéologie* as the science of ideas. Just as biology means the science of life, and geology the science of the earth, ideology was dedicated to understanding ideas and how we come to them. Today we would understand Tracy's work as a branch of psychology, but he preferred to place it under the rubric of zoology. Tracy, released from prison with the overthrow of Robespierre in 1795, found a home at the Institut National (the successor to the royal academies overthrown by the revolutionaries), where he and his fellow *idéologistes* became tightly linked to the principles of republicanism (i.e., limited, representative government bound by the rule of law; you know, the good stuff). They also had some metaphysical ideas that I'm not particularly enamored with, but that's not relevant to the story here.

In 1799 Napoleon returned from Egypt and launched a successful coup d'état, making himself dicta–, er, first consul. At first the new regime seemed like great news for the *idéologistes*, as Napoleon assiduously cultivated their support. Jean-Bapiste Say even left his job at *La Décade* and took a position in Napoleon's consular government. The *idéologistes* contributed to the creation of the new constitution under Napoleon.

But there's a funny thing about authoritarian tyrants. They can tolerate (sometimes) free-market intellectuals, small-d democrats, and liberal reformers for as long as they don't get in the way. So while Napoleon—once known, and not without justification, as the Great Liberator—was sympathetic to the *idéologistes* and their cause, he quickly turned on them when he wanted to seize and solidify power, and their principles proved inconvenient. Napoleon wished to be a true emperor, not a mere republican administrator answerable to men and their laws.

In very short order Napoleon realized that people of principle—any principle other than loyalty to him—were a threat to his plans. He considered the Royalists his greatest threat, but for political reasons it was easier for him to concentrate his ire on the *idéologistes* (the terror, after all, was still fresh in the popular mind). Napoleon's men started fueling rumors and planting accusations in the press that the *idéologistes* were really unrepentant Jacobins nostalgic for Robespierre, a cutting lie given how much the *idéologistes* despised Robespierre and his Terror. In January 1800, an article, in all likelihood planted by the government, coined the word ideologue:

> The civilian faction is also called by the name metaphysical faction or "ideologues." Flatterers of Robespierre, they drove him to death, by the very excess of power they allowed him. They used the Directory to proscribe talents which overshadowed theirs. They looked for heroes to bring down the Directory. Today they have hatched new plans.[5]

In December of the same year Royalists attempted to assassinate Napoleon with a bomb planted on the side of the road in Paris, in the famous *Machine infernale plot* (also known as plot of the Rue Saint-Nicaise). Napoleon escaped death by pure, dumb luck—though many others didn't. He parlayed the incident into even more popularity. He even went straight on to the opera after the explosion and received a standing ovation. At first Napoleon honestly believed the attack came from the "Jacobin" leftists, but he soon discovered that it was in fact a Royalist plot. Nonetheless, he used the bombing as an excuse to order the public executions of numerous Jacobins. Later, and more quietly, he had the Royalist plotters killed, too.

A little over a month after the bombing, Napoleon was claiming credit for coining the word "ideologue" and using it freely as an insult aimed at eggheads allegedly ensorcelled by abstractions and metaphysics, who were getting in the way of the practical administration of the state. He railed against the "Windbags and ideologues who have always fought the existing authority." Napoleon saw ideology as a threat to his power and used ideologue as an epithet, as a way to claim that those who held principles independent from the demands of power were in fact independent from reality. And, when convenient, Napoleon's indictment described most religious and philosophical thought as ideology.[6] Ideologues—real and imagined—over the course of the decade became the scapegoat for the failures of his regime.[7] In today's terms he blamed them for "gridlock." The word ideology ceased to refer to anything other than theorists idealists, and intellectuals divorced from reality. "As Napoleon's position weakened both at home and abroad, his attacks on ideology became more sweeping and vehement," writes historian John B. Thompson. "Nearly all kinds of religious and philosophical thought were condemned as ideology. The term itself had become a weapon in the hands of an emperor struggling desperately to silence his opponents and to sustain a crumbling regime."[8]

In 1808, in Erfut, Prussia, Napoleon warned the Prussians of the danger posed by the ideologues:

> They are dreamers and dangerous dreamers; they are all disguised materialists and not too disguised. Gentlemen. . . . [*sic*] philosophers torment themselves to create systems; they will search in vain for a better one than Christianity which, in reconciling man with himself, assures both public order and the peace of states. Your *idéologues* destroy all illusions and the age of illusions is for individuals as for peoples the age of happiness.[9]

In his speech to the Council of State in 1812 he proclaimed:

> We must lay the blame for the ills that our fair France has suffered on ideology, that shadowy metaphysics which subtly searches for first causes on which to base the legislation of peoples, rather than making use of laws known to the human heart

> and of the lessons of history. These errors must inevitably and did in fact lead to the rule of bloodthirsty men. . . .
>
> When someone is summoned to revitalize a state, he must follow exactly the opposite principles.[10]

Several things are interesting about all this. First, the ideologues themselves were in many respects the forerunners of the American Pragmatists. American Pragmatism was launched as essentially the science of ideas. William James, the founder of the movement (though Charles S. Peirce coined the term), wanted to move away from what he believed to be the mysticism and cant in philosophy and get right down to the questions of why we believe certain things and how we act on them. More on that in a bit, but it's a nice irony that arguably the very first Pragmatists were the first to get beaten over the head with the scare word ideologue.

Second, Napoleon himself was a consummate Pragmatist (indeed, if you search through biographies of him the word pragmatic is a near constant refrain). He didn't believe in labels. He only cared about what works.

Third, he despised the ideologues because they were divisive. Napoleon was no great fan of Christianity or the Church. What he liked was the social cohesion that came with them, the compulsion to conform to the Rousseauian general will that found sole expression in Napoleon himself. "In religion," Napoleon famously said, "I do not see the mystery of the Incarnation, so much as the mystery of the social order."[11] Even Napoleon's brother, Lucien, saw in Napoleon a dismaying rejection of principle. Years before his brother's rise to power, Lucien wrote, "I've long discerned in him a completely self-centered ambition that outstrips his love of the common good. I really believe in a free state, [hence] he is a dangerous man."[12] Lucien would later support Napoleon in his bid for power, but at one moment he allegedly pointed his sword at his brother and vowed to run him through if he ever violated the principles of *Liberté, Fraternité*, and *Egalité*. Alas, he never got the chance.

We need to leave Napoleon here, but one last point is worth making. Napoleon, as Ralph Waldo Emerson eloquently wrote, was a truly modern man. He represented the ascent of a host of new ideas, forces, and trends: the self-made man; the movement of history; the ability of great men to create their own values while destroying the values of others. For Hegel, Napoleon was the "world-soul." After laying eyes upon Napoleon, Hegel said, "It is indeed a wonderful sensation to see such an individual, who, concentrated here at a single point, astride a horse, reaches out over the world and masters it."[13] Nietzsche, another pragmatist of a kind—the kind who, in his words, "philosophizes with a hammer"—saw in Napoleon "the embodiment of the noble ideal."[14] Otto Von Bismarck, the inspiration to a generation of progressive and pragmatic ideologues, was an "adorer" of Napoleon's rule. The Iron Chancellor and the Little Corporal shared countless attributes and personality traits, chiefly their hatred for binding rules or principles.

Napoleon represents power as its own justification, because power works. It works in ways that are obvious and recognizable. And it demands respect from those who want it. Bertrand Russell summarized this inherent flaw in pragmatism when he noted that if taken to its logical conclusions, "ironclads and Maxim guns must be the ultimate arbiters of metaphysical truth."[15]

Karl Marx comes up more than once in other chapters to follow, so I don't want to dwell on him too much here. But he is important to this story in this regard: Marx adopts Napoleon's definition of ideology and adds his own twist by universalizing the idea of an ideologue. At least when Napoleon accused the ideologues of being unrealistically beholden to "shadowy metaphysics," he conceded that they embraced their views by choice. For Marx that choice is an illusion. An ideology isn't something you develop or embrace as an ongoing intellectual enterprise. It is something you are born into, that is imprinted on you by external forces. It is entirely a function of your class. He explains it here, but reading the passage will only give you a headache:

> The ideas of the ruling class are in every epoch the ruling ideas, i.e. the class which is the ruling *material* force of society, is at the same time its ruling *intellectual* force. The class which has the means of material production at its disposal, has control at the same time over the means of mental production, so that thereby, generally speaking, the ideas of those who lack the means of mental production are subject to it. The ruling ideas are nothing

> more than the ideal expression of the dominant material relationships, the dominant material relationships grasped as ideas; hence of the relationships which make the one class the ruling one, therefore, the ideas of its dominance.[16]

The only way to break the spell of ideology is to . . . agree with Marx. If you are working class and don't understand that you should be a Communist, then you suffer from "false consciousness." But fear not, you can be cured of this through diligent reeducation by Marxists.

This formulation opened up a lot of options for the left. It created a rationale for dismissing contrary evidence without having to contend with it. Because Marxism was "scientific," it allowed its proponents to claim there was only one side to the argument—theirs (see Chapter 18, Science). "Oh, that's just your class interests talking" is an abracadabra phrase that makes all substantive disagreements and inconvenient facts vanish—without even the mess of a puff of smoke.

This, as Hannah Arendt once observed, was one of the great innovations of Communists: the ability to dispute any fact by questioning the motives of the presenter. In the 1950s this argument was given even more scientific luster, as Marxist social scientists claimed that the conservative (i.e., fascist) mind wasn't merely a product of class consciousness but was in fact a diagnosable psychological disorder.

Anyway, enough with Marx for now. Suffice it to say that Marxism was a main, but hardly solitary ingredient in the intellectual stew that started to cook in the second half of the nineteenth century. Darwinism saturated everything. Nietzschean pragmatism—even though the word pragmatism didn't come until later—suffused intellectual discourse. For Nietzsche the man who threw off the accumulated dogmas of the past to move beyond Christianity, beyond tradition, beyond, even, good and evil, was the superman. And why not? Was God not dead?

In America, William James—decent, sober-minded, kindly William James—was working on his own American recipe of the same stew. It wasn't as exotically flavored nor as forebodingly thick. But it was a similar dish nonetheless. James and Nietzsche had similar ideas but very different styles. As a brooding Romantic German, Nietzsche felt the crushing weight of history all around him. All those cathedrals and candles! A beneficent American, James felt liberated from history without having to lift a finger. As Richard Rorty, one of the left's star philosophers, put it, "As a good American, and as someone who thinks of himself as a pragmatist, I am of course inclined to see pragmatism as having duplicated all the best of Nietzsche while avoiding all the bad."[17]

The Nietzscheans, Marxists, and Hegelians had to wrestle History to the ground like she was a wild animal. They came up with theories that tamed History and made it their pet or beast of burden, pulling humanity in a predictable direction. The beast was hitched to the new great causes: nationalism, socialism, the rule of experts and technocrats who understood with "scientific" certainty what history is and where it must go. The fight with capital-H history was an epochal struggle, requiring all able-minded men to muster for battle.

Meanwhile, in America, a country founded on the idea of putting the past behind it and starting over, where reinvention was both a birthright and part of the national character, History was at its back. Whereas in Europe History was a dragon to be slain, in America History could be ridden bareback through the sunny uplands of the New World. The Europeans were weighted down with pessimism, fatalism, and the sense of the tragic. In America anything was possible if you tried really hard. Nietzsche had his gloomy, blood-soaked, "will to power." James had his happy and upbeat "will to believe." It's all oddly reminiscent of George Carlin's riff on the differences between baseball and football: "Baseball begins in the spring, the season of new life. Football begins in the fall, when everything's dying." Baseball is a nineteenth-century pastoral game played in a park. Football is a military-technological struggle for territory played on a gridiron in a stadium. In baseball you make "errors." In football you get "penalties."

Anyway, you get it. The point is not that America's progressive intellectuals were in sharp disagreement with the Europeans on most of the big questions; it's just that they were cheerier about it, and William James, America's premier philosopher at the time, reflected this optimism more than anyone else. When Charles Peirce came up with his very complicated theory of pragmatism, James immediately latched onto it, popularized it, and made it his own. (Poor Peirce simply wasn't up to the task of safeguarding the term and eventually changed the name of his own philosophy to "pragmaticism.") James saw himself—again, like Nietzsche—as sorting out what to do in the aftermath of "God's Funeral"[18] but rather than a somber wake complete with dirges, James preferred something a bit more like the moving party of a New Orleans jazz funeral.

Indeed, there was something admirably jazzlike to pragmatism in its early days. The whole idea was to lighten up, to not take philosophy too seriously. Instead of looking for eternal truths we should concentrate on what works. Ideas were true if they were successful, or in his famous phrase, if they had "cash value." Instead of an "iron block universe" we should think of a universe with the "lid off."[19] He spoke of "possibilities" and the ability to make the world what you want. He took the hammer and tongs of European philosophical combat and made them into constructive tools for building a better society. "[D]emocracy," wrote James, "is a kind of religion, and we are bound not to admit its failure. Faiths and utopias are the noblest exercise of human reason, and no one with a spark of reason in him will sit down fatalistically before the croaker's picture."[20] What Americans needed to do was find a healthy expression for the "sick shudder of frustrated religious demand."[21]

The Moral Equivalent of Liberalism

One of James's greatest contributions to progressivism was the idea of the "moral equivalent of war." This has had real cash value for liberals over the last one hundred years. "Martial virtues," James wrote, "must be the enduring cement" of American society: "intrepidity, contempt of softness, surrender of private interest, obedience to command must still remain the rock upon which states are built." What James wanted was a way to figure out how to have war without war, to mobilize and galvanize people to drop their petty concerns and interests as if they were threatened by an outside foe. In other words, pragmatists care about what works, and war works. It works at getting people to shut up and listen, to follow orders, to make sacrifices and work together. More importantly, war legitimizes vast expansions of the state. Now if only we good and decent people can figure out a way to scare, enrage, or otherwise work up the people the way war does, we could really make something out of this country!

Like most people who've read James, I have a soft spot for the guy. He really was trying to work his way through the bloom'n' buzzin' confusion of the universe. And he was a decent enough fellow. The problem is that James was working in an environment where others were all too eager to redeem the cash value of his ideas for less sunny purposes. In Europe James's will to believe joined forces with Nietzsche's will to power and produced the ideas that led to Italian fascism.

Before that, a whole generation—the first generation—of American progressive intellectuals went to Europe, particularly Germany, to study. Thanks in large part to the growing fascination with Bismarck's "top-down socialism"—"a catalytic of American progressive thought," in historian Eric Goldman's words—they returned with an attitude that was far more philosophically serious than James's loosy-goosey, laugh-clown-laugh approach. A young Woodrow Wilson wrote that Bismarck's Prussia was the most "admirable system, . . . the most studied and most nearly perfected" in the world. Indeed, some nine thousand Americans had studied in Germany by the end of the nineteenth century. When the American Economic Association was formed, five of the first six officers had studied in Germany. At least twenty of its first twenty-six presidents had as well. In 1906 a professor at Yale polled the top 116 economists and social scientists in America; more than half had studied in Germany for at least a year.[22]

These progressives took the idea of a moral equivalent of war very, very seriously. Even before James came up with the conceit, progressives had been struggling for a way to convince Americans to lay aside the antiquated dogmas and outdated ideologies of individualism in favor of a new collective ethos. "[W]e must demand that the individual shall be willing to lose the sense of personal achievement," insisted Jane Addams in 1902, "and shall be content to realize his activity only in connection to the activity of the many."[23] Walter Rauschenbusch, the leading proselytizer of the progressive social gospel movement, declared, "New forms of association must be created. . . . Our disorganized competitive life must pass into an organic cooperative life." Elsewhere, Rauschenbusch put it more simply: "Individualism means tyranny."

And creating a moral equivalent of war was just the perfect way to get this organic cooperative life off the page and into American hearts and minds. Although the idea began as just the moral equivalent, when the opportunity for a real war loomed on the horizon, the progressives leaped at it with both feet. John Dewey, James's heir as the foremost practitioner of philosophical pragmatism, championed going to nonmetaphorical war, on the grounds that it would help do all of the things that James wanted from a moral equivalent of war. In less than a decade the optimistic and individualistic possibilities of pragmatism had now evolved into "social possibilities," specifically what Dewey called the "social possibilities of war." He complained that opponents of entering World War I failed to recognize the "immense impetus to reorganization afforded by this war" and implored them not to let the crisis go to waste.

After the war (covered extensively in my book *Liberal Fascism*), progressives returned to the Jamesian argument about the moral equivalent of war, now claiming that World War I proved that planning and social control had worked under Woodrow Wilson's war socialism. Therefore, the same techniques—command and control economics (i.e., "war socialism"), censorship, propaganda, etc.—should be applied in peacetime. "We planned in war" became the mantra of the intellectuals, furious with the Republican-led "return to normalcy" of the 1920s. And liberalism has never recovered. The search for a moral equivalent of war continues to define American liberalism to this day.

It is not a controversial observation, even to liberal historians of the New Deal, that FDR campaigned in 1932 promising to use the techniques of World War I to fight the Great Depression. Once elected he recruited a slew of Wilson administration veterans to re-create or revive the infrastructure of Wilson's "war socialism." The Securities and Exchange Commission was an extension of the Capital Issues Committee. The Reconstruction Finance Corporation was an updated version of the War Finance Corporation. The Civilian Conservation Corps was sold and run as a paramilitary organization inspired by William James.

The National Recovery Administration, an explicit revamping of Wilson's War Industries Board, was the crown jewel of the early New Deal. It was created by the National Industrial Recovery Act. "As in the great crisis of the World War," Roosevelt explained in 1933 while unveiling the law, "it puts a whole people to the simple but vital test: Must we go on in many groping, disorganized, separate units to defeat or shall we move as one great team to victory?" The NRA was run by General Hugh "Iron Pants" Johnson (an ironic nickname when you consider what "Hugh Johnson" sounds like when you say it fast), the man who oversaw the draft under Wilson. Johnson militarized it from the beginning. He issued the Blue Eagle—the symbol of the NRA—and FDR explained that it was like a military insignia that distinguished friend from foe. Johnson was a huge fan of Benito Mussolini, who was already running his own openly moral equivalent of war programs in Italy. Johnson used many of Il Duce's techniques, including staging huge military-style parades, complete with mandatory uniforms for workers.

Despite the fact that the New Deal was a failure, it remains the gold standard in liberal policy making. In fairness, such leading lights as Paul Krugman and Lawrence Summers concede that the New Deal didn't work. But their beaux ideal of a great economic recovery program was *World War II*—which is not exactly a sharp break from the moral equivalent of war argument.

Regardless, World War II or the New Deal or some combination of the two have remained the prism through which liberalism sees its calling. John F. Kennedy explicitly framed the New Frontier as an extension of the war generation's mission. His successor, LBJ, fashioned the Great Society as a revamped New Deal, complete with a moral equivalent of war campaign: the War on Poverty. "Our decision about energy will test the character of the American people and the ability of the president and the Congress to govern," Jimmy Carter told the nation, while wearing a fetching sweater. "This difficult effort will be the 'moral equivalent of war'—except that we will be uniting our efforts to build and not to destroy." Since then, environmentalists and various affiliated crusaders for green energy have invoked moral equivalent of war arguments with abandon. Thomas Friedman, who routinely waxes poetic on the advantages of China's "one-party authoritarianism," insists that we must fight global warming like it was World War II, because "green is the new red, white and blue." And let's not even pause on the whole "we need to be like the greatest generation" cliché.

Paul Krugman, America's foremost exponent of Keynesian economics, is constantly invoking war or the threat of war as an economic boon. "If we discovered that, you know, space aliens were planning to attack, and we needed a massive buildup to counter the space alien threat, and really inflation and budget deficits took secondary place to that, this slump would be over in eighteen months," he said on CNN. "And then if we discovered, oops, we made a mistake, there aren't any aliens, we'd be better—"

At this point Harvard economist Ken Rogoff interrupted. "We need Orson Welles, is what you're saying."

To which Krugman responded, "There was a 'Twilight Zone' episode like this in which scientists fake an alien threat in order to achieve world peace. Well, this time, we don't need it, we need it in order to get some fiscal stimulus."[24]

Krugman takes a similar position about World War II, which he claims pulled America out of the Great Depression (an argument largely dismantled by Arthur Herman, Robert Higgs, and Robert Barro), and a World War II–level intervention in the economy is required to fix our current woes. Similarly, after the September 11, 2001, terrorist attacks Krugman wrote that the economy would be boosted by everyone rushing "out to buy bottled water and canned goods."[25]

Meanwhile, President Obama came into office motivated by the mantra "a crisis is a terrible thing to waste." He routinely invokes moral equivalent of war arguments directly and indirectly, as do his supporters. During the Gulf oil spill he insisted the crisis "echoes 9/11." At a military base he proclaimed to military personnel, "This is an assault on our shores, and we're gonna fight back with everything that we've got!" That night he gave an Oval Office address offering his "battle plan" to fight the spill and suggested that we somehow owe it to our troops to rally around his energy agenda.

All of this is the natural product of American pragmatism, which vows that it is opposed to ideology. The desire to create a moral equivalent of war isn't an ideological agenda, they insist; it's simply what any pragmatic person would do.

The Devilish Dewey

The moral equivalent of war isn't the only manifestation of pragmatism's lasting impact on liberalism. (Pragmatism's impact on Obama is not a controversial claim, by the way. Harvard's James Kloppenberg's 2010 book, *Reading Obama*, celebrates the president as the incarnation of the pragmatic spirit: "Barack Obama embodies a surprising number of the central themes in the American political tradition, particularly as it has come to be known in the last half century. . . . Americans who prefer their principles stated with dogmatic certainty rather than with the humility and tentativeness appropriate for democratic deliberation might find Obama's conception of politics unpalatable.)"[26]

From the beginning American pragmatism set out to, in effect, rule by cliché. James's optimistic, relatively *practical*, philosophy was exactly what a generation of ideologues needed to clear the field of rival ideologies. In this it was a "philosophy and a psychology perfectly tailored to progressive needs," Eric Goldman writes in his classic *Rendezvous with Destiny*. William James's call for a new orientation of "looking away from first things, principles, 'categories,' supposed necessities; and of looking towards last things, fruits, consequences, facts," allowed liberals to attack all competing ideas as outdated dogmas no longer relevant. James's protégé, Horace Kallen, explained that Pragmatism "dissolves dogmas into beliefs, eternities and necessities into change and chance, conclusions and finalities into processes. But men have invented philosophy precisely because they find change, chance and process too much for them, and desire infallible security and certainty."

Taken on its own terms, pragmatism's folly is that it separates intelligence from wisdom. Its greatest sins are arrogance and deceit, including self-deceit. It is arrogant because it assumes the individual—particularly the expert—can know everything he needs to know without reference to received wisdom, historical precedent, tradition, dogma, etc. The pragmatists particularly loathed history, because it was a storehouse of old thinking with no relevance for the new age of science, slide rules, and data. Tricked by what they saw out their windows, they assumed that human nature had an expiration date—and that date was yesterday. "I speak in dispraise of dusty learning, and in disparagement of the historical technique," boasted Stuart Chase, the brain truster who reportedly gave the New Deal its name and yearned for an "economic dictatorship" in the United States, "Are our plans wrong? Who knows? Can we tell from reading history? Hardly."

Pragmatism's deceit comes in the form of actually believing this nonsense. There is a book screaming to be written on how the twentieth—and now twenty-first—century can be understood as a world-historical struggle not between Friedrich Hayek and John Maynard Keynes, as is so often claimed, but between Hayek and John Dewey. Hayek, more than anyone else, illuminated the knowledge problem. Simply put: No one person can ever know enough. Planners who think they can process all of the data from disparate sources across vast expanses of geography and culture are, quite simply, educated fools. The planners of the New Deal had convinced themselves that they were smart enough to grind out any problem so long as they had enough data. Worse, in their contempt for the "disorganized" character of capitalism, they were deeply hostile to markets and the informational power of prices. When prices went in the wrong direction the New Dealers took it upon themselves to out think the market. Hence the great pig slaughter of September 1933, when the government ordered the killing of six million pigs in a time of deprivation.

Hayek explained, and not just in the realm of economics, that knowledge is communal and collective. It is bound up in, and communicated by, traditions, customs, laws, prices, even language. There's a lot of philosophical and epistemological overlap between Hayek's philosophy and the pragmatists'—in terms of how we know and learn things as individuals. But on this core point the two could not be more different. Hayek understood that markets are collective, cooperative endeavors precisely because individuals are empowered to make their own decisions. Dewey believed the only way we could have a collective, cooperative system was if we took away the individual's ability to make his own choices. Citizens needed to be forced to become the kind of citizens Dewey believed would be productive. "Social arrangements, laws, institutions . . . are means of creating individuals. . . . Individuality in a social and moral sense is something to be wrought out," Dewey wrote.[27]

Hence, the great irony: Hayek, one of the greatest champions of individual liberty and economic freedom the world has ever known, believed that knowledge was communal. Dewey, the champion of socialism and collectivism, believed that knowledge was individual. Hayek's is a philosophy that treats individuals as the best judges of their own self-interests, which in turn yield staggering communal cooperation. Dewey's was the philosophy of a giant, Monty Pythonesque crowd shouting on cue, "We're All Individuals!"

If asked, I could offer a rousing indictment of Dewey's political ideology. He didn't like America very much, and his writings often have a whiff of anti-Americanism to them. He often seemed to think everyone was doing things better "over there," and over there could mean just about anywhere not here. He was certainly convinced that America was backward because it remained embarrassingly committed to what he called "ragged individualism." Indeed, as much as any one man could, he popularized the notion that "rights" are a fiction. "Natural rights and natural liberties exist only in the kingdom of mythological social zoology," he insisted. Rights can only be properly understood as tools of "organized social control" via a "socialized economy." Heck, *humans* are "nothing in themselves," according to Dewey. Experts under the authority of the state must be tasked with *creating* worthwhile men.

He was both impressed and flattered by the Soviet Union's great experiment, particularly the Soviets' fondness for his educational philosophy. And while his views on Soviet Marxism were, uh, nuanced, he was constantly looking for an indigenous socialist (nonviolent) revolution in America. This gave him a soft spot for self-proclaimed visionaries, revolutionaries, and rabble-rousers. He never voted for FDR when Norman Thomas, the Socialist Party of America candidate, was on the ballot. He found himself on the same side of many debates with Father Charles Coughlin (who we will see again later). He wandered from one fad to another, each time convinced that he'd simply applied the clearest, most empirical intelligence to the latest, most pressing problem. "I seem to be unstable," Dewey admitted in his old age, "chameleon-like, yielding one after another to many diverse and even incompatible influences; struggling to assimilate something from each and yet striving to carry it forward."[28] In other words, rather than bringing order to the blooming buzzing confusion of the universe, he was carried away by it like a bit of flotsam in the tide.

Which brings me to my primary objection to Dewey. It is not his ideology but his profoundly successful campaign to claim that he, along with his disciples and colleagues, had no ideology at all. He was an intellectual con man. Over the course of a very long, hugely influential career in education, philosophy, and political journalism, in which he served as a weather vane for leftist fads of all sorts, he always pretended to be free of cant, dogma, and ideology, when in fact he was weighted down by all three. He railed against "isms" and mocked the "stupidity of habit bound minds" in his opponents. All the while he did everything he could to advance a thoroughly socialist agenda—in kindergarten classrooms and college lecture halls—that was violently at odds with the American tradition. "Dewey," writes Tiffany Miller Jones, "arguably did more than any other reformer to repackage progressive social theory in a way that obscured just how radically its principles departed from those of the American founding."[29]

Part of his trick was being an absolutely terrible writer (a trick countless postmodern academics figured out and emulated). With considerable effort he could manage to be merely dry and boring. But his more substantial philosophical prose reads like a bunch of German words were dipped in maple syrup and dragged across a linty floor before being badly translated back into English by someone with a less firm grasp of idiom. Oddly, the denseness of his prose gave the impression of seriousness. Odder still, given that pragmatism seeks to make ideas "clear," and yet a lead-lined bucket of mud is more transparent than most of Dewey's work. Fortunately for him he didn't always go by the pragmatic label. He kept a lot of fake IDs in his philosophical wallet: naturalism, instrumentalism, functualism, and of course, empiricism.

And it worked. Dewey and his cohorts pulled off one of the great intellectual cons of the twentieth—and now the twenty-first—century. Like the old saw about how the greatest trick the devil played is convincing the world he didn't exist, American liberalism from the time of Dewey until the early 1960s managed to convince vast swaths of America that there was nothing ideological whatsoever to their worldview.

Cool Pragmatism

The 1960s, before the wackiness started, was the decade of John F. Kennedy's "cool pragmatism." JFK and his "whiz kids" were going to apply the latest scientific methods to settling political questions. They had punch cards and slide rules and everything! John Kenneth Galbraith's

1958 book, *The Affluent Society*, convinced policy makers that there was plenty of money to fix America; all it would take would be the right policies. In his 1962 Yale commencement address President Kennedy explained that "political labels and ideological approaches are irrelevant to the solution" of today's challenges. "Most of the problems . . . that we now face, are technical problems, are administrative problems," Kennedy insisted at a press conference the previous March. These problems "deal with questions which are now beyond the comprehension of most men."

The American public has soured on liberalism's claims of pragmatism since the 1960s. People understand that it is an ideological approach, even if many liberal ideologues deny it. But they still play this game. They're still convinced that their agenda is nonideological, focused simply on what works. This has put liberals in a terrible box. They desperately want to argue for ideological principles, but they've cut themselves off from the authority of those very same principles. Herbert Croly, founder of the flagship liberal journal *The New Republic* and author of the progressive bible, *The Promise of American Life*, responded to attacks that he and his magazine were supporting Mussolini too ardently by noting that *The New Republic* was "not an exponent of liberal principles." Indeed, "[i]f there are any abstract liberal principles, we do not know how to formulate them. Nor if they are formulated by others do we recognize their authority. Liberalism, as we understand it, is an activity."[30]

In other words, Croly was saying, we liberals are just so smart we can figure out everything from scratch. This is what pragmatism has bequeathed liberalism: intellectual deracination. Liberalism has become bookless, in the words of the longtime publisher of *The New Republic*, Martin Peretz. E. J. Dionne writes that "liberals and Democrats tend not to view themselves as the inheritors of a grand tradition. Almost on principle, they are suspicious of such traditions, of too much theorizing, of linking themselves too much to the past." Sure, they like to throw around words like "new progressive era" and "new New Deal," but they are utterly unwilling—and unable—to be bound by the inconvenient baggage of those precedents.

The steel spine of progressivism, with its calls for "social control" and "economic dictatorship" has given way to the invertebrateness of contemporary liberalism, which stands for nothing but empirically driven but unbounded do-goodery. Writers such as Michael Tomasky are forced to concede the amnesia of his fellow liberals while still insisting that liberalism is never wrong.[31] Why? Because according to Tomasky whenever liberalism goes off the tracks and turns into something bad or despotic, it's because real liberals have abandoned the project.

The result is an ideology that doesn't know why it upholds and cherishes its ideas. And if you don't know why you cherish your ideas, you're going to have a hard time recognizing when it's time to move on to something else. As William Voegeli puts it in his penetrating book *Never Enough*, contemporary liberalism is plagued by a lack of a limiting principle. By pragmatism's own metaphors, their philosophy is like an acid that dissolves dogmas. The problem with acid is that it never knows when to stop burning. That's why liberals are constantly discovering new crises that require more government solutions. Suggesting to activist liberals that maybe some day they could just go home and get a real job elicits nothing but bewilderment or rage when you bring it up.

Some early progressives foresaw the danger of "China Syndrome" pragmatism—where the acid just keeps burning. "These people are talking the relativism which will ruin liberalism yet," Charles Beard lamented of New Deal–era liberals. "Don't they know that the means can make the ends? Don't they realize that their method of arguing can justify anything? I wish we could find some way of getting rid of conservative morality without having these youngsters drop all morality." Nearly twenty years earlier the progressive J. Allen Smith complained of Wilson-era progressives: "The real trouble with us reformers is that we made reform a crusade against standards. Well, we smashed them all and now neither we nor anybody else have anything left."

In fairness, today's liberalism does have standards. But they all bend to the ultimate need, which is to justify the authority of liberalism.

3
NO LABELS

> I don't believe in labels. I want to do the best I can, all the time. I want to be progressive without getting both feet off the ground at the same time. I want to be prudent without having my mind closed to anything that is new or different. I have often said that I was proud that I was a free man first and an American second, and a public servant third and a Democrat fourth, in that order, and I guess as a Democrat, if I had to take—place a label on myself, I would want to be a progressive who is prudent.
>
> —Lyndon B. Johnson, television and radio address, March 15, 1964

In 2010, a group of self-proclaimed freethinkers and raging moderates founded an organization called No Labels. New York City mayor Michael Bloomberg was the guiding personality behind the enterprise. While the group was new, the idea was old. As we've seen, it goes all the way back to another famously short egomaniac, Napoleon.

The official motto of No Labels is "Put the Labels Aside. Do What's Best for America." Or at least that's one of them. For a group that doesn't like labels, they sure have a lot of mottoes. Anyway, their mission statement goes on: "We are Democrats, Republicans, and Independents who are united in the belief that we do not have to give up our labels, merely put them aside to do what's best for America." Elsewhere on their Web site the organization likens itself to the Korean Demilitarized Zone

(DMZ), which it describes as an area designed by North and South Koreans alike for "cool heads" to craft "elegant solutions." Likewise, No Labels wants to be a "Depoliticized Zone" that achieves the same purpose.

It's a metaphor that does not speak well of the No Labelers. The Korean DMZ is one of the most heavily mined and dangerous places in the world, with soldiers waiting for the slightest provocation to launch a devastating war, and where nothing fruitful in the affairs of men has happened for half a century.* Moreover, the DMZ is the demarcation point between the fundamentally decent, prosperous, and democratic nation of South Korea and the fundamentally evil, impoverished, and totalitarian criminal regime of the Kims. But other than that it's a boffo metaphor.

The No Labelers believe that labels get in the way of problem solving. Taken at its plainest meaning, this argument is incandescently stupid. "Label" is another word for "word(s)." And without words—i.e., language, communication, the sharing of complex ideas—we are back in the trees. I love people who say, "I don't believe in labels," as if labels are like unicorns or the tooth fairy or good flan. *Everything* we associate with civilization, decency, and progress depends on labels. If we cannot label something poisonous, people will die. When we label evil behavior with the word evil, we signal to the world that that is something you should not do. If a criminal rejects the label "murderer," that doesn't make him any less of one. But if we accept that murder is just a meaningless label we go a long way toward being a party to murder. If you cannot understand why having a blanket policy against labels is such a terrible idea, I urge you to march into your kitchen and peel the wrappers off all of your cleaning supplies, prescription drugs, and canned goods. Natural selection will take care of the rest in due time.

Now of course this is not what Bloomberg and his allies mean when they say they are against labels. What they mean is something supposedly much more sophisticated. The labels they oppose are things like socialist or Nazi or left wing and right wing. What they don't like about these terms is that they get in the way of pragmatic problem-solving.

And, to be sure, they have a point. Hurling undeserved epithets at people is not all that helpful or constructive. As William Galston and

---

*Though, ironically, the DMZ has been a boon for animals and wildlife.

David Frum, two in-house intellectuals of the No Labels "movement," write in the *Washington Post*: "[T]he political system doesn't work if politicians treat members of the other party as enemies to be destroyed. Labeling legitimate policy differences as 'socialist' or 'racist' undermines democratic discourse."[1]

Here we get closer to the heart of things. The No Labelers' real problem, it seems, is not with labels per se, but with lying, or more specifically, with defamation. If I call you a racist for opposing reparations for slavery or for opposing statehood for Washington, D.C., my offense is not in using the word racist but for using it inaccurately. Similarly, my sins may be numerous if I call you a Nazi for wanting to take away the perks of public employee unions, but the fact that I used the word is of no great import. The fact that I used it unfairly is. However, if you propose restoring slavery because blacks are unworthy of citizenship and I call you a racist, I've done nothing wrong at all. Indeed, I should be applauded for committing the simple yet noble act of telling the truth. And if you spend your days extolling Adolf Hitler and waxing lyrical about the benefits of rounding up and liquidating the Jews, what decent person will object if I call you a Nazi?

But this isn't what the No Labelers are actually pushing. It is merely the argument they are using to sell what they really want. And what is that? To clear away principled objections to what they want to do. They proclaim that they are against ideology—and sometimes they are even sincere—but what they fail to take into account is that they too are ideologues, objectively and on their own terms. When you hear politicians proclaim that we must get "beyond" ideology, that we must lay down labels, what they are really saying is that you must unilaterally put aside all of your philosophical and principled objections and get with *their program.* You never hear a politician proclaim that we must "put aside labels," "get past the partisan divide," and "stop the ideological squabbling" and then say, with equal passion, "That's why I am abandoning all of my principled positions and agreeing with you."

When people say, "We all need to put away our labels," what they really mean is, you must put away yours so that I may continue with my program unimpeded. It's like Rosie O'Donnell's gun control policy: Maybe you shouldn't have a gun, but her kid's bodyguard should.[2]

This is an ancient grift, a venerable con, a time-honored ruse used by ideologues to clear the field of opposition. Let us put aside all of our ideological priorities and accept my ideological priorities as fact and wisdom. Sometimes, as with John Dewey, this feint is carried out with impressive philosophical light shows. And sometimes it is pulled off with the sort of brazen effrontery (or plain old obtuseness) that is only possible when you take it for granted that your biggest fans are idiots.

In these cases I have in mind such creatures as Arianna Huffington, an intellectual huckster of the first order. Huffington has been playing this game for several years now. Whenever confronted with the fact that what she is spewing is little more than boilerplate leftism, she responds with a long-canned answer about how the left-right paradigm has outlived its usefulness. Here she is on CNN: "This whole framing as a right versus left debate—a liberal versus conservative debate—is completely flawed. It's obsolete. It's making it much harder for us to solve our problems as a country."[3] And here is Huffington ranting in one of the books with her name on it: "Someone please alert the media: not every issue fits into your cherished right/left paradigm. Indeed, that way of looking at the world is becoming less and less relevant—and more and more obsolete. And more and more dangerous."

This might have been a teeny-weeny bit more compelling an argument if it didn't appear in a left-wing screed of a book titled *Right Is Wrong: How the Lunatic Fringe Hijacked America, Shredded the Constitution, and Made Us All Less Safe (And What You Need to Know to End the Madness).* For Huffington the anti-ideologue, only one ideological perspective is too ideological.

What makes this a quintessential scam is that it uses the classic psychological trick mastered by all con men: making people feel dumb for being smart. Anyone who's been hoodwinked knows what I'm talking about. Jack buys the magic beans because he's beaten over the head with his own skepticism. The used-car salesman gets us to consider buying the special undercoating by making us feel dumb for being skeptical. "I can't believe you're falling for the whole 'don't get the extended warranty' myth," says the guy at the electronics store. The trick is to make you feel like you're in that old *Saturday Night Live* "Bad Ideas Jeans" commercial.

The same goes for this refrain to get people to give up labels of things they understand for ideas they disagree with. If we just call trial lawyers "community protection attorneys," they'll suddenly think they're not ambulance chasers anymore. If we call taxes the "dues" we pay for the privilege of living in America, they won't care how high we hike them. News flash: A nonrefundable deposit is not a deposit; it's a fee. If I mug you, do I get to stay out of jail if I explain that all of your money was simply a mandatory nonrefundable deposit? Airlines do the same thing. The ticket's only $100, but there's a $750 one-time seating fee.

Since politicians—liberal, and all too often, conservative alike—are certain that their policies are correct, they figure voters have to be either too stupid to see the truth or they have to be tricked into accepting what they don't believe. John Dewey begged the Socialist Party leadership to change their name but keep their policies. "The greatest handicap from which special measures favored by the Socialists suffer," Dewey declared,

> is that they are advanced by the Socialist party as Socialism. The prejudice against the name may be a regrettable prejudice but its influence is so powerful that it is much more reasonable to imagine all but the most dogmatic Socialists joining a new party than to imagine any considerable part of the American people going over to them.[4]

One person who took this advice, at least figuratively, is Van Jones, President Obama's erstwhile "green jobs czar." Jones explained in a 2005 interview that he was going to give up openly proselytizing Marxist-Leninism while still pursuing the ends: "I'm willing to forgo the cheap satisfaction of the radical pose for the deep satisfaction of radical ends." As historian Ronald Radosh notes, this was simply the latest effort of rebranding radical socialism so that it would be palatable to Americans, starting with Earl Browder and his claim that communism was simply "20th Century Americanism."[5]

A great many liberals believe in the "special measures favored by the Socialists," to borrow Dewey's phrase. Indeed, in their own publications and conferences they routinely say they favor socialism, or "social democracy," which is socialism. But the moment critics say liberals are socialists, it's considered a slander. But remember, these liberals don't *dislike* socialism. Even the ones who don't embrace it fully themselves admire the social democracies of Europe and want to emulate, say, the Labor Party in Britain. What they object to is anyone who doesn't like socialism calling them socialists.

When you ask them about this you get two answers. One is of the Deweyan variety. It goes something like this: "Labeling us socialists is just a scare tactic to frighten people from our agenda." In other words, the people are too stupid. The other argument is that conservatives understand socialism to be synonymous with Stalinism or Maoism. (It most emphatically is not. Mao and Stalin were socialists. Not all socialists are Maoists or Stalinists.) In other words, liberals are smart enough to use the word socialist intelligently but conservatives aren't.

Even if there were a lot of truth to the claim that conservatives don't understand what socialism is (I think it's a little true of some conservatives), both responses betray not only a staggering smugness but also a remarkable degree of insecurity. If liberals are so afraid of labels that they can't take their eye off them for one minute, what does that say about their ideology? If socialists want to improve the status of socialism in America, I think they'll have a tough road ahead of them. But the first place to start would be to own the label.

The same goes for the fake nonideologues of the No Labels crowd. Michael Bloomberg is a nannying, statist bully who, much like Napoleon, hurls around charges of ideological ensorcellment as a way to delegitimize political opponents he cannot defeat in open debate. He, like so many self-hating liberals, is convinced that there are millions upon millions of "socially liberal fiscal conservatives" out there in America for him to scoop up. The only problem is, they don't exist. They're the "jackalopes of American politics," in the words of my friend Kate O'Beirne. The press keeps telling us they exist out there in huge numbers, but when you go looking for them, they refuse to emerge from the bushes. In fairness, a great many people do describe themselves as social liberals but fiscal conservatives. But social scientists identify these people by a pithier label: Democrats.

And yet we're constantly told that if the Republicans could just give up their labels and their ideological obstreperousness, the jackalopes will rush to the GOP's big tent. The truth is that a handful of rich lawyers in

Priuses (or is it Prii?) will drive up to the front of the tent along with a few hundred Andrew Sullivan knockoffs, and forty million social and economic conservatives will head for the exits.

But why do they even bother with the social liberal, fiscal conservative talk in the first place? Because liberals are embarrassed by their own label. That's why they don't believe in labels—because the labels describe them accurately.

4

DOGMA

> If it be really true that men sickened of sacred words and wearied of theology, if this largely unreasoning irritation against "dogma" did arise out of some ridiculous excess of such things among priests in the past, then I fancy we must be laying up a fine crop of cant for our descendants to grow tired of.
>
> —G. K. Chesterton, *What's Wrong with the World*

The dawn of the Enlightenment, it was assured, spelled the end of the long night of dogma. Generations of superstition, tradition, and myth had accumulated like piles carpeting the Augean stables, proclaimed the *philosophes.* All that was necessary to liberate man was to clean out the muck and excrement. The war on dogma was intended to be both a collective endeavor and a personal one. Descartes, for instance, attempted to purge his mind of any and all notions, and then only to readmit those that he could personally verify with the tools of reason and logic. On a much broader landscape, the forces of Enlightenment set about to pry off the dead hand of the past so that mankind could escape the clutches of history and take flight on the wings of their ideals. As we've seen, perhaps even belabored, the pragmatists considered delegitimizing the authority of the past to be among their noblest endeavors.

Dogmas are ideals broken in by time and consecrated by experience. As such, what dogma lacks in inspiration it makes up for in sober reliability. But before anyone can suggest a dogma be tossed into the dustbin of history as an unnecessary relic of the ways things once were, it must first be born as an ideal—new, exciting, revolutionary.

As ideals, they are intoxicating. They can be, as Dostoyevsky put it, the "fire in the minds of men."[1] The Russian revolutionaries, disciples of their Jacobin forebears, insisted that the latticework of dogma supporting czarism institutionalized arbitrary abuses of power, torture, and cruelty. And they were right! And the defenders of the regime responded that overthrowing the status quo would usher in an age of cruelty and barbarism the likes of which humanity had never seen. And they were right, too! The dogma of the czars killed thousands. But the dogmas of Marxism, dressed in the uniform of science and reason, slaughtered and enslaved hundreds of millions.

Hitler was obsessed with the need to throw off the dogmas of Christianity's slave morality. "Christianity, of course, has reached the peak of absurdity," Hitler insisted in 1941. "And that's why one day its structure will collapse. Science has already impregnated humanity. Consequently, the more Christianity clings to its dogmas, the quicker it will decline." Der Führer was interested in scrubbing away old dogmas to replace them with ideals and "truth":

> From the tenderest age, education will be imparted in such a way that each child will know all that is important to the maintenance of the State. As for the men close to me, who, like me, have escaped from the clutches of dogma, I've no reason to fear that the Church will get its hooks on them.
>
> We'll see to it that the Churches cannot spread abroad teachings in conflict with the interests of the State. We shall continue to preach the doctrine of National Socialism, and the young will no longer be taught anything but the truth.[2]

Of course not all, or even remotely most, sworn enemies of dogma embrace genocidal ideals. But that is because they uncritically embrace an equally dogmatic aversion to mass murder. We create dogmas so that we may understand what is good and right in our everyday lives; hence the Greek root of the word "dogma": "seems good." When the academics proclaim we must cleanse humanity of its dogmas, what they are in effect arguing is that we must shed humanity of its humanity.

"Man can be defined as an animal that makes dogmas. As he piles doctrine on doctrine and conclusion on conclusion in the formation of some tremendous scheme of philosophy and religion, he is, in the only legitimate sense . . . becoming more and more human," writes G. K. Chesterton, the greatest defender of dogma properly understood in the English language. He continues:

> When [man] drops one doctrine after another in a refined skepticism, when he declines to tie himself to a system, when he says that he has outgrown definitions, when he says that he disbelieves in finality, when, in his own imagination, he sits as God, holding no form of creed but contemplating all, then he is by that very process sinking slowly backwards into the vagueness of the vagrant animals and the unconsciousness of the grass. Trees have no dogmas. Turnips are singularly broad-minded.[3]

Alas, this point has been lost on generations of brilliant turnips.

"Am I a criminal?" asked the late Jack Kevorkian. "The world knows I'm not a criminal. What are they trying to put me in jail for? You've lost common sense in this society because of religious fanaticism and dogma."[4] Franz Boas explained that the roots of his genius stemmed from the fact that his "parents had broken through the shackles of dogma."[5] "When people are the least sure," John Kenneth Galbraith assured us, "they are often the most dogmatic."[6] "Nothing is more dangerous," warned Stephen Jay Gould, "than a dogmatic worldview—nothing more constraining, more blinding to innovation, more destructive of openness to novelty."[7] When longtime *New York Times* columnist Anthony Lewis sought to sum up the lessons of his career he explained that the greatest enemy we face is "certainty": "[C]ertainty is the enemy of decency and humanity in people who are sure they are right, like Osama bin Laden and John Ashcroft."[8]

(This raises a few concerns: To begin, Lewis's conclusion raises a simple question: "Is Lewis really sure about this?" I mean, if you're certain that certainty is evil, what does that make you? More important, this is dangerous nonsense. If Osama bin Laden and John Ashcroft are both enemies of humanity and decency because they are certain of their beliefs, then so are Mother Teresa, Elie Wiesel, and Jesus. To suggest one is a threat to decency and humanity for being sure that Nazis or jihadists are threats to decency and humanity is the very definition of asinine sophistry.)

Dewey's student Horace Kallen helped invent the language of pragmatism because it "dissolves dogmas into beliefs, eternities and necessities into change and chance, conclusions and finalities into processes. But men have invented philosophy precisely because they find change, chance and process too much for them, and desire infallible security and certainty."[9]

President Obama paid homage to this grand tradition when he vowed in his inaugural an "end to the petty grievances and false promises, the recriminations and worn-out dogmas, that for far too long have strangled our politics." As with every progressive pragmatist, the past is the enemy and dogma its greatest weapon.

As we've seen, the self-styled empiricists of liberalism have convinced themselves that they are only concerned with what works. They are like rats behind the pied piper of data, and they will go wherever it leads them, regardless of ideology or convention. Bentley University economist Scott Sumner writes on his blog: "I can't think of any real world policy disputes facing Congress, now or in the past, where liberals did not take what they saw as the roughly utilitarian position. And I can see lots of cases where conservatives, dogmatic libertarians, or econ-nuts took non-utilitarian positions."[10]

The fact that Sumner cannot think of situations where liberals were nonutilitarians is not evidence that liberals are nonutilitarians. It is evidence that Professor Sumner hews to the dogmatic mythology that liberalism is simply the doctrine of clear thinking applied to politics. But one need not rehearse the countless ways in which liberalism sneaks its values into policy debates under the guise of utilitarianism (or realism, pragmatism, empiricism) to recognize how palpably untrue Sumner's interpretation of reality is.

The armies of liberalism pour out of these Trojan Horses to do battle for social justice at every turn (see Chapter 11, Social Justice). Head Start, among the holiest of social programs, has never worked, and each time this unwelcome fact presents itself it is greeted as proof that the program simply requires more money. The War on Poverty was less successful at reducing the poverty rate than ignoring it was. In 1966 the poverty rate was roughly 19 percent. In 1974, after the antipoverty programs were fully institutionalized, the poverty rate was 11.2 percent. Thirty years later, in 2004, when antipoverty spending was enormously greater, the poverty rate was 12.7 percent. And as of this writing, under Barack Obama it is over 15 percent (admittedly after a major recession, but also during a time of massive domestic spending and a relatedly weak recovery). Meanwhile, in the twelve years from 1949 to 1961—the supposedly scandalously apathetic Ike Age—poverty rates were cut roughly in half, from 41 percent to 21 percent. In other words, the cause of social justice was served more by a government that didn't bother with social justice.[11]

Science and reason are hailed as the greatest antidotes to dogma because they are a more concrete, more provable, form of truth. George Eliot writes in *Middlemarch*: "Science is properly more scrupulous than dogma. Dogma gives a charter to mistake, but the very breath of science is a contest with mistake, and must keep the conscience alive."[12]

Elliot was right, but it's worth noting that this is not an indictment of dogma part and parcel. It is true that many dogmas are built upon mistakes. But that doesn't mean the resulting edifice is not worthwhile. A ship may sink due to the blunder of the captain, but the resulting sunken wreckage beneath the waves may serve as a bountiful reef supporting a wealth of new life. So it is with humanity and her institutions. Columbus "discovered" America by mistake and the world is better for what was built upon that mistake. How many beloved children were born thanks to some capricious accident? We are told that the institution of monogamous marriage between a man and a woman was a mistake, unchartered by the laws of evolution and unlicensed by the conclusions of science. Maybe so. But what was built upon the rock of that "mistake" is not so easily or desirably undone even if we are willing to admit the existence of an error committed somewhere in the ancient recesses of prehistory. If tomorrow science tells us that it would make more sense to make stoplights green instead of red, the price of the resulting chaos would not be worth the gains in rational organization. Indeed, a reasonable man understands that the costs of ripping up the old and tried are often too expensive for the theoretical promises of the new and untried.

Lincoln's wisdom was only outstripped by his eloquence when he proclaimed in 1861, "The dogmas of the quiet past are inadequate to the stormy present. The occasion is piled high with difficulty, and we must rise with the occasion. As our case is new, so we must think anew and act anew. We must disenthrall ourselves and then we shall save our country."[13]

In his triumph Lincoln not only forged a new conception of our nation free of slavery, he forged *a new dogma* that it must never return to that evil. If all dogma is wrong, then it must always be considered a live proposition that slavery might in some circumstances be a worthwhile institution. Surely a mechanistic utilitarian could craft a perfectly consistent argument that the slavery of the few would maximize the happiness of the many. The only plausible utilitarian retort is that the many could not be happy while enjoying the fruits of slave labor. But such an argument hinges on the inconvenient fact that such unhappiness would be made possible only if the majority felt the sting of a properly formed conscience. And such a conscience can only exist when informed by a fundamental dogma about what is right and wrong. After all, the history of humanity unfolded for millennia with happy majorities benefitting from the miseries of an enslaved minority. It's a sign of civilizational progress that we—in the West, at least—believe that any happiness enjoyed at the expense of another's enslavement isn't a morally legitimate happiness.

William F. Buckley understood that dogma is a source of progress because it sets boundaries of acceptable discourse. He illustrated this point nicely when discussing a libertarian's idea of privatizing lighthouses. Buckley thought the idea absurd (and Buckley was famously wrong about that), but he noted that he wished the effort success, for "if our society seriously wondered whether or not to denationalize the lighthouses, it would not wonder at all whether to nationalize the medical profession."[14] Unfortunately, as my friend Mark Steyn has noted, we now have a world that is perfectly happy to discuss privatizing lighthouses even as we nationalize the medical profession.

But let's get back to science. The idea that dogma is necessarily at war with science is a misunderstanding of the former and a misapplication of the latter. Much of what is true of science is also true of dogma:

Both have many moral strikes against them. Science is the author of infinite boons to humanity and need not be put in the dock because it is also the accomplice to countless crimes. The light of reason hails from a flame that burns as often as it warms or illuminates. Likewise, dogma has kept societies backward and cruel, but it is also what keeps forward thinking and decent societies from becoming backward and cruel (see Chapter 18, Science).

Similarly, where dogma triumphs over science should be obvious. Science is silent on what should be done with the fruits of science. Science can cure illnesses and cause them, destroy cities and build them, save lives and take them. It is the realm outside of science, the realm of morality and religion, i.e., the realm of dogma, that tells us what is permissible and what is taboo. The scientist free of moral dogma is a cartoon villain who creates death rays for sport or ransom.

Dogma constrains how science should be done. The Hippocratic Oath, even in its original form, represents not a triumph of science but a triumph of moral absolutism. Whereas until the Hippocratic Oath (as Margaret Mead among others has argued) sorcerers and healers often wore the same hat, the advent of the oath marked the moment when doctors as a class became committed solely to preserving life. There's nothing within science per se that says medical researchers must not experiment on human subjects; it is the imposition of ethical dogma that constrains the scientist. The mandate "first do no harm" is as rankly ideological and dogmatic a precept as any, even more so. Most Republicans will accept tax increases in one area if offset in another. Many prolifers countenance exceptions for abortion in the cases of rape or incest, and, of course, for the life of the mother. Doctors make no such exceptions to the Hippocratic Oath—save, of course, when it comes to abortion—and only then when another dogmatic obsession trumps their oath.

Alas, this is not the only area where ideological forces corrupt science. Nowhere is this more obvious than in the battlefield of climate science, where the progressive protagonists insist that they are mere servants of the facts and their opponents are backward deniers of the unfolding apocalypse. Whenever a scientist follows the facts in a direction contrary to environmentalist dogma, he is no longer a real scientist.

Hence, when Al Gore's own scientific mentor cast a skeptical eye on the industry his work helped create, the pupil proclaimed that his former master had taken leave of his senses.

Indeed, green religious devotion runs so deep that adherents to the dogma of climate change must not only subscribe to the diagnosis of a fevered earth, they must show undying loyalty to the proposed remedy as well. It is true that the earth has gotten warmer since the Industrial Revolution, and it is probably true that mankind has contributed to that warming. How much of a contribution and how big a problem are still open questions, no matter how much saying so hurts the feelings of those who believe otherwise. It is also unclear what the ratio of costs and benefits might be. We've heard about the costs—real and alleged—ad nauseum: shrinking Arctic ice, floods, lost polar bears, etc. What gets less play are the potential benefits. In 2008, Thomas Fingar, then chairman of the National Intelligence Council, testified before the House Select Committee on Intelligence on the consequences of climate change. He explained that "net cereal crop yields likely will increase by 5 to 20 percent, for example, and most studies suggest the United States as a whole will enjoy modest economic benefits over the next few decades largely due to the increased crop yields." He also noted that the "growing season has lengthened an average of two days per decade since 1950 in Canada and the contiguous United States." New sea routes, primarily through the Northwest Passage, will be opened as well.

Regardless, there is nothing inherent to the claim that the earth is overheating that requires we follow a prescription of abolishing fossil fuels and smashing the internal combustion engine with the same zeal the iconoclasts applied to graven images. When a patient gets a fever we do not cure it by reverse engineering the habits that may have fostered the fever. We treat the ailment. Similarly, it is entirely possible that we could cure the earth by treating the symptom by, say, releasing particles into the air that would alleviate the greenhouse effect. Science has much to say on whether that would be a good idea. But unscientific dogmatists in lab coats conspire to keep the question from being asked. Hence, when a Nobel Prize–winning chemist suggested that geoengineering might solve global warming at a millionth of the cost of ineffective rationing strategies and alternative energy fantasies, the environmental community responded like Church elders presented with a proposal to disestablish the Church itself.[15]

More broadly, what is lost in these debates is the crucial distinction between science and scientism. The former is a value-neutral enterprise that seeks, through the scientific method, to understand and manipulate the reality of the physical world. Science is a procedure defined by systematic observation and measurement, followed by experiment, and then by the formulation, testing, and modification of hypotheses. It is not the source of moral truths, but moral truths must be informed by them. "The truth of our faith," observed Thomas Aquinas, "becomes a matter of ridicule among the infidels, if any Catholic, not gifted with the necessary scientific learning, presents as dogma what scientific scrutiny shows to be false."[16]

Scientism, meanwhile, is the act of seeing in science what is not there. It is an act of faith that elevates, nay makes divine, the authority of science to bolster the aims of its acolytes. The practitioners of scientism presume to tell us that we should live a certain way because science tells us we must. It reduces human existence to material causes and humans to bags of water, meat, and bones powered by electrical impulses. It is the ancient naturalistic fallacy updated with more contemporary lingo. Indeed, as the philosopher Edward Feser notes, scientism is itself a fallacy on its face, because it exempts itself from the scientific method. Scientism is not a testable proposition; it is an assertion of faith. No wonder the scientific socialists, technocrats, progressives, social psychiatrists, and environmentalists insist that science is on their side in the same way the mullahs and zealots proclaim that God is on theirs. They respond to inconvenient questions with the same dismissiveness as Bill Murray in *Ghostbusters* when he barks, "Back off man, I'm a scientist."

But at least the naturalistic fallacy assumes a creator, a larger wellspring of meaning, justice, and order. The fallacy of scientism creates priests answerable to no one and no thing other than the very dogma they mint. The fetus is an unhuman with no more rights than a ham sandwich because the new dogmatists wish it to be so, and they sell the proposition by saying science says they're right, the same way pagan priests insisted the viscera of goats indicated the will of the gods.

This is nothing new. When man loses God he sets about to make new gods. Or as the philosopher Eric Voegelin puts it, "[W]hen God is invisible behind the world, the contents of the world will become new gods; when the symbols of transcendent religiosity are banned, new symbols develop from the inner-worldly language of science to take their place."[17]

Likewise man creates dogmas because man needs dogmas. The light of reason illuminates the darkness and science provides us compasses to find our way. But it does not provide us with reasons to get out of bed in the first place. As John Dos Passos said, "The mind cannot support moral chaos for long. Men are under as strong a compulsion to invent an ethical setting for their behavior as spiders are to weave webs."[18] This is as true of criminals in prison as it is of monks in monasteries and scientists in laboratories.

5
SEPARATION OF CHURCH AND STATE

The principle of separation of church and state is as rooted an ideological precept as any that exists, whether you call it ideological or not. If you don't think so, it's probably because you already agree with the principle. Indeed, pretty much every position regarding the role of religion in society is seen as ideological by those who hold the opposing position. Obviously, if you're a member of the Christian Coalition, you probably think the ACLU is ideologically extremist, and vice versa.

But increasingly what counts for religious "extremism" is merely what until very, very recently was considered normal. For example, the American Atheists sued over the installation of the "9/11 cross"—a cross-shaped beam found at ground zero—at the National September 11 Memorial & Museum because "any government enshrinement of the cross was an impermissible mingling of church and state."[1] Anyone thinking otherwise must have overindulged in the Church wine, reasoned the AA, because "[t]he WTC cross has become a Christian icon. It has been blessed by so-called holy men and presented as a reminder that their god, who couldn't be bothered to stop the Muslim terrorists or prevent 3,000 people from being killed in his name, cared only enough to bestow upon us some rubble that resembles a cross. It's a truly ridiculous assertion."

The truth is that both the ACLU and the Christian Coalition are more ideologically similar than they are different. In any place in the world where freedom of conscience doesn't exist (Saudi Arabia comes to mind), the general notion that we should be free to worship as we please is greeted as profoundly and ideologically radical. The space between our alleged religious fanatics and our supposed atheistic fanatics is shockingly small. That's because our arguments are about the details of implementing a shared principle.

The separation of church and state has its roots in the West, with Jesus' injunction to "render unto Caesar the things which are Caesar's" (and only those things, it should be noted). But it took millennia of bloodshed and social upheaval for that idea to be translated into the recognizable practice we have today. When the Roman Empire fell in the West, the sole seat of political authority transferred to Constantinople, but the religious authority remained in Rome (though the Eastern Orthodox would say, more accurately, that it split). This meant that emperors and kings retained secular power in the West, but the Church was still the ultimate moral authority. For instance, when Emperor Theodosius slaughtered the Thessalonians, Archbishop Ambrose of Milan was so repulsed that he refused to give the emperor holy communion. "No fair!," (I paraphrase) the emperor cried. Insisting that David had done worse in the Bible. Ambrose replied, "You have imitated David in his crime, then imitate him in his repentance!" And so, off and on for eight months, the most powerful ruler in the entire world mimicked the biblical David, dressing in rags like a beggar in order to plea for forgiveness outside Ambrose's cathedral. One wonders if John Kerry would have submitted to a similar penance back in 2004, when bishops were threatening to refuse him communion should he present himself at the rail.

Over time the papacy's moral authority increased. Pope Leo III may have been forced to anoint Charlemagne as Rome's emperor, but by doing so he also cemented the notion that even kings were answerable to a higher authority. When Emperor Henry IV challenged Pope Gregory VII's power of investiture, he ended up, as legend has it, kneeling in the snows at Canossa for three days begging for forgiveness.

But the Protestant Reformation fractured Western Christianity, and with it the notion of a single source of temporal moral authority. Lutherans and Calvinists, contrary to a lot of glib commentary these days, were not moderates but ardent believers who wanted to overthrow the worldliness of the Catholic Church and replace it with more austere religious authority (see Chapter 21, The Catholic Church). Bloody religious wars ensued, with brutal massacres in the streets of European capitals. "In 1555," writes James Q. Wilson, "the Peace of Augsburg settled the religious wars briefly with the phrase *cuius regio, eius religio*—meaning that people in each state or principality would have the religion of their ruler. If you didn't like your prince's religion, you had to move somewhere else."[2]

The toothpaste was out of the tube. A riot of new denominations spread across Europe—Anabaptists, Quakers, Zwinglians, et al. More wars and social turmoil wracked Europe for the better part of a century. The Peace of Westphalia advanced the cause of religious liberty by carving out a few ideological and political harbors for freedom of conscience. In the words of C. V. Wedgwood, "[T]he essential futility of putting the beliefs of the mind to the judgment of the sword,"[3] was finally pecking its way into the European mind.

But the battle to clear space for the free exercise of conscience hardly ended there. Oliver Cromwell led a Presbyterian rebellion against the throne, but he understood that he didn't have the power to force his faith on all of his countrymen, and that trying to do so would be a fatal overreach. He needed to recruit adherents of other faiths to his cause. To this end he persuaded Parliament to respect liberty for "all who fear God." He even took tentative steps to welcome back the persecuted and exiled Jews of England.[4]

Then came the bloody trading of blows, faith, and thrones that marked the late seventeenth century. Ultimately Parliament passed the Toleration Act, permitting believers of various Protestant faiths to follow their religion so long as their loyalty to the crown was not in doubt. Even then, writes Wilson, "[t]heir members still could not hold government office, but at least they would not be hanged." Catholics and Unitarians, meanwhile, were not formally protected by law, but the English increasingly left them alone, too.[5]

The story goes on. Galileo had had his battles with the Church in Italy a half century earlier. The Puritans came to America to escape religious persecution. Again, these were not religious moderates (just ask the women who were hanged at Salem) but devout believers who craved the room to practice their religion as their consciences dictated.

Religious pluralism in colonial America continued to evolve. Maryland for Catholics, Georgia for Baptists, Massachusetts for Red Sox fans, and so on. The Founders barred the establishment of a religion by the federal government—in no small part because they remembered the repression of minority sects under the state church of England. But they saw no problem with the various American states establishing their own official churches. And they certainly had no objection to official displays of religiosity. One of the first acts by the new Congress was to hire a chaplain. Until well into the nineteenth century, the largest weekly church service in the United States took place in the U.S. Capitol building. At the request of President Jefferson, music was provided at federal expense by the United States Marine Band.[6]

Today you could argue—and if you don't I will—that the project of cleansing religion from the public square has gone too far. Whereas we used to have official national days of prayer and fasting, now we're almost at the point where we have a constitutional crisis if a kid says "God bless you" to a sneezing public-school teacher.

Whatever the right balance is between church and state, the point is that our overwhelming commitment to religious freedom isn't some purely abstract notion yanked out of a seminar discussion. As we've seen, whereas many academic debates can be over how many angels are on the head of a pin—wait, sorry, that's a theological question, how about, How many different kinds of evil are dead white European men?—ideological debates are not impractical distractions. They get at the core of what kind of civilization we want to live in. And there is no way to wall off religion from those debates. Yes, we can separate, to one extent or another, the role of religion in our society, but it is impossible to separate the role of religion—or the lack of it—in our own hearts. This is true at a very practical level insofar as it is impossible to know what someone's true motivations for any decision are. We can only judge people by the arguments that they make and the decisions that they take. But it's also true at a very high philosophical level.

It is beyond absurd to say that your religious faith informs your conception of the cosmos and your place in it, morality, and human purpose, but then also to say that your religious faith will have nothing whatsoever to do with your decision making as an elected official. This does not mean that you have to impose your religious views on others. John F. Kennedy confronted the issue of his Catholicism head-on and said it would not bind him to policies he deemed contrary to American interest. One can certainly gainsay some of his decisions, but most reasonable people would have a hard time detecting a relentlessly pro-Catholic bias.

One might even ask, "So what if a politician did have a proreligion bias?" I'm not talking about the unconstitutional imposition of Sharia or kosher laws for everyone. But what if a Catholic president had a soft spot for the wonderful work that parochial schools do? Or if a Druid president had a keen interest in forestry? Save the trees for they are our brothers and sisters! If a politician runs openly and honestly on his values, we should not be scandalized when those values inform his decision making, and we should not be surprised that his values are informed by his religion. In short, there's nothing essentially, fundamentally, wrong with religion guiding your politics.

Letting your politics guide your religion is another matter altogether. "I think that everything you do in public life has to be guided by your faith, affected by your faith, but without transferring it in any official way to other people," Senator John Kerry explained during the third presidential debate in 2004. "I believe that I can't legislate or transfer to another American citizen my article of faith. What is an article of faith for me is not something that I can legislate on somebody who doesn't share that article of faith."

That sounds reasonable enough, right? It's not how I would frame the issue, but it's a defensible position to be sure. Not surprisingly, this answer came up in the context of abortion. It is a dogmatic article of faith among many staunch defenders of abortion rights that abortion foes are driven by religion, and therefore banning abortion is an unjust religious imposition. "Keep your rosaries off my ovaries" and all that. And ever since Mario Cuomo's famous Notre Dame speech, Democratic politicians have been invoking the "Cuomo defense." In short, you can be *personally* prolife and still *publically* enforce prochoice policies. I find this to be a theological mess, but it is not my place to criticize others about their religious convictions.

But the whole thing comes off the rails of logic when Kerry says that his religious conviction is "why I fight against poverty. That's why I fight to clean up the environment and protect this earth. That's why I fight for equality and justice. All of those things come out of that fundamental teaching and belief of faith." Over and over during the campaign he zinged President Bush—or seemed to think he was zinging him—by pointing out that one must "demonstrate faith with deeds." And these were Kerry's deeds.

But wait a second. Kerry says his religious faith drives him to fight for the poor and the environment and all of that stuff. But when it comes to abortion, he suddenly cannot impose an article of his faith. Really?

I understand why abortion-rights activists see prolife policies as an imposition of faith (and I can see why a fetus would feel much the same way about prochoice policies, if he or she had a chance to live). But how are environmental or antipoverty policies driven by faith not an imposition of faith? If your faith tells you to pass (often misguided) environmental regulations that cost a father his job or a community its livelihood, you are making quite an imposition on others. Equality, in John Kerry's formulation, means denying some people opportunities for the benefit of others. And justice, however defined, usually involves guys with guns, courts, judges, prosecutors, and the like—all of whom are empowered by the state to use violence, even to kill you if necessary. Those sound like impositions to me. Indeed, as libertarians are fond of pointing out, pretty much all law comes with the implicit threat of violence. Don't believe me? Refuse to obey even the most picayune law and eventually a man in uniform with a gun on his hip is going to come talk to you about it.

President Obama is explicit in his overt claims that he is driven by a modern-day social gospel quest for social justice. One of his standard lines is that he is fulfilling the biblical injunction to be our brother's and sister's keeper. By the way, there is no such injunction. The only time the phrase "brother's keeper" appears is when Cain is trying sarcastically to dodge a murder rap. Some argue that Matthew 25:40 is what Obama and other liberals are getting at: "Verily I say unto you: Inasmuch as ye have done *it* unto one of the least of these my brethren, ye have done *it* unto me." But that's not a commandment to be your fellow man's keeper (keepers keep animals). Moreover, even if you're generous in how you interpret all of this, I'm unaware of any passage in the Hebrew or Christian bibles where God says that doing good to others means supporting bloated, inefficient, and often counterproductive government programs.

Regardless, the point is that Obama believes the bible tells him to push his agenda. Is that not an imposition of his faith? In his acceptance speech at the Democratic convention in 2008, he artfully replaced the idea of the American dream—individual opportunity, the pursuit of happiness—with the century-old progressive nostrum of "America's promise." At times, his rhetoric seems lifted straight out of the pages of Herbert Croly's *Promise of American Life.*

But to his credit, Herbert Croly was honest about the fact that the two visions are in fundamental opposition. The idea behind Croly's *Promise of American Life* was to move the country beyond the outdated nineteenth-century notions of rugged individualism in pursuit of the American dream. And it was an explicitly Christian enterprise. It was certainly the mission of the social gospel ministers, like Walter Rauschenbusch, but more revealingly, it was the mission of the technocratic progressive economists as well. Richard Ely, the leader of the University of Wisconsin progressives during their heyday and the founder of the American Economic Association—still the leading professional organization for American economists—was also the foremost lay leader of what was called the "Christian socialism" or "Christian sociology" movement.[7]

Ely believed and taught that every aspect of life should have Christianity injected into it. He held that Christians made a fundamental error by holding that salvation lies in the next life. When Jesus says that his kingdom is "not of this world," the correct translation, according to Ely, is "not of this age." And it was Ely's core conviction that the age of salvation could be reached through the judicious application of welfare-state policies. He wrote, in *Social Aspects of Christianity*, "I take this as my thesis: Christianity is primarily concerned with this world, and it is the mission of Christianity to bring to pass here a kingdom of righteousness and to rescue from the evil one and redeem all our social relations."[8] Woodrow Wilson shared this vision. "There is a mighty task before us, and it welds us together," Wilson told a YMCA conference. "It is to make the United States a mighty Christian Nation, and to Christianize the world."[9]

While there were some secular progressives, as a social movement it's almost impossible to speak of progressivism as anything other than a fundamentally Christian movement. And it sought to smash what we today would call the wall between church and state. Ely, for instance, hated the practice of seeing the world as "divided into things sacred and things secular" and asserted that "to a Christian all things must be sacred—his business as well as his church."[10] The American Economic Association (which initially brimmed with over sixty ministers as members) was to be a fundamentally religious organization that imbued all of its analysis and recommendations with a Christian vision that rejected laissez-faire economics as sinful and cruel. "God works through the State in carrying out His purposes more universally than through any other institution," Ely wrote. It "is religious in its essence" and "a mighty force in furthering God's kingdom and establishing righteous relations."[11]

So profound was the progressive insistence that there should be no demarcation between religion and politics that social gospel minister Walter Rauschenbusch proclaimed that if God couldn't be a liberal progressive then we needed a new god entirely. "[U]nless the ideal social order can supply men with food, warmth and comfort more efficiently than our present economic order," Rauschenbusch warned in his 1912 treatise *Christianizing the Social Crisis*, "back we shall go to Capitalism." Therefore, "[t]he God that answereth by low food prices," he proclaimed, "let him be God."

Taken seriously, this remains the essence of liberal political theology. Unfortunately, liberalism can no longer say so clearly. Bookless, liberalism lacks the vocabulary and the faith to connect these dots any longer. The god of lower food prices may not be the god of Abraham, Issac, and Jacob, nor that of the Jews or Muhammad, but the Jedi-like force of All Good Things is a liberal, and violating that faith is a sin.

Or as Senator Obama put it when he was asked "What is sin?"

Sin, he explained, is "[b]eing out of alignment with my values."[12]

Just so.

6
POWER CORRUPTS

In 1887, John Emerich Edward Dalberg-Acton—Lord Acton for short—penned his famous line, "Power tends to corrupt, and absolute power corrupts absolutely."[1]

Of all the truisms found in Bartlett's Familiar Quotations, this one may be the most revered as sheer genius among campus *philosophes*, op-ed Jeremiahs, and the carnival-stall barkers of cable news.

With very few exceptions, Acton's axiom is almost invariably aimed at anyone whom the speaker thinks cannot be trusted with power, but never at the ranks of those whom the speaker would very much like to see made ever more powerful. Republicans lament that power corrupts Democrats, and vice versa. But it is a rare day that we condemn the corruption of one of our own. Acton's Axiom is a cudgel to use on the other team.

However, the phrase is the engine of particularly acute hypocrisy among left-wing intellectuals. The same people who promise to "speak truth to power," will go to great lengths to explain why Castro isn't a dictator, why Stalin needs to be seen "in context," and why Yasser Arafat was an authentic champion of the powerless. Conservatives, meanwhile, own up to their corruption a bit more, recognizing that we are all cut from the crooked timber of humanity. The Right may allow for compromises with sons-of-bitches, but it usually concedes that they are in fact sons-of-bitches.

But more to the point, use of the phrase "power corrupts" is often a sign of the speaker's own corruption—and this is really what Acton had in mind in the first place.

Acton penned the line in a letter to his friend the Anglican bishop and historian Mandell Creighton. In 1887, Creighton had asked Acton to take a look at a history book he was working on. Acton chastised Creighton for his too sympathetic treatment of the Reformation era popes (i.e., the bad popes). Acton wrote:

> I cannot accept your canon that we are to judge Pope and King unlike other men, with a favourable presumption that they did no wrong. If there is any presumption it is the other way, against the holders of power, increasing as the power increases. Historic responsibility has to make up for the want of legal responsibility. Power tends to corrupt, and absolute power corrupts absolutely. Great men are almost always bad men, even when they exercise influence and not authority, still more when you superadd the tendency or the certainty of corruption by authority. There is no worse heresy than that the office sanctifies the holder of it.
>
> Here are the greatest names coupled with the greatest crimes; you would spare those criminals, for some mysterious reason. I would hang them higher than Haman, for reasons of quite obvious justice, still more, still higher for the sake of historical science.
>
> Quite frankly, I think there is no greater error. The inflexible integrity of the moral code is, to me, the secret of the authority, the dignity, the utility of History.
>
> If we may debase the currency for the sake of genius, or success, or rank, or reputation, we may debase it for the sake of a man's influence, of his religion, of his party, of the good cause which prospers by his credit and suffers by his disgrace. Then History ceases to be a science, an arbiter of controversy, a guide of the Wanderer, the upholder of that moral standard which the powers of earth and religion itself tend constantly to depress. It serves where it ought to reign; and it serves the worst cause better than the purest.[2]

While many know about this letter as the source of "power corrupts," the context of Acton's letter is forgotten—or, more likely, was never known—by the vast majority of people who invoke it. Acton, a devout if unorthodox Catholic, was responding specifically to the Catholic doctrine of papal infallibility put forth in 1870. Acton risked excommunication for his long battle against the doctrine of infallibility.

His objections were twofold, one theological, the other historical. It is the latter that is relevant for our purposes. Acton, a passionate liberal in the classic, British, sense of the word, feared that such a doctrine would erase the crimes committed by the Church. For Acton, history was a science, though not in the sense that we use the term today. He was not a positivist or a materialist, believing that the science of history was amoral or value-free. Rather, he believed that historical discipline required the application of judgment on the past, judgment informed by a permanent and immutable moral code.

We—and I mean everybody, liberals and conservatives alike—violate Acton's principles all the time. Conservatives make apologies for benevolent dictators. Liberals forgive totalitarian movements because of the principles to be found somewhere beneath an ocean of blood. The most obvious example of this tendency today is the liberal compulsion to forgive or simply ignore the cruel authoritarianism of the Chinese regime because they envy the efficiency of authoritarian rule. It is amazing how forgivable tyranny is when it implements the preferred policies of liberalism. Cuba's police state is a mere distraction from their stunning "success" at providing free health care!

But we also violate Acton's maxim closer to home as well. When Edward Moore Kennedy died from a brain tumor in 2009 at the age of seventy-seven, the collective reaction from the establishment, including not just partisan liberals but the vast bulk of the media, historians, and politicians, violated Acton's real message. James Fallows spoke for the crowd, calling Kennedy, "A flawed man, who started unimpressively in life—the college problems, the silver-spoon boy senator, everything involved with Chappaquiddick—but redeemed himself, in the eyes of all but the committed haters, with his bravery and perseverance and commitment to the long haul."[3]

But Fallows's passive reference to "everything involved with Chappaquiddick" is a rhetorical leap over a yawning moral chasm. There's no room here to sift through the farrago of lies and corruption that led to Kennedy's legal absolution for Mary Jo Kopechne's death. Still, some basic facts, not in dispute, are in order. Kennedy and some male friends—all, like Kennedy, married—spent a weekend at the Kennedy compound at Martha's Vineyard with the "boiler room girls": young single women who liked to have a good time, so to speak. After much drinking, Kennedy took Kopechne for a drive. Kennedy claimed to be driving Kopechne to the ferry, though the record doesn't support this. On the way to their destination, a drunk Kennedy drove his 1967 Oldsmobile off Dike Bridge and into Poucha Pond. Kennedy escaped from the vehicle, and after allegedly trying to save her, simply gave up and walked to the cottage where his friends were staying. He passed no less than four houses and a firehouse—all had phones.

Kennedy told his compatriots not to tell the other women about the accident; allegedly because he was concerned they might risk their lives needlessly to save their friend. Kennedy spent the rest of the night at an inn in Edgartown, making small talk about sailing with another guest. At 7:30 A.M. his compatriots asked whom he called to report the accident, and he said he hadn't called anyone. At 9:00 A.M. Kennedy formally called the police.

What followed after that were a series of public lies and subterfuges by Kennedy and the Kennedy machine in order to cover up the truth of the incident and preserve Kennedy's political viability. The judge who gave Kennedy the minimum possible punishment—a two-month suspended sentence—retired two days after the decision. The Kopechne family never sued, opting to be done with the matter as quickly as possible.

At his death it was reported that Kennedy often liked to ask people, "Have you heard any good Mary Jo Kopechne jokes?" Apparently this usually got a laugh from people who would be disgusted by such a question should it stem from an anonymous gas station attendant or schoolteacher.

According to many, it was thanks to the tragedy at Chappaquiddick that Ted Kennedy had such a long and fruitful career in the Senate. Mary Jo Kopechne's death ruined his chances to win the presidency. Some in their admiration of power find this a worthwhile trade-off. A writer for the Huffington Post wondered what Mary Jo Kopechne "would have thought about arguably being a catalyst for the most successful Senate career in history . . . Who knows—maybe she'd feel it was worth it."[4]

As a senator, Kennedy did many admirable things, and even more things his ideological compatriots found admirable. He was also a lout, a womanizer, and a drunk. His exploits were usually overlooked and forgiven because he was also a Kennedy, and Kennedys are powerful in every sense of the word. They do not merely wield power through elected positions and great wealth; they have a greater power: the power to corrupt others in their cause.

7
DIVERSITY

> Diversity has been written into the DNA of American life; any institution that lacks a rainbow array has come to seem diminished, if not diseased.
>
> —Joe Klein

> The next time some academics tell you how important diversity is, ask how many Republicans there are in their sociology department.
>
> —Thomas Sowell

> Well, I could be wrong, but I believe diversity is an old, old wooden ship that was used during the Civil War–era.
>
> —Ron Burgundy

There are highlights in everyone's career. For me the greatest moments are fairly easy to recollect: My first cover story for *National Review*, getting picked up as a syndicated columnist, various breakout moments during my stint as founder and editor of *National Review Online*, returning to the American Enterprise Institute (where I started my career in Washington as an intern) as a scholar, reaching number one on the *New York Times* bestseller list, becoming a regular panelist on Fox News's *Special Report*, and so on.

But in terms of sheer joy and mirth, all of these things pale in comparison to the news that Barbra Streisand canceled her *Los Angeles Times* subscription to protest their decision to hire me as a columnist for her hometown paper.

In fairness, her real complaint was that Robert Scheer, a left-wing gargoyle who'd spewed nonsense from the paper's parapets for years, had been removed from its lofty façade. The fact that I was one of the new columnists to replace him was simply salt in the wound. I suppose it was a bit like having your favorite archbishop replaced with a pagan priest.

"The greater Southern California community is one that not only proudly embraces its diversity, but demands it. Your publisher's decision to fire Robert Scheer is a great disservice to the spirit of our community," Ms. Streisand proclaimed in a mini-manifesto that was so syntactically impaired, if it was a horse it would have been shot. She continued:

> It seems . . . that your new leadership, especially that of [publisher] Jeff Johnson, is entirely out of touch with [your readers] and their desire to be exposed to views that stretch them beyond their own paradigms. So although the number of contributors to your op-ed pages may have increased, in firing Robert Sheer [*sic*] and putting Jonah Goldberg in his place, the gamut of voices has undeniably been diluted. . . .
>
> In light of the obvious step away from the principals [*sic*] of journalistic integrity . . . I am now forced to carefully reconsider which sources can be trusted to provide me with accurate, unbiased news and forthright opinions. Your new columnist, Jonah Goldberg, will not be one of those sources.[1]

Now, leave aside the fact that gamuts cannot be diluted and that "principal" is the initial sum of a loan. To dwell on such things would be like correcting Bluto in *Animal House* by telling him that the Germans did not, in fact, bomb Pearl Harbor ("Forget it, he's rolling"). Of far greater import is Ms. Streisand's conception of "diversity."

Let the record show that Robert Scheer's ethnic lineage and my own are remarkably similar. We both hail in large measure from the same stock of East European Jews and Germans. His parents worked in the garment industry, and so did my grandparents (on my father's side). Mr. Scheer is, by popular parlance, upper middle class and white. Oh, and I should add, without much fear of contradiction, that neither Mr. Scheer nor myself are female or gay.

So in terms of the most common understanding of diversity these days—racial, sexual, gender, or ethnic—swapping a Scheer for a Goldberg is a wash, little more than the equivalent of replacing an old mutt with a younger one. Certainly, Jesse Jackson or Al Sharpton would not be satiated in their demands for more diversity if one of their shakedowns resulted in this sort of personnel diversification.

So when in her role as the voice of the entire "greater Southern California community" she demands diversity, what does she mean? While it sounds like she desires a diverse range of views—she dubs Scheer an "often singular voice of dissent" (see Chapter 10, Dissent)—what she actually means by diversity is simpler. She means: "People who agree entirely with me."

When Barbra says she wants someone to stretch her paradigms (no doubt causing any one of her countless personal assistants and retainers to ask in a double take, "Stretch your what now?"), what she in fact desires are writers who reinforce them. After all, there's not a micron of ideological daylight between Scheer and Streisand. Indeed, the two are old friends, with Scheer serving as something of an ideological tutor.

But that is beside the point. At one level, for people like Streisand, diversity is a magic word. Anything good supports diversity and everything bad lacks diversity. (Ever notice how in movies the "good" street or prison gang or band of mercenaries is the one that's diverse? Those rapists and murderers can't be all bad. Look, there are two black guys and an Asian!)

But at a deeper level, diversity is about conformity. There's no shortage of horror stories about diversity run amok—from the first responders in the aftermath of Hurricane Katrina, who were forced to undergo sensitivity training before they could fish drowning people from flooded neighborhoods, to the fire departments that seem to spend more energy fighting for quotas than fighting fires. Some may recall that after 9/11 New York City was embroiled in a controversy over a statue commemorating the truly heroic contributions of the Big Apple's firefighters. The statue was supposed to replicate the iconic photo of three firemen planting a flag at ground zero. But there was a problem. The three firefighters who actually planted the flag were white. The sculpture had to be more diverse than that. When people complained, a representative of the black firefighters union opined, "I think the artistic expression of diversity would supersede any concern over factual correctness."[2]

I've always loved that term—"factual correctness"—because it captures perfectly the Streisandian attitude. "Factual correctness" has the same stink on it that the right puts on "political correctness." When confronted with the latest idiocy like, say, the demand to call seminars "ovulars," conservatives say, "Oh, that's just political correctness" and dismiss it out of hand. So when confronted with, say, *the truth*, the Streisandian left says, in effect, "Oh, that's just factual correctness, I'm not going to cave into *that.*" It brilliantly demotes the facts into just another perspective to politely consider but dismiss if necessary (it's amazing how pragmatism creeps up on cat's paws, isn't?).

Diversity is an abracadabra word that magically makes inconvenient facts disappear and forces everyone to get in line. Over two decades ago these stories were already old and their true significance already obvious. In 1990, when the University of Northern Colorado invited Linda Chavez to speak at their graduation commencement ceremony, the intellectual and former government official was honored. But in spite of being a minority and a proponent of bilingual education, she was a Republican, and hence unacceptable to the left's typecasting. So the students protested. The president of the university met with ninety-five protesting students—exactly 1 percent of the student body—and after the predictable group assault on his status as an insensitive white man, the president relented. In a statement he explained that she had been picked in the first place to demonstrate that the school was "sensitive to cultural diversity" and to "communicate the importance of cultural pluralism." And why not? After all this is a very successful female Hispanic—a "twofer," as they say.

But no. The diversity pick was not a diversity pick because Hispanics must embrace the homogeneity of a single worldview that takes it as a given that political correctness is more important than factual correctness. And so the president apologized for the school's "uninformed" decision and the "appearance of being grossly insensitive" that it fostered. Not just insensitive, but "grossly insensitive."

Ever since, such stories are so common that they serve as convenient filler for conservative publications and quick column topics for right-wing pundits. To the extent that they are covered in the mainstream press, it is invariably an occasion when the media wishes to join the mob, to prove its own commitment to diversity—hardly surprising given that the dying newspaper industry has some of the most rigid quotas in American life. Even as the newspaper as an institution has been crumbling around them, the members of the American Society of Newspaper Editors have collectively dedicated tens of thousands of hours to figuring out how to make their ranks more diverse. It's like a ship's captain watching the vessel fill with water and insisting that the top priority must be to form a bucket brigade that looks like America.

Ah, but diversity makes us stronger, say the newspaper editors and just about everybody else who seeks to barrel past argument to conclusions.

But is it true?

"Diversity makes us stronger" is almost, but not quite, an example of de Tocqueville's "clear but false idea."[3] Sometimes it is both clear and true. Stock portfolios are stronger when they are diversified. Steel, concrete, Asian fusion menus, iPod playlists, wardrobes, diets, and travel itineraries are all improved by a diversification of ingredients, choices, compounds, and components.

Of course, this can be misleading. By looking solely at the successful and worthwhile examples of mixing things up we run the risk of coming to the conclusion that diversifying per se is always an improvement. An omelet with red peppers and sausage is better than one with only red peppers. But an omelet with red peppers and kitty litter is not. Adding carbon to molten steel creates the stuff of samurai swords. Adding tapioca to molten steel is less advisable.

And so it is with people. Experts tend to suffer from groupthink. Because worldviews are shared, common conclusions are too easily reached.[4] Moreover, because experts tend to believe more than most in the absolute authority of experts, the average expert in the room will defer to the judgment of the superexpert. Groupthink errors have yielded some of the most momentous and calamitous events in history. Some recent examples include Pearl Harbor, the Bay of Pigs, the failure to find WMDs in Iraq, and, of course, the release of New Coke. This is an area where dissent *is* valuable.

One of the more fascinating counterintuitive facts of life is that the introduction of dumb people can make a group of smart people collectively smarter. Bluntly stated, some stupid people are too stupid to automatically defer to smart people. Remember the story about the truck that got jammed in the tunnel because it was too tall? All the experts were stumped. But some kid yelled, "Let the air out of the tires," saving the day. This is essentially the moral of the fable "The Emperor's New Clothes." Substitute kids with morons and you get the same thing. By my count, at least fifteen episodes of the TV series *House* have hinged on this basic insight. The problem is that for every time some idiot says "let the air out of the tires" he will also say things like "let's put our car keys in the microwave!" or "maybe we can teach grizzly bears to give us tongue baths." Eventually smart people understandably tune out dumb people and, over time, the fact that a dumb person disagrees is seen as proof that the group must be right. That's why the best way to avoid groupthink is to have a group of smart people with diverse perspectives, not simply with diverse pigmentations.

There are, of course, other instances in human affairs where diversity strengthens the group. Every good team of doctors contains different specialists. Every military unit has members with a diversity of skills distributed within it. Every magazine is made better by a diversity of writing talents and styles.

On the other hand, the National Basketball Association would be made vastly more diverse if a rigid quota of midgets and one-legged point guards was imposed upon it. But the game would not be improved, and any team that voluntarily adopted such a regime would have very long odds of making the play-offs. It would not strengthen the DVD sales of a porn flick if the content was sufficiently diversified that it included a long tutorial on gardening tips. The NAACP would not be a more effective organization if they adopted a hard quota of Klansmen at every meeting, and the cadres of America's school crossing guards would not be made stronger with a forced recruitment of more blind crossing guards.

This is a long way of saying the obvious: It depends. Diversity can strengthen a group or it can weaken it. The problem with the progressive obsession with diversity is that it is a very narrow understanding of the term applied universally. When Bill Clinton said he wanted a cabinet that "looks like America," he synthesized the problem perfectly. Superficially his cabinet was the most diverse ever, boasting a remarkable number of women, blacks, and Jews. In some instances, as in his search for a female attorney general, he was forced to run through one woman after another (something he was known for in a completely different context as well) as each new nominee ran into various problems getting through the confirmation process. Ultimately he stumbled upon Janet Reno, a staggering mediocrity who served both the country and the president poorly.

More to the point, his cabinet may have looked like America but it acted like what it was—a collection of uniformly liberal lawyers.

Checking off ethnic, religious, and sexual boxes was hardly new in American politics, a fact many conservatives often overlook. Gone may be the days when Italians and Irish demanded their seat at the table, but changing the categories of the various players hardly changed the game dramatically.

The real transformations are closer to the ground. American higher education has grown drunk on a highly distilled spirit called diversity. Lee Bollinger, the president of Columbia University, famously declared:

> Diversity is not merely a desirable addition to a well-rounded education. It is as essential as the study of the Middle Ages, of international politics and of Shakespeare. For our students to better understand the diverse country and world they inhabit, they must be immersed in a campus culture that allows them to study with, argue with and become friends with students who may be different from them. It broadens the mind, and the intellect—essential goals of education.[5]

It's a nice sentiment, but not very persuasive. Most of the greatest scientific and literary minds of the last two thousand years were products of educational environments that would hardly count as diverse according to the standards applied by today's diversity industry. Newton, Galileo, and Einstein had very little exposure to Asians and African

Americans. The genius of Aristotle, Socrates, and Plato cannot be easily correlated with the share of non-Greeks they chatted with around the office well.

Meanwhile, if a lack of diversity is an educational hardship, why aren't historically black colleges or all-women's schools in the diversity industry's crosshairs? Morehouse College is, by all accounts, an exemplary liberal arts college. It is almost entirely black and is all male. Where's the scandal? What is the problem? Of course there isn't one. And there shouldn't be, particularly if you believe that a deep diversity of institutions is preferable to a superficial diversity in any particular institution that is literally skin-deep.

But the reason why there's no scandal in the eyes of Lee Bollinger is that their true ideological agenda is not educational at all. On one level it is to construct a rationale for making racial preferences permanent. Racial and gender quotas were originally conceived of as a way to redress past wrongs. "You do not take a person who, for years, has been hobbled by chains and liberate him, bring him up to the starting line of a race and then say, 'you are free to compete with all the others,' and still justly believe that you have been completely fair," Lyndon Johnson famously declared in his 1965 commencement address to Howard University.[6]

Whatever the merits of that contention, and there were obviously some, the fact is that racial preferences are no longer about redressing past wrongs. Preferences are given to African immigrants, Hispanics, and women of myriad backgrounds, life experiences, and races—often with little or no regard for how many have lived lives economically and culturally identical to the WASP next door. Such spoils cannot be justified under the logic of the original affirmative action regime. Diversity is a way of getting around all of that.

But at a deeper level the agenda behind diversity is about power. It is a way to give permanent license to social engineers. If you make diversity a compelling state interest or social imperative, someone has to decide what does or does not count as beneficial diversity, and that someone is invariably a social engineer like Lee Bollinger. Hence, under Bollinger the University of Michigan assigned a numerical value to the race of applicants. Blacks, Hispanics, and Native Americans automatically got twenty points out of the one hundred needed to guarantee admission. An outstanding personal essay was worth three points. An exemplary personal achievement was worth five points, while scoring a perfect grade on the SAT was worth twelve points. In other words, a wealthy black kid with mediocre credentials would start out with the same qualifications as an Asian who aced the SAT, wrote a Hemingwayesque personal essay, and founded a chain of soup kitchens.

But, if you dare oppose such narrow schemes to play with demographics like old Soviet ministers of population, you are "against diversity," which in far too many circles is simply code for racist.

Not only is this a reprehensible form of moral bullying used to stigmatize people who may in fact value diversity but who also emphasize other, competing, values such as fairness, merit, or, simply, freedom. It is also a deeply pernicious form of reasoning that was once utterly recognizable as unfair discrimination not so long ago.

Before World War II, when four out of five winners of New York Regents scholarships were Jewish, notes historian David Brion Davis, most New York medical schools had a strict anti-Jewish quota—in the name of diversity. The dean of Columbia University's medical school defended his school's quota by arguing, "The racial and religious makeup in medicine ought to be kept fairly parallel with the population makeup."

Today Asians—and to a lesser but still significant extent Jews—face a similar problem. Their accomplishments and experiences—no matter how harrowing or impressive—count for less in admissions at countless universities (though not so much in California and other states that, via popular referenda, have banned racial quotas in admissions). Moreover, the diversity experiment on college campuses does not work as advertised. When minority students are admitted above their abilities they almost always perform poorly academically, which is one reason why drop-out rates for minorities are so high.[7]

Another point: Is it really true that diversifying a college population will inevitably result in large numbers of minorities interacting with whites? I've visited scores of colleges, and wherever I go, the tendency I've seen is for self-ghettoization. Black students eat with black students, whites with whites (Asians seem to split; some cluster with each other, some integrate more into the dominant white culture). And such self-sorting seems to be encouraged by faculties and administrators, who celebrate the creation of various ethnic centers and student associations categorized by race. If the point is to encourage interaction, why create a black student union at all? Meanwhile, students who want to break out of such ghettos often feel there is no place for them. They become isolated, alienated from a campus culture that celebrates diversity to the point where the social experience is cheapened.

This is a troubling parallel to the larger national experiment with diversity. Robert Putnam, a liberal sociologist at Harvard, famously (infamously, for some) found that as communities become more ethnically diverse they in fact become socially frayed. In a survey that included interviews with over thirty thousand people, Putnam found that as a community becomes more ethnically and socially varied, social trust plummets. People tend to "hunker down," in Putnam's words banding together with a shrunken and shrinking group of friends or alone in front of the TV. Trust in political leaders, the political process, and even voting decline precipitously. Volunteerism, from charitable giving to carpooling, deteriorates. Political activism increases as people look to government to solve problems that once might have been solved by a simple conversation across a coffee table or a shared fence between neighbors.

Note: Putnam did not find that diversity fuels racism; the vast bulk of the people interviewed for the study were not bigots. What he found was that diversity promotes alienation, disengagement, and social isolation. This all runs counter to a host of prevailing clichés and pieties (see Chapter 23, Understanding).

Tellingly, in Putnam's study and in others, Los Angeles ranks at the bottom of the list of communities in terms of social strength. Residents, not to mention political leaders, spout a lot of "happy talk" (to borrow a phrase from researchers of a similar study) about diversity even as diversity fuels a pervasive unhappiness with the health of the community. People like Barbra Streisand are a good example. Ms. Streisand flits by limo from one gilded cage to another. She famously demanded—through her representatives, of course—that employees of the MGM Grand avoid eye-contact with her when she performed there. When she sang in the United Kingdom, she demanded that her accommodations include peach-colored toilet paper to match her skin tone and a sufficient number of rose petals in the toilet bowl. Hotel staff is instructed not to speak with her unless given permission. There's a whole chapter dedicated to her in investigative journalist Peter Schweizer's *Do as I Say (Not as I Do): Profiles in Liberal Hypocrisy.* In Schweizer's detailed telling, Streisand treats common laborers little better than vassals even as she spouts liberal talking points about the burning need to improve the plight of the working man.[8]

Obviously Ms. Streisand is like this largely for reasons that are unique to her. And since she is very rich and powerful, she undoubtedly likes it that way. She can spout off ideas and subsidize politicians who will further implement her conception of how the world is supposed to work while never having to actually cope with the consequences. But for the rest of the greater southern California community, things are not nearly so cozy or comforting. By attempting to stretch their paradigms their living experiences have been cheapened to the point where, brother, they can't paradigm.

So in at least one sense, I owe Ms. Streisand an apology. Los Angeles is a gamut of voices. And because of the sort of pinched and shrill diversity she demands, the gamut of voices in her own hometown—much like the rest of the country—has been undeniably diluted.

8

SOCIAL DARWINISM

> The Conservative Movement, as its progenitors like to call it, is now mounting a full-throttled attack on Darwinism even as it has thoroughly embraced Darwin's bastard child, social Darwinism.
>
> —Robert Reich

> In any event, whether called social Darwinism or social Spencerism, the defense of the social and economic hierarchy of nineteenth-century America that the doctrine was intended to accomplish held little appeal for the men and women who were shaping the emerging fields of sociology, psychology, economics, and anthropology at the end of the century. The aim of social Darwinsim was frankly conservative; the rising social scientists were not.
>
> —Carl Degler

Social Darwinism isn't simply a cliché. It's magic, an alchemist's trick that transmogrifies the gold of freedom into the lead of Hitlerism. Leading intellectuals and journalists cavalierly employ it as placeholder for All Bad Things having to do with genetics, fascism, racism, evolution, free markets, or any human behavior that might be seen as callousness of a right-wing sort. Dropping Social Darwinism into a conversation is like flinging around Eastern philosophical mumbo jumbo (zen, tao, chi, etc.): Everyone recognizes the words; nobody really knows what they mean.

Mario Cuomo, in his famous 1984 Democratic Convention keynote speech—which "electrified," "galvanized," and "inspired" Democrats, who went on to lose forty-nine states in the general election—declared that "President Reagan told us from the very beginning that he believed in a kind of social Darwinism."[1] Walter Mondale, the Democratic nominee that year, insisted that Reagan preferred "Social Darwinism" over "social decency."

The same drum beats steady twenty years later: "It's called the Ownership Society in Washington," then senator Barack Obama explained in 2005. "But in our past there has been another term for it—Social Darwinism—every man or woman for him or herself."[2]

This all goes back, of course, to Herbert Spencer, widely held to be the "founder" of Social Darwinism. A writer for one British paper insists Spencer was "a downright evil man . . . whose passion for eugenics and elimination made him the daydreamer of things to come." Edwin Black, in his history of eugenics, *War Against the Weak*, writes that Spencer "completely denounced charity and instead extolled the purifying elimination of the 'unfit.' The unfit, he argued, were predestined by their nature to an existence of downwardly spiraling degradation."[3]

Such attacks are beyond common, as the historian George H. Smith has chronicled for years. But perhaps the most telling comes from Richard L. Schoenwald's psychological autopsy of Spencer in the 1968 summer issue of the esteemed journal *Victorian Studies*, in which the historian reveals that Spencer's twisted and deformed worldview stemmed from his fascination with shit. Literally.

Starting with Spencer's childhood, Schoenwald concluded that "Spencer's self-esteem had been undermined hopelessly in the oral and anal stages of his development; he could commit himself only to paper, not to a woman." As a baby Spencer rejoiced in his ability to "create excrement." He never forgave his parents' efforts at toilet training, which revoked "the anal freedom in which he had gloried." This "fearful attack from behind" left permanent scars, which is why, for example, Spencer would one day oppose public sanitation regulation, because he "saw in sanitary reform an attack on his magical anal producing powers."

To put it mildly, there's something about Herbert Spencer and Social Darwinism that gets under the skin of a lot of people.

Let's clear the brush away. Herbert Spencer, the British author, sociologist, and reputed creator of Social Darwinism, did not coin the term Social Darwinism. He was not a Darwinist (he had a separate theory of evolution), and he never called himself a Social Darwinist. Neither the term Social Darwinist nor the name Darwin appear in his 1851 book *Social Statics, or The Conditions Essential to Happiness Specified, and the First of Them Developed* which laid out his theory of the "fittest." Yale sociologist William Graham Sumner, Spencer's purported junior partner in Social Darwinism, did not call himself a Social Darwinist either, nor was he particularly indebted to Darwinism.

Simply put, there was no intellectual movement—at least not in America or Britain—called Social Darwinism, and the evil views attributed to so-called Social Darwinists were not held by its alleged founders. A survey of all of the leading English-language academic journals from the mid-1800s until 1937 produced not a single citation, mention, or argument that linked Spencer (dead by 1903) and Sumner (1910) to an intellectual movement called Social Darwinism.[4]

Even more amazing, in the entire body of Anglo-American scholarly publications—spanning more than a century—there is only one article that actually advocates—rather than criticizes—something called Social Darwinism.

Let me repeat that. Despite the fact that America's foremost historians, politicians, and journalists routinely invoke and demonize the intellectual movement called Social Darwinism pioneered by Herbert Spencer, there is only one academic publication or article that clearly and unequivocally advocates something called "Social Darwinism" *and it not only wasn't written by Spencer, it doesn't mention him either.*[5] And yet we are told by no less than the *Oxford English Dictionary* that Social Darwinism is "the theory that societies, classes, and races are subject to and a product of Darwinian laws of natural selection. *Often used to justify political conservatism, imperialism, and racism*" (my emphasis). And yet the *OED* fails to identify even a single use by a proponent of the idea. It's an amazing triumph of intellectual propaganda. "Everyone knows" that conservatives believe in Social Darwinism, but no one can point to a Social Darwinist. "Everyone knows" that Herbert Spencer founded Social Darwinism, but he did no such thing. It's like those famous help wanted signs that said

No Irish Need Apply that everyone remembers but historians have never found proof of.

But wait, it gets even more vexing. Social Darwinism is routinely used to describe both Hitler's genocidal racism and eugenic policies as well as mainstream American libertarianism (Social Darwinism is useful in this regard for creating terminological diversity in the liberal vocabulary. Simply repeating the word "fascist" gets tiresome). You too can be a Social Darwinist if you believe in small government and the free market. Or if you believe in herding the lesser races and the enfeebled into camps.

So how do we explain this? Let's start with its eugenic connotations. One important part of the answer is that Social Darwinism as a phrase was born in Europe and, over there, it was often used as an ugly and bastardized Nietzschean racial philosophy of the strong against the weak. Meanwhile, in America, it became associated with figures like Spencer and Sumner who were philosophical "radical individualists," or what today we would call libertarians.

In a sense, this shift is a reversal of what happened to the word liberal when it crossed the Atlantic Ocean. In Europe, where the word originated, liberal still means something like libertarian. But in the United States liberal has come to mean a moderately left-wing statist. That switcheroo took place in the late 1920s and early 1930s, because Progressives (and later, Communists) had so poisoned "progressive" that they had to change their brand.

Another piece of the puzzle stems from the fact that liberals overly revere Darwin (while many conservatives do not revere him enough, alas). And since he must not be blamed for anything bad done in the name of evolutionary theory, they peeled off from the pack that handful of nineteenth-century intellectuals and thinkers who were actual libertarians and blamed them for any and all of the fallout from Darwinism. Specifically, everything bad that comes out of evolution is hung on the notion of "survival of the fittest," a phrase Spencer coined. Indeed, you can find scores of letters to the editor and blog posts by disgruntled Darwin fans angrily explaining that Darwin didn't *invent* the phrase "survival of the fittest," and so therefore he cannot be blamed for eugenics, war, or any other cruelty associated, fairly or unfairly, with the doctrine of evolution. Meanwhile, Spencer, who believed almost none of the things he is said to have believed, is responsible for everything bad that resulted from Darwinism. It's an astoundingly weak argument.

Some claim Darwin never even uttered the words "survival of the fittest." While I'm not sure why that would be important, it's simply not true. Darwin just didn't say it *first.* Indeed, in later editions of *The Origins of Species*, Darwin replaced "natural selection" in some passages with "survival of the fittest." The waters get muddier still. That phrase was preceded by Thomas Malthus's "*struggle* for the fittest" and the "struggle for existence," and Malthus was a major inspiration for Darwin's theory of evolution. Malthus is also a darling of progressive thought, because his argument that humans cause scarcity is an inspiration for environmentalism, socialism, and other leftist doctrines. Here is Darwin in his own words from his *Autobiography*:

> In October 1838 . . . fifteen months after I had begun my systematic inquiry, I happened to read for amusement "Malthus on Population," and being well prepared to appreciate the struggle for existence which everywhere goes on from long-continued observation of the habits of animals and plants, it at once struck me that under these circumstances favorable variations would tend to be preserved, and unfavorable ones to be destroyed. The result would be the formation of new species.[6]

And here he is openly and deliberately applying Malthus in the updated 1859 edition of *The Origin of Species*:

> Hence, as more individuals are produced than can possibly survive, there must in every case be a struggle for existence, either one individual with another of the same species, or with the individuals of distinct species, or with the physical conditions of life. It is the doctrine of Malthus applied with manifold force to the whole animal and vegetable kingdoms; for in this case there can be no artificial increase of food, and no prudential restraint from marriage. Although some species may be now increasing, more or less rapidly, in numbers, all cannot do so, for the world would not hold them.[7]

Why survival of the fittest should be assigned the blame above and beyond so many other far more noxious notions and doctrines is beyond me, save as a way of passing the blame onto intellectual enemies. Its effectiveness as a verbal bludgeon cannot be denied, because it is taken as a given by almost all liberals that there's a direct line from Spencer to Hitler, all because of that phrase and the images of concentration camps that it conjures. That's largely why Spencer may be the single most unfairly vilified thinker of the nineteenth century. While hundreds of millions have been killed by the faithful application of Karl Marx's ideas, Marx still enjoys a deep reservoir of respect and an army of apologists. And, perhaps more shocking, Darwin is still found utterly blameless on that score, even though he was in fact the inspiration for a good deal of Marx's work. Marx reportedly wanted to dedicate *Das Kapital* to Darwin, but Darwin talked him out of it (this may be a myth, but it's clear that Marx was deeply influenced by Darwin). Meanwhile, poor Herbert Spencer, one of the chief architects of what is today called libertarianism, is routinely denounced as one of the most evil figures in human history.

Even more infuriating is the simple fact that American liberalism should be squarely in the dock for the ideas routinely laid at Spencer's feet. While Herbert Spencer was a laissez-faire liberal who wanted the state to mind its own business, ardently supported women's suffrage, and loathed slavery, many of the progressives and liberals who hated him were committed eugenicists and racists. The economists at the heart of progressivism were all eugenicists. Charles Van Hise, the president of the University of Wisconsin during its progressive heyday, founder of the conservation movement, and adviser to Teddy Roosevelt, believed, "He who thinks not of himself primarily, but of his race, and of its future, is the new patriot."[8] He added, "We know enough about agriculture so that the agricultural production of the country could be doubled if the knowledge were applied; . . . we know enough about eugenics so that if the knowledge were applied, the defective classes would disappear within a generation."[9]

The most famous intellectual at the University of Wisconsin was arguably E. A. Ross—coiner of the phrase "race suicide," and one of America's leading "raceologists" at the turn of the twentieth century. "The theory that races are virtually equal in capacity," warned Ross, "leads to such monumental follies as lining the valleys of the South with the bones of half a million picked whites in order to improve the conditions of four million unpicked blacks."[10]

The minimum wage was defended by progressive economists with explicitly Social Darwinist language. The fear was that since black and, especially, Chinese laborers needed so much less to get by, the unfittest might survive at the expense of the fittest (i.e., Whites). Or, as Ross put it, "The Coolie cannot outdo the American, but he can underlive him."[11] Raising the minimum wage to a white man's worth would help lock out the unfit and, hopefully, cause them to die out from destitution. "No consistent eugenist [*sic*] can be a 'Laisser Faire'[*sic*] individualist," wrote the hugely influential British socialist Sidney Webb, "unless he throws up the game in despair. He must interfere, interfere, interfere!"[12]

There's a tendency among liberal historians to claim that there were conservative eugenicists and liberal eugenicists, and the liberals were all decent because they just wanted to improve everyone's environment, while the conservatives were cruel, Spencerian racists who wanted to weed out the inferior races. But while it is surely the case that there were racists on what passed for the right, and even a few eugenicists, the more glaring truth is eugenics was overwhelmingly a phenomenon of the Left. Remember, progressives saw eugenics as compassionate policy making, not punishment. Conservatives and classical liberals were evil because they didn't care enough about the poor to sterilize them for their own good. When the debate about eugenics was most active, the world's foremost opponent was the Catholic conservative G. K. Chesterton, while the most famous eugenicists were socialists like H. G. Wells and George Bernard Shaw.

One can see this divide perfectly in Herbert Croly's effort to make peace between the two factions. For example, he wrote in an unsigned *New Republic* editorial in 1916:

> We may suggest that a socialized policy of population cannot be built upon a laissez faire economic policy. So long as the state neglects its good blood, it will let its bad blood alone. There is no certain way of distinguishing between defectiveness in the strain and defectiveness produced by malnutrition, neglected lesions

> originally curable, or overwork in childhood. When the state assumes the duty of giving a fair opportunity for development to every child, it will find unanimous support for a policy of extinction of stocks incapable of profiting from their privileges.[13]

In other words, once we get a fully realized welfare state up and running, we'll be able to pick out those who belong to the unredeemable stocks of the unfit from those who are unworthy because of poverty, at which point we'll be able to work on making the former group extinct.

Consider Oliver Wendell Holmes, the Supreme Court justice who was an impassioned eugenicist and believed that "building a race" was central to his entire worldview. The revered liberal lion of the court authored the *Buck v. Bell* decision, which held that the state had the constitutional right to forcibly sterilize unfit women (it was an 8–1 decision with all of the liberals, including Louis Brandeis and Harlan Fiske Stone, concurring, and only the archconservative Catholic Pierce Butler dissenting). Holmes later became a hero to progressives for his dissent in the *Lochner* decision, in which he mocked Herbert Spencer's libertarian views ("The Fourteenth Amendment does not enact Mr. Herbert Spencer's *Social Statics*," Holmes wrote).

What united all of these figures, from Croly and Holmes to Jane Addams and W. E. B. Du Bois, was their adherence to what the liberal historian Eric Goldman calls Reform Darwinism. But it was the libertarians who believed that the State had no role in choosing worthy and unworthy races who have come down in history as the racists and Hitlerites. The outright reversal and widespread ignorance of the historical record on this matter is a disgusting intellectual scandal that lives on to this day.

Which brings us to the poor "robber barons," the rich and successful champions of commerce from the nineteenth century who put the gild on the Gilded Age. The argument goes like this: Darwinism arrived on the scene around the same time that American capitalism took flight. The robber barons—who were neither robbers nor barons—therefore must have been inspired by Darwin's theories to justify their dog-eat-dog theories of capitalism.

We owe this argument almost entirely to Richard Hofstadter's book *Social Darwinism in American Thought, 1860–1915*, which first appeared as his PhD thesis in 1938 and subsequently as a book in 1944. It was Hofstadter who argued that the robber barons had found an ideological rationalization for their rapacious ways in Social Darwinism. Hofstadter writes:

> With its rapid expansion, its exploitative methods, its desperate competition, and its peremptory rejection of failure, post-bellum America was like a vast human caricature of the Darwinian struggle for existence and survival of the fittest. Successful business entrepreneurs apparently have accepted almost by instinct the Darwinian terminology which seemed to portray the conditions of their existence.[14]

Other historians were quick to follow. Merle Curti in *The Growth of American Thought* argued that Social Darwinism "admirably suited the needs of the great captains of industry, who were crushing the little fellows when these vainly tried to compete with them." Henry Steel Commager wrote in *The American Mind* that "Darwin and Spencer exercised such sovereignty over America as George III had never enjoyed."

And then there's Robert Reich, who has been regurgitating these arguments with an almost bulimic regularity. Social Darwinism, he writes,

> offered a perfect moral justification for America's Gilded Age, when robber barons controlled much of American industry, the gap between the rich and poor turned into a chasm, urban slums festered, and the wealthy bought off politicians. It allowed John D. Rockefeller, for example, to claim that the fortune he had accumulated through the giant Standard Oil Trust was "merely a survival of the fittest, . . . the working out of a law of nature and a law of God."[15]

Reich then adds: "The Modern Conservative movement has embraced Social Darwinism with no less fervor than it has condemned Darwinism."

It is less out of a respect for the author than an admiration for the concision of the passage's inaccuracy that I single it out as an example, for just about everything in it is untrue or misleading. Let's start again with the robber barons, enduring bogeymen in the liberal imagination. In the twelfth and thirteenth centuries there were actual robber barons—European feudal lords who shook down unfortunate travelers in their realm. In nineteenth-century America the term emerged as a catchall for brigands, highwaymen, and carpetbaggers. After the Civil War it was occasionally used to describe wealthy captains of industry.

But it wasn't until Matthew Josephson's intellectually bankrupt 1934 book, *The Robber Barons: The Great American Capitalists, 1861–1901*, that the term stuck as a description of those leeches of the liberal imagination. Josephson was a relentless partisan for socialist economics, and his book amounted to little more than a comic book without pictures. His unifying thesis was to take seriously Balzac's dictum that "behind every great fortune lies a great crime." He assumed that wealth was and is by its very nature felonious.

This didn't just go for individual robber barons but for the entire nation as a whole. Generations of left-wing historians and muckraking journalists cast the post–Civil War expansion as a time of unprecedented exploitation. America, in effect, had committed some kind of crime by prospering.

The truth, however, is that American prosperity during this admittedly rough-and-tumble period lifted millions of poor people out of poverty. What Reich describes as a period of runaway income inequality was in fact the single greatest explosion in economic growth in American history. Per capita GDP soared during the so-called Gilded Age. Milton Friedman concluded that the 1880s were the single most prosperous decade in American history. And from 1890 to 1910, U.S. GNP grew at 6 percent a year.[16] According to historian Burton Folsom, in 1870 America was creating 23 percent of the world's industrial goods, while Britain and Germany produced 30 percent and 13 percent, respectively. By 1900, America was in first place with 30 percent; Britain had fallen to 20 percent; and Germany had risen to 20 percent. In 1870, Britain was the world's chief steel producer; by 1900, Andrew Carnegie alone made more steel than all of Great Britain.[17]

Henry Hazlitt describes it as "a period of unprecedented expansion, of rising wages and falling prices, of increased longevity and startling increase of population, of rising living standards and the beginnings of production for, and consumption by, the masses. . . . But the historians were so preoccupied by the growing pains," notes Hazlitt, "that they overlooked the growth." Hazlitt points out that the famous progressive historians Mary and Charles Beard delivered

> a relentless bitter indictment of American business enterprise after the Civil War. But then, in a brief afterthought, they mentioned a few statistics which revealed the astounding national growth and material wellbeing of the period. Between 1860 and 1900 our population grew from 31 million to 76 million, a growth "unprecedented in Western history." Our national wealth, said the Beards, was only one third that of Great Britain in the year of Daniel Webster's death. Half a century later our wealth was one and a quarter times that of Great Britain. In half a century it had grown fivefold.[18]

One need not defend every so-called robber baron to defend the "age of robber barons" as a boon to mankind. Indeed, I will gladly concede that some robber barons cut too many corners if the Left will concede that many a robber baron was not so committed to capitalism as the standard myths suggest. Many robber barons went on bended knee to Washington asking for protection from the ravaging tides of capitalism. In 1909, Andrew Carnegie himself was asking for "government control" of the steel industry.[19]

So what does this have to do with Social Darwinism? Well, pretty much nothing, just like the robber barons themselves. Hofstadter, the historian who essentially invented the idea that American capitalism in the nineteenth century was inspired by Charles Darwin, never offered much by way of actual proof that his idea was accurate. A truly brilliant writer, he was like a chef who can make a few ingredients go a long way. He stretched out the broth in *Social Darwinism in America* by citing a handful of anecdotes and then making sweeping generalizations about them.

Thanks to a legendary effort in historical fact-checking, led by scholars Irwin Wyllie and Robert C. Bannister, Hofstadter's entire project has been dismantled.[20] Quite simply, the "robber barons" were not inspired by Charles Darwin or Darwinism. They did not see in Darwin a rationalization for their economic philosophies or business practices. Not only was there no self-declared school of Social Darwinists among academics and intellectuals, the alleged beneficiaries of their teachings had little to no interest in the subject whatsoever.

Now when you dismantle something you do not destroy it in every particular. A dismantled engine will still leave you with a carburetor, a drive shaft, etc. Similarly, Hofstadter & Co. can and do still cling to a few random quotes from second-order figures who were parroting the vernacular at the time. (Darwinian metaphors were all the rage in the late nineteenth century, in every field.) And they can certainly cite Andrew Carnegie, who was, legitimately, a true disciple of Herbert Spencer and a devotee of Darwinian thought.

The fact that Carnegie was an exception to the rule is of little regard to Hofstadter and others determined to attach Social Darwinism and the robber barons at the hip. So certain it couldn't be otherwise, both Hofstadter and Reich eagerly identify John D. Rockefeller as a Social Darwinist by referring to a speech where Rockefeller attributed his fortune to "merely a survival of the fittest, . . . the working out of a law of nature and a law of God." The only problem, of course, is that the line is actually from a 1902 speech by John D. Rockefeller *Junior*, son of the pious Christian entrepreneur who, for the record, had no use for Darwinism.[21]

To be fair, Reich simply repeated Hofstadter's mistake. And Hoftsadter made many. Quotes about "natural law" are repeated without noting that they are references to the laws of physics or God, not Darwinian evolution. Other references to evolution, say, in Thomas Mellon's memoirs, are taken as endorsements of Social Darwinism, when in fact they are only relevant to religion.

When you think about it, the idea that businessmen were inspired by a then novel biological theory should not have even passed the smell test. "Gilded Age businessmen were not sufficiently bookish, or sufficiently well educated, to keep up with the changing world of ideas," writes Wyllie. "As late as 1900, 84 percent of the businessmen listed in *Who's Who in America* had not been educated beyond high school."[22] Overwhelmingly, businessmen of the period were influenced by Christianity first and foremost, classical economics second, some self-help inspirational nostrums a distant third, and egghead notions about biology almost not at all. Cornelius Vanderbilt read one book in his entire life. It was *Pilgrim's Progress.* And he didn't get to it until he was past the age of seventy. "If I had learned education," Vanderbilt famously quipped, "I would not have had time to learn anything else."[23]

The response from informed liberals is often, well, yes, Social Darwinism is a misleading term if you mean that it was a school of thought—but it does accurately describe the behavior of the robber barons. Except that's not true either. To be sure, these were tough businessmen, but they were also some of the greatest philanthropists in world history; they created libraries, hospitals, conservation trusts, foundations, universities, and general purpose charities. Now why would they do that if they saw the world through the zero-sum prism of survival of the fittest? Because these men took their Christianity very, very seriously. As Wyllie notes, Christian ethics suffused the business world because even the well educated were taught in an explicitly religious context. Robert Harris, the president of the Chicago, Burlington, and Quincy Railroad, might be a good candidate to be a Social Darwinist if not for his expressed view: "As a general proposition, it seems to me that the strong should help the weak, now by one course and now by another; and in exercising authority to do it as we would wish it done to ourselves."[24]

Even the avowed Spencerist Andrew Carnegie was one of the most spectacularly generous philanthropists the world has ever seen. At the age of thirty-three he wrote a letter to himself, which read in part: "[T]he amassing of wealth is one of the worst species of idolatry—no idol more debasing than the worship of money."[25] He committed to retiring at the age of thirty-five so he could dedicate himself to philanthropy. He believed that the man who "dies rich dies disgraced." He missed his deadline but nonetheless became one of the most generous benefactors in the world and a committed pacifist.

Hofstadter claimed that Social Darwinism provided "one of the great informing insights in . . . the history of the conservative mind in America."[26] But as Robert Bannister painstakingly demonstrates, the truth is something close to the exact opposite. Liberals, progressives, and other champions of "reform Darwinism" were obsessed with Darwin and his theory's implications for society. It suffused their thinking in every respect (not least because it seemed so complementary with Hegelianism). And as a result, they *projected their categories of thought* onto their ideological opponents. Their obsessions with eugenics, with "fixing" society, with reform in all of its myriad particulars were driven by the great informing insight of Darwinism. And in their consummate arrogance and cocksure belief that they were the heroes of the tale, they simply concocted motivations for their opponents that did not exist. It's a familiar tale.

9
SLIPPERY SLOPE

It is seldom that liberty of any kind is lost all at once. Slavery has so frightful an aspect to men accustomed to freedom that it must steal in upon them by degrees and must disguise itself in a thousand shapes in order to be received.

—DAVID HUME, *OF THE LIBERTY OF THE PRESS*

Nor am I able to appreciate the danger . . . that the American people will by means of military arrests during the rebellion lose [their constitutional rights] throughout the indefinite peaceable future which I trust lies before them, any more than I am able to believe that a man could contract so strong an appetite for emetics during temporary illness as to persist in feeding upon them during the remainder of his healthful life.

— ABRAHAM LINCOLN, LETTER TO ERASTUS CORNING AND OTHERS (JUNE 12, 1863)

If we take the widest and wisest view of a Cause, there is no such thing as a Lost Cause, because there is no such thing as a Gained Cause. We fight for lost causes because we know that our defeat and dismay may be the preface to our successors' victory, though that victory itself will be temporary; we fight rather to keep something alive than in the expectation it will triumph.

—T. S. ELIOT, "FRANCIS HERBERT BRADLEY" (1927)

One wonders if someone had told whoever it was in the early nineteenth century who first made reference to the "slippery slope" something along the lines of: "You know, once you start talking about 'slippery slopes,' pretty soon we'll be on a slippery slope. There will be no turning back." Alas, no one offered such a warning, and the camel's nose got under the tent, the ship sailed, the horse got out of the barn and drove the wedge that toppled the first domino, which opened the floodgates, and now all we have left is boiled frog.

There is nary a statesman, scholar, or bricklayer who has not used, or opined on, the phrase "the slippery slope." There's a vast body of literature on the problem presented with SSAs (slippery slope arguments) and similar forms of inductive fallacies and arguments from analogy.[1] I will not rehearse it all here, because once you start, you just don't know where that sort of thing will end.

It should be conceded up front that there's nothing inherently liberal or progressive about slippery slope arguments. If anything, it is a small-c conservative form of argumentation used by people across the ideological spectrum. The basic SSA goes like this: If we permit A, we'll have to allow B, and pretty soon Xs, Ys, and even Zs will be getting married and having sex on Saturday morning TV or rounding up dissidents and honest citizens. (First, they came for the A, but I was not an A. Then they came for the Bs . . .) So that's why we can't give any of these damn As an inch, because we know the rest of the alphabetical integers will take a mile.

At some level, slippery slope arguments surely appeal to our caveman brains. The Neanderthal who never asked, "What could go wrong?" probably had a hard time passing on his genes successfully. Humans evolved in harsh environments, where anticipating how big problems stem from little ones was no doubt the key to making it through many a bad winter. Social organization itself is an evolutionary adaptation, and societies that stumble on successful cultures no doubt bequeathed to their progeny an innate instinct to protect them from reckless experimentation.

And in this sense slippery slope arguments make an important and valuable contribution to human progress. Only fools and revolutionaries fail to ask, "What could go wrong?" Hence the slippery slope argument is a fundamentally conservative mechanism in the sense that it promotes risk avoidance. But that doesn't mean it isn't used just as relentlessly by people on the left end of the ideological spectrum. Every Communist functionary who has been told to allow a little liberalization or a few market-based reforms has responded with a slippery slope argument that ended with a headlong rush to immoral capitalism. Every left-wing dictator who ponders giving his subjects an inch of freedom is quickly advised by his apparatchiks that the greedy people will demand a mile.

Likewise every lover of liberty frets that a small expansion of government into the realm of freedom will, like a metastasizing cancer cell, spread ever further. This offers one of the great insights into the wonder and glory of America and the greatness of her people. In much of the world, Europe included, the slippery slope argument in favor of restraining government's grip on our liberties has little to no purchase. Even in Great Britain, the wellspring of our own conception of liberty, it is widely accepted that the state can intrude wherever it is deemed prudent or progressive without much fear things will turn oppressive. For instance, every nook and cranny of the country is covered in surveillance cameras, and in some communities the government agents monitoring them can even use public address systems to chastise you for littering or to tell you to stop jaywalking.

Thanks to an earlier English fondness for intrusiveness, the colonies in North America became a haven for ornery types seeking to be left alone. The proto-Americans had a tendency to take what might be called preemptive offense at threats to their liberties. "In other countries [than the American colonies], the people . . . judge of an ill principle in government only by an actual grievance," Edmund Burke observed in 1775, but in America, "they anticipate the evil, and judge of the pressure of the grievance by the badness of the principle. They augur misgovernment at a distance and snuff the approach of tyranny in every tainted breeze."

Or at least that used to be the way Americans acted. Alas, the "positive liberty" doctrines introduced by the progressives diluted the ornery reaction of the American people to government intrusion. Still, to their credit, there remains a streak of antistatism even in our statists when it comes to (some) civil liberties. But when it comes to economic affairs, vast numbers of Americans have lost the ability to see small intrusions as down payments on much bigger ones to come. The Americans Edmund Burke spoke of would take one look at ObamaCare and see death panels lining up on the horizon like so many hostile Indians. Now even to raise the *concern* that such things are *possible* amounts to right-wing paranoia.

Ultimately slippery slope arguments are a mixed bag. They are useful as a way to reinforce good dogma, but they are also used to reinforce bad dogma. Similarly, they can scare us away from bad policies and good ones alike. There are good slippery slope arguments and bad ones for good ends and bad ends.

Whatever or wherever the source of slippery slope arguments, they all share the same weaknesses. For starters, they rest on bad reasoning, asserting that one thing will cause another thing that will cause another thing in a straightforward and foreseeable way like dominos falling in a straight line. Unfortunately, not even dominos are as reliable as you might think. Imagine you have lined up fifty dominos pretty well, but not perfectly. So let's say that if the domino at the front of the line falls it has a 95 percent chance of knocking over the one next to it. Presumably that means a whole lot of dominos will fall over when you knock over the first one. Then again, maybe they won't. Remember, there's a 5 percent chance that no more dominos will fall, and a 4.75 percent chance that only one more domino will fall. As more dominos fall the probabilities stack up that *this* domino will be the last one to fall. Statistically, there's a 92.3 percent chance that fifty or fewer dominos will fall, and on average you should expect no more than twenty dominos to topple.

Now assuming you're not drunk or wearing mittens, you can likely arrange dominos so that they have a higher probability of toppling their neighbor than 95 percent. But humans are a lot more complicated than dominos, and complex societies are a lot more complicated than any single human. The notion that you can predict that action A will cause a chain of events to proceed in a straight alphabetical line until you get to Z is highly unlikely.

But wait a second, aren't there a million good examples of slippery slope arguments being validated? Yes, and no. As Eugene Volokh illustrates in "The Mechanism of the Slippery Slope,"[2] antismoking activists routinely say they simply want to make one simple reform and that's it. He cites two press clippings, seven years apart:

> [Regarding legislation to outlaw cigarette machines.] Sandra Starr, vice chairwoman of the Princeton Regional Health Commission, . . . said there is no "slippery slope" toward a total ban on smoking in public places. "The commission's overriding concern," she said, "is access to the machines by minors."
>
> —"Princeton Proposes Ban on Many Cigarette Machines," *New York Times*, September 5, 1993

> Last month, the Princeton Regional Health Commission took a bold step to protect its citizens by enacting a ban on smoking in all public places of accommodation, including restaurants and taverns. . . . In doing so, Princeton has paved the way for other municipalities to institute similar bans.
>
> —*The Record* (Bergen County), July 12, 2000

Similarly, in the 1990s antismoking activists insisted they weren't setting a dangerous precedent, and they'd never go after, say, junk food. Today they're all going after junk food. Slippery slope vindicated, right?

Not really.

The problem with the slippery slope cliché is not that it doesn't describe a real problem; it's that it describes a real problem *poorly. Of course* precedents matter. But slippery slope metaphors can be pernicious because they discount, even remove, the dynamism of human agency. They even remove the dynamism of amphibian agency.

To wit: Consider the boiling frog we always hear so much about from politicians and activists. As the saying goes, If you put a frog in tepid water and slowly turn up the heat, it will stay in the pot until it's poached. But if you throw the frog into a boiling pot, it will leap out. The lesson is usually that crises that creep up on us incrementally are more pernicious than ones that are recognizable all at once. Now, the metaphorical principle may or may not be true. One can certainly think of cases where it is and where it isn't.

But as for the poor boiled frogs, we know this is in fact not true. Professor Doug Melton, of the Harvard University Biology Department, told *Fast Company*, which investigated the parable of the boiled frog, "If you put a frog in boiling water, it won't jump out. It will die. If you put it in cold water, it will jump before it gets hot—they don't sit still for you." After conducting a series of tests in which frogs leaped from the water once it got uncomfortable, J. Debra Hofman, research associate at MIT's Center for Information Systems Research and coauthor of "Implementing Radical Change: Gradual Versus Rapid Pace," explained, "There are certain cases where gradual change is almost preferred." More to the point, she added, "The change myth assumes a very narrow view of people. If frogs can do it, people definitely can."

That's right. When a domino hits another domino, there's no chance that there will be a domino backlash where the dominos band together to fight back against the scourge of domino toppling. Yes, the falling of the first domino increases the odds that the next one will fall, just as legalizing gay marriage does make legalizing polygamy more likely. But the similarity ends there, not least because humans aren't dominos, and we cannot compute the probabilities of human actions nearly as easily. If the government funds Catholic schools, then opponents of funding of religious schools will say it's a slippery slope, and we'll have to fund all religious schools, including jihadist madrasas and Satanic academies. But that's not true. Rather, if we give money to Catholic schools then some people will *say* we have to give money to jihadists and Satanists, because fairness and consistency requires that we do so. These people will fall into four general groups: jihadists, Satanists, lawyers, and idiots. And it is the duty of all good men to marshal the energy and will to tell jihadists, Satanists, lawyers, and idiots: "No."

Consider civil liberties, the foremost breeding ground of slippery slope arguments. There have been countless moments in American history when civil libertarians, on both the right and the left, have insisted that we must not do something to avoid careening down the slippery slope. Now if the slippery slope were the phenomenon they claim, America today should be a police state. But it hasn't worked out that way.

With the arguable exception of the Civil War (and, of course, the institution of slavery), the lowest point in American civil liberties wasn't during the Bush years, or the Nixon years. It was during the administration of Woodrow Wilson—who oversaw the censoring of scores of publications, the incarceration of political prisoners, the imposition of loyalty oaths, dissemination of sweeping propaganda, and the wholesale and often bloody intimidation of dissenters. At any time during this period one could have raised the specter of the slippery slope—and many decent people did. But guess what happened next? The country swung back to normal. The American people threw out the progressive Democrats responsible for the bedlam and voted in Republicans who ran on the platform of a "return to normalcy." It fell to the Republican president Warren Harding to show clemency to the political prisoners held by the Wilson administration.

This raises one of the most underappreciated dynamics of the American political system, and of democracy generally. Regular elections are circuit breakers. They stop—or at least can stop—the acceleration of slippery slope impulses. A change in party power often—though perhaps not often enough—halts the transmission of error. Totalitarian systems have no such circuit breakers—no checks and balances—and, hence, good intentions more easily snowball into evil results.

It is those areas of American life most immunized from democracy and partisanship that are most susceptible to slippery slope problems precisely because they are not democratically accountable. Bureaucracy is a superconductor of bad ideas. No democratic or market-based system would ever shut down lemonade stands; the circuit breaker would kick in long before the cops made some six-year-old girl cry.

It is when the circuit breakers are turned off or bypassed—for instance, during a war—that slippery slope problems flourish.

Fast-forward to World War II, when FDR put one hundred thousand Japanese Americans in camps on the West Coast. Surely some decent person looked at that scandal and said, "Good lord, this is putting us on the slippery slope to tyranny," or words to that effect. But it didn't. Internment was wrong on the merits, but it did not open the floodgates to far worse. Fast-forward again to the early 1950s. Whatever your view of the McCarthy era, it certainly didn't put us on the slippery slope to something worse. Why? *Because the American people didn't want to go someplace worse.* At various times over the last seventy years, Congress, the courts, and the American people have collectively flipped the circuit breaker. For all of the anti–Patriot Act hysteria under George W. Bush (which, remarkably, subsided with the election of Barack Obama, who successfully won its reauthorization and expanded its use), it has not put us on anything like the slippery slope we were told it would. Is there room for abuse? Sure. Should the law be repealed? Someday, yes. But to date most of the objections to it are hypothetical, because the actual use of it—catching terrorists—is both popular and legitimate in the eyes of the American people.

So long as one remembers that the slippery slope isn't a *thing* but a metaphor, it's not so bad. It's when people believe that it describes an actual phenomenon, a mechanism of historical progression, that the slippery slope becomes an invitation to surrender. If you take it as a given that losing an inch means you've already lost the mile, then you will give up after losing the inch. That is precisely what the other side wants you to do: give up prematurely. If you go through life thinking the slippery slope is real, you will make it real. If you go through life a happy warrior, believing every good fight is worth having because it is good, and every defeat is temporary, you might have other problems, but you won't have the problem of premature capitulation.

Edmund Burke is often quoted as saying words to the effect of "All that is necessary for evil to triumph is for good men to do nothing." My friend—and Burke scholar—Yuval Levin says there's no record of Burke having ever said it. What comes closest is Burke's observation in *Thoughts on the Cause of the Present Discontents*: "When bad men combine, the good must associate; else they will fall one by one, an unpitied sacrifice in a contemptible struggle." Regardless, Burke was right. All that is necessary for slippery slope arguments to triumph is for good men to do nothing.

10
DISSENT

> No matter that patriotism is too often the refuge of scoundrels. Dissent, rebellion, and all-around hell-raising remain the true duty of patriots.
>
> —Barbara Ehrenreich, *The Worst Years of Our Lives: Irreverent Notes from a Decade of Greed*

"*Dissent is the highest form of patriotism.*"

Like an artificially designed molecule, there's something about the phrase that allows it to slip through mental defenses and implant itself deep within the liberal mind. During the eight years of the George W. Bush presidency, this was a banner slogan of American liberalism.

"This is not the first time in American history when patriotism has been distorted to deflect criticism and mislead the nation," proclaimed Senator John Kerry while running to replace the "divisive" President Bush. Kerry continued, "No wonder Thomas Jefferson himself said: 'Dissent is the greatest form of patriotism.'"

"It is not unpatriotic to tell the truth to the American people about the war in Iraq. In this grave moment of our country," asserted Ted Kennedy, the man who rendered Kerry the junior senator from Massachusetts for nearly three decades, "to use the words of Thomas Jefferson, 'Dissent is the highest form of patriotism.'"

"We need to stop slicing this country in half, and saying those who support this act or this politician are 'good' Americans, and the rest are not," thundered Mitch Albom of the *Detroit Free Press.* "Sometimes 'dissent is the highest form of patriotism.' I didn't make that up. Thomas Jefferson did."[1]

All this might prove more convincing if Jefferson had actually said it—which he didn't.

As Mark Steyn has had great fun pointing out: Thomas Jefferson never said "dissent is the highest form of patriotism," at least according to the good people at the Jefferson Library. That fact gives a certain added buffoonish poignancy to this headline from the *Capital Times* of Madison, Wisconsin: THOMAS JEFFERSON GOT IT RIGHT: "DISSENT IS THE HIGHEST FORM OF PATRIOTISM." And teaching children how to be thoughtful and effective dissenters is the highest form of education."[2]

Steyn traces the fakery back to a 1991 quote from Nadine Strossen, who at the time was head of the ACLU, an organization with a vested interest in putting the Founders' imprimatur on relentless knee-jerk complaining. Others have erroneously credited Howard Zinn. The oldest reference I can find in major newspapers is a 1969 line from then New York mayor John Lindsay, who was congratulating anti-Vietnam protesters at Columbia University for their patriotism. (He was booed after he left the stage, and Paul Boutelle—a cab driver and Socialist Workers Party mayoral candidate known after 1979 as Kwame Montsho Ajamu Somburu—vilified him in absentia. The crowd loved that.) But the oldest source anywhere is apparently, of all things, a book called *The Use of Force in International Affairs.*[3]

Bear in mind that even if Jefferson had said it, it would be no less dumb.

Just curious: If a marine throws himself on a grenade while fighting for his country, would you feel confident that you'd keep your teeth if you said something along the lines of, "Wow. What a hero. A true patriot. He's almost as patriotic as that college professor who, from the comfort of his air-conditioned office, called the Marines baby killers and war criminals."

The protective coating of the phrase "dissent is the highest form of patriotism" is clearly provided by the word "dissent." It's a word that often elevates buffoonery on its own. But when it's tethered to patriotism it transmogrifies the lead of jackassery into the gold of stouthearted rebellion. Dissent in and of itself is nothing special. As anybody who has tried to get something constructive done can attest, dissent for its own sake is often one of the highest forms of asininity. The reflexive contrarian who cares not what he is contradicting is quite simply the most useless of citizens and annoying of coworkers. The guy who says, "Frankly, I don't care that the boat is taking on water. We shouldn't start bailing out until we've fully discussed our leadership structure" is a dissenter, and he is an ass for it.

"They laughed at Columbus, they laughed at Fulton, they laughed at the Wright Brothers," observed Carl Sagan. "But they also laughed at Bozo the Clown." Most lone dissenters are alone not because they are dissenters but because they are loons. Yes, we revere some exceptions, but we revere them because they were *exceptional—and because they were right.* Unfortunately, we live in a country where we increasingly lavish attention on people solely because they break from the emaciated and gasping corpse we call orthodoxy these days. Jack Kevorkian is treated like a Thomas More figure by HBO, when the reality is he was simply a ghoul who really enjoyed getting attention by killing desperate people.

In short, the merit of any dissent is dependent upon what the dissenter is dissenting *from*—and *why*. (Just as the merit of any consensus is wholly dependent upon what people are collectively consenting to.)

Even more so, the *patriotism* of dissent depends entirely on what the dissenter is dissenting *from*—and *why*. As John O'Sullivan once noted, tongue firmly in cheek, "Dissent is the highest form of patriotism. Treason is the highest form of dissent. Therefore treason is the highest form of patriotism." QED.

The American Communists who infiltrated American institutions and, on Stalin's orders, opposed American entry into World War II were not patriotic for doing so. And when Hitler betrayed his "partner in peace" and invaded Russia, those same American Communists did not become patriotic overnight by suddenly supporting the war either. Alternatively, the progressive historian Charles Beard opposed U.S. entry into World War II, just as the Communists did, and he was just as wrong on the merits of the question. But his motives were for the most part decent and patriotic. In other words, dissent *can* be patriotic but merely dissenting doesn't make you patriotic. Some of the chanting Occupy Wall Street protesters out there recycling their urine and filming gay porn movies in tents might also be interested in helping America, but many are simply motivated by an apish desire to join the crowd or a nihilistic yearning to take a sledgehammer to the foundation of a country they just happened to be born in.

The whole subject of assessing—or questioning—the patriotism of people leaves liberals particularly queasy, which, after all, partly explains why the phrase "dissent is the highest form of patriotism" is so appealing. It's a heads I win, tails you lose proposition, because it offers a free pass to say the most terrible things about your country and claim to be a patriot in the process. Dissenter: "I hate America." Normal Person: "Why are you so unpatriotic?" Dissenter: "How dare you question my patriotism!?"

This is the logic of the wife beater who insists that his spouse left him with no choice but to abuse her. In a rhetorical way it's even worse, because the one who questions the love a man has for the wife he beats is never cast as the villain. But question a fellow American's love of country, and all of a sudden you're the bad guy.

You can understand why this seems so odd to normal Americans. Imagine there's someone who believes it might do America "a ton of good to have our butts kicked" (in the words of left-wing novelist Tom Robbins). Or this person might believe that the world would benefit from "a million Mogadishus" and that "the only true heroes are those who find ways to defeat the U.S. military" (in the words of then Columbia professor Nicholas De Genova). Or this person might believe that America is "just downright mean," brimming with people with "broken souls" and hasn't done anything worthy of eliciting pride in her lifetime (Michelle Obama). Or he might believe that because of "Ameri-KKKs" racism at home and cruelty abroad we shouldn't say "God bless America" so much as "Goddamn America!" (Reverend Jeremiah Wright).

Now according to a large number of people, if you were to say that such a person was driving around with something less than a full tank of patriotism, that would make you a McCarthyite, a demagogue, maybe even a fascist.

To understand why this is absurd, just replace "America" in the above quotes with just about any remotely similar noun. "The only true heroes are those who find ways to defeat *the New York Yankees*!" *Cleveland* is "down right mean!" "It's not God bless my *K-car*, but God-damn my *KKK-car*!" And so on. In any of these instances a reasonable person might "question" a given individual's love for the Yankees, Cleveland, or K-cars. But no reasonable person can ever—ever!—question the patriotism of anyone else without being the worst kind of villain. Indeed, when listening to the Left it sometimes sounds as if it's reasonable to question whether or not Ethel and Julius Rosenberg were guilty of giving atomic secrets to the Soviets, but don't you dare question their patriotism!

Even more confusing is the stance of mainstream liberals when it comes to patriotism. Many respected intellectuals will dismiss or forgive the ravings of the hard left on the grounds that dissent is patriotic even as they concede that the actual content of the dissent may be unpatriotic. But ultimately, anti-Americanism doesn't much interest them. What drives them crazy, however, is what they consider to be unwarranted *pro*-Americanism, or what is commonly referred to as "American exceptionalism." My longtime debating opponent Peter Beinart writes that calling America the greatest country in the world is a "lunatic notion."[4] Michael Kinsley, meanwhile, was so flabbergasted by the stupidity of voters who opposed Obama that he saw fit to pen yet another essay on how America is not the greatest country ever for *Politico*; it was titled "U.S. Is Not Greatest Country Ever."[5]

Subtle.

Again, imagine a man who relishes going out of the way to point out how his wife isn't all that special. You might think that guy isn't wholly committed to her. And if a woman said, "My daughter's fine, but she's really no better than any other kid," you might think she's lacking in the maternal-love department. This illustrates a truth about how love works. At some basic level, if you love something, you must find it preferable to something else, perhaps everything else. Your reasons can be subjective, or simply impossible to identify or quantify. Love, true love, is a mystery. Indeed, I put it to you that men who marry women solely because they meet a checklist (blond hair: check! Green Bay Packers fan: check!) aren't really in love. They may grow to love their spouse, but that happens only when they come to appreciate what makes her different from a mere manifestation of categorical bullet points.

This doesn't mean love of wife or country requires deceit or unthinking agreement. "'My country, right or wrong,'" Chesterton famously observed in *The Defendant*, "is a thing that no patriot would think of saying except in a desperate case. It is like saying, 'My mother, drunk or sober.'" And while the quote is not taken too violently out of context, it does leave out the part where Chesterton says that any decent man would share his unfortunate mother's troubles for the rest of his life. Why? Because he loves his mother. Similarly, the patriot who believes his country is wrong is right to say so. But that does not mean that saying your country is wrong automatically makes you a patriot—or right.

I am not saying that all liberals do not love America. What I am saying is that they are hopelessly confused about how to think about and, therefore, express their love of her.

We could, but should not, leave it there. Because confusion does not exhaust the problems liberals have with patriotism. Chesterton may have said "my country right or wrong is something no patriot would say." But Orwell got closer to the truth of true patriotism when he said, "My country right or left." This is the formulation today's liberals have a much more difficult time grappling with.

When America elects a left-wing president, the tendency for conservatives is to like the government less and the country more. This is because liberal presidents tend to want to change America while conservative presidents tend to talk about the need to change the government. And when America elects conservative presidents, the Left tends to express its love for government more (and lament how it is being discredited by conservatives) and its fondness for America less. Every four years the stars in the firmament of liberalism start talking about how they might need to leave the country if the Republican is elected. They almost never do, alas, but the fact that they talk that way is indicative of their obsession with politics above everything else.

For all the whining about how Republicans use patriotism as a wedge against their opponents, the reality is more complicated. Liberals are uncomfortable with the topic of patriotism because their core philosophical impulses are to make America a different country than it is. This is not an evil impulse, and it can certainly manifest itself in patriotic ways. More importantly, it can manifest itself in humane and decent ways. But at the most basic level love is about acceptance. If you are constantly trying to change the person you claim to love into someone he or she is not, there comes a point when it's reasonable to ask whether you really, truly, deeply love the person for who he or she is. Barack Obama campaigned promising to "fundamentally transform" America.[6] We would not think a husband who promises to "fundamentally transform" his wife has a healthy love for her.

By the same token, it is simply untrue, as a historical matter, that liberals don't resort to what we call McCarthyite tactics. Throughout the twentieth century progressives cast the bulk of their program as an effort to impose "100 percent Americanism" from coast to coast. For a time their greatest bogeyman was the "hyphenated American"—i.e., German-Americans, Italian-Americans, etc. "There is no such thing as a hyphenated American who is a good American," declared Teddy Roosevelt. "The only man who is a good American is the man who is an American and nothing else." Naturally, the Wilson administration was the worst. "Any man who carries a hyphen about with him carries a dagger that he is ready to plunge into the vitals of this Republic whenever he gets ready."

"When I hear a man advising the American people to state the terms of peace," Clarence Darrow explained while working as a propagandist for the Wilson administration, "I know he is working for Germany." In a speech at Madison Square Garden he said, "[A]ny man who refuses to back the president in this crisis is worse than a traitor."[7] FDR and his surrogates routinely suggested that opponents of the New Deal were unpatriotic "malefactors of great wealth" and the like.

The very idea that liberals have always stood foursquare against anything that smacks of McCarthyism is simply a self-serving myth (indeed, McCarthy himself began his career as a Democrat and rose in Wisconsin state politics as a progressive Republican). The Left has always made allowances for McCarthyite tactics when it is one of their enemies getting grilled. The House Un-American Activities Committee, after all, was founded by a progressive Democrat, Samuel Dickstein, to investigate German sympathizers. During the barely remembered Brown scare of the 1940s everyone from real Nazi supporters—the German American Bund, for example—to misguided isolationists was targeted and harassed. Much like Wilson, FDR believed that any domestic dissent was treachery and insisted that his department of justice persecute his opponents. At the height of the madness Walter Winchell read the names of isolationists on the radio, calling them "Americans we can do without."[8] American Communists in this period readily named names and compiled lists of alleged German sympathizers. After the war, when Harry Truman ran for president in his own right, he won the election only after insisting that his opponent was a stooge frontman for a Hitlerite plot. In 1964, liberals peddled the idea that there was some vague connection between Barry Goldwater and the Nazis. CBS's Daniel Schorr even reported that Goldwater's planned vacation in Europe was actually a clandestine effort to link up with Nazi elements in "Hitler's stamping grounds." During the war in Kosovo, former *New York Times* columnist and dean of left-wing civil libertarians Anthony Lewis dubbed Republicans in Congress the "disloyal opposition" for their dissent from Clinton's effort (dissent that makes the recent Democratic stance toward the Iraq war seem like cheerleading).

But that's ancient history, right? Well, look at what happened the moment Barack Obama was elected. Suddenly dissent stopped being the highest form of patriotism. In the summer of 2009, then speaker of the House Nancy Pelosi and then majority leader Steny Hoyer insisted that the town hall protests against the Affordable Care Act were "un-American." Indeed, the moment a populist, grassroots movement—aka the Tea Partiers—sprang up against Barack Obama, dissent suddenly transformed from the highest form of patriotism to the lowest form of racism. "Let's be very honest about what this is about," noted self-trained political scientist and Oscar-robbed star of *Mystery Men* and *Wet Hot American Summer* Janeane Garofalo to a nodding Keith Olbermann. "This is not about bashing Democrats. It's not about taxes. They have no idea what the Boston Tea party was about. They don't know their history at all. It's about hating a black man in the White House. This is racism straight up and is nothing but a bunch of teabagging rednecks. There is no way around that."[9]

Obviously, if Hillary Clinton had been elected president in 2008 instead of Barack Obama and crammed the same policies through Congress, no remotely serious person would expect the opponents of ObamaCare to say about HillaryCare 2.0, "Oh, well. It would be a huge problem if a black man was pushing these policies. But, you know, since

Hillary is white, it's okay." But just because something is ludicrous on its face doesn't mean it won't gain popularity if it confirms or reinforces the existing biases of the Left.

When they can, liberals use patriotism as a sword and indignation over having their patriotism questioned as a shield. When used in combination, it's a formidable tactic intended to conceal the fact that they love their country when it's left, but not when it's right.

11
SOCIAL JUSTICE

In these days of difficulty, we Americans everywhere must and shall choose the path of social justice . . . the path of faith, the path of hope and the path of love toward our fellow man.

—Franklin Delano Roosevelt, "Campaign Address at Detroit, Michigan," October 2, 1932

I am certain nothing has done so much to destroy the juridical safeguards of individual freedom as the striving after the mirage of social justice.

—Friedrich A. Hayek, *Economic Freedom and Representative Government* (1973)

In that classic of American cinema, *Caddyshack*, Danny—the protagonist—desperately wants to win the annual Bushwood Country Club scholarship set aside for impressive young caddies. He meets with Judge Smails, who is charged with awarding the scholarship. He has the young caddy's future in his hands (which is awkward, because Danny was recently caught in flagrante delicto with the judge's niece).

Smails, eager to demonstrate that he's as fair a judge of character as he is of greens, explains his thinking:

> You know, despite what happened, I'm still convinced that you have many fine qualities. I think you can still become a gentleman someday if you understand and abide by the rules of decent

> society. There's a lot of . . . well, badness in the world today. I see it in court every day. I've sentenced boys younger than you to the gas chamber. I didn't want to do it—felt I *owed* it to them. The most important decision you can make right now is what you stand for—goodness . . . or badness.

Danny, eager for a scholarship, chooses "goodness."

I mention this scene because it captures the essence of what most people mean when they invoke the idea of social justice. A cry for social justice is usually little more than an assertion "for goodness." "Progressive" has become a euphemism for "all good things." But sometimes the p-word is too vague. So if you press a self-declared progressive—"What does that mean?"—they'll respond, eventually, with something like. "It means fighting for social justice." If you ask, "What does social justice mean?" you are likely to get an exasperated eye roll, *because you just don't get it.*

Social justice simply *is* goodness, and if you can't see that, man, you're either unintentionally "part of the problem" or, well, you're for "badness."

I once met an ex-cop getting a master's degree in a criminology program at a major university. He explained to me that he had a hard time fitting into the culture of the program because the faculty seemed so concerned with do-goodery instead of stopping the forces of do-baddery. The chair of the department explained that they teach criminal justice but they consider their true mission "social justice."

Not only is social justice good, it's heroic. After the horrific and senseless Norwegian massacre by Anders Behring Breivik in July 2011, Jalees Rehman, MD, took to the *Huffington Post* to claim that Breivik targeted the teenagers on Utoeya Island in Norway because they promoted "values such as tolerance, social justice and peace. Their participation was a sign of their commitment to further improve our society, and in this sense, they are heroes similar to the firefighters and policeman [*sic*] who died during the September 11, 2001, attacks in the line of duty."[1]

Social justice is one of those phrases that no mission statement—at least no mission statement of a certain type—can do without. One simply cannot be in the do-goodery business without making reference to the fact that you're fighting for social justice.

Here's the AFL-CIO: "The mission of the AFL-CIO is to improve the lives of working families—to bring economic justice to the workplace and social justice to our nation. To accomplish this mission we will *build* and *change* the American labor movement."[2] The Service Employees International Union (SEIU)—a labor union two million members strong that enjoys close relations with President Obama and his administration (former SEIU president Andrew Stern was the most frequent visitor to the White House during the first six months of the Obama presidency, which no doubt is why his presidency got off to such a great start)—asserts: "We believe we have a special mission to bring economic and social justice to those most exploited in our community—especially to women and workers of color." In case that's unclear, they go on: "We must build political power to ensure that workers' voices are heard at every level of government to create economic opportunity and foster social justice."[3]

We expect as much from labor unions, and no less from academia. A recent *Harvard Crimson* editorial explains that you should give the college money because "it largely succeeds as a mechanism for social justice."[4] Well, okay then, where's my checkbook?

Just type "social justice" into a search engine alongside almost any institution's name and you'll find such twaddle. The Ford Foundation gave the Newseum a grant "for a Web site incorporating videos, interactive games and primary resources in a curriculum-based structure for classroom use and to organize a forum on journalism and social justice."[5] In 2010 the Smithsonian held a conference on "A Deeper Diversity, the Nation's Health: Renewing Social Justice and Human Well-Being in Our Time."[6] The Muslim American Society, the organization founded by and through which the Muslim Brotherhood operates in the United States, declares on its Web site that it "hopes to contribute to the promotion of peace and social justice."[7] Even the American Nazi Party, not wanting to be left out of all the fun, identifies "[s]ocial justice for White Working Class people throughout our land" as one of their two main tenets.[8]

All these organizations (and by no means only these) claim that social justice sits at the center of their mission, and yet rarely does any organization go on to explain what they mean by it, other than connoting some sort of implied goodness. This is from the home page of the Yale Social

Justice Network: "The Social Justice Network at Yale is a coalition of organizations and individuals working for social justice and social change at Yale, in New Haven, and beyond. SJN is dedicated to building a community among and reaching out to those who identify themselves as working for social justice, while helping activists develop skills necessary to acheive [*sic*] this change."[9] Got it?

Beyond simply being a placeholder for goodness, progressively defined, what does social justice mean specifically? What are the action items of social justice? Securing gay rights, gay marriage in particular, has to be near the top of that list. After the New York State Legislature passed a bill legalizing civil marriages for same-sex couples in June 2011, Governor Andrew Cuomo took the podium to alert the masses that the Empire State had "reached a new level of social justice" and that "this state, when at its finest, is a beacon for social justice." New York is for goodness.

This raises one of the really neat things about social justice. Once you become a poster child for it, you also become an expert on it. Indeed, the lesbian, gay, bisexual, and transgender (LGBT) movement considers itself to be such an authority on questions of social justice that they often feel compelled, nay obliged, to weigh in on all sorts of issues beyond what some not fully fluent in social justice issues might think outside their bailiwick. Invoking the "longstanding commitment to all forms of social justice of the LGBT community," the presidents of the Gay & Lesbian Alliance Against Defamation (GLADD) and the National Gay & Lesbian Chamber of Commerce (NGLCC) sent a letter to the chairman of the Federal Communications Commission (FCC) in May 2011 urging it to support "President Obama's vision of an America in which everyone has high-speed access" by allowing the merger between AT&T and T-Mobile.[10]

I remain a bit hazy on how, exactly, high-speed Internet access is a requirement of social justice, or for that matter of specific concern for gays. Perhaps the merger between AT&T and T-Mobile will mean that no one will ever again have to say, "Can you hear me now?" when they come out of the closet?

But this does help illustrate the problem with social justice. It becomes like The Force in *Star Wars*. Who are Jedis? They are good people who are strong with The Force. What is The Force? It is what Jedis are strong with. The social justice syllogism goes something like this: 1) We are liberals. 2) Liberals believe it is imperative that social justice be advanced wherever we find it. 3) Therefore, whatever we believe to be imperative *is* social justice. And there's the corollary: If you oppose liberals in advancing what they want, you are against not just liberals but social justice itself.

Fortunately, some folks are willing to offer some specifics about what full-spectrum social justice looks like. The Green Party, for example, lists social justice as one of the four main pillars of their platform. They even provide a handy list of all the different themes and policies that count toward advancing it, including such broad topics as women's rights, labor, education and the arts, environmental justice, universal health care, and "a commitment to ending poverty" through "welfare." Each of these is then explained at some length, as you might expect. But there are also the more granular offenses to the advanced conscience, such as justice for the native Kanaka Maoli of Hawaii, including the need for "open dialogue among all residents of Hawai'i on the sovereignty option of full independence" (that would mean "secession," if you're not reading too closely) to remedy the "illegal annexation" of Hawaii—er, sorry Hawai'i—in 1898.

It's quite a grab bag, really. If you believe in social justice, according to the Greens, you should support "[e]liminating all laws that seek to restrict or censor artistic expression, including the withholding of government funds for political or moral content" (this will be hailed as fantastic news for the more artsy members of the Ku Klux Klan); the promotion of "new traditions and images of men becoming fully involved in all aspects of the family planning process"; that "[y]oung people should have input into the direction and pace of their own education, including input into the operation of their educational institutions"; and that "[a]ll people have a right to food, housing, medical care, jobs that pay a living wage, education, and support in times of hardship."

What hardship could there be, one wonders, what with all the free food, housing, medical care, education, and well-paying jobs?

Now you may object that this is the agenda of the Green Party, which is of course going to be pretty out there ideologically. Perhaps. But a reasonable response is that because the Green Party is out there, it can actually afford to explain what social justice means. In other words, they can let everyone out of the clown car of social justice and let them stretch their legs a bit. Moreover, it's not like there are a lot of competing and more reasonable definitions out there. Rather, the closer to the mainstream an organization gets, the less it will *explain* what social justice *is*, and the more they'll just let those in the know interpret the code for themselves.

Regardless, even members of the Green Party understand that Rome wasn't ruined in a day. An agenda like this takes time and effort over lifetimes. That's why it is so important to *teach* social justice to future generations, so they can carry the torch that will one day burn Western civilization to the ground. And you cannot teach social justice without first training the teachers to teach it.

This was the idea in 2000 when the National Council for Accreditation of Teacher Education, which accredits about half of the colleges of education in the country, introduced a new set of standards for accrediting schools that incorporated the latest trend of "disposition evaluation." According to the NCATE, the dispositions of the teacher candidates should be measured in order to determine which candidates are most likely to be successful as teachers. But which dispositions ought to be evaluated? Surely not the disposition to take a nip out of that bottle of peppermint schnapps in your desk drawer during recess.

Well, according to the NCATE, the dispositions to be measured are those that are "guided by beliefs and attitudes related to values such as caring, fairness, honesty, responsibility, and social justice." How, exactly, one can measure a "disposition for social justice" remains unclear. And while the NCATE dropped these "disposition standards" in 2006 when they fell out of vogue, many education colleges still apply these standards in their student, teacher, and new hire evaluations.

Sparked by an incident at his own Brooklyn College School of Education, where a student was penalized for not demonstrating a sufficient "disposition for social justice," Professor KC Johnson has done yeoman's work documenting education programs across the country that include "social justice dispositions" in their evaluation of soon-to-be-molders-of-young-minds. Among the most aggressive with its requirements for the social justice disposition is Brooklyn College, which identifies—like the Green Party—social justice as one of the four pillars of their conceptual framework. They explain: "We educate teacher candidates and other school personnel about issues of social injustice such as institutionalized racism, sexism, classism, and heterosexism (Fine et al, 1996; Nussbaum, 1999); and invite them to develop strategies and practices that challenge [such] biases."

Similar statements can be found in scores of education colleges around the country. For example, the School of Education at the University of Colorado, Boulder, requires students to demonstrate a "shared commitment to *evidence-based policy and practice and to democracy, diversity, and social justice*" (their emphasis). The education program at the University of Kansas expects its students to be "more global than national and concerned with ideals such as world peace, social justice, respect for diversity and preservation of the environment." Graduates from the University of Maryland, Baltimore County, are expected to be "leaders in their schools as well as advocates for democracy and social justice." The education program at the University of South Carolina aims at "preparing educators to have a sincere understanding and appreciation of diversity as we challenge ourselves and others to work for social justice."[11]

This is the beauty of the phrase social justice. It means everything to those who care about it and it means nothing to those whose eyes glaze over when they hear what they think is mere boilerplate. The "social justice disposition" that these colleges are "measuring" has nothing to do with the substance of the disciplines being taught—or that are supposed to be taught—and everything to do with filtering out those who aren't part of the movement without having to admit to discriminatory policies.

So far we've just been dancing around the heart of social justice's historic and core meaning: spreading the wealth around. The *Oxford English Dictionary* lists "distributive justice" as a synonym of social justice, and defines it as "justice at the level of a society or state as regards the possession of wealth, commodities, opportunities, and privileges."

Before we go any further, a very brief (and thus overly simplified) history of how the term emerges in its current context is in order.[12]

The phrase social justice began as a technical term within Catholic theology—coined by Catholic moral theologian Luigi Taparelli d'Azeglio in an 1840 treatise on natural law. Taparelli was concerned that with the growing popularity of various social contract theories of the nineteenth century (Rousseau's in particular), people might lose sight of the "the social fact" of humanity. Simply put, we humans are social beings. We are born into families, and live in communities. An individual belongs to more institutions—more "societies"—than just the State. In other words, there isn't just civil society, there are civil *societies.* And those societies maintain a level of autonomy apart from that of the State. We form groups and associations in order to obtain basic goods and complete tasks that would otherwise be very difficult, if not impossible, to accomplish.

These intermediary associations act as both bridge and buffer between the individual and the State. The associations of "lower society" maintain their own autonomy so long as they do not threaten to destroy the unity of the "higher society"—i.e., the State. The State, in turn, has a responsibility to not "destroy the inner unity" of those associations, but rather respect their freedom and autonomy within the society. In other words, the government cannot trample the structure of social ecosystems that make life worthwhile.[13]

Against the backdrop of the dramatic rise in the size, scope, power, and authority of the nation-state system, Taparelli worried that the traditional language of "legal justice"—i.e., plain old justice, according to most people—might reinforce the erroneous and dangerous idea that the only society that exists is the one that people call the State, constraining the autonomy and spiritual authority of, among other things, the Church. Recall that later Mussolini would define fascism as "everything within the state, nothing outside the state"[14]—a view that earned the condemnation of the Church for "statolotry," or the sinful worship of the state.

To remedy this misunderstanding, Taparelli introduced the phrase "social justice" as a way to emphasize that much of the important stuff lay outside the realm of the State. It had nothing to do with redistributing wealth (never mind fighting for gender equity). Taparelli thought of and employed social justice in a completely different way than almost everyone, Catholic and otherwise, does in contemporary society.[15]

The concept percolated within the intellectual machinery of the Church for years. Another priest-philosopher, Antonio Rosmini-Serbati, popularized it in his *Constitution of Social Justice.* Eventually, advisers to Pope Leo XIII suggested he take up Taparelli's idea of replacing the phrase legal justice with social justice in his 1891 encyclical, *Rerum Novarum*. Being a good Thomist, Leo decided not to make the swap. Twenty-one years later, a former student of Taparelli's by the name of Ambrogio Damiano Achille Ratti was named Pope Pius XI. And nine years after that, he celebrated the fortieth anniversary of *Rerum Novarum* with a social encyclical of his own that fully embraced the language of social justice, and thus introduced it formally into the Catholic lexicon.[16]

It needs to be understood that pretty much the whole intellectual world was fixated on the adjective "social" back then. The "social question" was the central question of the late nineteenth and early twentieth century. What was the social question? You name it. Urbanization, unification, industrialization, democratization, deracination, and consolidation: These trends worked with and against each other to churn nearly every settled assumption about how the world works. The rise of "mass society," the crumbling of monarchy, and the economic transformation of traditional agriculture meant pretty much everything was "in play." Today we think of socialism as a purely economic doctrine of one kind or another. But when the term gained widespread currency, it had a more inclusive connotation, suggesting how people should *live*, not just how people should work or be compensated for work.

Social justice got thrown into this intellectual blender. Many theologians became involved in the late-nineteenth-century movement known as Social Catholicism, and unlike their (classically) liberal counterparts, who held that charity in the form of alms giving ought to be the primary way to help those in need, the Social Catholics argued that social justice demanded more charitable economic arrangements. Of course, only the state itself could impose such arrangements. And so social justice developed a political and ideological charge that was never intended by its formulator—but would prove wildly useful as a rallying cry for progressive economic policies.

When planted in American soil social justice grew into something even more warped. The phrase kept a religious connotation, but it evolved into a more explicitly political and economic doctrine, thanks largely to two left-wing American priests, Monsignor John Ryan and Father Charles Coughlin. Ryan was the most respected liberal Catholic intellectual and theologian in America during the early twentieth century. He spearheaded the use of social justice to mean the moral obligation of the state to ensure the well-being of all citizens, and of the poor, vulnerable, and elderly in particular. His 1906 book, *A Living Wage*, largely introduced the concept to American progressives. He insisted that *Rerum Novarum* had changed the living wage "from an implicit to an explicit principle of Catholic ethics." Later, and not surprisingly, he became one of FDR's biggest supporters, earning the nickname "Monsignor New Deal" for his sharp-edged rhetoric:

> It should be obvious that insurance against unemployment and old age is an elementary measure of social justice. The sum of the matter is that these and several other enactments of the New Deal constitute moderate measures of economic reform which were long overdue in the United States. They are mild installments of too long delayed social justice. If they are denounced as communistic, it is simply because this is the most damaging epithet that can be hurled against them by beneficiaries of social injustice.[17]

It's a small sign of how deeply the Manichean categories of Marxism had seeped into liberal argumentation. If you feared that guaranteed income was "too communistic," it can only be because you are a beneficiary of "social injustice."

But Ryan was a pussycat compared to the "little flower," Father Charles Coughlin, when it came to championing the need for social justice policies in America. Coughlin—a cliché unto himself insofar as he is routinely described as the "right-wing radio priest"—was well to the left of Roosevelt and Ryan. Early in his career as a pundit of sorts he was one of FDR's most influential defenders. It was "Roosevelt or Ruin" in the 1932 election. The New Deal was "Christ's Deal," for had not FDR promised to "drive the money changers from the temple" in his inaugural address? Coughlin quickly became disillusioned with the New Deal. Not, mind you, because he thought the New Deal was too intrusive or too leftist, but precisely because it was not aggressive enough in fulfilling all the socialist requirements of social justice.

In 1934 Coughlin founded the National Union of Social Justice and outlined sixteen requirements of social justice, only some of which according to him were being fulfilled by the New Deal. Among the articles of faith for this new superlobby:

- That every citizen willing to work and capable of working shall receive a just and living annual wage which will enable him to maintain and educate his family . . .
- Nationalizing those public necessities by which their very nature are too important to be held in control of private individuals[18]

The following month Coughlin issued another seven principles to elaborate exactly how the NUSJ would combat the horrors of capitalism and modern commerce. Among them: The government must guarantee the production of "food, wearing apparel, homes, drugs, books and all modern conveniences." "This principle," Coughlin rightly explained, "is contrary to the theory of capitalism."[19]

In the years leading up to the 1936 election, Monsignor Ryan and Father Coughlin—once friends and political allies (Ryan once said Coughlin was "on the side of the angels"[20] for his work in social justice)—became embroiled in a public battle for the political hearts and minds of the Catholic faithful. Ryan argued that Roosevelt was a champion and the New Deal an embodiment of social justice. Father Coughlin, however, was convinced Roosevelt still favored "pseudo-capitalistic monetary policies," and campaigned against his reelection with vigor:

> The great betrayer and liar, Franklin D. Roosevelt, who promised to drive the money changers from the temple, had succeeded [only] in driving the farmers from their homesteads and the citizens from their homes in the cities. . . . I ask you to purge the man who claims to be a Democrat, from the Democratic Party, and I mean Franklin Double-Crossing Roosevelt.[21]

In other words, by the time FDR was reelected in 1936, the only live debate on how to fulfill the requirements of social justice was whether moderately liberal policies were enough to get the job done, or if it required even more radical government intervention and redistribution.

This use of social justice—an empty vessel to be filled with any and all leftist ideals, and then promptly wielded as a political bludgeon against any and all dissenters—is precisely what F. A. Hayek had in mind in his *Mirage of Social Justice*, the most extended, and definitive, assault on the topic to date. Hayek came out swinging: "I have come to feel strongly that the greatest service I can still render to my fellow men would be that I could make the speakers and writers among them thoroughly ashamed ever again to employ the term 'social justice.' "[22]

No one should be surprised that the twentieth-century heir to Adam Smith would have a problem with the concept of social justice. But why describe it as a *mirage*? To begin, Hayek wisely identified justice in the classical sense as a particular action of *persons*. "[O]nly situations that have been created by human will can be called just or unjust. . . . Social justice," Hayek concludes, "does not belong to the category of effort but that of nonsense, like the term 'a moral stone.' " Whining about how high unemployment is "unjust" is dangerously misleading nonsense. Justice creates a claim on others. So who is being unjust? The employers who cannot afford more workers? The consumers who refuse to create enough demand to justify more workers? The government for not taxing innocent parties to pay for labor that isn't needed and that they did not vote for? Social justice assumes rights—social rights, economic rights, etc.—that cannot be enforced.

It's a brilliant and fun read that I can't summarize adequately here, but it's important to note his overriding conclusion: It makes no sense to speak of social justice in a free society, because to do so assumes that we should not in fact live in a free society, at least not as classically understood.

Think of it this way. The Bill of Rights is framed in the negative because your rights are prior and independent from the government. "Congress shall make no law . . ." infringing on this or that right. A "social justice bill of rights" might begin, "Government must provide . . ." a home, car, job, French bulldog puppy, whatever. You cannot truly "have" such rights, because you are not born with them. How can you be born with an "inalienable right" to a home? Why not an inalienable right to a hovercraft or a jetpack?

In a society that relies upon the invisible hand of the free market, social justice is a nonsensical concept, in precisely the way saying "let the market decide" would make no sense in, say, North Korea today. The only way for social justice to make sense is if you operate from the assumption that the invisible hand of the market should be amputated and replaced with the very visible hand of the State. In other words, each explicit demand for social justice carries with it the implicit but necessary requirement that the State do the fixing. And a society dedicated to the pursuit of perfect social justice must gradually move more and more decisions under the command of the State, until it is the sole moral agent.

Of course, this opens up Hayek (and me by extension) to an obvious rejoinder. Hayek was working from the assumption that we do, and more important, should live in a free society, in the classical, free-market, limited government sense. That is the ideological prior conclusion, as it were, from which he launches his attack on the stupidity of social justice. I will stipulate that it is my ideological foundation as well (a shocking revelation, I know). So if you're a progressive activist for social change and social justice, or of just plain "goodness," in the Smailsian sense, you are free to respond that the concept of social justice is worthwhile *only* if you look at it from an equally specific ideological perspective—one that affirms the vast role the State must play in bringing about the just society.

And that's the point. Social justice is not a nonideological concept that simply draws on ethics or morality or the overall need for goodness in society. No, it is a deeply ideological set of assumptions that most practitioners of social justice refuse to openly and sincerely acknowledge.

The funny thing is, liberals used to acknowledge the point frankly. Here's our friend Herbert Croly, the founding father of modern liberalism:

> The idea of individual justice is being supplemented by the idea of social justice. When our constitutions were written, the traditions of English law, the contemporary political philosophy and the economic situation of the American democracy all conspired

> to embody in them and their interpretation an extremely individualistic conception of justice—a conception which practically confided social welfare to the free expression of individual interests and good intentions. Now the tendency is to conceive the social welfare not as an end which cannot be left to the happy harmonizing of individual interests, but as an end which must be consciously willed by society and efficiently realized. Society, that is, has become a moral ideal, not independent of the individual but supplementary to him, an ideal which must be pursued less by regulating individual excesses than by the active conscious encouragement of socializing tendencies and purposes.[23]

The fundamental problem with social justice is that there are no limiting principles to it. It is an open-ended license for the forces of goodness to do what they think is right *forever*. It is an empowering principle for the high moral ground in all political debates. There are no boundaries, no internal checks, no definitional roadblocks. It's social justice for as far as the eye can see. And the forces of social justice can see way past the arbitrary borders of the United States, or any state.

No wonder then that the Crolyite vision of replacing individual justice with social justice has found a home at the United Nations. In November 2007, the UN General Assembly declared that starting in 2009, February 20 would be celebrated annually as the World Day of Social Justice (shop early for those hard-to-find social justice gifts!). The intellectual lodestone inspiring this new holiday was a 157-page report produced by their Division for Social Policy and Development entitled: "Social Justice in an Open World: The Role of the United Nations."

"Social Justice," the authors of this page-turner declare, "is not possible without strong and coherent redistributive policies conceived and implemented by public agencies." But that's downright Jeffersonian compared to the more concentrated and pernicious asininity to follow. They warn: "Present-day believers in an absolute truth identified with virtue and justice are neither willing nor desirable companions for the defenders of social justice."[24] Translation: If you actually believe in the antiquated notion that rights exist outside the schemes of governments and social planners, if you think that the concept of justice endures beyond the relativistic standards of whatever the forces of goodness say this week, then you cannot be seen as an ally of the great, wise, and noble global social justice coalition.

In one sense, this is all just very funny. It's a bit like that scene in *Miracle on 34th Street* when the judge declares that Santa Claus must exist because the U.S. Postal Service says so. The United Nations—that insufferable nest of crapweasels and kleptocrats—holds that if you believe in "an absolute truth identified with virtue and justice" then you are no friend of the cause of social justice. Which, I suppose, is true.

What is infuriating, however, is that if social justice simply means goodness, then anybody who disagrees with the UN or its affiliated cadres of social justice seekers, must of necessity be a champion of badness. Not only that, but we subscribe to an ideology of badness while the forces of social change just want to do what's right.

Ultimately, social justice is about empire building. The Roman Empire was sustained by "the idea of Rome," which always fell far short of the reality. Nonetheless, it sought to create hierarchies of thought and virtue, define what was acceptable and civilized and what was barbarian and backward. Of course, anyone looking with an objective eye at what Rome countenanced could find much that was backward and barbaric. But the idea of Rome somehow sanitized and elevated it all. It gave the advancing Roman soldiers the aura of superiority and sophistication. At least the Romans brought material improvements with them (or as John Cleese says in *The Life of Brian*, "apart from the sanitation, the medicine, education, wine, public order, irrigation, roads, the fresh-water system, and public health, what have the Romans ever done for us?)"

Meanwhile, what does social justice bring with it? On virtually every front where social justice claims the high ground, it does so by appealing to the authority of a mirage and grounding its arguments in nothing firmer than an ill-defined sentiment. Intellectually, it has no more weight than a gesture, no more substance than a wish. Yet those who fight for it do not care; indeed, they like it that way, because it prepares the battlefield for them. They promise to deliver a better world but haven't the foggiest idea how to provide it. The Romans knew how to build roads and toilets; all the centurions of social justice know how to provide is someone else's money. It's imperialism fueled by guilt and sustained by smugness.

But it is successful. These centurions and citizens of social justice run our schools, our charities, our newspapers, and, if they have their way, our world.

12
COMMUNITY

> This is the moment when we must come together to save this planet. Let us resolve that we will not leave our children a world where the oceans rise and famine spreads and terrible storms devastate our lands.
>
> —Senator Barack Obama, Berlin, July 24, 2008

> If you make—not have—$1 million a year, should you not participate in the sense of community of our country? I'm willing to put that on the table.
>
> —Representative Nancy Pelosi, April 14, 2011

> The lion and the calf shall lie down together, but the calf won't get much sleep.
>
> —Woody Allen, *Without Feathers*

"Government is simply the name we give to the things we choose to do together." This adorable pseudoinsight, widely attributed to representative Barney Frank of Massachusetts, has become increasingly popular in recent years, particularly among those who voted for Barack Obama on the grounds that they are the ones they've been waiting for.

Government isn't an abstraction, they insist. It's not a theoretical construct. Those blowhards on cable and talk radio? They're nuts when they talk about "the state," "tyranny," "fascism." They just don't understand. Government is about us. It *is* us. In other words, government doesn't just help other people; it makes you, Joe and Jane Taxpayer, feel good about yourselves for supporting ever larger government.

Logically, the idea that "government is simply the word for those things we choose to do together" is an obvious fallacy. We do many things together, some of them involve the government, most don't. An estimated 111 million people watched the 2011 Super Bowl. Weren't we as "together" for that as we are for, say, an OSHA hearing on the efficacy of toilet flush regulations?

Even if you allow for poetic license, this idea is a mess. We aren't all employees of the government, and so we don't all do what the government does together. We do all benefit together from a few things—a very few things—the government does, such as: ensuring the health of the water supply, enforcing the rule of law (broadly understood), and defending America from foreign enemies. But we don't really do those things together, do we? Consider the military, one of the few national institutions truly intended to serve all Americans equally. Military service clearly is not fulfilled by everyone, even if everyone pays for it. Indeed, one of the reasons we honor the fallen on Memorial Day and those who served on Veterans Day is precisely because we don't all do it together. Those who wear the uniform carry the extra load so the rest of us don't have to. The Korean War Memorial that reads "Freedom isn't Free" might be more accurate if it said "This Freedom brought to you by the Army, Navy, Air Force, and Marines"—but it's too hard to make that rhyme in a Toby Keith song.

And even when considering those very few things that benefit everybody, or nearly everybody, it's a misunderstanding of our form of government to suggest that they are good or worthwhile because everybody agrees on their merits. We do not have a system of government that depends on the consent of everybody. In fact, no system ever has the consent of everybody, but plenty of systems have claimed they have support from everybody and have tried to prove it by killing anybody who disagreed.

We have a system of government that depends on the *consent* of the *majority* of citizens. And even then, majorities do not always win the day—nor should they. We have a Bill of Rights and a Supreme Court precisely so that the majority cannot always win. At least theoretically, the majority cannot revoke my freedom of religion, speech, or association.

It cannot take away my property nor rescind my right to bear arms. Now, obviously, in practice the majority can sometimes do these things, but only for reasons that pass various constitutional tests. But those tests are invariably applied when at least someone disagrees enough to go to court to complain.

More to the point, when Barack Obama or Barney Frank say that government is just a word we use for those things we all do together, they're doing so inevitably to make the case for spending money on things: entitlements, high-speed rail, Head Start, windmills, teacher salaries, mohair subsidies, whatever. And it is hardly the case that we're "all in it together" when it comes to paying for these things. The average person on Medicare gets three times more out of it than they paid in.[1] The rest is carried by other taxpayers, living and unborn. Sixty percent of households get more from the U.S. government than they pay into it.

But even if all of us paid for government equally, what would that mean? When you cut a check for your share of the Department of Sanitation's budget, do you pump your fist in the air afterward, brimming with a sense of accomplishment? Or do you feel like you cut a check for a necessary service? Does knowing that you paid for the Fire Department make you feel the same way it would if you joined a bucket brigade and helped put out a fire yourself? The simple fact is there is no such transitive property to paying taxes.

Consider some snippets from MSNBC's "Lean Forward" ad campaign. In one installment we see Rachel Maddow standing in front of the Hoover Dam. She begins midsentence, tearing into a straw man like Michael Moore into a bowl of Fiddle Faddle: "When people tell us no, no, no we're not going to build it. No, no, no, America doesn't have any greatness in its future. America has small things in its future. Other countries have great things in their future. China can afford it. We can't. You're wrong, and it doesn't feel right to us, and it doesn't sound right to us, because that's not what America is."

It's not clear which of the infinite parallel universes Ms. Maddow is living in, but in our corner of the multiverse, if you wanted to build the Hoover Dam today it would not be conservatives shouting "No, no, no" (assuming such a project made economic sense). Meanwhile, you can be sure that liberals like Maddow and her fans would not only be saying "no, no, no," they'd be throwing in some, "Hey hey, ho ho, this damn dam has got to go"s for good measure, as they handcuffed themselves to trees and proclaimed the sanctity of some endangered grasshopper or rare moss.[2]

In another clip she testifies: "I feel like we have sort of an amazing inheritance in terms of what our grandparents and our great-grandparents thought to leave us. When they were building the infrastructure that is the spine of this country, they knew that the benefit of it would redound to us; they knew it. What are we doing?"

It's telling that she speaks to a *feeling* about what our grandparents and great-grandparents left us. Feelings rank high in the hierarchy of rhetorical authority, precisely because they cannot be easily refuted with reason. But let us take this feeling seriously.

Yes, it is certainly nice that our forefathers paid for the interstate highway system (critical infrastructure nevertheless reviled by many environmentalists), but is that really the inheritance that makes America great? This is the sort of thing any Communist peasant could say about Stalin or Ceauşescu who, after all, built some awfully impressive public-works projects. It is the sort of thing Romans said about the aqueducts and Egyptians about the pyramids, in order to wave away complaints about conquest, tyranny, and slavery. What separates our great projects from those of other civilizations are the values—moral, legal, constitutional—of those who produced them. It is the difference between inheriting a mansion from your father or grandfather and inheriting the values that enabled your grandfather to afford one.

What Maddow and her compatriots are really up to is a branding exercise. Just as admen try to convince dumb teenagers that their life will turn into a music video if they drink a certain beverage, progressives are trying to suggest that we can all fill the holes in our souls with a sense of accomplishment and community—greatness, even!—by paying higher taxes for more public-works projects, more generous entitlement checks, and faster passenger trains.

At the political level what Maddow, Frank, Obama & Co are doing is simple bait-and-switch marketing. Citizens are told that if they empower politicians and bureaucrats with votes and tax dollars, they'll get something magical in return: meaning. A major problem with this is, it's simply not true. The most alienated, deracinated, cynical people in modern human history are those people who outsourced the intellectual heavy lifting in life to the State, which in turn foisted the literal heavy lifting back to them. The people of the Soviet Union were, all in all, a miserable lot. Public spaces weren't hubs of civil society; they were places to defecate, steal, and exploit others. Whether in Moscow or, for that matter, Chicago, the hallways of public housing projects are often a Hobbesian realm of devil take the hindmost.

Moreover, at the philosophical level, what they are talking about is not government but the State, and the two things are not the same. The government in the Anglo-American tradition is for the most part a necessary evil. The State, in the European, and specifically German-historicist, tradition imported by progressives in the late nineteenth and early twentieth centuries is something different altogether. Under the Constitution the government is a well-defined institution charged with certain important but limited responsibilities. It delivers mail, protects the borders, levies taxes, fights wars, etc. To be sure, it plays an important symbolic role in our lives as well, and helps define what it means to be an American. But it is ultimately silent on what it means to be a human being.

The State, on the other hand, is a far more ambitious and all-encompassing entity. With the State we really are all in it together. Hillary Clinton writes in *It Takes a Village* that civil society is just a "term social scientists use to describe the way we work together for common purposes." But this is closer to the opposite of what civil society means. Civil society is that sphere or realm where individuals, groups, and institutions interact for private purposes. It is in this place where that thing called "life" most visibly takes place. Under tyrannical regimes civil society is kept as constrained as possible, because everything is political, everything is the State's business. That's why dictators curtail free association and why dissidents are forced to conspire secretly while playing soccer or chess.

Sometimes the only place where civil society is allowed to flourish is around the kitchen table, and sometimes not even then. In the Soviet Union children were taught to inform on their parents. Robert Ley, head of the Nazi German Labor Front, famously said the only private person in Germany was someone who was asleep.

According to the political philosophy that inspired the progressives, Communists, and Fascists, the "State," in the worlds of F. W. Hegel, "is the actually existing, realized moral life. . . . The divine idea as it exists on earth." As he proclaimed in *The Philosophy of History*: "[A]ll worth which the human being possesses—all spiritual reality, he possesses only through the State." Richard Ely, intellectual mentor to Woodrow Wilson, Theodore Roosevelt, and Robert La Follette, translated Hegelianism into an American theology of the State. "God works through the State in carrying out His purposes more universally than through any other institution," Ely wrote. It "is religious in its essence" and "a mighty force in furthering God's kingdom and establishing righteous relations." The only legitimate reason to restrain the State's right and authority to intervene in society, according to Ely, lay in the limits of its "ability to do good."[3]

Alas, most progressives don't grasp the distinction between government and State and treat the words and concepts interchangeably. They see the government as the vessel for the nation's soul and its aspirations, the repository and reservoir of our meaning. The simple fact is that the Founding Fathers never dreamed that government was the path to self-fulfillment. And yet the progressive marketers of liberalism are determined to make the government that spent nearly $3.5 trillion in 2011—pushing our national debt past $15 trillion—into some kind of church or nationalized calling for the sorts of high school girls who say, "If we all try our hardest, we can make this the best yearbook ever!"

13
TEN GUILTY MEN

> There is nothing new in the realization that the Constitution sometimes insulates the criminality of a few in order to protect the privacy of us all.
>
> —Justice Antonin Scalia

Joe is an accountant. Joe has lived an upright and decent life. One day Joe is accused of murder. The trial sparks a great controversy. Cable news networks throw out much of their regular programming to debate questions of guilt and innocence, circumstantial evidence, alibis, and justice. Ad rates for erectile dysfunction pills and gold skyrocket.

As sure as night follows day, someone will say, "Better ten guilty men go free than one innocent man" be punished, imprisoned, or executed. This is what Alan Dershowitz said during the O. J. Simpson trial. No doubt it's what he would say if his client ever succeeded in fulfilling his vow to find the "real killers," and Dershowitz found himself trying to free murderers once again.

And to be fair, Dershowitz is just one of an army of distinguished legal minds to offer this pithy aphorism. The legendary English jurist William Blackstone—the *fons et origio* of much of our common law—said, "Better that ten guilty persons escape than that one innocent suffer." In fact, this 10 to 1 formula has become known as the "Blackstone ratio" or "Blackstone's formulation." In a brilliant study, "*n* Guilty Men," legal scholar Alexander Volokh traced the idea that it is better to let *n* number of guilty men free from Abraham's argument with God in the book of

Genesis over the fate of Sodom to the writings of the Roman emperor Trajan, to the legal writings of Moses Maimonides, to Geraldo Rivera. Most often in these formulations *n* equals ten, but sometimes it can be less. "It's better to turn five guilty men loose than it is to convict one innocent man," says Thomas Berry Bruce, the ex-Mississippi executioner and roadside fruit stand operator. And sometimes it can be more. In 1471 English chief justice John Fortescue put the number at twenty: "Indeed I would rather wish twenty evildoers to escape death through pity, than one man to be unjustly condemned." (Though Fontescue didn't necessarily want the evildoers to go free, just to avoid the executioner's block).[1]

But as Volokh concludes after his exhaustive adventure across millennia and civilizations, Blackstone's ratio stands as "the father of criminal law."[2]

There's only one problem: It's not true. Or to be more accurate, it's unproven.

Of course, it depends on what you mean by "better." Better for whom?

I think it's better for dogmatic reasons. But for the empiricist, the nonideologue, the antidogmatist, the fellow who concerns himself solely with what works, it is demonstrably false that we're better off when the guilty go free.

Let's go back to Joe for a moment. Joe, before he was a defendant, was an accountant. It was his chosen career. What does that mean? Well, in this case (and most like it) it meant he spent many years doing what accountants do: filing taxes, adding up columns of numbers, etc. He was, in short, a *career* accountant.

Now let's ponder these ten guilty men. We know they are guilty precisely because it is asserted as a given. It is the very premise of the phrase "better ten guilty men." So I don't need to prove their guilt to anybody. These are guilty men. Guilty of what? Crimes. That too is stipulated. No distinction is made about what kinds of crimes these guilty men have committed. The formulation is not "better ten men guilty of nonviolent misdemeanors go free than one innocent go to jail." It is simply that it would be better if "guilty men"—any guilty men—go free.

Well, we know a few things about criminals. Most do not commit a single crime. It is believed that for every single criminal act we know about, assign blame for, prove, and convict, that perpetrator has possibly committed dozens, even hundreds of other crimes. We also know that a great many criminals—particularly violent criminals and sex offenders—commit more crimes when they are released from prison. We call these people "career criminals."

In other words, career accountants do taxes over and over again and career criminals commit crimes over and over again.

In a groundbreaking study, Marvin Wolfgang (whom the British *Journal of Criminology* described as "the most influential criminologist in the English-speaking world") looked at the records of all of the boys born in 1945 in Philadelphia and who attended school (around ten thousand). He found that just under 7 percent of the boys in Philadelphia committed more than half of all the crimes of that cohort.

Moreover, he followed the Class of '45 for three decades, until 1975. Dismayingly, most did little jail time. On average, the fourteen murderers in the group spent a mere four years in prison. When interviewed, these worst of the worst admitted that they'd committed anywhere from eight to eleven crimes for each offense they were arrested for. That is not to say they were arrested for eight to eleven crimes. They got away with eight to eleven other crimes for each crime the police knew about. Wolfgang found that if each boy in the criminal 7 percent had stayed just one more year in jail, Philadelphians would have suffered seventy-two hundred fewer *serious* crimes.[3]

Wolfgang's was just the first of a vast body of social science research showing that a small number of criminals commit a wildly outsized share of the crimes.[4] A Rand study interviewed more than two thousand prisoners serving time for robbery in California, Texas, and Michigan. Almost all said they'd committed a lot more crimes than the ones they were convicted for. The half who confessed to committing the *fewest* burglaries said they averaged about six a year. But the most active criminals—the top 10 percent—averaged more than 230 per year. That's one crime every thirty-eight hours. The bottom half of robbers averaged five a year, the top performing 10 percent of robbers averaged 87.

And then there are the costs of crime. According to a study in the *Journal of Forensic Psychiatry & Psychology*, Iowa State's Matt Delisi and his coauthors found: "The most violent and prolific offenders singly produced costs greater than $150 million–$160 million per year in terms of victim costs, criminal justice costs, lost offender productivity, and public willingness-to-pay costs. A 1998 study found that "the total external costs of a life of crime are estimated to range from approximately $1.5 million to $1.8 million per person. Of that amount, about 25 percent are tangible victim costs, 50 percent lost quality of life, 20 percent criminal justice costs, and 5 percent offense productivity losses."

So let's go back to Joe the accountant. Let us imagine for the sake of argument that people are serious when they say "better ten guilty men go free than one innocent man go to jail." Further, let us imagine that we could actually put this idea into practice. Joe, the innocent accountant, will be able to return to his wife, two adorable kids, and lovable golden retriever. But doing so will require letting ten guilty men go free. And not just any ten guilty men, but ten of the men all the empirical research tells will commit many, many more crimes. Those ten rapists and murderers will collectively commit scores, maybe even hundreds more rapes and murders. They will create hundreds, even thousands, of grieving families and friends. They will inflate the climate of fear on the streets. They will cost society untold millions in health care, security, and criminal justice costs. Oh, and let us not forget that those ten men will be in effect pardoned for the crimes we know they committed. Your raped daughter, your murdered father: They will go without meaningful justice, just so Joe doesn't have to endure any more injustice.

Or we can let Joe rot in prison and let those ten guilty men stay where they are.

Not surprisingly, Jeremy Bentham, the author of utilitarianism, recognized the dilemma of ten guilty men. In *A Treatise on Judicial Evidence* (1825) he writes:

> At first it was said to be better to save several guilty men, than to condemn a single innocent man; others, to make the maxim more striking, fixed on the number ten, a third made this ten a hundred, and a fourth made it a thousand. All these candidates for the prize of humanity have been outstripped by I know not how many writers, who hold, that, in no case, ought an accused person to be condemned, unless the evidence amount to mathe-

> matical or absolute certainty. According to this maxim, nobody ought to be punished, lest an innocent man be punished.[5]

Obviously, this is nonsense on stilts, to borrow a phrase from Bentham himself. But if we are to take the logic of *n* guilty men seriously, we have to ask why it is nonsense. After all, we can be sure that there is, somewhere in our vast penal system, an innocent man rotting behind bars. After all, we know from the revolution in forensic genetics that the falsely accused are routinely freed from prison. The only way we can be absolutely sure that such crimes are never repeated is to let everyone out of prison and then close them down for all time.

Now you might say we've reached the point of *argumentum ad absurdum.* The reasonable man would respond that the "better ten guilty men" principle isn't a literal policy proposal. It is an illustration of a principle.

And you would be absolutely right. It is a *principle.* The principle is that the society should err on the side of the accused. It is a statement of how our system of criminal justice should be oriented and a reflection of the bedrock dogma of all civilized societies that innocent men and women should not be punished for crimes they did not commit. Even Increase Mather proclaimed during the Salem witch trials that "it were better that ten suspected Witches should escape, than that one innocent person should be condemned."[6]

The problem is that as a principle it is utterly and totally uncontroversial. I've never met a soul who disagrees with the proposition that we should have safeguards to protect the rights of the falsely accused. Our entire legal system rests on this idea. We are all, figuratively speaking, children of the "father of criminal law."

The reasons why the principle is important are too numerous to list. Bentham himself acknowledged that a society built around the idea that it is tolerable to punish the innocent will not prosper. It is a bedrock contract of society, more important and older than notions of democracy that justice be done to all. But, and this is crucial, that contract is not a suicide pact. Hence the folly of releasing an army of rapists and murderers in order to ensure a single Joe the Accountant is treated fairly. Just governments have an obligation to protect citizens from violence—by other citizens or by a capricious and arbitrary government official or ruler. All morally serious people understand this. Which is why they also understand that in an imperfect world, trade-offs are inevitable. Distinctions have to be made, lines drawn. If we took the principle of *n* guilty men as sacrosanct, we would require that the accused be found guilty not beyond a reasonable doubt, *but beyond all doubt.*

Such a system would not be impossible to impose, but it would be impossible to sustain, because it would require letting teems of rapists, crooks, and murderers free in order to ensure that the innocent are never, ever, wrongly punished.

So rather than institutionalize folly, we do the best that we can. We create rules that give the benefit of the doubt to the accused. We give them lawyers. We bind prosecutors to rules of evidence. We appoint judges bound to oaths of fairness and empanel juries to weigh the evidence to the best of their ability. We allow for appeals, sometimes without end. Even so, mistakes are unavoidable. Hopefully they will be mistakes made with the best of intentions and in good faith. In short, our entire system of justice is a cathedral built upon the foundation of Blackstone's formulation.

Hence, when teaching law students or civics classes this basic principle of our justice system, it is entirely fine to state, "Better ten guilty men go free than one innocent be punished." It never hurts to pour another layer of cement in the foundation of that cathedral.

But the phrase becomes pernicious and dangerous when it is used to change the subject from actual and specific questions of guilt or innocence. If Joe the Accountant is innocent he is innocent, and it does not matter what we do with guilty men. And if Joe is guilty, he is guilty. Too often, when people invoke *n* guilty men what they are in fact trying to do is change the subject. They corral an abstraction—"the system"—because they are uncomfortable arguing the facts in question. The implication is that they are arguing with somebody. But who are they arguing with? Not the judge, nor the prosecutor, nor the loved ones seeking justice for the dead, nor the other guests on a cable talk show. It is a debater's talking point preloaded with its own straw man. As such it is a way to fend off an argument rather than a means of making one.

That's why the only intelligent response to someone who says, "Better ten guilty men go free . . ." is, "Okay. So what?"

14
LIVING CONSTITUTION

> You know, I believe the Constitution is a living and breathing document and that there are liberties found in the Constitution such as the right to privacy that spring from the document, itself, even though the Founders didn't write specific words saying this, this, and this, because we have interpreted our founding charter over the years and found deeper meanings in it, in light of the subsequent experience in American life of the last 211 years of our republic, and a strict constructionist, narrow-minded, harkening back to a literalist reading from 200 years ago, I think that's—I think that's a mistake.
>
> —Al Gore, March 14, 2000

You know Lady Justice, right? No, not personally. But you know the statue. It's the one of a woman wearing a blindfold and holding a scale. She stands in front of countless courthouses across America. She's an amalgamation of various Greek and Roman divinities, starting with Themis and her daughter Dike. Themis was the goddess—a Titan, if you want to get technical—of order. Her name means "divine law," and she represented the just and right customs laid down by divine authority. After Themis set the divine law, her daughter, Dike, delivered it to men. She led her sisters, the Horae, in her determination to deliver impartial and fair justice to the mortal world. She even carried scales to balance the facts and competing claims of those seeking justice.

Depictions of Lady Justice changed with the conceptions of justice itself. Inspired by the Greek poets, the Romans conceived of Justitia, a goddess of justice who wielded scales in her left hand and a double-edged sword in her right hand. The scales represented fairness and balance to both sides in any dispute, the sword the might and power of reason. By the fifteenth century Justitia had evolved into Lady Justice, complete with her iconic blindfold, which represents her objectivity. From then on statues of Lady Justice proliferated across Western civilization, and the phrase "Justice is blind" settled into the popular consciousness (though it probably dates back to Roman times). In 1601, we see the first usage of *Fiat justitia ruat caelum*: "Let justice be done though the heavens fall."[1]

The notion that justice must be impartial and universal, showing neither favor nor animus to rich or poor, became one of the most revolutionary and liberating ideals in the history of humanity. As with any ideal, nobody has ever perfectly implemented it, but the conviction that one should try was the engine of human progress for millennia, toppling the divine right of kings and laying the groundwork for democracy and the rule of law. That's why Lady Justice stands vigil outside our own Supreme Court and is given full expression in the Supreme Court justices' oath of office. Each justice vows to "administer justice without respect to persons, and do equal right to the poor and to the rich, and that I will faithfully and impartially discharge and perform all the duties incumbent upon [me] . . . under the Constitution and laws of the United States. So help me God."

But, hey man, times change.

So argued the progressives. Drunk on a rich cocktail of Hegel, Darwin, and Dewey, they believed that they were smart enough to scavenge what they thought useful from the whole mule cart of Western civilization, and then throw the rest of it off the cliffside of history, clanging and banging its way down the memory hole. They would start over. Fresh. Blank sheet. They would rebuild Lady Justice, stronger, faster, better (cue bionic man sound effect). Here's *New Republic* editor Herbert Croly writing of Lady Justice's need for a total makeover.

> In the past, common-law justice has been appropriately symbolized as a statuesque lady with a bandage over her eyes and a scale in her fair hands. The figurative representation of social justice

> would be a different kind of woman equipped with a different collection of instruments. Instead of having her eyes blindfolded, she would wear perched upon her nose a most searching and forbidding pair of spectacles, one which combined the vision of a microscope, a telescope, and a photographic camera. Instead of holding scales in her hand, she might perhaps be figured as possessing a much more homely and serviceable set of tools. She would have a hoe with which to cultivate the social garden, a watering-pot with which to refresh it, a barometer with which to measure the pressure of the social air, and the indispensable typewriter and filing cabinet with which to record the behavior of society. . . . [H]aving within her the heart of a mother and the passion for taking sides, she has disliked the inhuman and mechanical task of holding a balance between verbal weights and measures.[2]

Alas, this book doesn't come with illustrations, because I would rather enjoy commissioning an artist's rendition of a woman outfitted to look like a cross-dressing hybrid of Mr. Gadget and Granny Clampett from *The Beverly Hillbillies*, as the great symbol of progressive jurisprudence.

The "living constitution," as the phrase is used today (i.e., distinct from the very different conceptions of, say, Britain's "unwritten Constitution" or the "living tree" doctrine of Canada's constitution), is a direct descendant of Croly's time. Its chief architects were the by now familiar figures, Woodrow Wilson, Oliver Wendell Holmes, and the rest of the cast of *That 1910s' Show*. Wilson believed that the old Newtonian conception of the Constitution needed to be replaced by the Darwinian idea of an *evolving* Constitution.

It's difficult to exaggerate the impact of evolution on intellectuals in the late nineteenth and early twentieth centuries. Evolution didn't just create new lines of thought; it seemed to provide scientific confirmation for ideas already deeply entrenched among intellectuals (the dynamic repeated itself when Einstein's Theory of Relativity was taken to be more scientific confirmation of moral, legal, and ethical relativism). "Evolution germinated ideas wherever it penetrated, and it penetrated everywhere," observed one historian.[3] "The most fundamental things in our minds were," Richard Ely, the intellectual guru of the Wisconsin school of progressive economists and historians, recalled of his generation of intellectuals, "on the one hand, the idea of evolution, and on the other hand, the idea of relativity."[4] In July 1909, John Dewey penned an essay for *Popular Science*, "Darwin's Influence Upon Philosophy," in which he concluded:

> [P]rior to Darwin the impact of the new scientific method upon life, mind, and politics, had been arrested, because between these ideal or moral interests and the inorganic world intervened the kingdom of plants and animals. The gates of the garden of life were barred to the new ideas; and only through this garden was there access to mind and politics. The influence of Darwin upon philosophy resides in his having conquered the phenomena of life for the principle of transition, and thereby freed the new logic for application to mind and morals and life.[5]

For Woodrow Wilson, power was a good in and of itself. He believed the artificial checks on presidential power were unnatural and ran counter to the tide of history. Holmes, likewise, felt that the courts had no business imposing economic rules enshrined in the Constitution if majorities and their representatives didn't like them. "Experimentalism," advised the pragmatists, was the key to all human progress, so any good Constitution must give social planners the power to experiment (this is why FDR tried to pack the Supreme Court with yes-men who would back his "bold consistent experimentation"). Don't look backward, the progressives shouted from page and pulpit, for the past has nothing to teach us. "Progress!" exclaimed Wilson. "Did you ever reflect that that word is almost a new one? No word comes more often or more naturally to the lips of modern man, as if the thing it stands for were almost synonymous with life itself.... Progress, development,—those are modern words. The modern idea is to leave the past and press onward to something new."[6]

And that was why, Wilson argued, governments must have unchecked power, and why "[l]iving political constitutions must be Darwinian in structure and in practice." Wilson was the first American president to openly proclaim the Bill of Rights to be a dead-letter relic.

Those who still held it dear were bound up in mere "Fourth of July sentiments."[7]

He was also the first president to hold that the president must have a "vision" for re-forming the United States. To that end, an enlightened Constitution must conform to those charged with imposing that vision, not the other way around. The pursuit of happiness was no longer an individual right but a state-driven agenda to be foisted upon a once free people. Quite simply, Woodrow Wilson subscribed to a treasonous theory of the law.

He was hardly alone. Across the progressive landscape the treason of the intellectuals was on full display. Charles Beard did lasting damage to the standing of the Constitution by arguing in his hugely influential *Economic Interpretation of the Constitution of the United States* that the Founders imposed a counterrevolutionary Constitution on the American people. According to Beard, the Founders enacted a system that protected their elite economic interests. His scholarship was slipshod and dishonest, as Forrest McDonald, Robert E. Brown, and other historians would finally demonstrate in the 1950s (economic self-interest and status played no significant role in the votes at the Constitutional convention or among the voters who ratified the Constitution).[8] In Dewey's *Ethics* (cowritten with James Hayden-Tufts) the authors lament that America's Constitutions—i.e., the federal and state constitutions—"are full of . . . distrust of popular cooperative action. [The authors] did not and could not foresee the direction of industrial development, the increased complexity of social life, nor the expansion of national territory. Many measures which have proved indispensable have had to be therefore as it were smuggled in . . . by 'legal fictions' and by interpretations which have stretched the original text to uses undreamed of."[9]

These deliberate "legal fictions" and absurdly elastic interpretations were smuggled in at such a rate and with such audacity that they eventually became the reigning clichés of American legal life. Oliver Wendell Holmes, Jr., proclaimed that the "provisions of the Constitution . . . [are] organic living institutions."[10] Supreme Court Justice Felix Frankfurter wrote in a 1952 case, "The Constitution, we cannot recall too often, is an organism."[11]

One could go on at great length about the intellectual roots of all this, and no doubt my own interest in the subject matter is less than wholly healthy.* But an easier way to understand what the "living constitution" means and has always meant is to simply think of it as Felix the Cat's magic bag. Under this understanding of the living constitution, if a liberal roots around in there long enough and works hard enough at it, he can find anything he wants in the Constitution. In July 2011, George Will asked a panel of liberal "experts" on the Constitution if it was constitutional to force people to join Weight Watchers. The experts could not bring themselves to say no. The consensus: It's constitutional if the Supreme Court says it is.[12]

During the 2000 presidential campaign, when Al Gore was asked what kind of judges he would appoint to the bench, he said that they'd be the sort of magic-bag riflers "who understand that our Constitution is a living and breathing document," and who grasp that "it was intended by our Founders to be interpreted in the light of the constantly evolving experience of the American people."[13] One such fellow is Ninth Circuit judge Stephen Reinhardt, who admits: "The judgments about the Constitution are value judgments. Judges exercise their own independent value judgments. You reach the answer that essentially your values tell you to reach."[14] U.S. Supreme Court Justice Sonia Sotomayor, proud of her Puerto Rican heritage, believed that "a wise Latina woman with the richness of her experiences would, more often than not, reach a better conclusion" than some plain old white guy.[15]

Why? Because she would have special empathy—a magic word for members of the living constitution cult—for certain types of people at the margins of the society. It was this conviction that led President Obama to nominate her for the Supreme Court in the first place. "We need somebody who's got the heart, the empathy, to recognize what it's like to be a young teenage mom, the empathy to understand what it's like to be poor or African American or gay or disabled or old," Obama announced during his campaign, "and that's the criterion by which I'll be selecting my judges."[16] A few years earlier, then senator Obama opposed the nomina-

---

*And if you want to explore all of this further, I recommend Bradley C. Watson, *Living Constitution, Dying Faith: Progressivism and the New Science of Jurisprudence* (Intercollegiate Studies Institute Press, 2009).

tion of U.S. Supreme Court Chief Justice Roberts on the grounds that he lacked empathy. In the "truly difficult" cases, Obama reasoned, a judge must rely upon "one's deepest values, one's core concerns, one's broader perspectives on how the world works, and the depth and breadth of one's empathy." In short, "the critical ingredient is supplied by what is in the judge's heart."[17]

This all sounds lovely. If you were looking to fill the position of king or czar or numinously wonderful gay next-door neighbor on a sitcom, Obama's criteria might make for a pretty good summation of what you're after. But judges aren't kings or czars, they're *judges.* If the truly defining qualification for judges are their values or their level of empathy for certain aggrieved groups, then why bother sending lawyers to the Supreme Court in the first place? The very instance of a case making it all the way to the Supreme Court is already a sign that it is among the "truly difficult" ones. If heart is all that matters, why not assemble a panel of philosophers, ethicists, and social workers, or a mix-and-match grab bag of superterrific people like on a special episode of *Oprah*? This might seem ridiculous, but with a living, ungrounded Constitution as your guide, it is almost impossible to make a grounded argument for why such a system would not be desirable, if not preferable.

Oh, come on, complain the serious defenders of the living Constitution. First of all, this depiction of the living Constitution is a straw man. For instance, Michael C. Dorf, a law professor at Cornell University, says that conservatives are simply making it up when they complain that living constitutionalists are imposing their own values.[18] It's difficult to take this rejoinder too seriously when the liberal, con-law professor, who also happens to be president of the United States, plainly says that's what he is looking for.

More to the point, it's quite obvious that believers in the "organic" Constitution do exactly that. Oliver Wendell Holmes found the forced sterilization of Americans constitutional in *Buck v. Bell* because that was his preferred policy approach, as historian William Leuchenburg has demonstrated at length.[19] "Three generations of imbeciles is enough," Holmes wrote without regard to legal reasoning or precedent. Shortly afterward, Holmes wrote to Harold Laski, "I . . . delivered an opinion upholding the constitutionality of a state law for sterilizing imbeciles the other day—and felt that I was getting near the *first principle of real reform*."[20] Why "the first principle of real reform" requires the State be able to sterilize whomever it wishes, or why judges should concern themselves with advancing the first principles of "real reform" in the first place, Holmes does not say.

Dorf has a second argument that, while more interesting and sophisticated, is no more persuasive. "Living-Constitutionalists," he writes, "believe that while the original understanding has some bearing on the Constitution's contemporary meaning, it is not the whole story. For living-Constitutionalists, the act of ratification by people who are long dead, and whose numbers did not include any women or enslaved African-Americans, does not suffice to make the Constitution effective today. For us living-Constitutionalists, the Constitution's current authority derives at least in substantial part from the fact that we the living people accept it as authoritative." And since we the living are the ones who matter, then "the way in which contemporary Americans understand the Constitution's language" is really important. "Understood in this way," he continues, echoing arguments made by Cass Sunstein and others, "the notion of a living Constitution is simply an effort to interpret the Constitution, not to replace it."[21]

Again, it's an interesting argument, and perfectly progressive in its thinly veiled contempt for both the past and the idea that we can be born into a bond we didn't vote on ourselves. But ultimately this is a lot of smoke and mirrors deployed to conceal Felix the Cat's magic bag. Simply calling it "interpretation" instead of "replacement" doesn't mean that in practice the former is not synonymous with the latter. If you can find new rights and powers for the government in the document no one ever imagined before, then interpretation *is* replacement. And again, if judges are nothing more than polysyllabic barometers of the zeitgeist, why appoint judges at all? There are plenty of pollsters better equipped to understand what Americans think about the Constitution. Indeed, why have a Supreme Court if all such questions should be decided democratically?

But hold on, Dorf and others all concede that *some* things in the Constitution are binding. "Originalists and living-Constitutionalists both agree that where the constitutional text is clear, it controls. For example," he writes, "Article II states that no person under the age of 35 can be President, and no champion of the living Constitution would argue that nonetheless an especially precocious 32-year-old should be deemed Presidency-eligible simply because she dislikes the textual limit."[22] Elena Kagan trotted out the same argument in her confirmation hearings.

Well, great. If all we need are people who can identify where "the text is clear" all the more reason to appoint people from random walks of life. I have no doubt that your average poor, gay, black plumber is perfectly smart enough to read and comprehend the bits of the Constitution where the "text is clear." You don't need some fancypants law degree to know that the Constitution says you must be thirty-five years old to be elected president. So why find judges who merely feel empathy for plumbers or gay men or blacks or poor people when you can appoint the real thing?

As for the trickier bits that aren't spelled out in the text, why not put them up to a vote? By all means, let's have a referendum on which God-given rights unpopular people have at the height of their unpopularity. What could go wrong?

There you go again, warns the progressive, taking things too far when the living Constitution is such a moderate, sensible policy. All these conservative hang-ups must have something to do with an abiding fear of change. "We do not insist that our medicine, our technology, or even our entertainment, all remain in an obsolete state; why would we demand that the law be given such treatment?" asks *Slate*'s legal editor Dahlia Lithwick. "It seems absurd to suggest that we can change the speed limit to reflect improved technology but we cannot interpret the Constitution to reflect improvements in society."[23] Woodrow Wilson said it better when he just shouted "Progress!"

Now rather than rehearse all of the reasons why this is cockeyed nonsense, let me switch courses somewhat and say that I would take these sentiments seriously if they were sincere. But the "living Constitution" is a quintessential tyrannical cliché precisely because the bad faith of its adherents is so glaring. Give the original progressives their due; at least they were honest about what they were after. Today's living constitutionalists insist that their project has a rich and serious intellectual lineage, but don't you dare write or say anything that suggests that its intellectual history is actually relevant. They want to claim all of the authority of an intellectual tradition without having to defend or even acknowledge that tradition's roots in Darwinism, Hegelianism, and various efforts to make Lady Justice look like Robocop with a garden rake.

Meanwhile, the very same living constitutionalists are the first people to hide behind old Lady Justice's skirts and invoke the original intent of the Founding Fathers as soon as it becomes advantageous. During the Bush-era debates over the Patriot Act (which ceased being the fighting wedge of fascism when Barack Obama adopted its core provisions), one leading liberal after another suddenly discovered the enduring wisdom of the Founders. One after another they took to the Senate floor to quote Benjamin Franklin's warning that those who would trade liberty for security will get neither. Well, if the living constitutionalists are right that the Founders couldn't have foreseen the technological and social changes that would unfold two centuries after ratification, why must we rely on their wisdom when it comes to fighting terrorists? Surely the Constitution must adapt to new and unforeseen challenges?

Another example: Lawrence Tribe, a stout defender of the Constitution's organic malleability, suddenly invoked the unchanging meaning of the commerce clause in defense of ObamaCare: "Since the New Deal, the court has consistently held that Congress has broad constitutional power to regulate interstate commerce," the Harvard professor writes in the *New York Times.* "This includes authority over not just goods moving across state lines, but also the economic choices of individuals within states that have significant effects on interstate markets. By that standard, this law's constitutionality is open and shut."[24] Aha. So apparently the Constitution died in the mid-1930s and must evolve no more?

But nowhere is this "living for me, but dead for thee" Deweyan legal fiction more transparent then in the Left's view of constitutional amendments. I can't count how many times I've met liberals who've defended the living Constitution on the grounds that if it didn't adapt and change blacks would still be slaves and women wouldn't have the vote. What these cultured *ignorami* fail to acknowledge is that women got the vote and blacks were emancipated with—wait for it!—constitutional amendments, a broadly democratic procedure carefully spelled out in—you guessed it—the original Constitution.

Conservatives do not oppose changing the Constitution; they simply prefer to change it through constitutional mechanisms. But the moment conservatives propose amending the Constitution to adapt to changing times, liberals suddenly proclaim horror at the suggestion that we would "tamper" or "tinker" with the glorious genius of the Founding Fathers. Now that America has a welfare state that actively attracts immigrants to take advantage of our generous entitlements, some propose amending the Constitution to get rid of automatic birthright citizenship (making us more like the European countries liberals normally insist we must emulate). The immediate response is indignant horror. "I think it's horribly dangerous to open up the Constitution, to tamper with the Constitution,"[25] shrieked Representative Raul Grijalva, in response to proposed changes to the Fourteenth Amendment. Here's Angela Kelley of the liberal Center for American Progress on Senator Lindsey Graham, who proposed such an amendment: "He's not one to tamper with the Constitution, so I'm surprised he would even suggest this."[26] "While everyone recognizes that there are problems with our immigration system in this country," Elizabeth Wydra of the progressive Constitutional Accountability Center chimed in, "my perspective is: Let's try to fix this through legislation and not tinker with the genius of our constitutional design."[27]

Senator Patrick Leahy, the chairman of the Senate Judiciary Committee, routinely waxes lyrical about the living, breathing, vitality of the Constitution—that is, whenever the question at hand is whether we should appoint progressive lawyers to the bench. "The chairman of the Republican National Committee criticized you last month for agreeing with Justice Thurgood Marshall's observation that our Constitution as originally drafted was imperfect," Leahy told Elena Kagan during her confirmation hearings. "The criticism surprised me, because everything you read about the Founders, they knew that they would lay down something that would not cover every foreseeable thing. I mean, how could they possibly foresee what the country is today? They were—they wrote in broad terms. They couldn't foresee every challenge."[28]

True enough! But when conservatives propose amending the Constitution to require a balanced budget, Leahy all but puts on a powdered wig and proclaims himself the unyielding champion of the Founders' original intent. "I respect the wisdom of the Founders to uphold the Constitution, which has served this Nation so well for the last 223 years. Let us not be so vain to think we know better than the Founders what the Constitution should prescribe."[29]

In short, the living constitutionalists want a monopoly on what the Constitution means. It is a golden goose for progressives, an unalterably sacred text for everyone else.

15
LET THEM EAT CAKE

> On Monday, President Obama released his budget for fiscal year 2012. The president's budget targets the concerns and the need to invest now for a better future for our families, communities and our great country. On the other hand, the Republican budget that was released last Friday is severe and irresponsible because it gives tax benefits for the wealthiest few, while destroying jobs and harming middle class families, young adults, seniors and even veterans. Are the Republicans saying, "Let them eat cake"?
>
> —Representative Charles Rangel, February 17, 2011

From the monarchs of eighteenth-century Europe, to the "robber barons" of nineteenth-century America, to the conservative leaders (political and otherwise) of today, perceived indifference to the plight of the have-nots has been denounced as a sign of cold-heartedness far and wide by those who extol the redeeming power of compassion and empathy.

A less frequent, but still quite common, indictment is that those in power are not scrooges, but arrogant fools. Their stinginess stems from a deep-rooted ignorance about how the world really works. Harry Hopkins, the head of the WPA, told a conference of mayors in 1936: "There are plenty of business men who realize that when millions are in actual need it is stupid for the top one-tenth of one per cent of the people to be getting as much income as the entire bottom 40 percent. It is as stupid as it was in the days of Louis XVI when Marie Antoinette said: 'If they have no bread, let them eat cake.'" That same year, Franklin Roosevelt denounced Republicans for saying to the poor, "Let them eat cake."[1]

In 1968 Mario Puzo reviewed *The Jeweler's Eye* by William F. Buckley. "The great thing about reading Buckley," Puzo explained,

> is that one comes to really understand why so gallant a nation as France lopped off so pretty a head as Marie Antoniette's. "Let them eat cake" is an infuriating phrase in any language and this collection of [Buckley's writings] . . . boils down to those old blue-blooded words of wisdom—with the same effect.[2]

In 1971 when Spiro Agnew gave a speech defending the profit motive, Democrats denounced it as "Marie Antoinette economics." In 2008, Pat Buchanan denounced the Republicans' "'Let-them-eat-cake!' coldness" to American automakers.[3]

The first problem with these, and thousands of other such indictments: Marie Antoinette never said "Let them eat cake!" Nor was she indifferent to the plight of the poor.

The legend comes from Rousseau's *Confessions*, in which he wrote that a "[g]reat princess" had declared, "*Qu'ils mangent de la brioche*" while the people were starving. Unfortunately "*Qu'ils mangent de la brioche*" doesn't mean "Let them eat cake!" It means, more or less, "Let them eat buns." More specifically, it means let them eat very snooty, expensive buns. The phrase was turned into a deliberate propaganda tool to incite riots, intellectual and literal, against the monarchy.

Moreover, *Confessions* was written in 1768, two years *before* Marie Antoinette moved to France, and the line appears in Rousseau's journal notes years before Antoinette was even born. Assuming Rousseau didn't just make it up (which would be highly plausible, since Rousseau was hardly a stickler for the facts), some historians think he must have been referring to a comment made by Spanish queen Marie-Thérèse who, alas, would have offered the offending phrase some hundred years earlier. Indeed, several sources have her saying, "*Que ne mangent-ils de la croûte de pâté?*" (Why don't they eat the crust of a meat pastry?). Meanwhile, other historians have fingered yet other culprits for this now timeless expression of gold-cocooned ignorance, including a thirteenth-century archbishop of Canterbury, who employed the phrase to characterize the general indifference of the wealthy. Clearly, the question of who said "Let them eat cake!" is one of history's greatest examples of "too good to check."

But the dubious authorship of the phrase barely captures the deeper problem with this now timeless cliché.

First, some context: Eighteenth-century France had the bakery equivalent of the Northeast Dairy Compact. (And, the French being slow to change, still have it—though it was broadly liberalized in the 1980s.) The system required bakers to sell cheap bread and artificially low prices and, if the baker ran out of the cheap stuff, they were required to sell more expensive fare—like *brioche*—at the same price as the cheap bread. The intent of this second policy was to prevent greedy bakers from making too little bread or using cheap bread as a loss-leader for more expensive products. Since everyone *deserved* bread, the aristocrats reasoned, everyone should *have* bread. But since the royalty couldn't be expected to spend their own money on the masses, they simply insisted that bakers carry the burden.

Economically, this wrought havoc on the all-important bread market. For many bakers, it was akin to telling car dealers that have to sell their used AMC Pacers and other low-end cars at a near-loss and, should they run out of Pacers, the dealers must then sell Porsches and BMWs at the same low price. Under such a system, dealers might keep a manageable supply of cheap cars on their lots, but you can be sure they would not keep a very large inventory of luxury cars on hand, should the supply of the cheap ones run out and they were suddenly forced to sell them at a loss in the name of justice.

To declare "*Qu'ils mangent de la brioche*," wasn't so stupid after all. This is in fact what the law *required*. Marie Antoinette, if she said it at all, may well have been simply demanding that the "profiteering" bakers should follow the law and feed the people the more expensive bread, or buns—even though the ultimate result would have been to crush the bakeries financially, and hence make starvation even worse. In short, the system that made a statement like "Let them eat cake!" seem like a plausible suggestion to the aristocracy was in fact *the very system that created the bread crisis in the first place.* What would someone like Marie Antoinette care about the effect regulation had on the market? She got her own bread when and how she wanted it, and, economics be damned, the poor people should have it thus, too.

So, while "Let them eat cake" has come to symbolize how rich do-gooders think rich conservatives see the world, it actually signifies how rich do-gooders screw things up by creating "compassionate" schemes that only make things worse for the poor.

Consider housing laws. Cities with generous and compassionate laws intended to prevent homelessness invariably create *more* homelessness. In Washington, D.C., the City Council passed an ordinance in 1984, guaranteeing shelter for everyone. Within two years the number of homeless families living in government shelters rose 500 percent. One woman called D.C. authorities telling them she had just enough savings to cover the flight for her and her children and asked them to reserve her free housing for her.[4]

Rent control laws have a similar effect. The wealthy as well as the subsidized middle class support efforts to "help" poor people afford their rent. But whenever and wherever such schemes are put in place, the amount of affordable housing shrinks and, as a consequence, rents skyrocket. Studies of rent control in places like Cambridge, Massachusetts, and Berkeley, California, find that the chief beneficiaries of such policies are concentrated among the ranks of the highly educated, not the undereducated poor.

(An even more dramatic illustration can be found in the grotesque higher education price "bubble" inflated over the last generation. It is liberal dogma that everyone should go to college and public policies have been crafted to make this utopian scheme as close to a reality as possible. As a result, tuitions have skyrocketed. According to *Money* magazine, "After adjusting for financial aid, the amount families pay for college has skyrocketed 439 percent since 1982. . . . Normal supply and demand can't begin to explain cost increases of this magnitude."[5] Economist Mark Perry found that from 1997 to 2007 home prices increased by 68 percent creating the housing bubble that crashed the economy in 2008. Meanwhile, over the same period, college tuition and fees rose by 83 percent. "In fact," writes Perry, "college tuition and fees have never increased by less than 73 percent in any ten-year period back to the 1980s. And in the decades ending in 2009 and 2010, college tuition increased by more than

90 percent."[6] Does anyone—anywhere—believe that the quality of the product has kept pace with the price rise? Anyone?)

The notion that today's rich are the most likely to say "let them eat cake!" is a form of cultural propaganda. To be sure, there are many wealthy and politically conservative individuals who are out of touch with the hardships of poverty. But the most obvious inheritors of the cocooned arrogance and self-indulgence we associate with members of the monarchical courts of Europe are to be found not in boardrooms, but among the most celebrated liberals of American life: Hollywood celebrities.

Few CEOs surround themselves with courtiers the way your typical diva does. And none hires out a private retinue of vassals, tutors, and hangers-on more than the pampered glitterati who recreate a private court no less opulent and self-indulgent than the entourages of seventeenth-century France. If you're lucky enough to witness one of these movable feasts in person, it becomes immediately apparent that the otherworldly opulence of the denizens of the pages of *US Weekly* and *People* magazine dwarfs that of even our greatest captains of industry.

From medieval times through the end of the Enlightenment, kings and queens draped their monarchies with sumptuary laws and rules of grammar to communicate to all, including themselves, that they were special. The only place in America where such arrangements endure is in the oxygen-enriched confines of Hollywood doyens (and those outposts of modern medievalism known as college campuses).[7] Jennifer Lopez bars people from photographing her elbows.[8] Mariah Carey has an assistant whose only job is to hand her towels. Also, wherever Mariah goes, her courtiers must first remove posters of rival "divas," lest they offend her delicate sensibilities: Thou shalt have no divas before me![9] Kim Basinger is "allergic" to the sun and requires an assistant to carry an umbrella to protect her on the off chance she might be exposed to dangerous solar radiation.[10] John Travolta is reported to have a staff of twelve assistants. When he signs up to do a film he often demands that the studio cover the costs of his entourage. For one film shot in Paris, he demanded that Mandalay Entertainment fly and house "more than a dozen assistants, trainers, makeup artists, stand-ins, security guards, massage therapists, stunt doubles and drivers." He demanded that his personal chef be retained and he wanted approval of *the catering staff for the rest of the cast and crew.* When he filmed *The General's Daughter* he arrived with an entourage of "25 personal assistants, including masseurs, acupuncturists, nutritionists and fortune tellers." According to Mike Nichols, who directed Travolta in *Primary Colors*, sitting down with the actor is "not unlike taking a meeting with Henry VIII. When John Turteltaub met with him to work out details of the movie *Phenomenon*, "There were 13 people at this meeting, all to talk about John's feelings about the script. It was like setting up the Treaty of Versailles."[11]

Sylvester Stallone—who, in fairness, supports Republicans—once refused to continue with an interview until his hotel room was painted a more "likable" peach.[12] Mike Myers almost quit the filming of *Wayne's World* because he didn't have any margarine for his bagel.[13] Sean Penn had an assistant swim the dangerous and polluted currents of New York's East River just to bring him a cigarette.[14] Only members of Jennifer Lopez's double-digit entourage are permitted to gaze into the windows of her soul. Various stars travel with full-time aromatherapists, masseuses, acupuncturists, and, one presumes, court jesters. Oprah Winfrey has a bra handler. Sylvester Stallone, Tom Cruise, and, of course, Barbra Streisand are just a handful of the folks who think they're on the same plateau as Japanese emperors, Turkish pashas, and medieval kings.

Unlike businessmen or inventors, actors value their emotions above all things. So if you feel that poor people should have more, it must be so. The "pleasure of the king" was the law under Henry VIII and so it is with modern-day royalty who can afford their self-indulgence both financially and *culturally*. Almost no Fortune 500 CEO could stop a business deal because his bagel lacked margarine. Everyone understands this intuitively. But our intuition probably obscures the explanation. The businessman wouldn't do such a thing not because he could not afford to, but because the culture of business does not tolerate such behavior. The culture of artistic success demands that whims be indulged, emotions set free to express themselves without the interruption of fact.

Is it any wonder that any human so ensconced in the spun silk of self-indulgence would lose the ability to grasp the rigid scaffolding of the real world? Unlike the self-made riches of the so-called robber barons, the wealth of these dauphins is derived not from the mined riches of terra firma but from the vaporous clouds of their own feelings.

The artistic rich can utter incandescent idiocies and be applauded for thinking outside the box. Sheryl Crow famously proposed on her Web site that all of us should be limited to one square of toilet paper per bathroom visit. "Although my ideas are in the earliest stages of development, they are, in my mind, worth investigating. One of my favorites is in the area of conserving trees which we heavily rely on for oxygen," she wrote. "I propose a limitation be put on how many squares of toilet paper can be used in any one sitting," she continued. "I think we are an industrious enough people that we can make it work with only one square per restroom visit, except, of course, on those pesky occasions where two to three could be required."[15] See, it's just that easy. Oliver Stone, an avowed admirer of Cuban socialism and the director of the anticapitalist screed *Wall Street*, owns palatial homes in various locales. When interviewed by *Architectural Digest* in 1993 at his magnificent Spanish colonial villa in Santa Barbara, Stone was asked if he felt any guilt about his opulent lifestyle while still claiming to be a despiser of all things capitalist and bourgeois. "That's a Western Christian trip," he responded.[16] Of course, his own response to any economic question is in effect "Let them eat cake!"

Michael Moore, self-proclaimed champion of the working man and best friend to organized labor, is a notoriously unpleasant boss who treats his staff like peasants. He describes his office as "a nonstop rock-'n'-roll party for the proletariat," but went to great lengths to keep his employees from unionizing. When they did join the Writers' Guild, staffers had to routinely implore their union reps to force Moore to pay what he owed. "If you had . . . a reunion of people for whom working for Michael was the least pleasant professional experience of their lives," noted a former Moore producer, "it might be necessary to rent a large stadium."[17]

Much is made of the fact that wealthy environmentalists can afford the costs of their preferred public policies—they will lose neither their vacation homes nor the ability to fly to them in a world with draconian carbon taxes or green eminent domain. But not nearly enough is made of the fact that their real successes lay not in distorting the markets but in distorting the culture. When Catherine Zeta-Jones married Michael Douglas, her lawyers demanded and got a $5 million "straying fee" in the highly probable circumstance that he, as a "recovering sex addict," might get the Jones for someone else's Zeta.[18]

Or take the all-too ironically named Madonna. It's an understatement to say Madonna was a champion of cultural libertinism. She launched her career as a peripatetic evangelist of slattern chic. She taught twelve-year-old girls to embrace their sexuality, and to throw off all those bourgeois hang-ups about sex, marriage, heterosexuality, whatever. And when it came time to settle down and have a husband and kids, she could, quite simply, afford to. But what happened to the lower-middle-class girls from Jersey City who took her advice? When on tour, Madonna has an entourage of hundreds. When not on the road her retinue drops to less than a tenth of that, but there are still enough hands on deck. "I don't have any problems with [diapers]," she has explained, "because I have never changed one."[19]

If this pathology only led to these modern aristocrats building temples to their own egos, indulging in Dionysian excess and employing cadres of sycophants, there would be little or no harm. But today's secular royalty will not content itself with personal contentment. They feel compelled to export values only the very rich and very admired can afford. A plumber, and more importantly his children, cannot so easily carry the freight of serial broken marriages. Nor can society afford to have a generation of children think "if it feels good, do it" is a productive way to live. Madonna can afford to have as many children as she wants, indeed she can afford to buy "surplus" children from poor Africans. But the middle-class woman who lives for the moment may well have some extra diapers to change as a result.

Worse, some of the new aristocrats adopt a policy of *droit de seigneur*—the lord's right—to live outside the rules of others. Roman Polanski, who drugged a thirteen-year-old girl in order to have sex with her and then fled the country after accepting a plea bargain, is as good an example of Acton's warning that power corrupts not just the powerful, but the voluptuaries of power (see Chapter 6, Power Corrupts). Normally, the rule is that women don't make up such allegations. But despite the fact that she testified to the grand jury that he committed forcible rape, none of Mr. Polanski's peers seemed to care. Numerous actors, directors, and producers, not to mention heads of state, writers, and leading journalists, all defended Polanski upon his arrest on the grounds that this all happened long ago, the victim has "forgiven" him, and—most important—

Polanski has made some wonderful films. Whoopi Goldberg insisted that what Polanski did wasn't "rape-rape" but rather the sort of rape that important people sometimes get away with. Such instances shed light on the self-image of the true ruling classes.

Alas, the greater damage caused by the new nobility is rarely this obvious, because it does not usually manifest itself in the form of rape in a hot tub. Rather it manifests itself in a class, governed by its own unfiltered appetites, insisting that everyone can eat cake, just like them.

16

VIOLENCE NEVER SOLVES ANYTHING

> I object to violence because when it appears to do good, the good is only temporary; the evil it does is permanent.
>
> —Mohandas Karamchand Gandhi

Imagine you are being raped. As you struggle to get free of your attacker, your hand finds the assailant's gun on the floor. Your fingers pull it to your grip and you bring it up to point at your assailant. Then, suddenly, it dawns on you! "Violence never solves anything!" You immediately lay down the gun and endure the unendurable wishing there was some way out of your predicament.

"Violence never solves anything" is one of the greatest examples of something transparently untrue nonetheless serving as profound and high-minded. Violence has been a necessary solution to myriad problems. The problems of madmen on killing sprees are often solved with the judicious application of bullets. Indeed, if violence never solved anything, police would never have guns in the first place. Violence used, or at least threatened, by "peacekeepers" must solve *something*, otherwise so many people who so often say "violence never solves anything" wouldn't love them so much. Many of the greatest evils conceived by men were put to an end with violence. The global slave trade, condoned without controversy for centuries in the Muslim and Christian worlds alike, was ultimately abolished because a few Christian souls in Britain ultimately convinced their fellow countrymen to crush the practice by force. In

America, it took a Civil War to end the institution of slavery. Perhaps war was avoidable, and it was certainly regrettable, but only a fool would say it wasn't part of the solution to the problem of slavery in the United States.

It is an unpleasant thought to contemplate violence as a morally neutral phenomena. Something deep within us cries out in protest at the notion that violence is a mere tool devoid of moral content in and of itself. This is undoubtedly so because decent people of all political persuasions recoil at human suffering as a thing in itself. It also runs counter to the best of the Enlightenment tradition which assumes that men are open to reason, and reason can rightly inform conscience without recourse to violence. But unpleasant truths do not cease to be true because they are unpleasant.

"Those who 'abjure' violence," George Orwell wrote in 1945, "can only do so because others are committing violence on their behalf."[1] This insight, hardly original to Orwell, is the fundamental, irrefutable fact of all civilizations at any time in history. Max Weber in his *Politics as a Vocation*, wrote that the state has a "monopoly on violence" (*Gewaltmonopol des Staates*). Weber meant it as much as an observation as a theory. The State, both modern and premodern, determines the legitimate use of violence. This is true of evil regimes and just ones. Indeed, one of the best ways to differentiate a just state from an unjust one is how violence is regulated.

In a decent society the police have a right to use as much violence as necessary, and no more, against the illegitimately violent. The military has an obligation to use violence, when necessary, to deter threats from without. Citizens may use violence in some cases—self-defense being the most obvious example—or employ private security only when doing so is in accordance with the law. But it is the state that determines the scope and definition of those laws.

Certain breeds of libertarian and anarchist are fond of observing that the state is ultimately about force, by which they mean violence. They'll point out that if you refuse to pay your taxes or even mow your lawn long enough, eventually after much paperwork, men with guns will come to your home and make you do—or pay—what is required of you. The problem with this observation is not that it is wrong, but that those who espouse it think it is an *indictment.* Law without the possibility of force is not law. Or, as Hobbes noted, "covenants, without the sword, are but words, and of no strength to secure a man at all."[2]

In other words, to say violence can't solve anything is to say that the law cannot solve anything. Without the ultimate threat of force, law becomes simply a wish expressed with legalistic formality. I am for laws against child rape. To be for laws against child rape means also being in favor of police with guns stopping, apprehending, or securing for punishment men who rape children. To be for the former but against the latter is to be against child rape in principle but for it in practice.

While the libertarian is offended by the reality of law, the liberal is in denial about it. It is a common device of liberal rhetoric to replace "tell" with "ask." It's "only right that we ask everyone to pay their fair share," President Obama says about his burning desire to raise taxes on the wealthy (somewhat unfulfilled as of this writing). *The New York Times* followed suit in a front page headline OBAMA TAX PLAN WOULD ASK MORE OF MILLIONAIRES.[3] But Obama's plan is not to "ask" more of millionaires, it is to *tell* millionaires to pay more. After all, taxes are not voluntary. Now it's true that we use the word "ask" in funny ways. Football coaches "ask" more of their players, which is a polite way of saying that they demand more. But the state is different. If you defy your football coach, you're off the team or don't get to start in the big game. If you defy the government, eventually men with guns will come to your home and force you to either pay up or go to jail. If you resist, it is likely they will hit you or shoot you.

Still, since I believe that some amount of taxation is necessary I believe that a necessary amount of law enforcement is necessary as well. Hence I believe that violence solves the problem of people not paying their taxes. I could run through all the steps again, but suffice it to say you can't solve the problem of tax cheats and delinquents without guns or Billy clubs.

This sort of rudimentary state violence is one of the great drivers of peace in human history. As Steven Pinker documents in his *The Better Angels of Our Nature: Why Violence Has Declined,* the first kings (the human manifestation of the State) disliked tribal raids, vendettas, and murders between their subjects for the same reason a rancher dislikes violence among his livestock: there's no profit in it. In the pre-state era before the rise of the first feudal kings, 15% of the populations died from violence. After kings imposed order—violently!—such deaths dropped to around 3 percent. This process accelerated into and through the Middle Ages as small kingdoms merged into the first nation-states and empires. Trade, the greatest driver of peaceful coexistence, increased as the rule of law prospered. Contracts make trade possible and contracts must ultimately be enforced at the point of a gun (or sword or really pointy spear).

Of course, most people who say violence never solved anything say it in a very specific context: When America might do something violent. For instance, when some evil regime slaughters domestic opponents, even whole peoples, in order to hold on to power, a certain breed of pacifist says there's nothing we can do about it other than to "work diplomatically," rally "world opinion," or impose sanctions. After all, violence never solved anything. In the vast majority of cases these remedies do little to nothing to halt the violence. Often, the sanctions end up hurting innocent civilians while leaving the regime unscathed. And, sometimes, the sanctions even help the regime solidify power because the government is in control of the food supply. This describes countless situations from North Korea today to Saddam Hussein's Iraq. The hitch is that the violence being waged by the regime solves all sorts of problems—*for the regime.* And our refusal to use violence is the one thing that guarantees the continuation of the problematic regime. This is a particularly acute challenge when the problematic regime is in fact at war with us.

This was Orwell's fundamental insight into pacifism. "In so far as it hampers the British war effort," Orwell wrote in 1941, "British pacifism is on the side of the Nazis and German pacifism, if it exists, is on the side of Britain and the USSR. Since pacifists have more freedom of action in countries where traces of democracy survive, pacifism can act more effectively against democracy than for it. Objectively the pacifist is pro-Nazi."[4] The following year he observed in *Partisan Review* that "Pacifism is objectively pro-Fascist. This is elementary common sense. If you hamper the war effort of one side you automatically help out that of the other. Nor is there any real way of remaining outside such a war as the present one. In practice, 'he that is not with me is against me.'" (When George W.

Bush said something similar, not aimed at domestic opponents of war, but at foreign regimes who harbored terrorists, he was denounced as a fascist for agreeing with Orwell.)

The people who say violence never solved anything usually say it in tandem with the old saw that "might doesn't make right," which even at most relevant is a non sequitur. Flexibility doesn't make right, either. Archbishop and Nobel Peace Prize winner Desmond Tutu, on the eve of the UN vote authorizing force in Iraq, cowrote an essay for the *International Herald Tribune* against war. "The current moment confronts the world with a terrible decision: will we stand by reason and law or act in force and aggression? . . . At stake is whether might makes right."

Left out of his analysis is that even the United Nations, to which he was appealing, enshrines the notion that might makes right into its fundamental charter. The permanent members of the UN Security Council have final authority not because they are the wisest or "rightist" nations, but because they are (or were, at the end of World War II) the mightiest nations. And, ultimately, it is the might of those nations that give the laws of the UN relevance and force.

Regardless, it is true that might doesn't make right. But might doesn't make *wrong*, either. This point seems to be lost on a lot of people, particularly the sorts of people who brag incessantly about "speaking truth to power" as if the powerful are incapable of knowing the truth or being decent and the powerless are somehow noble and righteous. No doubt there are some noble and righteous powerless people, but some of the most disgusting, vile, and dangerous people reside in the ranks of the powerless as well. Growing up in New York City in the 1970s I was never mugged, frightened, or harassed by very powerful people. I can't say the same of the destitute, deranged, or deviant characters who roamed the streets in those days. The root cause crowd might be right; powerlessness may drive some people to do evil things—terrorism, thievery, kidnapping, drug dealing, etc.—but that doesn't make what they do any less evil.

The thinking on the international stage often seems to be that because America *can* work its will, it should not be allowed to. This is the sort of logic that says it is unjust for a teacher to intervene to stop a bully from tormenting a weaker student because the teacher is so much more powerful than the bully.

The comparative success of Western civilization is not simply the result of might making right, it is the result of right *creating* might. "Let us have faith that right makes might," Abraham Lincoln beseeched, "and in that faith, let us, to the end, dare to do our duty as we understand it." By no means was the West without sin. But so many of the sins uniquely attributed to the West—slavery, imperialism, racism—are universal sins of humanity. Take slavery, arguably the oldest and most evil human institution. "On the issue of slavery," writes Thomas Sowell, "it was essentially Western civilization against the world." And "what was peculiar about the West was not that it participated in the worldwide evil of slavery, but that it later abolished that evil." That because "it was essentially European imperialism which ended slavery." Specifically, it was the conservative Christian abolitionist ideology, centered in Britain, which forced the end of slavery, at least in the West. In North Africa and the Middle East, where slave trading was an ancient practice, it took longer. White Europeans were still sold in Egyptian markets until the 1880s.

Anti-Western, or postcolonial, intellectuals and activists bring up the West's rap sheet not because we were uniquely complicit in slavery, colonialism, and imperialism, but because we are uniquely vulnerable to such guilt mongering. "I think it would be a good idea," Mohandas Karamchand Gandhi famously replied when asked what he thought of Western civilization, as if Indian civilization was without sin. To this day, left-wing poseurs have this line stuck to their refrigerators or use it for yearbook quotes as if it is a brilliantly insightful and humorous bon mot, when in reality the joke is on them.

Gandhi was in many respects the pioneer of exploiting Western self-loathing. For many pacifists, "What Would Gandhi Do?" is a more important question than "What Would Jesus Do?" and for good reason. Jesus did believe that violent self-defense was sometimes justified (that's why he instructed his followers to carry swords). Gandhi did not.

"The Mahatma"—which means, "great soul"—was undoubtedly one of the most idiosyncratic world leaders in modern memory. Particularly given the prevalence of New Age pieties these days, he has become a saint of sorts. A true ascetic, Gandhi voluntarily eschewed luxurious pleasures. He found satisfaction in more humble pastimes. Indeed, among his greatest joys and fascinations was the successful bowel movement. Paul Johnson notes that the first question he asked of his female attendants every morning was "Did you have a good bowel movement?" One of his favorite books, which he reread often, was *Constipation and Our Civilization.* Deprived of a sense of smell, which no doubt impaired his sense of taste, his vegetarian diet was centered around the goal of a successful digestive cycle. Spices, flavor itself, were to be avoided for Gandhi saw eating as a utilitarian affair.

He had the same attitude toward nearly all the spices of life as well. He came to believe intercourse was a regrettable necessity justifiable solely for the production of children. He embraced the *Brahmacharya*, a spiritualized celibacy that accelerated his estrangement from his wife. By his middle years he took to sleeping with naked women (including his own grandniece) in order to test his capacity for self-denial, and claimed to have only one seminal emission, entirely by accident, in his sleep at the age of sixty-six. He felt great shame for his failure.

Sometimes his beliefs amounted to more than victimless eccentricities. Gandhi refused to let British doctors give his wife a life-saving shot of penicillin, ostensibly on the grounds that she should not have alien substances injected in her body. His fastidiousness was a death sentence for her. And yet he was willing to accept quinine when he himself later contracted malaria. He also let British doctors perform an appendectomy on him, another alien intrusion to be sure.

He was, in short, a peculiar duck. To his credit, unlike most of the iconic, cultish leaders of the twentieth century, he was not power-mad, nor cruel (though his wife may have differed with that). Gandhi benefited from his oddity. His personal asceticism conveyed a moral authority and legitimacy to his political views they did not deserve on the merits. In a way he was the mirror opposite of the sinful preacher who preaches against sin. The preacher is wrong for what he hypocritically does behind closed doors, not for what he says to millions. Gandhi was often admirable for what he did behind closed doors, but that does not mean he was always correct in what he instructed his followers.

For instance, his advice on both personal diet and public agriculture was not merely impractical and gloomy. Had his ideas been translated into public policy they would have subjected millions of Indians to even worse starvation and even more pervasive poverty than they were already enduring. Gandhi's social and economic vision was perhaps best described as Tolkienesque. Technology was the enemy of decency, the perfect political unit was the Arcadian village, a subcontinental Shire where, instead of hobbits, Hindus would work individually on their tiny looms.

Of course, you would not know this from the film that helped cement the Gandhian legend. For instance, in *Gandhi* the movie, audiences are led to believe that his first hunger strike was to protest the British police's horrific slaughter of a crowd of peaceful Indian protestors. But Gandhi's first hunger strike was devoted to protesting a British effort to grant the Untouchables—India's lowest and most oppressed caste—greater rights and freedoms, including providing them with access to a form of affirmative action. That wouldn't play as well on the big screen, alas.

The filmmakers were merely picking up on a practice begun by the British foreign office. Simply put, Gandhi was a creature of the system he sought to overthrow. For years the British Empire used Gandhi as the most convenient nationalist. Unlike other anticolonial activists, Gandhi worked assiduously to prevent violence. "The true oddity," writes Richard Grenier, "is that Gandhi, this holy man, having drawn from British sources his notions of nationalism and democracy, also absorbed from the British his model of virtue in public life. He was a historical original, a Hindu holy man that a British model of public service and dazzling advances in mass communications thrust out into the world, to become a great moral leader and the 'father of his country.'"

Gandhi's accomplishments were great, but absent the context of a liberal empire, he would have accomplished little or nothing. He was "not a liberator, but a political exotic," writes Paul Johnson, "who could have flourished only in the protected environment provided by British liberalism."[5] The reason there was never a German Gandhi to stare down the Nazi regime is that the Nazi regime was immune to such appeals. Orwell observed that "it is difficult to see how Gandhi's methods could be applied in a country where opponents of the regime disappear in the middle of the night and are never heard of again. Without a free press and the right of assembly, it is impossible not merely to appeal to outside opinion, but to bring a mass movement into being, or even to make your intentions known to your adversary. Is there a Gandhi in Russia at this moment? And if there is, what is he accomplishing?"[6]

Hence, Gandhi's brand of nonviolence was not a universal standard for all of humanity but was instead an exceedingly parochial, even backwater, idea. The Gandhian conception that violence never solves anything worked because nonviolence was an effective tool against the British conscience and a country exhausted by war with Germany. Violence wasn't the answer for colonials in India. But, suffice it to say, violence *was* the answer for American colonists dealing with the same British Empire a century and a half earlier.

Gandhi's commitment to nonviolence led him to what can only be described as incandescently dumb positions. The Mahatma implored the British to surrender to the Nazis (and not the other way around). "I would like you to lay down the arms you have as being useless for saving you or humanity," he told the British. "Let [the Nazis] take possession of your beautiful island with your many beautiful buildings. You will give all these, but neither your souls, nor your minds."[7]

Fortunately there were no takers.

A starker illustration of the futility of Gandhi's prescriptions can be found in his advice to the Jews. Asked what the Jews should do in response to the cruelty visited upon them by Gandhi's "friend" Adolf Hitler, the answer was simple: Commit mass suicide. Gandhi—who despised the idea of a Jewish homeland in "Arab Palestine"—believed that the Jews shouldn't allow the Nazis to bully them out of Germany. Hence he advised German Jewry to stand up to the Nazis with Gandhian civil disobedience. He believed that such defiance would "have aroused the world and the people of Germany to Hitler's violence." When his biographer asked him, "You mean that the Jews should have committed collective suicide?" Gandhi replied, "Yes, that would have been heroism."[8]

Even after the war, when the full extent of the Holocaust was being realized, Gandhi never recanted his position that "the Jews should have offered themselves to the butcher's knife. They should have thrown themselves into the sea from cliffs." The Jews died anyway, Gandhi explained; at least if they'd followed his advice they would have died significantly. Theologians, ethicists, and philosophers can debate which aspects of this response are the most offensive. Heroism, after all, is ultimately in the eye of the beholder. What is not open to debate is the stunning naiveté of Gandhi's universal philosophy of peace. How likely is it that Jewish mass suicide would have "aroused the world" to Hitler's violence, when the *mass murder* of the Jews did not. Moreover, of what use is arousing world opinion when Gandhi's preferred course of action is surrender? If all you propose is to call attention to violence but do not believe that force is ever justified to stop it, why bother?

Still Gandhian nonviolence is preferable to the sort of violence employed by today's self-proclaimed anti-imperialists: Muslim terrorists. If the Palestinians, for instance, took Gandhian nonviolence to heart, they'd be living in their own state already. But instead they've opted for terrorism and bloodshed. When Hamas blows up pizza parlors or sends assassins to slit the throats of babies in their sleep, the "violence never solved anything" chorus remains remarkably mute. When Israel takes lawful action to prevent or punish such attacks, that is the cue for the very same chorus to kick in. That's because, as ever, the claim that "violence never solves anything" is not a universal truism; it is a selective attempt to manipulate the conscience of those with might not to do right.

17
MIDDLE CLASS

So say the Asian, the Hispanic, the Jew,
The African and Native American, the Sioux,
The Catholic, the Muslim, the French, the Greek,
The Irish, the Rabbi, the Priest, the Sheikh,
The Gay, the Straight, the Preacher,
The privileged, the homeless, the Teacher.

—Maya Angelou, "On the Pulse of Morning"

What do all of these folks say? I'm not too sure. But you can figure that out for yourself if you want to by reading Maya Angelou's "Inaugural Poem" delivered at Bill Clinton's swearing-in as the forty-second president of the United States. This passage serves as a less than ideal example of the Left's obsession with identity politics—the idea that we are all locked into our status as gay, straight, black, white, etc. But there are three reasons why I've chosen it. First, it's notable that at the inauguration of a president of the United States, the poem listed just about every flavor of humanity ever captured in a Benetton ad, but never once mentioned *Americans*. Second, it highlights the intense cognitive dissonance of the American Left.

And third: It rhymes, which is nice.

Let's circle back to number two. Bill Clinton won the Oval Office in large part because he refused to fall into the trap that so many Democrats before him had. Namely, the Democratic Party had become (and largely remains) the tail on the dog of special interests, particularly labor unions, racial grievance peddlers, feminists, limousine liberals, and the rest of the usual suspects. He cast himself as a different kind of Democrat, who wanted to "end welfare as we know it" and offer a "hand up not a hand out." He attacked the brilliantly self-parodying rapper Sister Souljah, distanced himself from Jesse Jackson took time off from the campaign to oversee the execution of a mentally retarded man and, most importantly, talked relentlessly about the "middle class."

Hence, the cognitive dissonance. You see, Bill Clinton and his advisers mastered the art of using the term middle class to win elections for a party that is obsessed with categorizing people in terms that negate the very idea of a middle class. Moreover, once elected, and all in the name of "protecting" the middle class, they put in place programs and championed ideas that undermined the stability of the middle class.

"Middle class" is a confounding term. Everyone uses it. Everyone claims to know what it means and who it describes, and yet it is almost entirely useless as a term of economic precision and deeply misleading as a term of political identity. In 2008, both Hillary Clinton and Barack Obama ran for president with policies predicated on the assumption that 98 percent of Americans were, in effect, middle class.[1] It tells you something that a party widely associated with its concern for the poor talks about the middle class far, far more. When President Obama was speaking at the 2008 Democratic convention—to his most passionate ideological comrades-in-arms, no less—he talked at length about giving tax breaks to the middle class. He didn't even mention the word "poor."[2] John Kerry's 2004 convention speech mentions the middle class six times, and discusses it at length. Kerry mentions the word "poor" twice, once to mention that Bill Clinton helped reduce poverty, once to mention that Bush increased it. Scorecard for Al Gore's convention speech in 2000: Tax cuts for the middle class, yes. Direct mention of the poor, no.

This is not to say Democratic politicians don't care about the poor. I'm sure they do. But they also understand that even the poor—at least the *voting poor*—tend to think of themselves as the middle class, or aspire to be members of it. So when they talk about the middle class versus the rich, what they in fact mean is *everybody* versus the rich. In other words, being *for* the middle class, at least in many contexts, is just code for being *against* the rich. This has profound and pernicious public policy implications (to which we'll return).

But there's another meaning to the middle class: "middle America," traditional America, flyover America, Main Street, Norman Rockwell America. It means the America of old-fashioned values and norms, the part of the map that got edited down to next to nothing in that famous *New Yorker* magazine cover depicting the Manhattanite's view of America from Ninth Avenue. Democrats can never—ever—be caught appealing to what the hard campus Left calls "white America," because white America is the very thing that the campus Left sees as the author of all of our problems and the primary target of all progressive reforms. That's why the term "middle class" comes in so handy. It is a way of appealing to the heartland in terms that cannot be effectively faulted by the gargoyles on the parapets of the ivory tower.

This is not to say that the gargoyles don't look down upon the middle class. Despising the traditional-minded, religious, hardworking middle class—once known to elite, effete, intellectual types as the "bourgeoisie"—has been the great and abiding pastime of the very same elite and effete intellectual types for centuries. Stendhal said that small businessmen made him want to "weep and vomit at the same time." Hatred of the bourgeoisie is "the beginning of all virtue" proclaimed Gustave Flaubert.[3] I learned from David Brooks that Flaubert even signed his letters "Bourgeoisophobus" to signal just how much he despised "stupid grocers and their ilk."

At first, America was not a hospitable climate for bourgeoisophobia. The founders were split not on the question of whether the bourgeoisie was good or bad, but which bourgeoisie to love the most. The Hamiltonians had a vision for America as a "commercial republic." The Jeffersonians had a vision of America as a democracy of self-sustaining yeoman farmers. It took generations of wealth accumulation for America to produce an entire class of intellectuals who could hate the middle-class country that produced them.

In the early 1920s, American liberals turned their backs on the country that sought a "return to normalcy." Disgusted with the triumph of the "Babbitts"—the pejorative label for middle-class philistines, taken from the main character of Sinclair Lewis's novel of the same name—a slew of articles and books appeared denigrating "middle America" as dimwitted, backward, and irredeemably provincial. The progressives of the Teddy Roosevelt and Woodrow Wilson years had an abiding faith in the power and wisdom of public opinion, particularly when molded by "experts." But once public opinion turned against them, they turned on the public. Harold Stearns, a once promising *New Republic* writer and Wilson administration functionary, edited a collection of essays in *American Civilization* that amounted to a seething indictment of American backwardness.[4]

The Nation ran a whole series of articles under the heading "In These United States" purporting to reveal that Manhattan was an island of sophistication in a vast wasteland of American backwardness.* This was the era when it became an article of faith that the artist must hate the society in which he lives, that he must be "a public enemy" in the words of H. L. Mencken, and that the "*vox populi* is, to him, the bray of an ass." The writers for *The Nation* ridiculed what is today called "fly-over country"—which back then was really "train-through country" or perhaps "cruise around country"—with relentless condescension. Chronicling his impressions of Minnesota, Sinclair Lewis lamented that the "Scandinavians Americanize only too quickly!"[5] Perhaps not surprisingly, the South was an object of particular scorn. One writer believed that Mississippi could only be saved by an invasion of civilizing, cultured, missionaries from the North. Another scratched his head to ask what, if anything, Alabama had ever contributed to humanity.

The Midwest and West were hardly spared either. The story of Colorado was a tale of "continuous colossal waste." The famed Kansan-progressive William Allen White lashed out that his state's own culture of self-improvement was now backward, too. The "dour deadly desire to fight what was deemed wrong" had arrested Kansas's artistic development. "No great poet, no great painter, no great musician, no great writer or philosopher" could be found in the Sunflower State. All that existed was the "dead level of economic and political democracy." The Ohio-born

* I am indebted to Christopher Lasch's seminal *The True and Only Heaven: Progress and Its Critics* (W.W. Norton & Company, 1991) for his discussion of this period.

novelist Sherwood Anderson asked: "Have you a city that smells worse than Akron, that is a worse junk-heap of ugliness than Youngstown, that is more smugly self-satisfied than Cleveland?"

All in all, the cultural elite of the 1920s had firmly convinced themselves that they were, in Christopher Lasch's words, "a civilized minority in a nation of Babbitts, Rotarians, and rednecks." Undoubtedly, self-loathing played an important role in this bigotry toward middle America. Sinclair Lewis was lashing out at the small town world that bred him. He spent much of his life searching for the refined life he was sure was out there. In the process he wrecked marriages, friendships, and his own career. In self-imposed exile in Italy, Lewis drank himself to an early grave in 1951. His self-loathing was only outmatched by that of his obituary writers.

Harold Stearns went off to Paris to escape American provincialism, only to become a legendary drunk and moocher, who barely repented his disdain for his home country before he died. Sherwood Anderson died in Panama, having perforated his gut with the toothpick from a martini.

There is certainly some significance to the fact that so many of these writers were condemning their own communities and home states. In a sense, progressivism nurtures and is nurtured by a tendency to loathe what is near and love what is far. Those who escape the provincial must justify their own betrayal of their roots. The same story, but on a generational scale, played itself out to some extent in the 1960s when the New Left's chief complaint (before they latched on to the civil rights movement) was how good they had it. Comfort, it seemed, was a sin. The opening line from the Students for a Democratic Society's 1962 Port Huron Statement says it all: "We are people of this generation, bred in at least modest comfort, housed now in universities, looking uncomfortably to the world we inherit."[6] Betty Friedan, one of the founding mothers of modern feminism, was a devoted Communist journalist who deduced that her critique of bourgeois America would have more bite if she passed herself off as a humble housewife speaking truth to power instead of the Berkeley-educated activist she was. In *The Feminine Mystique*, she indicted the traditional middle-class home as "a comfortable concentration camp" where women were held captive.[7] That the biggest difference she recognizes between being a Jew at Buchenwald and being June Cleaver is the degree of "comfort" says more about Friedan than it does about anything going on in 1960s suburbia.

This line of thinking also helps demonstrate that the second wave of feminism was in no small part launched as a Trojan Horse for an older and more familiar Marxist assault. It may have evolved into something different and more mainstream, but the DNA is there.

And since we're on the subject of Marxism, we might as well deal with it here since anyone venturing into the realm of class must at some point pull over at Karl's Funland and throw some darts at the balloons, squirt water in the clown's mouth, and tease the dancing monkeys.

According to most conventional discussions of Marxist theory, there are only two classes: the workers and the owners, or the proletariat and the bourgeoisie. "By bourgeoisie," explains Marx in *The Communist Manifesto*, "is meant the class of modern Capitalists, owners of the means of social production and employers of wage-labor." The proletariat, meanwhile, are "the class of modern wage-laborers who, having no means of production of their own, are reduced to selling their labor-power in order to live."[8]

The problem even for Marx, never mind his intellectual heirs, is that whenever one actually looks at people as they actually live, it turns out that there are a lot more classes than just two.[9] That's why Marx is, to borrow a term from social science, such a hot steaming mess. In *Das Kapital* he writes that there are in fact *three* classes: The capitalists, proletarians, and the landowners. But then pretty soon Marx had to add the petty bourgeois and the peasants to his list of classes. That makes five.

No wait, it's six, actually, because he divided the peasants into two types: The lowly serfs and the landowning peasants. The landowning peasants were proletarians but didn't know it. Since their mortgages were taken out from the capitalists, they were really wage earners with undeservedly high self-esteem. The nonlandowning peasants, meanwhile, were members of the "barbarian class." The petty bourgeois—small shopkeepers and the like—didn't own the means of production, but they did employ wage earners. Where do they belong? Well, Marx is pretty sure they belong among the capitalists, but since they seemed to be disappearing he calls them a "transition class."

Then there are the "ideological classes"—who are sometimes the handmaidens of the capitalists and sometimes their own class, it depends apparently on which side of the bed Marx got up from that day. Sometimes he talks about the "ruling classes." In Britain they are the "aristocracy," "the moneyocracy," or "finance aristocracy" and the "millocracy." There's also the "lower-middle-class," which draws its members from the ranks of the petty bourgeoisie, depending on what they do, what they make, or how much they earn.

Then, of course, there's the "lumpenproletariat," my favorite of the umpteen classes found in Marx's allegedly two-class system. The *Communist Manifesto* defines them as "the dangerous class, *the social scum, that passively rotting mass thrown off by the lowest layers of old society.*"[10] But I prefer the fuller definition in *The 18th Brumaire of Louis Bonaparte*, which includes a list of all the members of the lumpenproletarian coalition that, according to Marx, formed the brute squad (to borrow a phrase from *The Princess Bride*) of the Bonapartist regime:

> [D]ecayed *roués* [cads, lechers, and rakes] with dubious means of subsistence and of dubious origin, alongside ruined and adventurous offshoots of the bourgeoisie, were vagabonds, discharged soldiers, discharged jailbirds, escaped galley slaves, swindlers, mountebanks, *lazzaroni* [an Italian term for goons-for-hire], pickpockets, tricksters, gamblers, *maquereaux* [pimps], brothel keepers, porters, literati, organ grinders, ragpickers, knife grinders, tinkers, beggars—in short, the whole indefinite, disintegrated mass, thrown hither and thither, which the French call *la bohème.*[11]

If that's too archaic, think of the henchmen Hedley Lamarr wanted to enlist to his cause in *Blazing Saddles* (minus, of course, the Methodists): rustlers, cutthroats, murderers, bounty hunters, desperados, mugs, pugs, thugs, nitwits, halfwits, dimwits, vipers, snipers, con men, Indian agents, Mexican bandits, muggers, buggerers, bushwhackers, hornswogglers, horse thieves, bull dykes, train robbers, bank robbers, ass-kickers, shit-kickers, and Methodists.

Regardless, the takeaway is that when talking about the lumpenproletariat, the thing to remember is that, as Obi-Wan Kenobi said of the denizens of the Mos Eisley spaceport: "You will never find a more wretched hive of scum and villainy."

The reason Marx's analysis suffered from such an incontinent stream of classes is that humanity is simply not easily, reliably, or sufficiently categorized by class. In his myopic arrogance he insisted on imposing a single mode of analysis on humanity. It would be like dividing the entire world into those who are left-handed and right-handed. Yes, you would learn and highlight some very interesting things about the differences and interactions of southpaws and decent humans (I don't trust left-handed people!), but that would hardly unlock the mysteries to every realm of life. Like the proverbial Martian visitor who would rationally deduce that humans were slaves to dogs because we pick up their feces, Marx's obsession with defining everyone as *homo economicus* caused him to ignore many of the most important facts of life. It is a lesson that not only Marxist economists would do well to learn: To look upon the interactions of the priest and the confessor, mother and child, doctor and patient, soldiers and their comrades, musicians and their audiences as exclusively, or even primarily, economic transactions is to cram the square pegs of your ideology into the round holes of reality.

(This was the genius of fascism's appeal. Mussolini, a committed Marxist socialist for most of his life, realized that the Italian masses liked the idea of a command economy, but they also liked the idea of being *Italians.* Marxists insisted that factory workers in Florence should have more solidarity with factory workers in Minsk than with the grocery store owner down the block.)

Europeans—and later Asians—found Marxism particularly plausible because class was always a more salient concept on the continent. But Marx mistook cultural arrangements for "scientific" categories. In the United States class played—and continues to play—far less of a role. For most of the nineteenth century, the average American was an owner—or co-owner with his family—of his own means of production. In fact, prior to the Civil War only a fifth of the population lived in cities, and most people lived on their own farms. With the advent of urbanization and industrialization, the working classes—i.e., the proletariat—grew quickly. They also rapidly carved out a lifestyle that made them if not fully bourgeois (whatever that actually means), then certainly prosperous enough not to feel exploited. Moreover, the working classes saw literally millions of their children enter the upper classes simply by dint of their hard work. The notion that class was an iron cage locking people into a permanent struggle with the ruling classes simply never caught on. Indeed, the majority of those in nineteenth-century American ruling classes—both political and economic—were not born into that status but earned it. As David Brooks writes, "Marx told us that classes inevitably conflict, but sometimes they just blur."[12]

Europe had a history of serfdom, Americans left that behind (with, of course, the obvious and odious exception of slavery, an institution which has also proved confounding to traditional Marxists, because it centers on race, not class). Yes, America has had its periods of labor strife—giving false hope to Marxists and other flavors of socialist that the party was about to get started—but ultimately the conflicts in America have been along different fault lines: racial, regional, cultural, and philosophical. And most of them haven't been bloody, but political. In his famous 1906 book *Why Is There No Socialism in the United States?* Werner Sombart asked, "Why is there no socialism in the United States?" Library shelves groan with books answering that question, but the short answer is quite simple: Because this is the United States, damn it.

To be sure, class is not an exclusively Marxist term, even if all discussions of class have an oily Marxist residue to them akin to the greasy film on the tables at a Chuck E. Cheese's. Marx's great rival in academic debates about class was Max Weber, who defined class not so much in terms of income, but social authority. Weber's vastly superior analysis held that a given society's organization of classes was contingent on a specific culture, and that income had far less to do with the rankings than the Marxists thought.[13] Priests in seventeenth-century France, for example, may not have been particularly wealthy, but they were certainly more influential than the comparatively prosperous blacksmith guild. Lady Gaga is not influential because she's rich, she's rich because she's influential.

In America, the so-called new class of professors, journalists, education bureaucrats, social workers, and activists makes far less money than the typical orthodontist but has far, far more influence over our culture. Perhaps this is one reason why the term rich is routinely defined in the fine print of Democratic proposals as income just slightly above what the more successful workers in these fields make. As Megan McCardle has noted, there's an amusing tendency among liberal financial journalists to call for taxing the rich at rates "just above the level a top-notch journalist in a two-earner couple could be expected to pull down."[14]

Bill Clinton was a quintessential member of this new class (and you thought I forgot about him). A man never much interested in making money (until he left the Oval Office), he was from his teen years onward fixated on politics. His wife, too, was a consummate champion of the "helping professions." Clinton's political success lay in brilliantly updating the Nixonian formula of treating the vast, mostly white, American middle class as an identity politics group without ever conceding that was what he was doing. Inspired by the book *The Real Majority*, written by the political scientist Richard Scammon and (my old boss) Ben Wattenberg, then a Democratic strategist, Richard Nixon appealed to the "silent majority" of middle America, which Scammon famously defined as "unyoung, unpoor, unblack." Wattenberg and Scammon always intended their analysis to be used by Democrats to win elections, but a Nixon aide by the name of Pat Buchanan saw its merits while the Democrats, still descending into McGovernism, couldn't. Nixon won reelection in a landslide.

Twenty years later the lesson finally sank in. Bill Clinton marketed his 1992 campaign around the theme of "Fighting for the Forgotten Middle Class." The brilliant trick, however, was that by 1992, according to Clinton's pollster Stan Greenberg, fully 90 percent of Americans considered themselves to *be* middle class. In other words, it was a term that seemed to be about "class" but was in reality about everything except class. It was an appeal to classically bourgeois values masquerading as class warfare. The background issues in 1992 were as much crime, welfare, race riots, cultural rot as they were about the "economy stupid." But a Democrat couldn't talk about those issues directly, at least not without offending his base or the white middle-class voters he needed to win. Middle-class anxieties were, are, and always have been about more than mere economic concerns. We know this not least because what the cultural elite hated least about the bourgeoisie was *their money*. What they loathed were their values, and merely resented that middle-class values were remunerative. Clinton's populist appeal to the middle class was a dog-whistle signal to white voters telling them, in effect, "I get it." He wasn't subtle about it.

"And so, in the name of all those who do the work and pay the taxes, raise the kids, and play by the rules, in the name of the hardworking Americans who make up our forgotten middle-class," Bill Clinton announced at the 1992 Democratic Convention, "I proudly accept your nomination for President of the United States." And after the thunderous applause died down: "I am a product of that middle-class, and when I am president, you will be forgotten no more." Translation: This is not the lumpenproletariat's Democratic Party anymore.

The first two years of the Clinton presidency revealed the dilemma the dog has when he finally catches the car. He ran as a man championing middle-class values, but he violated that pledge when he was seen as making the issue of gays in the military his first priority in office. His battles with feminist "bean counters" (his term) and his personal style lent the impression that he knew what to say to get elected but his heart was still with the damn hippies. His wife's talk about a new "politics of meaning" only reinforced the perception.

Thanks to Republican victories in 1994 and his own reptilian instinct for political survival, Clinton eventually found his way back to the center, and then hugged it for dear life for the rest of his presidency. He reluctantly embraced Republican-led welfare reform. He poll-tested his vacation itineraries so as to seem more middle class (he preferred Martha's Vineyard but his pollster Dick Morris tested that with voters and advised him it was too elitist. Better to go camping in Wyoming). And he successfully marginalized middle-class resentments against him by railing against the dangers of "angry white men."

American affluence has always been a vexing challenge for liberalism. Just as the hard left loathed the bourgeois' "comfort," mainstream liberalism despises their complacency. In the 1950s old-style mainstream liberalism had overseen a massive explosion in American prosperity after World War II—thanks to both good fortune and effective policies. But now what? Perhaps liberalism had run its course?

"The fear that liberalism would be thanked for its service and given a gold watch became more acute as the American economy soared after World War II," notes William Voegeli. He continues:

> In 1957, the year before John Kenneth Galbraith published *The Affluent Society*, Arthur Schlesinger tried to redefine liberalism's mission for such a society. He wrote that the New Deal's establishment of the welfare state and Keynesian management of the economy heralded the completion of the work of "quantitative liberalism." Its logical and necessary successor should be "qualitative liberalism," which would oppose the drift into the homogenized society. It must fight spiritual unemployment as [quantitative liberalism] once fought economic unemployment. It must concern itself with the quality of popular culture and the character of lives to be lived in our abundant society.[15]

Just because the extinction of liberalism was a real anxiety among liberals doesn't mean that there was ever a real chance that liberals would actually pack it in. If history shows anything about the progressive mindset it's that there's always more work to do. Very soon after Schlesinger offered his diagnosis of and prescription for the liberal dilemma, John Kenneth Galbraith would indeed write *The Affluent Society*, which in turn would lead to the Great Society programs which set about not only to transform society in myriad ways, but to do so with a sense of panicked urgency. Ever since, the new class activists in and out of government have recommitted themselves to transforming society through law and bureaucratic diktat, popular culture and K-through-PhD indoctrination.

Not all of these efforts have been wrong or pernicious in intent or result. One of the wonderful things about American culture is that it is fundamentally bourgeois, so it tends to "bourgeoisie-ify" even the most marginal cultural trends. One need only look to see how queer—and straight—theorists who once dreamed of "smashing monogamy" now celebrate the fact that gay men and women can spend their days as committed couples raising children and working to pay off their mortgages. For all of the effort by the campus left and their emissaries in the larger culture, identity politics alone—be it racial or gender quotas, barmy historical revisionism, or grievance peddling in all of its predictable forms—is not strong or compelling enough to overpower the force of our culture or the countervailing pressure to "work hard and play by the rules" that capitalism encourages.

"The great secret of education is to direct vanity to proper objects," Adam Smith observed in his first book, *The Theory of Moral Sentiments.*[16] Smith isn't talking about manipulation or brainwashing. He's not invoking Marxist notions of "false consciousness." No, he's talking about *educating* people, and you can only educate with the truth. Everything else is indoctrination. Smith believed that the free market and, more broadly, the free society, directs men's vanity toward its proper objects, the virtues of prudence, restraint, industry, frugality, sobriety, honesty, civility, and reliability. Freedom teaches the virtue of "self-command" which, he writes, "is not only itself a great virtue, but from it all the other virtues seem to derive their principal luster."[17]

And this is the great and tragic irony. The hurly-burly of America's cultural politics, while important, even vital, can never unravel the implicit social contract of capitalism which says that if you follow the virtues Adam Smith laid out, you will do just fine. If you teach those values to your kids, they will do better than you. That is true of whites, blacks, Hispanics, gays, and everybody else Maya Angelou listed in her no doubt brilliant poem. That in a nutshell is the American dream. There are no guarantees, but odds are in your favor.

Indeed, that's the hitch. It is *because there are no guarantees in a free society that you develop the habits that are essential to success in a free society.* Freedom makes many things harder, which is to say it makes many things more valuable. Without wading into the nitty-gritty of every policy proposal out there, the simple fact is that the Democratic agenda of "fighting for the middle class" amounts to subsidizing the middle class. Both as a philosophical goal and a cynical political strategy, FDR sought to turn vast constituencies—labor unions, blacks, widows, big business, et al.—into clients of the state. FDR wanted to go further, but couldn't before he died. Nonetheless, the "interest-group liberalism" he left the party with served it well, politically, for more than a generation. It only became a liability for Democrats when mainstream Americans came to realize how it was undermining the health of the overall society, culturally and economically. That realization put Ronald Reagan in office.

The Democratic Party since Clinton has tried to "transcend" interest-group liberalism by treating the whole middle class as a monolithic interest group. From housing policy, to student loans, to health care, the philosophy driving the Democratic Party amounts to middle-class social democracy. It's not evil. And, though it makes the libertarian inside me scream in agony to say it, it's not altogether wrongheaded. A modern society does have an obligation to figure out how to care for those who cannot care for themselves, be they sick, poor, or elderly. That doesn't require centralized, state-driven policies. Nor does it require policies that undermine the Smithian virtues. But it does require some policies.

The problem with the contemporary liberal approach is that it amounts to middle-class welfare. Not only can we not afford it economically, the middle class cannot afford it morally. To miss out on the opportunity to cultivate the Smithian virtues is to eat the seed corn of social capital. Liberals to be sure don't see it that way. They see it as an effort to make life easier, to expand the realm of "positive liberty" that John Dewey envisioned and FDR hoped to implement with his "economic bill of rights." Here's Nancy Pelosi explaining how the Affordable Care Act (i.e., ObamaCare) would stimulate the economy: "We see it as an entrepreneurial bill, a bill that says to someone: 'If you want to be creative and be a musician or whatever, you can leave your work, focus on your talent, your skill, your passion, your aspirations because you will have health care. You won't have to be job locked.'"

Never mind that the causal link between socialized medicine and entrepreneurism is not exactly firmly established. The larger point is that the liberal vision of an advanced society is one where it is finally rich enough to liberate the middle class from their comfortable bourgeois lifestyles and to subsidize their conversion to bohemian ones. If you want to be a "musician or whatever" it's okay, because we'll tax the rich enough so that you don't have to worry about life's essentials (like health care or housing or food or your kids' education) anymore. In other words they are going to win their centuries'-old war on the middle class by subsidizing the bohemian lifestyle to the point where it no longer pays to be bourgeois. It probably won't work in the long run. But in the short run, it will bankrupt us all, not only financially, but morally as well.

18
SCIENCE

Now, we don't know who will win next year's presidential election. But the odds are that one of these years the world's greatest nation will find itself ruled by a party that is aggressively anti-science, indeed anti-knowledge. And, in a time of severe challenges—environmental, economic, and more—that's a terrifying prospect.

—Paul Krugman, "Republicans Against Science," *New York Times*, August 28, 2011

More intelligent individuals may be more likely to acquire and espouse evolutionarily novel values and preferences (such as liberalism and atheism . . .) than less intelligent individuals.

—Satoshi Kanazawa, London School of Economics and Political Science, "Why Liberals and Atheists Are More Intelligent," *Social Psychology Quarterly*, March 2010

Disparate conservatives share a resistance to change and acceptance of inequality. Hitler, Mussolini, and former President Ronald Reagan were individuals, but all were right-wing conservatives because they preached a return to an idealized past and condoned inequality in some form. Talk host Rush Limbaugh can be described the same way.

— John Jost, Stanford University's Graduate School of Business; Arie Kruglanski, University of Mary-

LAND AT COLLEGE PARK; JACK GLASER, UNIVERSITY OF CALIFORNIA, BERKELEY GOLDMAN SCHOOL OF PUBLIC POLICY; AND FRANK SULLOWAY, OF UC BERKELEY, "POLITICAL CONSERVATISM AS MOTIVATED SOCIAL COGNITION," PSYCHOLOGICAL BULLETIN, AMERICAN PSYCHOLOGICAL ASSOCIATION, JULY 22, 2003

They do that because they were born that way."

If you say that about homosexuals, you are tolerant and realistic.

If you say it about blacks, you are racist (unless you're black).

If you say it about Jews, you're anti-Semitic, unless it's in the context of criticizing Israel, in which case you're simply telling "hard truths" everyone else is afraid to say.

If you say it about women, you may or may not be sexist, depending on who is manning (er, Womanning) the feminist battle stations at the moment.

If you say it about men, you just might be a writer for *Esquire.*

But if you say it about conservatives, you're a scientist.

If the tyranny of clichés can be understood as the use of allegedly nonideological insights to advance starkly ideological understandings of the world, then "science"—and what it allegedly tells us—is the mother of tyranny (figuratively speaking of course). From climate change to embryonic stem cell research to early childhood education, patently ideological agendas are camouflaged under the tarp of scientific rhetoric while plainly legitimate scientific findings are dubbed "pseudoscience" when they prove inconvenient. Second perhaps only to "health," science is routinely used as a false flag of reasonableness carried by those who allegedly only care about "the facts," but are in fact concerned about something else.

A host of liberal activists and intellectuals are deeply invested in the idea that conservatives are "antiscience." Obviously, not all of these people argue in bad faith. But many argue in very selective good faith. They pick and choose the benchmarks of what constitutes being proscience. So, for example, if you disagree with not only the diagnosis of climate change but the proposed remedies for it, you are antiscience. Before it became clear that culling stem cells from human embryos was essentially unnecessary, it became a matter of faith that opposition to creating life to destroy it wasn't a matter of conscience, but evidence of antiscience views. And of course, there's the issue of "creationism," which is a very comfortable terrain for liberals to argue on for obvious reasons (the earth is not six thousand years old), even if the political relevance of the underlying questions are ultimately trivial.

But it is quite easy to play this game the other way. Why can't the measure of being proscience hinge on the question of heritability of intelligence? Or the existence of fetal pain? Or the distribution of cognitive abilities among the sexes at the extreme right tail of the bell curve? Or if that's too upsetting, how about drawing the dividing line between those who are pro- and antiscience along the lines of support for geoengineering? Or—coming soon—the role cosmic rays play in cloud formation? Why not make it about support for nuclear power? Or Yucca Mountain? Why not deride the idiots who oppose genetically modified crops, even when they might prevent blindness in children? Defenders of embryonic stem cell research insist that opponents want to deny people life-saving remedies. This is a horrendous slander on several levels, but if that is the relevant metric, how are we to deal with the armies of activists who oppose the use of DDT, which could save millions from malaria?

During the Larry Summers fiasco at Harvard, comments delivered in the classic spirit of open inquiry and debate cost Summers his job. Summers speculated that there might be more male geniuses than female ones. Some evidence apparently suggests men are overrepresented among morons and brainiacs, while the average woman is smarter than the average man. Scientists got the vapors because he violated the principles not of science but of *liberalism*. During the Gulf oil spill, the Obama administration dishonestly claimed that its independent experts supported a drilling moratorium. The experts emphatically did not and said so in public protest. The president who campaigned on basing his policies on sound science ignored his own handpicked scientists. According to the GAO he did something very similar when he shut down Yucca Mountain.

The idea that conservatives are antiscience is self-evident and self-pleasing liberal hogwash. It is also hogwash that liberals are intrinsically opposed to science. The reality is that each side sees science for what it is: a tool. In this case they see it as a tool to advance larger arguments. Liberals tend to be constrained by their exaltation of egalitarianism, conservatives tend to be constrained by what pro-lifers would call the sanctity of life. There's nothing inherently wrong with either value-system and reasonable people can have reasonable arguments about where their principles need to bend. It is a scientific fact that fire burns things. One is not denying science when one seeks to ban arson. No doubt, we could learn something useful by conducting horrific experiments on live human beings. But conservatives and liberals alike oppose such practices not because they are against science but because ethical considerations trump the pursuit of knowledge at all costs. If Democrats came out tomorrow in favor of human vivisection and Republicans opposed it, Republicans would not suddenly become antiscience. Rather, Democrats would suddenly become *wrong*.

Obviously, politicians—of both parties—routinely hide behind convenient studies and cherry-picked data and activists—again, of all ideological stripes—have their share of junk science. And while I would cherish the opportunity to take a swatter to the swarm of Naderite botflies that claim they are simply giving human voice to the otherwise cold empiricism of the scientific method, the best illustration of the deeper problem is in the always new science of conservative phrenology.

Okay, it's not technically phrenology (the old science of measuring head shapes to determine intelligence and character) anymore. The scientists have put away their calipers and replaced them with MRI machines and gene sequencers. The modern-day phrenologists are a mixed bag of political scientists, psychologists, geneticists, and neuroscientists. A generous soul would describe it as a cross-disciplinary field aiming to identify the inborn traits that determine our political views. A less generous—but perhaps more accurate—take would say this is a white-smocked effort to explain away conservatism as a mental defect, genetic abnormality, or curable pathology.

The field has exploded in the last decade. And, in truth, some of the findings have been intriguing. In their 2008 paper, "Two Genes Predict Voter Turnout," James H. Fowler and Christopher T. Dawes found that "individuals with a polymorphism of the MAOA gene are significantly more likely to have voted in the 2004 presidential election."[1] And researchers reexamining the Minnesota twin studies—surprisingly these have nothing to do with baseball players—have found that political outlook has a nontrivial amount of heritability. It seems there may be genetic and/or biological components to certain political orientations. You can't predict what politician a person will support from his genetic markers or from his PET scans, but you can make some informed guesses about how he or she sees the world.

One need not gainsay the scientific endeavor to call attention to the remarkably large amount of equine excrement in many of its manifestations and applications that have emerged from this otherwise innocuous finding. For instance, in one particularly famous study, researchers at NYU and UCLA—all committed liberals—asked subjects to take a test. Here's how the authors of the study explain the test:

> [E]ither the letter "M" or "W" was presented in the center of a computer monitor screen. . . . Half of the participants were instructed to make a "Go" response when they saw "M" but to make no response when they saw "W"; the remaining participants completed a version in which "W" was the Go stimulus and "M" was the No–Go stimulus. . . . Responses were registered on a computer keyboard placed in the participants' laps. . . . Participants received a two-minute break halfway through the task, which took approximately 15 minutes to complete. . . .
>
> Each trial began with a fixation point, presented for 500 ms. The target then appeared for 100 ms, followed by a blank screen. Participants were instructed to respond within 500 ms of target onset. A "Too slow!" warning message appeared after responses that exceeded this deadline, and "Incorrect" feedback was given after erroneous responses.[2]

If your eyes glazed over, basically the test asked subjects to spot Ms and Ws on a screen for a fraction of a second. (500 ms—"milliseconds"—is one half second. 100 ms is a tenth of a second.) It turns out that the liberals—as per the authors' definition—did somewhat better on the test than the conservatives. What does that mean? Well, according to the authors, it means: "Liberals are more responsive to informational complexity, ambiguity and novelty." Liberals are also "more likely than are conservatives to respond to cues signaling the need to change habitual responses." Meanwhile, "a more conservative orientation is related to greater persistence in a habitual response pattern, despite signals that this response pattern should change."

Translation: Conservatives are literally too stupid to be spell-checkers at an M&M factory because they won't be able to understand that the occasional W is just an upside down M, particularly when they start coming off the conveyor belt really fast like in the chocolate factory episode of *I Love Lucy*.

Shamelessly egged on by David Amodio, lead author of the study, the mainstream press ran with these findings as if they had found the key to unlocking the mysteries of politics. *The Guardian* dutifully declared, "Scientists have found that the brains of people calling themselves liberals are more able to handle conflicting and unexpected information."[3] The *Los Angeles Times* announced in an editorial that the study "suggests that liberals are more adaptable than conservatives" and "might be better judges of the facts."[4] Imagine a liberal driver and a conservative driver, Amodio told the *Times*. "If he's a liberal," the editors conclude, "he is more likely to be alert to a detour. If he's a conservative, he's more likely to, well, stay the course."

"Stay the course" was, at the time, a reference to the Iraq war. Get it? And we all know that such liberal lions like Lyndon Johnson or John F. Kennedy would never, ever think of staying the course in a quagmire. And it must have been the old liberal in Ronald Reagan that caused him to suddenly reverse course and pull troops out of Beirut.

In another study,[5] researchers telephoned 1,310 residents of Lincoln, Nebraska. Out of that number, slightly more than 10 percent (143) of them had strong political views and were willing to come into a university lab for testing. In the end, 46 of them finished the test. The researchers measured the reactions of the subjects to disturbing images—maggots in a wound, spiders on a face, a dazed man covered in blood—as well as their responses to sudden loud noises. The authors found a statistically significant correlation between the fear responses of subjects and support for various "Protective Policies." According to the authors:

> Individuals with measurably lower physical sensitivities to sudden noises and threatening visual images were more likely to support foreign aid, liberal immigration policies, pacifism, and gun control, whereas individuals displaying measurably higher physiological reactions to those same stimuli were more likely to favor defense spending, capital punishment, patriotism, and the Iraq War. Thus, the degree to which individuals are physiologically responsive to threat appears to indicate the degree to which they advocate policies that protect the existing social structure from both external (outgroup) and internal (norm-violator) threats.[6]

In both cases, the samples are tiny and extremely vulnerable to filtering bias. Perhaps liberals are simply more deferential to academic authorities and therefore have calmer responses when the expert in the lab coat busts out the calipers or electrodes? Maybe liberals are more interested in pleasing their inquisitors? Perhaps skeptical conservatives are constantly wondering "What the Hell are these people doing?" Perhaps the findings reflect some other underlying but unappreciated causation such as religious attitudes?

As for the more ludicrous "M versus W" study, it's difficult to know where to begin. The study purports to measure the subjects' comfort with complexity and ambiguity, but as *Slate*'s science columnist William Saletan notes, the study actually excludes complexity and ambiguity and instead measures the reaction time to a binary visual acuity test: seeing Ms and upside down Ms. Almost by definition, conscious thought has no role in a video-game test measured in milliseconds. How can liberals be deemed to be more intellectually supple based on this nonsense? Would Socrates be better at spotting rogue Ws on a screen than the average mouth-breathing teenage gamer?

As ridiculous as some of this is, it doesn't mean that these researchers are all just a bunch of Jacobins in smocks. Some are clearly judicious, committed professionals. And for every outlandish claim or study, there's another scientist pointing out the numerous flaws and holes in their work.

Besides, it's not preposterous to believe that there's ample nature to go with the nurture when it comes to our political views. Scientists know that we are not blank slates. We are hardwired as a species to believe and act in certain ways. In fact, conservatives have been saying as much for several millennia now—think original sin and human nature—while the Left has repeatedly bought into the idea we are born Rousseauian noble savages, or at least that the crooked timber of humanity can be straightened in a progressive fashion.

In other words, this is not a new story. The right is often accused, not always inaccurately, of thinking it has "God on its side." This claim, according to various narratives, is a terrible thing for a long list of obvious and less than obvious reasons. It causes the self-declared chosen people to turn their opponents into enemies and their enemies into demons. It breeds witch hunts and closed-mindedness.

Well, for the Left science has long been a god. Friedrich Hayek called this misuse of science as "scientism"—the assumption and claim that scientific principles can be smuggled into the world of nonscience. As we've seen, part of the genius behind Marxism's brand was its claim to be scientific. It came along at the dawn of "God's funeral" when Western Civilization was casting about for a new source of certainty, a new infallible insight to the direction and meaning of history. It's a largely forgotten insight to both Marx and Engels that they came to their communism via their atheism, and not the other way around. They hated God and sought to replace Him with a more reliable competitor. The Marxist god of science was the sole source of truth. Those who disagreed were denying not merely a "better way" but "objective" reality.

This was why the concept of "false consciousness" was so essential to communism. Any worldview, any ideology, that ran contrary to the atheist gospel of scientific socialism was delusional. Recognizing and accepting class consciousness was the secular equivalent of being born again for Jesus. Georges Sorel, the intellectual John the Baptist of both Italian Fascism and Russian Leninism, recognized that the science of Marxian scientific socialism was nonsense, but it worked extremely well as a political religion. He argued that *Das Kapital* should be seen as an "apocalyptic text . . . as a product of the spirit, as an image created for the purpose of molding consciousness."[7] This created the rationale for the Leninist vanguard of the proletariat, the intellectual high priests of Marxism who took it upon themselves to shape attitudes and wage a merciless war on backward thinking. They had the god of science on their side and that freed them up to say or do anything to deliver mankind to the next stage of history and, eventually, a new Kingdom of Heaven on Earth—the ultimate goal of the revolutionaries. "I suddenly realized that the devout Russian people no longer needed priests to pray them into heaven," wrote John Reed, the American Communist journalist in his chronicle of the Russian Revolution, *Ten Days That Shook the World*. "On earth they were building a kingdom more bright than any heaven had to offer, and for which it was a glory to die."

Not every socialist was a Marxist, in the same way that not every Protestant is a Lutheran. But these ideas were in the water. In America the progressives had their own version of the kingdom of Heaven, their own scientific gospels, their own hymns at God's funeral. The pragmatists, too, sought liberation from the old dogmas. The eugenicists set to work at weeding out the old blood lines of those unfit for the next great leap forward in history. The social gospellers sought not to defenestrate Jesus but to rebrand him as "the first socialist." But one thing united all of these disparate denominations of the church of scientific determinism: those who did not share the faith were a problem, a problem that needed to be solved.

In the late 1940s, Theodore Adorno, the Marxist sociologist and philosopher, was the lead author of perhaps the most influential—and most shoddy—piece of social science of the twentieth century. Ultimately published as a book entitled *The Authoritarian Personality*, the study purported to "prove" that holding conservative or right-wing views was a mental defect. Using the notorious "F-Scale" test (the F stood for Fascist), Adorno and his colleagues purported to have come up with an objective test to determine how protofascist—or just plain fascist—a person was. The problem was that the test—as well as the long interviews the researchers conducted—worked from the assumption that traditionalism and devotion to a strong family were both symptoms and causes of fascism (Adorno and his Frankfurt School colleagues were convinced that Nazism was spawned by the traditional German family). If that wasn't bad enough, a test designed to find totalitarian tendencies treated Communists—including outright Stalinists—and conventional American liberals as almost indistinguishable. In fact, Adorno thought that anyone who saw similarities between Nazism and communism was suffering from delusions. A methodological mess, *The Authoritarian Personality* used next to no statistical sampling and relied on tendentious interview techniques, loaded phrases, and ideological question begging.

While *The Authoritarian Personality* had its diligent critics, it electrified the liberal academic nervous system. Richard Hofstadter, one of the most influential liberal historians of the twentieth century, drank deep and long from Adorno's elixir, arguing that all political arguments could be boiled down to cheap psychological motivations. Charles Beard was a pioneer of this approach as well, arguing that the Founding Fathers were motivated by little more than their class consciousness as rich landowners. In 1958, Herbert McClosky, a trailblazer in the field of "political behavior," published his famous "Conservatism and Personality" study in the American Political Science Review. His extensive "research," complete with the "latest methods," found that the conservative "fears change, dreads disorder, and is intolerant of nonconformity," and he tends to "derogate reason and intellectuality and . . . eschew theory." These "personality types" were drawn from the ranks of "the uninformed, the poorly educated, and . . . the less intelligent," but also that they were "inflexible and unyielding" and "intolerant." To boot, the conservative "derogates reason."

How can you reason with people who are hardwired to "derogate reason"?

Throughout the 1960s, this arrogant bigotry masked as science leached into the popular political culture, finding expression in editorials, books, and even films (the General Jack D. Ripper character in the movie *Dr. Strangelove* and his phobia about Communists sapping our precious bodily fluids was a perfect satirical stand-in for the work of Adorno, McClosky, et al.). In 1964, over a thousand mental-health professionals thought nothing of signing a statement that Senator Barry Goldwater was not "psychologically fit" to be president of the United States—without ever having met him. Why? Because he was a conservative. The organizer of the petition took out an ad in the *New York Times* announcing this very scientific finding. Goldwater sued—and won.

Today textbooks from grade school to grad school are chockablock with subtle variations of this clinical bias, working from the assumption that conservatism is something to be educated out of students. In 2003, researchers at UC Berkeley's Institute of Personality and Social Research published "Political Conservatism as Motivated Social Cognition" in the *Psychological Bulletin*—one of the most prestigious journals of academic psychology. The study did no original research. Rather, it performed a meta-analysis of previous studies, some eighty-eight in all, and found—shockingly!—that conservatism is, as much now as ever was, a kind of mental defect. The methodology was the academic equivalent of shouting into an echo chamber and discovering that there are indeed echoes inside.

The press release issued by Berkeley explained that:

> Disparate conservatives share a resistance to change and acceptance of inequality. Hitler, Mussolini, and former President Ronald Reagan were individuals, but all were right-wing conservatives because they preached a return to an idealized past and condoned inequality in some form. Talk host Rush Limbaugh can be described the same way, the authors commented in a published reply to the article.[8]

Ahah. So Hitler and Mussolini—who both sought to socialize their economies, ban guns, ban dissent, ban freedom of every kind—were just like Reagan and Rush Limbaugh, who hold diametrically opposite positions in virtually every regard. Hitler was obsessive about economic and social equality—for all Germans. Mussolini never for a moment relinquished his adamantine faith—forged as a leader of the Italian Socialist Party—that he was a revolutionary. What's more, both men were devoutly atheistic enemies of Christianity, and yet the literature going back to Adorno and McClosky tells us that religious dogmatism is the soul of conservatism.

The actual paper is no better. What about authoritarian personalities like, say, Castro and Stalin? Easy! They too were conservatives. The authors write:

> There are also cases of left-wing ideologues who, once they are in power, steadfastly resist change, allegedly in the name of egalitarianism, such as Stalin or Khrushchev or Castro (see J. Martin,

> Scully, & Levitt, 1990). It is reasonable to suggest that some of these historical figures may be considered politically conservative.[9]

We are in the funhouse now. If your algorithmic whirligig spits out the finding that Joseph Stalin—the global leader of communism for two decades—and Fidel Casto—the global dashboard saint of recrudescent left-wing asininity, may now be reasonably "considered politically conservative" it's time to take the gadget out to a field and smash it with baseball bats like the printer in the movie *Office Space.* And remember: in no way were Stalin and Castro "against change." Stalin transformed eastern Europe, imposed revolutionary changes from above, attempted to create the "New Soviet Man," erase religion, and slaughtered millions. During this time the cream of the American Left defined opposition to all of this as backward and fascist.

Of course, it shouldn't be a surprise that the whirligig spit out a refined version of the garbage shoved into it. Again, there's surely some merit to the idea that our psychological wiring or our genes contribute to our political worldview. But the idea that it deeply informs our ideological precepts is deeply problematic. As I write this the Republicans are being routinely denounced for their "radical" desire to "fundamentally change" America's social contract by reforming Medicare, Medicaid, and Social Security. America's most prominent liberals have a white-knuckled grip on the status quo and fear change as ferociously as any conservative ever did. They spew poetry about the "legacy of FDR" and suggest that anyone who doesn't agree is somehow unpatriotic. Does that make them conservatives?

The market, which conservatives and libertarians want to radically expand at the expense of government, is the most powerful force for change in human history, Christianity included. And yet the supposed "market fundamentalists" are terrified of change? We are constantly told that conservatives are enthralled to extreme ideological notions and yet the whirligig says that we "eschew theory." Please.

The clearest sign that this is all a con built on a lie masquerading as science is that the overwhelming majority of this "research" seeks to find why *conservatives* are the way they are. A truly dispassionate approach would yield as many papers trying to decipher why the hell liberals are the way they are. In other words, all of this works under the assumption that liberals are normal, and conservatives are abnormal.

In fairness, some researchers do assert that liberals are the deviants—the evolutionarily superior deviants. Satoshi Kanazawa of *Psychology Today* argues that liberalism is genetically abnormal and its rise is a direct result of the fact that liberals are smarter than conservatives. He defines liberalism "in the contemporary United States as *the genuine concern for the welfare of genetically unrelated others and the willingness to contribute larger proportions of private resources for the welfare of such others*" (emphasis in original). And because mankind evolved in close-knit hunter-gatherer tribes such a worldview is "genetically novel."

Kanazawa goes on to write that, "apart from a few areas in life (such as business) where countervailing circumstances may prevail, *liberals control all institutions.* They control the institutions because liberals are on average more intelligent than conservatives and thus they are more likely to attain the highest status in any area of (evolutionarily novel) modern life." It's an engaging essay to be sure, but it's also barmy. It assumes that institutions designed to attract ideologically like-minded people are proof of liberal intellectual superiority because they attract and retain ideologically like-minded people.

The Achilles' heel of his argument can be found in his parenthetical concession that there are a "few areas in life (such as business)" where his theory falls apart. Why is business—a huge sector of American life—a contradiction to his thesis? The reason should be obvious: The institutional ideological filters do not screen out conservatives. In business, the bottom line is, well, the bottom line and not an affinity for social engineering, liberal group think, or progressive do-goodery. As a result there's no bias against conservatives. Liberals can succeed on Wall Street if they don't let their liberalism get in the way of profits. Conservatives can succeed on Wall Street if they don't let their conservatism get in the way of profits. The same goes for many institutions not driven by profit motives, like the military, law enforcement, engineering, and the hard sciences. In short, Kanazawa's argument makes complete sense if you ignore all of the things that better explain the phenomena he's describing: Culture, history, sociology, and plain old facts. Anybody who's actually looked at how academia, Hollywood, or publishing works understands that the gatekeepers aren't simply keeping stupid conservatives out; they're keeping conservatives out, period.

There are other problems with this argument. Christianity, while genetically novel, is not novel in a historic sense, and it is by his definition intrinsically liberal. After all, at the core of Christianity is the faith that we are all children of God. Also, it is a wonder that Kanazawa never considered the implications of his argument when it comes to issues of race. Blacks are woefully underrepresented in the leadership of institutions. Replace "conservative" with "black" and you have, on liberalism's own terms, a quintessentially racist argument. He might respond that there are institutional biases against blacks. But that would raise some real problems, too. After all, why should such biases exist if these institutions are run by liberals? The response would have to invoke all sorts of arguments and facts that reside outside of his crude genetic reductionism. Well, the same is true for conservatives, perhaps even more so. Liberal institutions have dedicated their vast brain power to attracting more minorities into their ranks, and to date they've failed. But they also spend considerable portions of their intelligence on keeping conservatives out of their institutions and they've succeeded.

The evidence for this bias is broad and deep. According to a 2005 tally, registered Democrats at Stanford and Berkeley outnumber registered Republicans by a ratio of 7 to 1. In all the California schools surveyed, the ratio between Democratic and Republican professors of neuroscience is a staggering 13-1. Only the departments of sociology, ethnic studies, and performing arts are more lopsided.[10] Psychologist and author Shawn Smith responding to Kanazawa writes that the field of psychology, "which is unquestionably dominated by liberals, has developed an ugly habit of falsely maligning the political right. Through respectable-looking 'research' we sling mud with flawed data and tendentious methodology."[11]

"These bogus studies," he continues, "build on each other to create an inbred, incoherent body of literature that will be cited with unquestioning faith by the next conservative-bashing researcher. And there are plenty of them. A simple PsycINFO search for the word 'Democrat' returns 324 articles. 'Republican' yields more than double, at 688 articles. Clearly, psychologists have deemed conservatives worthy of a special level of research. The bulk of that research is 'unflattering,' in the words of Professor Richard Redding, J.D., Ph.D."

Frank Sulloway, the coauthor of "Political Conservatism as Motivated Social Cognition," demonstrates how this bogus research becomes self-justifying. In a *Los Angeles Times* story about a different study—which he touted as significant, not surprising since it bolstered his own findings—Sulloway declared, "There is ample data from the history of science showing that social and political liberals indeed do tend to support major revolutions in science."[12] There's much stupidity here, given that many of the political liberals he's referring to held views that would mark them as conservatives on any of the F-scale type tests. Moreover, as Saletan notes, "When new ideas turn out to be right, liberals are vindicated. But when new ideas turn out to be wrong, they cease to be 'revolutions in science,' so it's hard to keep score of liberalism's net results."[13]

Indeed, a more evenhanded statement would be: "There's ample data from the history of science to show that liberals tend to support every fancypants new idea that comes down the block, including both successful ones like the pasteurization of milk, and incredibly evil ones like forced eugenic sterilizations." And a more honest researcher would ask: "Why are liberals always keen on heralding the Next Big Thing without any skepticism?"

As with any institution or field cosseted by groupthink, all additional biases become self-fulfilling. Already some of the scientists involved in this much hyped research have set up political consultancies where they promise to not only test brains for ideological leanings, but advise politicians and similar clients on how best to navigate all of the abnormal minds out there.[14]

The fact that liberals are more likely to embrace this stuff might be an inducement for the scientists involved to tell their potential clients—and boosters in the press—what they want to hear. And the fact that liberals are open-minded about a scientific endeavor that confirms all of their biases only reinforces the notion that liberals are open-minded and "proscience."

The hypocrisy of liberals in all of this is beyond even quantification through meta-analysis. Liberals routinely insist it is outrageous to speculate about the genetic basis or heritability of intelligence or other traits among different races and sexes, while at the same time they are giddy to entertain the notion that conservatives have broken brains—based solely on the fact that they are conservatives. One can certainly understand the trepidation about some of these taboo subjects. But how on earth to explain the enthusiasm for studies that in effect medicalize political differences?

The short answer is that this is just the latest in a long string of examples of the Left looking for ways to dismiss opposing arguments rather than grapple with them. According to science, conservatives believe those things because, like pedophiles and psychopaths, they just can't help themselves. And once you've taken that to heart, it becomes all the easier to understand why conservatives reject science when it comes to more prominent ideological priorities of the Left. Conservatives aren't skeptical about global warming because there's any science on their side; it's simply because they're hardwired to be Neanderthals. Indeed, since a great many liberals—like a great many conservatives—don't grasp the complexities of many scientific questions, they simply take it on faith that their experts are right, and since we all know liberals believe in science, that must mean that conservatives do not. Everything is so much easier when you have a god made in your own image on your side.

19
YOUTH

I got a baby's brain and an old man's heart,
Took eighteen years to get this far.
Don't always know what I'm talkin' about,
Feels like I'm livin' in the middle of doubt.
Cause I'm Eighteen
I get confused every day
Eighteen, I just don't know what to say
Eighteen, I gotta get away

—Alice Cooper, "I'm 18"

There is a little discussed fact, well established in the social science literature: Young people tend to be stupid. In fact, as a statistical matter, the younger you are, the more likely it is you will be ignorant and, frankly, dumb. While there's a lot of noise in the data, it's clear that all the way at the left end of the x axis every newborn person is what psychometricians call "a complete moron" and that condition only improves as you get less young.

This is not to say that we are born "blank slates" as René Descartes suggested. We do come with a lot of preloaded software, but that's mostly in the form of our operating system. Socrates' dialogue with Meno and the film *Baby Geniuses* notwithstanding, we simply don't *know* much when we are born. And it takes time to load our hard drives. The current scientific consensus is that the human brain doesn't finish developing until the age of twenty-five. Until then—and some would say even after—our brains are a battlefield between cognition and glandular impulses. Even young geniuses—those whiz kids who discover new chemical compounds, solve ancient mathematical conundrums, invent new places to put cheese on pizza—tend to be noticeably dimmer in other spheres of their lives. They make poor romantic decisions, overeat food that is bad for them, buy cars they can't afford, and wear Members Only jackets on first dates. Some studies have even found that large numbers of them vote for Ralph Nader.

Now, it's not entirely young peoples' fault; they were born that way. Moreover, they tend not to care for the simple reason that, all things being equal, it's a lot more fun to be young than to be old. Of course, that's not always true. Young people are also meaner to each other than older people. This is particularly sad because young people are vastly more insecure and sensitive than older people.

It helps if you think of youth as a drug. "Young people are in a condition like permanent intoxication," explained Aristotle, "because youth is sweet and they are growing." F. Scott Fitzgerald concurred. "Everybody's youth is a dream, a form of chemical madness." When you're a baby, everything is just wild. It's like you're high all the time. Your mood swings are crazy. Everything tastes so, so, so good, or so, so, so bad. Even the most trivial objects—car keys! A box of Kleenex!—can elicit joy. Liberated from every social convention, you see nothing wrong with soiling your pants, hurling food, picking your nose, or throwing a temper tantrum at the slightest insult or offense. In childhood, the high levels out a bit. You're slightly more open to reason. But you're still like a dog finding joy in incredibly simple things, like running around for no apparent purpose.

But you're still pretty dumb, though. Your financial literacy is close to zero. Throwing away your life savings on candy or comic books seems entirely reasonable. Jumping off tree limbs, playing with matches, running with scissors: It doesn't occur to you that this is all idiotic behavior. But again, you don't care because by adult standards you're higher than a moon bat.

Teen years are both better and worse. Even as your brain is starting to work out the basics of cause and effect and your long-term time horizon extends from hours to days to, if you're really mature, weeks, your body is doing all sorts of bizarre things. Like a stoner who can't contain his excitement over the prospect of watching a *Dr. Who* marathon with a case of Krispy Kreme donuts and an economy-size jug of off-brand chocolate milk, your ability to prioritize your time and energies is woefully impaired. Sure, at school you can learn about long division, the pluperfect tense, and crop rotation in the fourteenth century, but you'd much rather talk about the Situation on MTV's *Jersey Shore.* Or you might be a more substantive lad or lass and commit yourself to more serious fare, like multiplayer video games or perhaps even reading a book, such as Frank Herbert's *Dune.* After all, they do say that the Golden Age for science fiction is sixteen.

Regardless, as just about everybody reading this knows, it's an exciting, confusing, thrilling, and terrifying time ably chronicled by that ill-appreciated bard of the modern era, Alice Cooper, in his ballad "I'm 18." And it is precisely at this age that we say you can vote. I'm not categorically opposed to eighteen-year-olds voting. It's simply that in a properly ordered society, we would allow such people to vote on a case-by-case basis, if at all. We do not give drivers' licenses to people based upon their age. We say qualified—i.e., *tested*—drivers are *eligible* to apply for a license when they reach a certain age. The same, by the way, goes for military service. One is eligible to enlist or be drafted at eighteen, you don't automatically get a uniform and a gun on your eighteenth birthday.

The argument that carried the day when America was debating lowering the voting age to eighteen from twenty-one was that it was outrageous for young people (men, really) to "fight and die" to protect democracy but not participate in it at home. To which I say, fair enough. If you sign up to wear the uniform, you can have a waiver and vote early. I don't think that reform alone would put us in *Star Ship Troopers* territory. Besides, I believe that *nobody* should vote unless they pass a basic citizenship test. That goes for eighteen-year-olds and eighty-year-olds. If you can't pass the test we require of immigrants to become Americans, you shouldn't be able to vote either. One man, one vote, should be changed to one man, one *opportunity* to vote. But that's an argument for another time.

It is great fun to make these arguments to youth activists because they're so accustomed to having their propaganda applauded by condescending adults. When I tell them I'm not particularly enamored with the youth, they look at me the way my old basset hound would when I tried to feed it a grape: With total unblinking incomprehension. Then they get confused, furious, and anxious. "But . . . but . . . we are the future."

And that reminds me of the great story about Ronald Reagan, who was confronted by a bunch of screaming hippies back in his days as governor of California. They swarmed his car yelling at him for cutting education funding or some such. One fellow—who I like to imagine looked like Shaggy from *Scooby Doo*—held up a sign to Reagan's car window saying "We are the future!" Reagan quickly grabbed a pen from his suit pocket and wrote something down on a piece of paper and thrust it to his side of the window so the kid could read it. It said: "I'm selling my bonds."

For generations now, but particularly since the rise of the baby boomers, we have institutionalized the idea that young people are simply fantastic for no other reason than that they are young. It has become part of our formal educational philosophy to tell kids they are awesome for no apparent reason. When I was a kid, Saturday morning cartoons were punctuated with public service announcements informing me, "The most important person in the whole wide world is you—and you hardly even know you." Fred Rogers of *Mr. Rogers Neighborhood* used to end every episode by telling kids, "You make every day such a special day." He added, "You know how—by just your being you. You are the only person in the whole world like you, and people can like you for who you are." News flash: Some kids don't make every day such a special day.

Today the payoff is all around us. In a recent study, "Egos Inflating over Time," Jean Twenge of San Diego State University and a team of psychologists found that—you guessed it (Good for you! Gold star!)—egos are inflating over time. In particular, they concluded that America's youth are the most self-absorbed since testing began. Math, science, and English scores have stagnated, but self-regard is off the charts.[1] Way to go teachers! Twenge's findings have been corroborated and confirmed not only by other academics but a host of journalists as well. CBS's *60 Minutes* featured a whole segment on how so-called Generation Y is so full of itself that employers don't know how to communicate with their youngest workers. New employees expect to be told how wonderful they are at every turn. This is the best photocopying I've ever seen! Great job taking my phone messages! Everyone gets a trophy!

This is all the natural consequence of a political culture that nurtures the notion that young people are not only a special class but a source of special insight. Listen to liberal politicians talk about young people. It's like they're talking about business consultants from McKinsey. "They get this stuff . . ." "Young people understand that . . ." "The youth 'get it.' . . ." And, to be sure, young'ns will always be quicker on the uptake when it comes to deciphering new-fangled whirligigs and thingamajigs.

But much of what passes for the wisdom and insight of youth actually stems from the basic fact that young people are ignorant. Take the Hans Christian Andersen classic about "The Emperor's New Clothes." As the story is told, it's a fairly sweet commentary on the pretensions and pieties of the aristocracy. Still, the boy who points out that the emperor is naked does so because he's ignorant of social conventions. Because it's a fable for children, the story ends well. But it doesn't take much to imagine a more realistic narrative where the vain emperor has the child and his parents dragged off to his dungeons and dismembered. Meanwhile, in real life, the most common "emperor has no clothes" moments are not instances of stunning insight, but of mortifying embarrassment caused by the ignorant rudeness of children. Kids point out that Mrs. Smith "sure does drink a lot of wine." They announce loudly that Mr. Jones smells like cabbage and old cigarettes. Then everyone stands around, mortified.

Politically, it's worth recalling that the first modern "youth movements" of the twentieth century fueled both Italian Fascism and, more circuitously, German National Socialism.[2] It only makes sense that it would be so. Fascism, at its core, is a cult of action, unity, and contempt for the "system." All youth movements share these values. Because what the youth lack in experience and knowledge they make up for with passion and energy. America's youth movements are no exception. "In America," quipped Oscar Wilde, "the young are always ready to give those who are older than themselves the full benefit of their inexperience."

This is not to say that young people don't have their place in politics. When they bring their enthusiasm to existing institutions it is nothing short of invigorating. When they ask uninformed questions they provide a service by forcing their jaded elders to reexamine what they know or merely *think* they know. And on occasion they will bring fresh eyes to old problems, which is often (though hardly always) helpful. Besides, any movement or ideology that fails to attract new generations of adherents will, by definition, die out. "If something cannot go on forever," Herb Stein famously observed, "it will stop." And old institutions cannot go on forever without new people. Hence organizations and institutions committed to larger ideals and traditions that seek to recruit youth to their cause are fine with me. College Democrats, Young Republicans, the Catholic Youth Organization, Young Presidents' Organization, Young Americans Foundation,* and countless other similar groups are essentially fine with me, insofar as they are trying to recruit new members to an old cause ("We need the dues!").

With those caveats in mind, let me just say I find the political fetishization of youth and the whole effort to create a "youth politics" or "youth movement," alternately ludicrous and repugnant. Youth politics are the cheapest form of identity politics. They are the fake Rolex of ideological causes. At least with the identity politics of race and gender the categories are for the most part permanent. If you hire a black guy, he's going to stay black for the rest of his life (Michael Jackson being a notable exception to the rule). Young people aren't nearly so reliable.

Ever since the 1960s, young liberal activists have been working to convince themselves and everyone else that it is a requirement of youth to be liberal. This is a very old notion. Recall that famous line from Churchill about how if you're not a liberal at 20 you have no heart, and if you're not a conservative at forty you have no brain. Despite my almost unhealthy admiration for Winston Churchill, I've never liked this formulation, perhaps because I've always been a conservative of one flavor or another and I like to think I have a heart as well. Also, I've never understood why liberals are so eager to embrace this notion. "Yay! People who are ignorant and overly emotional support *us*! People with experience, maturity, and intelligence agree with *them*."

But it's also simply and patently untrue. Young people are not inher-

* Full disclosure: I have delivered many paid speeches on behalf of the Young Americans Foundation. I have been happy to do so.

ently liberal. Yet liberals—and the incredibly cloying youth activists who work for them—keep expecting otherwise. When the voting age was lowered from twenty-one to eighteen, the predicted hordes of progressive young people did not materialize to carry George McGovern to victory in 1972. Half of the eighteen-to-twenty age group stayed home, and the other half split about down the middle (52 percent McGovern, 48 percent Nixon). Though one should note that the youth vote was McGovern's best demographic.

And that should tell you something. As a matter of gross generalization, the eighteen-to-twenty-four-year-olds who cast ballots for McGovern did so as "youth voters," the ones who cast votes for Nixon were, simply, voters who happened to be young. What I mean is that liberal baby boomers have a messianic self-conception of their role in American life. They believe in a kind of secular astrology that holds that *when* you were born is as important, even more important, than where, what, or who you were born. They believed the hogwash spouted by a tiny, tiny minority of young activists, mostly living around New York City and Berkeley, that there was in fact a "youth movement" aborning. Worse, in their narcissism and nostalgia, they've never let go of the idea of youth as a political identity.

"Medicare had passed. Head Start had passed. The Civil Rights Act, the Voting Rights Act, the first African American justice [was appointed to] the United States Supreme Court. We felt like we were all in it together, that we all had responsibility for this country . . . ," explained Howard Dean in a 2003 interview with the *Washington Post* about the role the 1960s played in his worldview. "[We felt] that if one person was left behind, then America wasn't as strong or as good as it could be or as it should be. That's the kind of country that I want back.

"We felt the possibilities were unlimited then," he continued. "We were making such enormous progress. It resonates with a lot of people my age. People my age really felt that way."[3]

No. *Liberal people* Howard Dean's age really felt that way. Or to be more precise, a small fraction of liberal people with backgrounds similar to Howard Dean's felt that way. Other liberals felt there wasn't enough progress being made. You could look it up. But Dean in his splendid arrogance thinks that because he and his friends felt that way, everyone must have. In this you can glimpse the core impulse behind so much exaltation of youth in our politics. It's about power. If you can convince young people to see the world a certain way—or convince them to use a certain kind of toothpaste—you can hold on to them for the rest of their lives. So marketers, political and generic, condescend to young people, telling them how smart and discerning they are when what they really mean is closer to the opposite: they are impressionable.

Indeed, the emphasis on turning out the youth vote has little or nothing to do with the idea of getting more youthful input into our democratic system and everything to do with getting the politically and historically illiterate to vote in higher numbers for Democrats. There is no way on God's green earth all of these Hollywood "activists" would be haranguing young people to vote if they thought young people would actually vote in large numbers for Republicans. It's very similar to the role the black vote plays in Democratic politics. Because blacks vote overwhelmingly for Democrats, the party can afford to simply send buses into black neighborhoods and drive them to the polls, confident that 9 out of 10 of the votes will be for the Democrat. This also explains the constant crisis-mongering about the return of "Jim Crow" and similar nonsense.

A similar logic is at work with youth politics. Liberals yammer endlessly with high-minded platitudes about the importance of getting young people involved "in the process" and touting turnout as a public virtue in its own right. But the reality is that this rhetoric is intended to boost turnout among young liberal voters who tend not to vote very much. And while it is false to say that young people are inherently liberal (Reagan carried the youth vote by 20 points in 1984), it is true that liberal young people are easily seduced by naked appeals to youth.

In short, if you're the sort of person who takes "Rock the Vote" seriously, odds are you're either an aging baby boomer stuck in a nostalgic cocoon like Howard Dean, a cynical political consultant, or a doe-eyed youthful ignoramus who thinks the country desperately needs the full benefit of your ignorance.

20

OUNCE OF PREVENTION

> [I]nsurance companies will be required to cover, with no extra charge, routine checkups and preventive care, like mammograms and colonoscopies—because there's no reason we shouldn't be catching diseases like breast cancer and colon cancer before they get worse. That makes sense, it saves money, and it saves lives.
>
> —PRESIDENT BARACK OBAMA, REMARKS TO A JOINT SESSION OF CONGRESS, SEPTEMBER 9, 2009

"An ounce of prevention is worth a pound of cure." So said Ben Franklin (some 500 years after English Jurist Henry de Bracton said something very similar). And who can argue? What people tend to forget (or more likely never knew to begin with) is that he employed this slogan in the context of his role as the founder of the first fire insurance company in America. It doesn't mean he was wrong, but it's at least worth remembering he was making pounds of profit from ounces of other people's prevention.

Prevention can, of course, be worthwhile. It can also become an obsession and a license to spend a pound on prevention when a cure would only cost you an ounce.

Before we get to the concrete examples in public policy, consider the man who washes the after-dinner dishes, and wants to prevent creating a mess with the water that might spill on the floor or the countertop around the kitchen sink. It is very hard to wash dishes while taking care not to splatter or spill anywhere. Better to be a little messy—and more efficient—while doing the job and then correct your excesses with this amazing invention called the sponge. In other words, cures are often cheaper than prevention.

Moreover, prevention itself is not an unlimited principle. If it was, the guardrails on our highways would be one thousand feet tall.

Nowhere is Franklin's homespun wisdom more routinely invoked than in the realm of health-care policy. But surely Franklin was right when it comes to medicine. After all, didn't old Ben also say "An apple a day keeps the doctor away"?[1]

Yes, prevention for individual people or households is often, very often, less expensive than the cure. But in terms of public policy, what is cheap for individuals is not necessarily cheap for society. Ever since health economist Louise B. Russell wrote "Is Prevention Better Than Cure?" there have been hundreds of studies showing that system-wide prevention efforts very often cost more than they save.[2]

For instance, Norwegian medical researchers tracked 50,000 Norwegian men and women over twenty-five years. Forty-one percent of the men who smoked more than a pack of cigarettes a day for the full two and a half decades died between the age of forty and seventy. Among female smokers, 26 percent died. Among those who never smoked, the mortality rate was 14 and 9 percent, respectively. In short, even among those who smoked heavily, chances were that you'd make it past seventy. So, if the government acted "wisely" on the principle that an ounce of prevention is worth a pound of cure and required all smokers to undergo regular checkups for smoking related illnesses, it might have mandated chest X-rays and other tests for an absolute majority of people who would never die from smoking in the first place.

Now, many people will argue that it's still worth it to intervene early because any effort to fight smoking will save lots of lives. This is true, and as a matter of morality and medical ethics that's hard to dispute, and I wouldn't want to. But that is totally different than saying it will also save money.

Think about it—nearly every person who dies before they retire saves society money, because that way the government gets to pocket their Social Security and Medicare tax payments without paying anything back out. Moreover, the older you get, the more medical costs you accumulate. From a purely actuarial perspective, all of these people—Barack Obama, Bill Clinton, Michael Bloomberg—who claim that our health-care system needs to be reformed because our life expectancy is too low (it's not), miss the point that if we dramatically increased life expectancy in this country we would lose money on the deal, because that would mean dramatically increasing the length of time old people collect retirement benefits and increase the number of claims they make on the health-care system.

Your life is extremely valuable to you and to your loved ones, but for Uncle Sam's bean counters, you hit the point of diminishing returns the moment you stop paying taxes and start collecting taxpayer subsidies. You want to live longer because you want to live longer. And so for *you* an ounce of prevention is worth a pound of cure. But the math is reversed for the government; healthy people cost more than sick people. And, eventually, everybody gets sick and dies. That's why researchers have found time and again that over the course of a lifetime smokers and obese people (and particularly smoking obese people) cost less than healthy people. Politicians who insist that prevention will save lives are right. Politicians who insist that saving lives always saves money are wrong.

This doesn't mean we should adopt some Soylent Green remedy where we off the aged and turn them into protein-rich crackers for the productive workers. "People are important, their health is important, and we want to make their lives better in a variety of ways," Russell explained to the *Washington Post* in 2008. "The point of the medical-care system is to serve people. It is not the point of people to serve the medical-care system."[3] And yet that is exactly how many health-care bureaucrats see things. They want to get health-care costs down by rationing health care so as to ensure "the health of the system" first and foremost. This is like caring more about keeping your mechanic employed than the safety of your car.

And that is where a well-intentioned worldview becomes sinister. Underlying the desire to keep "the system" healthy is a desire for the experts to determine how others should live and, ultimately, to determine who should live. In health-care systems where the government handles all of the costs the government inexorably is forced to choose who is deserving of certain medical treatments and who is not. In Canada and the United Kingdom, you can't get some surgeries or treatments if you are overweight or past a certain age, not because of relevant medical concerns but because the government has decided you're not worth the investment. Funding for IVF treatments is increasingly rationed, which means that the government can tell certain people that they can't have children, in a sense deciding who can and cannot be born.

The liberal response to such arguments is that the market or insurance companies decide such questions now. After all, it's not like poor people have a right to affordable elective knee surgeries or fertility treatments. There are a number of problems with this argument, but one stands above all others: The government is *the government.* If you don't have enough money to buy an ad on a radio station, your free speech rights have not been violated. But if the government says you can't take out an ad because it doesn't like what you have to say, your rights *are* being violated. Similarly, when the government pays for all health care and then says you can't get a hip replacement because, well, you aren't worthy of one, that is a deeply troubling revision to the social contract.

This is where the tyranny in the cliché becomes manifest. Under progressive government, once you medicalize an issue, you politicize it. Michael Bloomberg, New York's seemingly endless mayor, has targeted everything from tobacco and trans-fats to street vendor bathroom breaks and insufficient rates of breast-feeding in the Big Apple. He does these things, with the endorsement of all the enlightened experts and commentators, on the grounds, in whole or in part, that he is preventing costly health problems down the line. That it is the "compelling interest" of the government to do so.

But what clearly motivates Bloomberg, in no small part, is the desire to tell people how they should live. The esteemed enemy of "labels" insists that is not the case. The proud non-ideologue is simply following the evidence. But that evidence is, at minimum, hotly contested and often flatly wrong.

But even if it was right, who is he to determine how others might live? The same condescension is on display when President Obama's Energy Secretary Steven Chu explains that taking away the option to purchase incandescent light bulbs is no big deal because "*we are taking away a choice that continues to let people waste their own money.*"[4] This follows on a long parade of decisions to prevent Americans from "wasting" their own money on large cars, cigarettes, tasty animal products, and so on. It's the same worldview that causes Barack Obama to despise tax rates that allow too many Americans to keep money they don't "need."

It's an old mind-set. When Herbert Hoover was the dutiful progressive food administrator in the Wilson administration during WWI he proclaimed that "Supper is one of the worst pieces of extravagance that we have in this country."[5] At least Hoover—who banned all sorts of foodstuffs from the American table—had the excuse that we were fighting a war. The problem is that progressives yearn to be wartime administrators even when we are not at war.

Forced deprivation during wartime is an old principle with much merit—*when it is warranted.* In *Democracy in America*, Alexis de Tocqueville warns: "It must not be forgotten that it is especially dangerous to enslave men in the minor details of life. For my own part, I should be inclined to think freedom less necessary in great things than in little ones." He goes on to note that in the "great things," the burden of (temporarily) lost freedom must inevitably fall "upon a small number of men." For example, in war we understand that some men (and now women)—aka soldiers—surrender the bulk of their liberties to protect the liberties of everybody else.[6]

This principle has been turned upside down by the Nanny Staters who see tyranny in such things as conscription, abortion, and surveillance of terrorists, but see nothing wrong with snapping on the metaphorical rubber glove and shoving their hands to the wrist in the posteriors of everyday people *for their own good.* If the survival of the country is at stake, who can object to the draft? If an eight-month-old fetus is in fact a baby, who can object to extending the protections of the constitution to it, even at the cost of inconveniencing the mother? But what business is it of the government to tell me what kind of potato chips I can eat?

This is the true danger of turning prevention into a governmental crusade: There's no end to it, no limiting principle. The complex of health-care activists, trial lawyers, and meddlers has become so entrenched and institutionalized that no aspect of life is beyond their

Sauron-like gaze. If it's bad for you, the government might just have to intervene, no matter how trivial the offense seems.

"Subjection in minor affairs breaks out every day and is felt by the whole community indiscriminately," de Tocqueville continued. "It does not drive men to resistance, but it crosses them at every turn, till they are led to surrender the exercise of their own will." On countless fronts, the natural pastures of daily liberty have become circumscribed by dull-witted but well-meaning bureaucrats slapping down the paving stones of good intentions on the road to Hell. But the good news is that the guard-rails getting us there are very, very high.

21
THE CATHOLIC CHURCH

Abhor that arrant Whore of Rome,
And all her blasphemies;
And drink not of her cursed cup,
Obey not her decrees
—"John Rodgers Verses," New England Primer, 1688

[I]n the Vatican—we have only to recall the Inquisition—the hands that are now raised in appeals to the Most Merciful are crimsoned. They have been steeped in blood!

—J. W. Draper, *History of the Conflict Between Religion and Science*

In this world we have seen the Roman Catholic power dying . . . for many centuries. Many a time we have gotten all ready for the funeral and found it postponed again, on account of the weather or something. . . . Apparently one of the most uncertain things in the world is the funeral of a religion.

—Mark Twain, *Following the Equator: A Journey Around the World*

The best—and most Burkean—line from the film *Animal House* is easily Delta House president Robert Hoover's passionate protest over his fraternity's expulsion from Faber College: "But sir, Delta Tau Chi has a long tradition of *existence*, both to its members and the community at large."

For the conservative, a "tradition of existence" can be a strong defense. Like sunken ships that over time become overgrown reefs for teeming colonies of sea life, some things increase in value simply by being around long enough. Social capital has a compound interest rate all its own. But old things also attract old barnacles, hard to remove and easy to confuse with the structure itself.

So it is with a slew of untruths that have evolved into defining clichés of our age. Not surprisingly, many have to do with overturning, demeaning, or diminishing the role of the Catholic Church or Christianity—and thereby Western civilization—in world history. The intent behind some of these clichés doesn't always rise to the level of an outright agenda. Sometimes simple benign ignorance is to blame, sometimes something more malignant. But underlying all of it is the notion that the Catholic Church or Christianity held humanity back for thousands of years and that it continues to do so today. Everyone likes to say that we must learn from history, but that's difficult to do when the history you're learning from didn't happen.

A Muslim Martin Luther?

Some ideas are just too good to think through. Since September 11, calls for a "Muslim Martin Luther" to reform the Islamic world can be heard with metronomic regularity. In *Ivory Towers on Sand: The Failure of Middle Eastern Studies in America*, Martin Kramer's brilliant indictment of the academic establishment, he notes that scholars of the Arab and Muslim world "were so preoccupied with 'Muslim Martin Luthers' that they never got around to producing a single serious analysis of bin Laden and his indictment of America" prior to 9/11. Worse, the faith-based conviction that the Muslim Martin Luther was around the corner was simply a rehash of biases that were common half a century ago. "The resort to the Reformation comparison in the 1990s," Kramer writes, "was but one more example of how academics kept recycling old analogies, probably without even being aware of it."[1]

As Kramer goes on to document, waiting for the Muslim Luther was a bit like waiting for Godot, because none of the candidates for the title panned out, either because they had no support in the Middle East or because they weren't in fact the moderate pluralists their boosters in the West hoped they'd be.

But the real problem with all this talk about a Muslim Martin Luther is that the analogy fails on both ends. Not only are there no Muslim Martin Luthers, Martin Luther wasn't "Martin Luther," or rather, wasn't the Martin Luther that progressives imagine him to be.

The idea seems to be that Martin Luther was some sort of moderate, soft-spoken reformer, a champion of tolerance and open inquiry. Indeed, it's telling that if you search the Internet for "Muslim Martin Luther" a sizable fraction of the results are discussions of the need for a "Muslim Martin Luther King, Jr.," as if the two figures are interchangeable. To be sure, the arrival on the scene of a Muslim Martin Luther King—an MLK to replace a KSM or OBL—would indeed be a wonderful development. Any popular movement toward nonviolence and pluralism in the Middle East would be a step forward. But the conflation of Martin Luther and Martin Luther King demonstrates some profoundly muddled thinking.

The real Martin Luther, a fiercely pious Catholic monk, did not want to split Christianity or break from the Church. He wanted to reform it. He objected that the Church was too "worldly," too corrupt, too modern, technological, rational, and intellectual. "Luther despised both intellectualism and good works," argued Erik von Kuehnelt-Leddihn, though that might be overstating it. What Luther despised was the claim that eggheadery or good deeds could substitute for faith. "Before, man could be saved *sola fide*, by faith alone."[2] Luther was even skeptical of philosophical scholasticism, believing it was tainted by the paganism of the Greeks and Romans. He loathed religious innovation and yearned to return to what he believed to be the "true faith" and the pure life of the early Church. Luther the "reformer" was a brilliant theologian but no religious moderate. He was a truer believer than most Catholics of the time (or so he would contend). One time he spilled a few drops of consecrated wine and immediately fell to the ground to lick them from the floor.

Just because the Reformation was modernizing doesn't mean the reformers saw themselves as modernizers. In fact, much of the Reformation simply seems modernizing because it was carried aloft by "modern" trends. For example, Luther's revolution may not have taken root had he not opted to address his fellow Germans in their native tongue rather than in Latin. And had the printing press not existed, it's doubtful Protestantism would have spread so rapidly. Perhaps most important, Luther and his fellow theological revolutionaries arrived—and not entirely by coincidence—as the nation-state was emerging as the primary political unit of European society.

The Reformation, and the battles that followed, were not between pluralism, moderation, and tolerance on one side and oppression and orthodoxy on the other. They were about determining how man should live in accordance with God's will. The reformers saw themselves not as 2 percent milk Christians who need attend church only on Christmas and Easter but as the true believers. Going by the definitions used by the sorts of people today searching for a "Muslim Martin Luther," they would be considered fanatics and zealots.

In riots of puritanical iconoclasm Lutherans and Calvinists burned paintings, smashed statues, and ransacked allegedly corrupt churches. If you visit museums in Switzerland you'll find one or two surviving canvasses from whole schools of painting, the rest having been consigned to bonfires by Zwlinglian or Calvinist mobs. The Dutch had their *Beeldenstorm*, or "statue storm"—also known as the "iconoclastic fury" (a fantastic name for a rock band or league of anarchist superheroes) in which religious statues across the country were pulled down in a mass frenzy. But by whatever name, the story was the same. The Protestants sought to cleanse and purge Europe of the worldly excesses and corrupt practices (including graven images) of the Catholic Church.

Theocratic regimes, morals police, executions, terror—these were all tools used by various forces of Protestantism during the early Reformation (and, in fairness, the Catholic Church often gave as good as it got). Obviously the Catholic Church saw early reformers as heretics. But the heretics believed other dissenting reformers were heretics, too. Calvinists attacked Zwinglians, Zwinglians drowned Anabaptists, Anabaptists put saran wrap on the toilet bowls of Calvinists.

This is not to say that Luther's revolution wasn't valuable. Over the long run Luther helped shepherd humanity to the uplands of history. Without Luther there is no Protestant work ethic and no Scottish

Enlightenment and none of the needed reforms within the Catholic Church. And while I have no interest in weighing the theological arguments at the heart of all this, Protestants would fairly claim that without Luther millions upon millions of souls would not be nearer to God. But the relevant point for this discussion is that the tolerance and pluralism ushered in by the Reformation wasn't necessarily part of the Protestant agenda. Rather it was the result of a bloody stalemate between opposing forces in a cataclysmic, century-spanning struggle.

Those yearning for a "Muslim Martin Luther" don't realize there are Muslim Martin Luthers all over the place, and they've been fomenting religious oppression and cruelty in the Middle East and terrorism abroad for generations now. What might be called the Muslim Protestant Reformation began a century ago, as the old Turkish caliphate of the Ottoman Empire crumbled from political, economic, and theological decay. The new Islamic Puritans wanted to restore Islam to its glory days, to a past that probably never existed. The Salafists seek a return to the Islam that existed during the first three generations after Muhammed. Ascetic, intolerant, opposed to intellectualism and innovation, the Salafists, Taliban, and Wahhabis of the twentieth and twenty-first centuries are roughly—and only roughly—analogous to the Calvinists, Lutherans, and Zwinglians (not necessarily in that order) of the fifteenth and sixteenth centuries.

Even this comparison leaves out a hugely important point: Christianity is not analogous to Islam in many fundamental theological respects. Christianity is not a religion of the sword, even if it has been misunderstood as such at times. Christianity began as a faith of peaceful martyrs who died for love. Islam began as a faith of invading soldiers who died for land. This does not mean that Islam has no peaceful traditions, or that Christianity has always lived up to its ideals, but at a theological level these are hugely important distinctions.

In 1925 Ibn Saud, a patriarch of the Saudi dynasty and a follower of the puritanical Wahhabi sect of Islam, ordered the destruction of the sacred tombs and mosques of Muhammed and his early followers. They razed Muhammed's home and the graves of the prophet's mother and first wife. The prophet's tomb was barely spared, thanks only to popular opposition. In recent years Saudi authorities have rededicated themselves to destroying the ancient art and architecture of Mecca and Medina out of the same puritanical zeal. A similar fanaticism inspired the Taliban to blow up the Bamiyan Buddhas and to ban music and even kite flying. The Iranian Revolution of 1979 was a Shia version of the Protestant Reformation of the shah's worldly, open, and modern Iran.

In short, Islam doesn't need any more Muslim Martin Luthers; it needs a pope. The Catholic Church didn't disappear after the Reformation (as you might have noticed). Instead, it launched the counterreformation under the guidance of Pope Pius III, who called the Council of Trent to address the accusations of Luther (among others) and initiate a worldwide movement of administrative reform within the Church. That process became institutionalized.

The Church adapted and had the authority and discipline to impose those adaptations. Where is there a similar institution in the world of Islam? Even when you look at some of the Muslim world's oldest institutions you still often find Holocaust deniers, apologists for terrorism, and enemies of modernity. Because these institutions don't have the power to change the attitudes of the so-called Arab street they become tools of the Arab street.

Unfortunately for Islam, the Ottoman caliphate vanished entirely in 1924, leaving nothing and no one to play the role of caliph. Islam needs a central authority that speaks for the interests of the larger Islamic world. It need not have religious authority over all Muslims, but it should have moral authority among Muslims and non-Muslims alike. There are those who say Islam itself is the problem, and expecting a caliphate to modernize and temper Islam is gravely naïve. They may be right, though I remain unconvinced. If they are right, then that is yet another reason why the quest for a Muslim Martin Luther is folly. Regardless, Islam right now has no large, authoritative institution with a "tradition of existence" that can temper the forces of zealotry and puritanism sweeping through the Muslim world.

Instead, would-be Muslim Martin Luthers and mini Mahdis issue more fatwahs than Luther had theses, telling why vast numbers of nonbelievers must be slaughtered or converted, why Islam will conquer the world, and how theological backsliding or compromise is a crime punishable by death.

The Crusades

The great irony is that the zealot-reformers who want to return to a "pure" Islam have been irredeemably corrupted by *Western* ideas. Osama bin Laden had the idea that he was fighting the "new crusaders." When George W. Bush once, inadvertently, used the word "crusade," jihadists and liberal intellectuals alike erupted with rage. It was either a damning slip of the tongue whereby Bush accidentally admitted his real crusader agenda, or it was a sign of his stunning ignorance about the Crusades. Doesn't he know what a sensitive issue the Crusades are? Doesn't he know that the Crusades belong alongside the slaughter of the Indians, slavery, and disco in the long line of Western sins?

After all, it's been in the papers for a while. In 1999, Muslim leaders demanded that Pope John Paul II apologize for the Crusades. "He has asked forgiveness from the Jews [for the Church's passivity in the face of the Holocaust], so he should ask forgiveness from the Muslims," Sheikh Ikrima Sabri, the grand mufti of Jerusalem, told the *New York Times.*[3] Across the country sports teams have been dropping their crusader mascots because they're offensive to . . . someone. Wheaton College changed their seventy-year-old team name from the Crusaders to the Thunder (no word from Thor worshippers yet as to whether they are offended). Even Campus Crusade for Christ opted to change its name to Cru partly because the word crusade has become too radioactive. "It's become a flash word for a lot of people. It harkens back to other periods of time and has a negative connotation for lots of people across the world, especially in the Middle East," Steve Sellers, the organization's vice president told *Christianity Today.* "In the '50s, crusade was the evangelistic term in the United States. Over time, different words take on different meanings to different groups."[4]

I'll say. Until fairly recently, historically speaking, Muslims used to brag about being the winners of the Crusades, not the victims of it. That is if they talked about them at all. "The Crusades could more accurately be described as a limited, belated and, in the last analysis, ineffectual response to the jihad—a failed attempt to recover by a Christian holy war what had been lost to a Muslim holy war," writes Bernard Lewis, the greatest living historian of Islam in the English language (and perhaps any language).[5] Historian Thomas Madden puts it more directly, "Now put this down in your notebook, because it will be on the test: The crusades were in every way a *defensive war.* They were the West's belated response to the Muslim conquest of fully two-thirds of the Christian world."[6]

At first the larger Muslim world didn't much care about the Christian reclamation of Jerusalem and the Holy Land. The jihad to repel the crusaders didn't start in earnest until the European forces pressed on into the Muslim Holy Lands approaching Mecca and Medina. Even then the Muslim world considered the fight to reclaim Jerusalem a sideshow. The real fight was in the East, where caliphs were rolling up victory after victory in the old Byzantine Empire. In 1291, the Muslims expelled the last of the crusaders, and all remaining Christians and Jews in the Islamic world lived as second-class citizens (though often better than Muslims or Jews might have in many parts of Christendom). By the sixteenth century, Islam's empire covered all of North Africa, Asia Minor, Arabia, and much of southern Europe. Had Islamic forces not been turned back outside the Gates of Vienna, Christianity itself may not have survived. (The battle ended in victory for the Christians on September 12, but it was the day before, marking the apex of Muslim rule, that would stick in the minds of many Muslims for the next 318 years.)

By that point the Crusades period was several centuries in the rear-view mirror, and most Muslims considered them one of their many, if minor, victories.

"In the vast Arabic historiography of the Crusades period," writes Lewis, "there is frequent reference to these invaders, who are always called 'Franks' or 'infidels.' The words 'Crusade' and 'crusader' simply do not occur." Lewis notes that the word only starts to gain wide currency in the Middle East in the nineteenth century, when Western notions of imperialism seep into the Muslim mind. And that's the irony. In the nineteenth century Europeans (and Americans) invoked the Crusades to justify their imperialist agenda. When imperialism fell into disrepute in the twentieth century, the Crusades fell with it. But the idea that twelfth-century Muslims—or even eighteenth-century Muslims—saw the Crusades as European imperial aggression is nonsense.[7] "In other words," Madden explains (writing back when bin Laden wasn't fish food), "Muslims in the Middle East—including bin Laden and his creatures—know as little about the real crusades as Americans do. Both view them in the context of the modern, rather than the medieval world. The truth is that the crusades had nothing to do with colonialism or unprovoked aggression. They were a desperate and largely unsuccessful attempt to defend against a powerful enemy."[8]

Lost in much of this discussion is that Christianity is not a Western faith imposed on the Middle East by the West. It was a faith born in the East that spread to the West. The Holy Lands were Christian for centuries before Muhammed was even born. The Crusades were launched not as a war of conquest but as a war to save Christians from Muslim persecution and conquest. Atrocities in the name of Christ were undoubtedly committed, as were atrocities in the name of Islam. One need not condone all of that. Indeed, one can single out Christianity for its hypocrisy, since the crusaders at times violated their ideals of love, forgiveness, and charity, while Islam was under no such restraint.

Regardless, to this day the Crusades myth saturates policy and academic debates as if everyone knows what they were really about. Leading textbooks continue to describe the Crusades as the dawn of Western colonialism and imperialism rather than an effort to beat back Eastern colonialism and imperialism. According to the authors of *Western Civilizations: Their History and Their Culture*: "the Crusades opened the first chapter in the history of western colonialism. . . . Western colonialism in the Holy Land was only the beginning of a long history of colonialism that has continued until modern times."[9] The often in error but never in doubt *New York Times* columnist Maureen Dowd wrote in 2003 that Bush's foreign policy had backfired because the "neocons . . . have created new terrorist-breeding swamps full of angry young Arabs who see America the same way Muslims saw Westerners in the Crusades: as Christian expansionist imperialists motivated by piety and greed."[10]

It's a bizarre turn. Robert Frost defined a liberal as someone too broad-minded to take his own side in a fight. In their desperation not to take their own side, today's anti-imperialists take at face value the flawed arguments of nineteenth- and twentieth-century imperialists just so they can condemn their own country for its imperialism. And, in their condescension, liberal commentators assume the West was always in the position of the aggressor, the hegemon, the empire builder, and that we have nothing to offer to the rest of the world but apologies. They lecture the rest of us about the burning need to understand and empathize with the frustration of the Arab street, and for Westerners to see things through their eyes so we don't breed even more terrorists (see Chapter 23, Understanding).

Meanwhile, the Muslim fanatics we are hectored to understand are recognizable to liberals precisely because they've been colonized by the same Western clichés.

Stopping the Witch Hunts

A similar dynamic can be found for the Church's various "internal Crusades" against heretics, freethinkers, Jews, and other members of the coalition of the oppressed. These crusades go by the clichéd shorthand: The Inquisition. The word is so freighted with ominous implications that merely using it suggests someone is being unfairly railroaded. If a witness on the stand or before a congressional committee complains that he is being dragged before "an inquisition," the implication is that something unfair or nefarious is going on. And suddenly the person trying to get the facts is forced to defend himself for even trying.

Communists loved to invoke the Inquisition during the Red Scare. See for example such subtly titled books as *Red Scare: Memories of the American Inquisition*, *The Boss: J. Edgar Hoover and the Great American Inquisition*, or *The Inquisition in Hollywood: Politics in the Film Community, 1930–60.* "Red Scare" itself is another such phrase that suggests an unfair ganging up on the accused. But scares can at least be based on facts. The avian flu scare, the anthrax scare after 9/11—these were driven by a real threat. The phrase "witch hunt" is even more loaded, because it assumes that there's no good reason to have an inquisition in the first place. After all, there's no such thing as a witch. That's nonsense when it comes to the McCarthy period. Joseph McCarthy was a bully and an often irresponsible loudmouth. But he was right about a very important point: There were Communists in our midst working to undermine America. Maybe not as many as McCarthy insinuated. But certainly more than those on the Left who say it was all just a witch hunt, will admit.

Let's turn to the original witch hunts of Europe. It is a fascinating, surprising field of study. Unless you are very up to date on the research it is almost surely the case that nearly everything you know about the subject is almost wholly untrue. One has to say "almost" because nearly any contention about a phenomenon that spanned wildly diverse cultures and eras will find some anecdotal support. But what is clear beyond any doubt is that the fantasies of feminists, atheists, and Wiccan propagandists (which is not to say all Wiccans), anti-Catholic bigots, Hollywood screenwriters, and some leading theorists of the Third Reich are all staggeringly wrong.

There is a bizarre yearning to claim that in the name of fighting heresy, the Church oversaw wholesale slaughter in order to impose Christianity on reluctant populations. "The witch-hunting cost the German people hundreds of thousands of mothers and women, cruelly tortured and executed," insisted Nazi SS chief Heinrich Himmler.[11] Adolf Hitler was obsessed with the witch-hunting "atrocities" committed by the Catholic Church. He blamed the joylessness of vast swaths of the Germanic world on the witch burnings of the Inquisition. "Clearly," he explained, "one must not forget that these areas are still feeling the weight of several centuries of religious oppression."[12]

Coming from a different perspective, in her *Revolution from Within* Gloria Steinem laments the "killing of nine million women healers and other pagan or nonconforming women during the centuries of change-over to Christianity."[13] Or consider the more mainstream but scandalously slanderous novel, *The Da Vinci Code*:

> The Catholic Inquisition published the book that arguably could be called the most blood-soaked publication in human history. "*Malleus Maleficarum*"—or *The Witches' Hammer*—indoctrinated the world to "the dangers of freethinking women" and instructed the clergy how to locate, torture, and destroy them. Those deemed "witches" by the Church included all female scholars, priestesses, gypsies, mystics, nature lovers, herb gatherers, and any women "suspiciously attuned to the natural world." Midwives were also killed for their heretical practice of using medical knowledge to ease the pain of childbirth—a suffering, the Church claimed, that was God's rightful punishment for Eve's partaking

> of the Apple of Knowledge, thus giving birth to the idea of Original Sin. During three hundred years of witch hunts, the Church burned at the stake an astounding five million women.[14]

Aside from the fact that there was indeed a book called *Malleus Maleficarum*—"the hammer of the witches"—everything in this passage is a hateful lie or ignorant nonsense. For the record, the best, most scholarly estimates are that somewhere around *forty-five thousand* people—not five million, and not just women (in Iceland, 90 percent of the witches were men)[15]—were killed as witches.[16] The *Malleus Maleficarum*, primarily written in 1486 by Heinrich Kraimer, a Dominican inquisitor, was purported to be the essential guidebook to identifying, trying, torturing, and killing witches. For generations it has been cited as the central evidence that the Catholic Church was a merciless persecutor of innocent women. The truth is that the Church rejected the book instantly and censured its authors. The more relevant fact is that the Catholic Church never much cared about witches, and for the most part intervened in the business of trying witches—and other alleged heretics—in order to halt bloodshed and hysteria by secular authorities and the laypeople of Europe.

In the last few decades scholars have stopped relying on the vast reservoir of propaganda about witches—and witch hunts—and started delving into the records of local towns and villages across Europe. It turns out that the most irresponsible parties in the persecution of alleged witches were not Catholic officials but neighbors of the accused, followed closely by ignorant secular authorities. Women were just as likely to turn in other women for witchcraft as men, and victims were not particularly likely to be folk healers, midwives, or keepers of some ancient tradition. Laura Miller, who surveyed the literature for *Salon* magazine in 2005, notes that accusations of witchcraft usually centered around pregnant women, births, miscarriages (only half of all babies survived to their first birthday), deformed children, and other maladies that could be ascribed to petty superstitions like the "evil eye."[17]

Most witch trials were conducted not by the Church but by the local lords and other nobles at the behest of the mob. In fact, one reason the word "inquisition" is associated with witch hunts as much as it is stems from mere terminological inexactitude. Witch trial documents often recorded a sentence "by inquisition," which simply meant "inquiry" or "investigation," but subsequent historians assumed it meant a capital-I Inquisition sanctioned by the Church.

Local officials were sometimes reluctant, other times eager to appease the people with a good witch trial. The problem was that the nobles were often just as ignorant and backward as the mob yelling "burn her!" They were reliably ill equipped to handle such cases. Innocent women were tortured and executed on absurd evidence interpreted through even more absurd reasoning. In this, the witch trial in *Monty Python and the Holy Grail* is dismayingly accurate ("If she weighs the same as a duck . . . she's made of wood!").

It was against this backdrop that the Church felt it had to intercede, to bring order, reason, and an end to such spectacles. The Church saved thousands of innocent people from horrific sentences by secular authorities. As a rule, the Church did not burn witches or heretics, contrary to popular conception. That's something the mobs or their lords did.

Also, while there were certainly witch trials throughout the Catholic Church's history, witch hysteria was essentially a product of the Reformation. "[T]he onset of large-scale witch trials," writes historian Joseph Klaits, "corresponds almost exactly with the uneven spread of reforming impulses across Christendom."[18] "During the 16th century, when the witch craze swept Europe," concurs Thomas Madden, "it was those areas with the best-developed [Catholic] inquisitions that stopped the hysteria in its tracks. In Spain and Italy, trained inquisitors investigated charges of witches' sabbaths and baby roasting and found them to be baseless. Elsewhere, particularly in Germany, secular or religious courts burned witches by the thousands."[19]

Hence this basic rule of thumb: Where the Catholic Church's authority was unquestioned, there were fewer—or no—witch trials. And when they did occur, they were saner and gentler. But where its authority was contested or nonexistent, there were more—and more barbaric—trials. Secular courts delivered death sentences. Catholic inquisitions rarely sentenced people to death, preferring dismissals or excommunication or penance.

The myth popularized by Dan Brown, Gloria Steinem, and Hitler that the Church was interested in beating back rival pagan faiths makes no sense for numerous reasons, not least the fact that the areas in question had by that time been converted to Christianity for over a thousand years. Jenny Gibbons, an avowed neopagan scholar of the subject, notes in a devastating essay, "Recent Developments in the Study of the Great European Witch Hunt": "Today, we know that there is absolutely no evidence to support this theory. When the Church was at the height of its power (11th–14th centuries) very few witches died. Persecutions did not reach epidemic levels until after the Reformation, when the Catholic Church had lost its position as Europe's indisputable moral authority."[20]

None of this erases the fact that the witch trials were an obvious barbarism. But the modern bias against institutional power and religious authority has caused us to get the causation horribly wrong. These crimes were not driven by the corrupting madness of absolute power and the Church's institutional dogmatism. Rather they were fueled by the demands of popular mobs a weakened Church could no longer hold at bay.

The Inquisition: What a Show!

We're not even close to done with the Inquisition yet. Historians specializing in the subject have all but given up trying to dispel popular misconceptions about the Inquisition (and I have no illusions that I will be any more successful than the professionals). The first misconception is that there was a single thing called the Inquisition. In fact, there were numerous individual inquisitions in countless countries over several centuries. There was an institution within the Church called the Inquisition, or the Supreme Sacred Congregation of the Roman and Universal Inquisition (Official title was *Suprema Congregatio sanctæ romanæ et universalis inquisitionis*[21] now known as the Congregation for the Doctrine of the Faith. But there were also various Inquisition movements as historians call them—the Medieval Inquisition, the Portuguese Inquisition, the Roman Inquisition, etc. There was also the famous inquisition of Galileo mentioned earlier.

Let's begin with the Medieval Inquisition. This too is a blanket term for a series of responses to heretical Christian movements in Europe in the twelfth century initially launched by Pope Lucius III in 1184. Here again the same general dynamic of the witch hunts applied. It was the secular authorities who punished heresy with death, and it was the people themselves who did most of the rounding up of heretics. The image of the Church looking under beds for heretics—so useful for defenders of Communists and others—is simply a distortion (and yes, of course, there were anecdotal exceptions).

Local lords, clerks, and bureaucrats had no idea how to determine whether someone was a heretic, unless of course the heretic made things extremely easy for the official by saying something like, "Hey, I am a heretic!" or driving a mule cart with a SATAN IS MY CO-PILOT! bumper sticker. That's why the Church was called in to provide expert advice on the question, like a theological CSI team. Most accusations of heresy under the Medieval Inquisition ended in either acquittal or a suspended sentence. Persons found guilty of "grave error" were for the most part permitted to confess their sins, perform penance, and thus be returned to the Lord's grace.

Believe it or not, most priests and monks were not, like the bishop of Hereford in *Robin Hood*, money-grubbing frauds. They were actual Christians who took an abiding interest in the souls of their flocks. And so they tended not to excommunicate total strangers on the basis of hearsay, hysteria, and innuendo.

Moreover, they weren't exactly eager to see people executed without a good reason. Indeed, the Church didn't put people to death for heresy, never mind burn them at the stake (which is not to say that it didn't endorse secular sentences when it found them warranted). Capital punishment for heresy was a secular sanction imposed by secular authorities (recall that St. Thomas More, alas, burned heretics when he was chancellor of England under Henry VIII).

The thing to keep in mind is that kings derived their authority by divine right, so heresy was perceived as a threat to their legitimacy (and charges of heresy were a useful means of eliminating political challengers). "The simple fact," writes Madden, "is that the medieval Inquisition *saved* uncounted thousands of innocent (and even not-so-innocent) people who would otherwise have been roasted by secular lords or mob rule."[22]

Ultimately, though, when you say "Inquisition," most people think only of the Spanish Inquisition. And to the extent they think of it at all, they probably think of Monty Python's hilarious running sketch that begins with: "Nobody expects the Spanish Inquisition!" Or, they remember Mel Brooks's funny but wildly fictional treatment at the end of *History of the World Part I.*

In a sense, the truth of the matter lies somewhere in between the two renditions. In the Monty Python sketch the inquisitors are led by the fearsome Cardinal Ximénez and his entourage of blood-red cloaked goons. In one famous scene (easily found on YouTube) the inquisitors interrogate an old woman, demanding that she confess her heresy. When she denies she's a heretic they threaten to torture her with soft cushions. When the poking of the cushions fails, they ominously call for—dum dum dumm!—"the comfy chair!" At the other end of the spectrum there is Mel Brooks's bizarre fantasy of what appear to be Hasidic or Ashkenazi Jews being mercilessly tortured with hot pokers and iron maidens.

Here is the truth: There was torture in the Spanish Inquisition, though surprisingly little—indeed, considerably less torture than in secular jails. In "only" 2 percent of the cases under review of the Spanish Inquisition was torture employed. No torture was permitted to last more than fifteen minutes, and in "only" 1 percent was torture used twice. It was never used a third time. A total of 1 percent of the cases ended in execution. Now, I put the word only in quotation marks for the simple reason that any use of torture is offensive and any use of torture to compel confessions of faith is beyond abhorrent. But, as I'll discuss in a moment, one has to ask, "Abhorrent compared to what?" The practices of the Muslims? The monarchies of Europe? The traditions of Asia or Africa? Such barbaric practices were a staple for roughly 98 percent of human history, and the fact that we have moved beyond them today is a thing to celebrate. But it is both Whiggish and arbitrary to single out the Church or the Spanish Inquisition as a unique offender. It's like singling out the Dutch for wearing shoes in the sixteenth century. If the dungeons and torture chambers of the Inquisition were so barbaric, why did some criminals profess their own heresy just so they could be transferred from the far crueler secular prisons to those of the Church?

But let's get back to those tortured Jews in the Mel Brooks version of the Inquisition. Not only is it absurd that Spanish (Sephardic) Jews be depicted as European (Ashkenazi) Jews—Sephardic Jews of the time would have looked more like turban-wearing Arabs—it's absurd that there are Jews in the scene at all!

No Jews were tortured in the Spanish Inquisition. Open Jews had nothing to fear from it whatsoever. The issue to be decided by the Inquisition was whether *conversos* (and Moriscos, i.e., converted Muslims) were in fact *Catholics.*

The *conversos* were descendants of Jews who had converted to Christianity in response to the rise of anti-Semitism in Spain in the fourteenth century. The ancient madness of Jew hatred arrived in Spain later than in most European lands (as a generalization, Jews have always been treated better in the Latin countries of southern Europe than in the north or east), but when it did break out it was particularly virulent. Waves of anti-Jewish hysteria erupted across the country, sometimes fueled by various kings or local Church leaders, sometimes against their wishes. Jewish quarters suffered murderous pogroms. Jews were told they must convert or leave the country. Hundreds of thousands opted to leave. Many stayed, hoping to ride out the madness. And some converted to Catholicism, becoming *conversos,* or "converts." The *conversos*—baptized Catholics of Jewish descent—thrived in Spain for nearly a century. They were an odd bunch, all things considered. Though they were practicing Catholics, they nonetheless dressed as Jews, observed many Jewish customs, and took special pride in being indirect descendants of Jesus. Madden recounts that when the *converso* bishop of Burgos, Alonso de Cartagena, prayed the Hail Mary, he would add with pride, "Holy Mary, Mother of God and my blood relative, pray for us sinners."[23]

Their success was resented both by the "Old Christians" as well as by the Jews who had refused to convert in the first place. Both groups fueled vicious conspiracy theories about *conversos* being "secret Jews" (crypto Jews sounds even more sinister). "Modern scholarship has definitively shown that, like most conspiracy theories, this one was pure imagination," writes Madden. "The vast majority of *conversos* were good Catholics who simply took pride in their Jewish heritage. Surprisingly, many modern authors—indeed, many Jewish authors—have embraced these anti-Semitic fantasies."[24]

When combined with more typical anti-Jewish hysteria, the situation in Spain rapidly escalated, and it reached a fevered pitch in the 1470s. In 1478, Queen Isabella and King Ferdinand persuaded the Vatican to sanction an inquisition into the status of the *conversos*, giving birth to the Spanish Inquisition. However, the whole enterprise was ultimately run under the authority of the crown, not the Vatican (as had become the custom at the time). Ferdinand, who relied on Jewish and *converso* advisers, believed that the investigation would not amount to much. He was wrong. False accusations multiplied. The same spirit that caused German businessmen to turn in Jewish competitors to the Nazis infected many of the old Christians. The throne encouraged well-publicized burnings of heretics. It was a repugnant spectacle; a conclusion shared by Pope Sixtus IV who, in April 1482, wrote the bishops of Spain:

> [I]n Aragon, Valencia, Mallorca, and Catalonia the Inquisition has for some time been moved not by zeal for the faith and the salvation of souls but by lust for wealth, and that many true and faithful Christians, on the testimony of enemies, rivals, slaves, and other lower and even less proper persons, have without any legitimate proof been thrust into secular prisons, tortured and condemned as relapsed heretics, deprived of their goods and property and handed over to the secular arm to be executed, to the peril of souls, setting a pernicious example, and causing disgust to many.[25]

It was not a proud or honorable moment for European Christianity or the Church—a fact the Vatican has never denied and for which it has formally apologized. Ferdinand, now utterly ensorcelled by anti-Semitic fervor, replied that the pope had been bribed with *converso* blood money. He and Isabella appointed Tomas de Torquemada to oversee the Inquisition. The Vatican hoped—in vain, alas—this would restore order to the madness. It was not until 1507, when Francisco Jiménez de Cisneros was appointed to run the Castile Inquisition, that something approaching sanity was restored. But by this point, Ferdinand and Isabella had already expelled the Jews from Spain. Some returned as *conversos* and had their property and rights restored. But the horrible stain on Spain's honor and, to a lesser extent, the Church's had indelibly sunk in. Over the course of the 350-year Spanish Inquisition some four thousand souls were put to the stake. It is worth noting that as horrible as this chapter of human history is, it is not nearly so horrible as portrayed by centuries of propagandists—first aided by the invention and spread of the printing press in the Protestant North, later by *philosophes*, secular humanists, atheists, and various flavors of socialists.

Looking back on this record some would understandably say, If that's an exoneration of the Church, I'd love to see what an indictment looks like. But my point is not to exonerate the Church from its misdeeds but to put them in context. The Church has much to atone for, and to its credit it has, repeatedly, openly, and with conviction. But to listen to various voices warning of the rise of "theocracy" in America, it seems all one has to do is say "The Inquisition" to settle all sorts of unstated, undeveloped, and unproven arguments. When one wants to proclaim that organized religion is the enemy of decency and humanity, it is easy to invoke the Inquisition or the witch trials as lazy shorthand. Religion, we are constantly told by its foes is an excuse to spill blood and set man against man. "I call Christianity the one great curse," proclaimed Nietzsche, "the one great intrinsic depravity, the one great instinct of revenge, for which no means are venomous enough, or secret, subterranean and small enough—I call it the one immortal blemish on the human race."[26] And when Christianity is on trial Catholicism is in the dock. Of course, it's also called the "opiate of the masses," a crutch for the weak-minded and superstitious. This is similar to the double bind conservatives are always caught in. We're caricatured as morons in every aspect of life save one—our capacity to orchestrate incredibly elaborate and sinister conspiracies.

But look at it from the flip side. The story of humanity is the story of man lifting himself out of the muck of blood spilled for the slightest advantage. Rousseau's noble savage never existed, not among the American Indians and not in the caves of Europe. The archeological record is abundantly clear that early humans, including allegedly peaceful farmers, routinely resorted to murder to settle differences, seize property, slaves, and women. Something like half of the remains of cave-dwelling men and other hunter-gatherers found in regions across the globe show signs that their lives ended through violence.[27] Ancient burial grounds overflowing with the skulls of men, women, and children punctured or crushed by stones, axes, sticks, and spikes testify to the fact that mankind has clawed slowly from barbarity.

Hatred of the Church, sometimes understandable, often deranged, is too often the hallmark of men whose will to power drives them to clear the field both of competing sources of authority as well as any institution that gives voice to conscience. From the Jacobins to the Kulturkampfers, to the Nazis and the Bolsheviks the witness of Christian faith has buzzed the ears of evil men to the point of distraction. In one of countless pithy ditties against religion, Voltaire proclaimed a decade before his death in 1778 that Christianity "is without a doubt the most ridiculous, the most absurd, and the most bloody [idea] to ever infect the world." He may have been a hero of free inquiry and civil liberties, but if only he had lived a little longer, he'd have seen the antireligious movement to which he lent his intellect unleash the Terror and kill in a few short years tenfold the number of men killed in three hundred years of the Spanish Inquisition. Or consider that the deaths from the Inquisition in the thirteenth century amounted to something like three per year. Between 1939 and 1945 the virulently anti-Catholic Nazis averaged that many every ninety seconds.

The Marxists who claimed to be ending the masses' addiction to religion then proceeded to slaughter those same masses at a rate unprecedented in the history of human life. The Church was intolerant of heresy to be sure, as one would expect of a *church,* but the exoneration rate of the Inquisitions is a monument to human decency and restraint compared to the inquisitions of the Communist world, which consigned men and *populations* alike to miserable deaths based on the diktats of a secular faith that the murderers in power made up as they went along. Catholic heretics had the right to a trial. Under communism whole populations did not.

John Reed, the heroic liberal journalist played by Warren Beatty in the incandescently asinine film *Reds,* dismissed complaints that the Bolsheviks were killing *fellow socialists* with a wave of his hand. "I don't give a damn for their past. I am concerned only in what this treacherous gang has been doing during the past three years. To the wall with them! I say. I have learned one mighty expressive Russian word: '*razstrellyat*' [*sic*] (execute by shooting)." Again this was the same man who wrote about his epiphany on the occasion of attending a Bolshevik funeral: "I suddenly realized that the devout Russian people no longer needed priests to pray them into heaven. On earth they were building a kingdom more bright than any heaven had to offer, and for which it was a glory to die."[28]

The celebrity atheist Sam Harris says that "the moment you shift the conversation to God, and the moral structure of the universe as decreed by religion, then all of a sudden all bets are off. You pretend to know things you absolutely and obviously cannot know."[29] But there are things that you can believe without knowing: that good is greater than evil; that lives have value; that rights exist; that the faith that God is watching you is a better check on evil than some utilitarian credo. Beliefs such as these have pulled us from the bloody muck. The forces that have known everything—or everything they needed to know—with scientific certainty have in the course of a century racked up a greater death count than all of the bishops of Rome combined.

As a fairly secular Jew I cannot and will not speak to the theological questions, in part because I do not want to, but mostly because I do not have to. The core problem with those who glibly invoke one cliché after another about the evils of organized religion and Catholicism is that they betray the progressive tendency to look back on the last two thousand years and see the Catholic Church—and Christianity generally—as holding back humanity from progress, reason, and enlightenment. They fault the Church for not knowing what could not have been known yet and for being too slow to accept new discoveries that only seem obvious to us with the benefit of hindsight. It's an odd attack from people who boast of their skepticism and yet condemn the Church for being rationally skeptical about scientific breakthroughs.

In short, they look at the tide of secularism and modernity as proof that the Church was an anchor. I put it to you that it was more of sail. Nearly everything we revere about modernity and progress—education, the rule of law, charity, decency, the notion of the universal rights of man, and reason were advanced by the Church for most of the last two thousand years.

Yes, compared to the ideal imagined by atheists and secularists this sounds like madness.

But isn't the greater madness to make a real force for good the enemy because the self-anointed forces of perfection claim to have some glorious blueprint for a flawless world sitting on a desk somewhere? It is a Whiggish and childish luxury to compare the past—or even the present—to a utopian standard. Of course there was corruption, cruelty, and hypocrisy within the Church—because the Church is a human institution. Its dark hypocrisies are the backdrop that allow us to see the luminance of the standard they have, on occasion, fallen short of. The Catholic Church was a spiritual beacon lighting the way forward compared to the world lit only by fire outside her doors.

Recall that the fall of Rome loomed large in everyone's imaginations, remaining fresh in the collective memory even centuries after. It was a powerful reminder that things didn't always get better with the passage of time. The conviction that Augustine's wheel of history only moved in a forward direction had been shattered by the collective battle-axes of barbarian hordes (Roman roads were the only reliable ones in Europe a thousand years after the sacking of Rome).

Where the Church was strong, civilization was strengthened. Where the Church was weak or absent—at least prior to the Reformation—mankind was more likely to operate according to its more barbaric default settings. Europe wasn't some land of enlightened, white-robed philosophers as depicted in Raphael's *School of Athens.* It was filthy, dark, and cruel—just like the rest of the world. The Church survived not because it was conniving and mercenary but because good men who *believed* more than they *knew* did their best to light the darkness. Many failed. Many shined that light in the wrong direction or in the right direction too late. But for all of the Church's failings—including, in all likelihood, transgressions against my own ancestors—the Church believed that it is better to light the candle than curse the darkness. And that is why it has a long tradition of existence, and so much more, to be proud of.

22

SPIRITUAL BUT NOT RELIGIOUS

YOUR KARMA RAN OVER MY DOGMA. You've no doubt seen the bumper sticker. The pun is easy to get, but the underlying point is more elusive. Most of the time, like so many bumper stickers, it's little more than a smug declaration of superiority whose appeal derives more from the appearance of cleverness rather than the reality of insight.

I have asked any number of people what it's supposed to mean. Beyond "I dunno, it's funny," the consensus goes something like this: In "Eastern" philosophy (which should mean Hinduism or Zen Buddhism but may well mean yogaism, or perhaps the state of enlightenment one attains after seeing *Kung Fu Panda* a half-dozen times while stoned) we believe in karma, while in Western theology you believe in something called "dogma." Under karma we are rewarded for our good deeds and punished for our bad ones, in this life and our next lives as humans or grasshoppers or carpet mold. But the meat-eating adherents to imperialist Western theologies of Christianity and Judaism unthinkingly take orders from ancient texts or their invisible sky god. Eastern religion is flexible, open-minded, kind, and "spiritual." It offers no dogmatic opposition to a three-way with your wife's Pilates instructor. Western theology is cramped, constipated, and mean.

It's a triumph of Hollywood marketing that this perception is so widely held. After all, it is hardly as if Christianity and Judaism are silent on the questions of how to live a good life that pleases God and perhaps turns on your karmic cruise control. According to actual experts, karma can for the most part be boiled down to "you reap what you sow," or as

Paul tells the Galatians "whatsoever a man soweth, that he shall also reap" (Galatians 6:7). And Jesus says: "'Thou shalt love the Lord thy God with all thy heart, and with all thy soul, and with all thy mind': This is the first and great commandment. And the second is like unto it: 'Thou shalt love thy neighbor as thyself.' On these two commandments hang all the law and the prophets" (Matthew 22: 37-40).

As for the Hebrews, it's a similar tale. When Rabbi Hillel was famously asked to summarize the Torah (while standing on one leg, no less) he replied, "That which is hateful to you, do not unto another: This is the whole Torah. The rest is commentary—[and now] go study."

Meanwhile, one often gets the sense from listening to Western liberal Buddhists—particularly of the Hollywood variety—that no such investigation is required. The idea of karma is all you need to know. Be nice, and everything good will follow. The problem, as the Jesuits and rabbis will tell you, is that one's conscience (i.e., the part of the mind that determines what is right and wrong) must be informed by reason. A child raised by Saddam Hussein will have a conscience, a sense of right and wrong, but we know it won't track too well with the teachings of the Dalai Lama or the pope, that is, unless I missed their respective pronouncements on the desirability of human rape and animal mutilation and vice versa (if you doubt this, Google "Uday and Qusay Hussein").

Karma is certainly a more benign philosophy than some others I can think of. One wouldn't expect riots in response to a saucy cartoon of Buddha in a Danish newspaper. If a storefront preacher vowed to burn a copy of the *Buddhavacana*, it's unlikely the State Department would have to issue warnings to Americans around the world about the potential for violent blowback (just as if you burned a copy of the *Watchtower*, the worst thing the Jehovah's Witnesses might do is come to your house and bore you to death). I certainly wouldn't fear wearing a yarmulke in the Buddhist sections of Paris.

But it's worth noting that the very concept of karma is in fact a form of dogma. Sincere Buddhists believe it is true, doctrinally, literally, dogmatically true. And there is nothing wrong with that, because there is nothing wrong with dogma. The notion that karma liberates the individual from Western, closed-minded dogmatism is true insofar as its adherents have simply changed dogmas. If I converted from Judaism to

Christianity, I would be switching one dogma for another. If I then switched to Buddhism, I would be switching dogmas again. The fact that Buddhism, at least the Western fashionable variety, is more lenient and liberating is not evidence that it is not dogmatic; it is merely evidence that it demands a whole lot less work from its adherents.

Hillel's answer has a nice echo to Buddhism in that it sounds awfully subjective. If you find something hateful, don't do it to anybody else. The difference is that for the Jew that doesn't mean you can rest on your laurels. You must study *why* it is hateful and, just as important, you must investigate what is truly hateful and what is not. The phrase "the rest is commentary" sounds dismissive in English, but it was not meant that way. Hillel believed it was vital for you to study the Talmudic commentary, which takes a lot of time and effort, and is why so many "spiritual" people have taken to studying the "Kaballah" instead. I put Kaballah in quotes because the real Kaballah is a branch of Jewish mysticism that even the most learned rabbis aren't supposed to even attempt to grapple with until they are at least forty years old. For Madonna it's a fun waste of an afternoon. Or as the Jenna Maroney character on NBC's *30 Rock* says, "It mixes the fun part of Judaism with magic."

The same goes for much of what passes for Buddhism in the West. Obviously there are many sincere and informed Buddhists in America. And even many of the champions of the watered-down lifestyle Buddhism we associate with Hollywood and yoga fetishists with silly bumper stickers have made useful contributions on issues such as the oppression of Tibet.

But at a very basic level, the fascination with Buddhism and "Eastern philosophy" is really no more than an age-old desire to appeal to the authority of what we don't understand to support what we already believe. It's a lot like the folks who complain about how we do things in "this country," as if they know how things are done in other countries. As the Dalai Lama himself has admitted more than once, he has become a global brand of mystical niceness. Or, as no less a theologian than Sharon Stone says, he's "the hardest-working man in spirituality." When he signed on to Apple's "Think Differently" campaign the Dalai Lama explained, "I am what you want me to be. I am a screen saver for computers? People can use me as they want."[1] Indeed they will.

According to dogmatic Buddhism, abortion and homosexuality are bad (abortion, he says, is "an act of killing"). But he doesn't talk about that in the West, because it would hurt his brand. When he released his book in Great Britain, his editors successfully got him to water down his pro-life beliefs and cut his references to homosexuality entirely. No less than *Salon* magazine described him as "Gandhi meets P.T. Barnum, minus the elephants."[2]

Let's leave the Dalai Lama alone for a minute, since he is basically a decent chap. Consider instead *Avatar*, the highest grossing film of all time. The film was a CGI exoskeleton of trite Hollywood tropes—*Dances with Wolves*, *Pocahontas*, et al.—covered in a digital 3D epidermis. Heroic noble savages are tied together by a spiritual Gaia-like life force and must fend off the evil, white, land rapists, with the aid of a white man who has been reborn as one of the natives. This was an old idea when I first saw *A Man Called Horse* thirty years ago. Indeed, the "genius" of the film wasn't to offer a controversial narrative about environmental spiritualism. The genius was in finding a way to peddle precisely the sort of New Age propaganda Hollywood (and, for that matter, the public schools) have been peddling for nearly half a century now. What would have been truly controversial and subversive to the prevailing Hollywood ethos would have been to make the heroes born-again Christians or, even better, Hasidic Jews.

When conservatives panned the unoriginality of James Cameron's script—tellingly, a script he had written twenty years earlier—defenders of the film went ballistic about the inability of conservatives to appreciate spirituality. This is a hard charge to take seriously from the same quarter that routinely mocks religious believers for being, well, believers.

I love having conversations with people who deride organized religion as so much superstition and magic, but who don't have any problem with superstition and magic when it is *disorganized*.

There are vast numbers of people on the left who hold two positions simultaneously: 1) Organized religion is a sham and a source of evil in everyday life; and 2) There are rich mystical, spiritual, and supernatural forces at work in the universe working apart from traditional religions. A great many feminist theorists endorse a hodgepodge of faiths, from Wicca to Gaia theory. New Agers snort and guffaw at traditional religion while at the same time worshipping crystals and blathering on about how they were scullery maids in the fourteenth century.

This worldview infects popular culture in myriad ways. Consider one admittedly minor example. When Disney came out with *The Princess and the Frog* it was hailed as a progressive triumph because the protagonist was a black princess. I have no objection to that. But the actual plot of the film rests on the prevalence of voodoo in New Orleans. Dr. Facilier, the villain of the tale is, in the words of Rod Dreher, "a big, bad French Quarter voodoo daddy who tries to manipulate evil spirits to do his bidding." As Dreher notes, New Orleans is saturated with Catholic mysticism, but rather than draw on that tradition, Disney felt it had to go another way: "a kooky Atchafalaya Oprah" of a white magic priestess. "My complaint is not religious," Dreher writes, "but artistic. Disney's politically correct aversion to Christianity hollows out the potential for spiritual grandeur that ought to have infused this lovely film," opting instead to go the safer route of clichéd dreck. "It's not so much anti-Christian prejudice as it is fear of real faith, and a failure of imagination. And when it comes to creating film fantasy, that's an unforgivable sin."[3]

When then first lady Hillary Clinton introduced her "politics of meaning," she was derided for trying to concoct a New Age spirituality that just so happened to support her political agenda in all of its particulars. Charles Krauthammer called it a "cross between Jimmy Carter's malaise speech and a term paper on *Siddhartha* . . . delivered with the knowing self-assurance, the superior air of a college student manifesto."[4]

Norman Lear, founder of People for the American Way, rushed to her defense. "The sophisticates of our politics, our culture and the media," Lear opined, "are embarrassed to talk seriously about the life of the spirit. . . . Our obsession with numbers, the quantifiable, the immediate, has cost us our connection with that place in each of us that honors the unquantifiable and eternal—our capacity for awe, wonder and mystery; that place where acts of faith in a process larger than ourselves, prove ultimately satisfying in the fullness of time."[5] It was an odd complaint coming from the man who devotes so much time, energy, and money to the idea that we must construct a high wall between church and state.

The oddness can be explained by the simple fact that spirituality is what liberals invoke when they want to combine the fun part of liberalism with magic.

23
UNDERSTANDING

> Peace cannot be achieved through violence; it can only be attained through understanding.
>
> —Ralph Waldo Emerson

In Monty Python's *Life of Brian*, the People's Front of Judea could not abide the Judean People's Front, never mind the Judean Popular People's Front or the obviously ridiculous People's Front of Judea. In one scene the People's Front of Judea hatches a plan to kidnap Pontius Pilate's wife, only to run into members of the Campaign for Free Galilee. They immediately begin to fight over which group first had the idea to kidnap Mrs. Pilate. Finally, Brian cries out that they must stop their squabbling and unite "against the common enemy." The assembled rebels then shout as one: "the Judean People's Front!"

But even this brief moment of solidarity quickly unravels as the two factions resume their fighting, with two Roman soldiers watching the whole spectacle. Finally, Brian is the only one left alive. Then the Romans capture him.

The absurdity of the scene is hardly an indictment against its plausibility, for few inanities are more widely held than the notion that increased understanding must lead to peace and solidarity.

How often do we hear variations of this idea that understanding brings peace? It's a staple of the liberal view of the world that peace comes with mutual understanding; when people get to know each other, they don't kill each other. "If we could just get both sides in a room to talk this out . . ." is the beginning (and end) of wisdom for this crowd. If only X could walk a mile in the shoes of Y. Meanwhile, as discussed earlier, the corollary to all of this is that violence only begets more violence. It's almost as if the Pax Romana, the Pax Britannica, and the Pax Americana were all the results of intensive group therapy sessions in which the leaders of these regimes simply hugged out all their differences.

The fetishization of understanding as a cure-all is a pristine example of radically utopian thinking hiding in plain sight under the camouflage of a harmless cliché. Look around the world today for the sources of the most intractable, bloody, and passionate strife. Is it ever between groups that don't understand each other? Palestinians watch Israeli TV. They work alongside Israelis. Many Palestinians speak Hebrew, and many Israelis speak Arabic. They share thousands of years worth of overlapping history, culture, and cuisine. And yet, according to a recent poll—conducted by Stanley Greenberg and sponsored by a propeace process and pro-Palestinian outfit—73 percent of Palestinians agree with the Koranic injunction to slay Jews where they hide, referenced in the Hamas charter.[1] If only they understood each other better!

The simple fact is that Israelis and Palestinians understand each other far better than American or Western activists understand either, and that more understanding has only led to more hatred.

The evidence is overwhelming on the global scale. Greeks and Turks, North Koreans and South Koreans, Serbs and Croats, Crips and Bloods, Irish and English, Irish Catholic and Irish Protestant, Springfielders and Shelbyvillians, Red Sox fans and Yankees fans: It is almost always the peoples who understand each other best who have the worst conflicts.

Meanwhile, there have been no significant conflicts between Poles and Guatemalans, or between Ukrainians and Native Americans. The Crips don't give a moment's thought to the American Society of Engineers and the Bloods do not spend their days planning drive-by shootings against the Belgian Lesbian Chess Master Association.

Russell Jacoby demonstrates in his book *Bloodlust* that throughout human history civil wars have always been bloodier and crueler than wars with "external" enemies.[2] For example, in Thucydides' account of the lead-up to the Peloponnesian War, he chronicles how the battle for

Corfu (then Corcyra) set off a wave of bloodshed that dwarfed what you might expect in a mere war. When the Athenians arrived off the coast, the pro-Athenian faction set out to massacre their domestic enemies. For a full week the Athenians waited in the harbor as the Corcyreans "continued to massacre those of their own [fellow] citizens. . . . There was death in every shape and form," according to Thucydides. "[P]eople went to every extreme and beyond it. There were fathers who killed their sons; men were dragged from the temples or butchered on the very altars." "Blood ties became more foreign than factional ones," adds Jacoby, as whole families divided against themselves.[3] Did the families not understand each other?

Consider the schism between Pakistan and India, arguably the most likely source of the world's first nuclear war. Both are relatively new countries but were essentially the same nation for most of their existence. When they were both part of British India—and various other empires—their heritage was, for the most part, a common one. Today, of course, Pakistan is constitutionally an Islamic country (the name means "Land of the Pure"—that is, pure Muslims), while India is predominantly Hindu, though constitutionally secular (though it's worth remembering that there are nearly the same number of Muslims in India today as there are in Pakistan).

More to the point, ethnically, culturally, historically, and geographically, Pakistan and India have far more in common than they have separating them. Pervez Musharraf, the former president of Pakistan, was born in India. One of India's leading Hindu nationalists, L. K. Advani, hails from what is now Pakistan. Like millions of Indians and Pakistanis, these leaders understand both the grievances of their neighbors and their arguments. And yet these two countries are constantly flirting with armed conflict when they're not actually at war.

Meanwhile, let's not forget it wasn't a Muslim who assassinated Gandhi, but a Hindu. It wasn't an Arab who killed Yitzhak Rabin, but a Jew.

Hatred and animosity from ancient Mesopotamia to the present day has more often than not been driven by what Sigmund Freud dubbed the "narcissism of minor differences." (In fairness. he was developing the work of British anthropologist Ernest Crawley, who conceived the concept first.) He first used the phrase in an essay, "The Taboo of Virginity," to describe males' fear of women as alien and scary. It is "precisely the minor differences in people who are otherwise alike that form the basis of feelings of strangeness and hostility between them," Freud wrote in 1919. He developed the idea into a theory of geopolitics in his classic *Civilization and Its Discontents.* Hatred of your neighbor is simply more "natural" than hatred of the true stranger. "It is always possible to bind together a considerable number of people in love, so long as there are other people left over to receive the manifestations of their aggressiveness."[4]

The evidence of the phenomena is all around you. College professors who agree on everything except who deserves the better parking space and the importance of sexual mores in the novels of Sinclair Lewis hate each other with the heat of a thousand burning suns. In the 1990s Republicans tended to revile Bill Clinton in no small part because he moved his party rightward. On the Internet you can see the phenomenon in all its hypocritical splendor. Some on the left will dismiss Islamic fanatics who burn women, crush homosexuals, behead Jews, and throw acid in the face of schoolgirls. But if some right-wing pundit makes the slightest politically incorrect gaffe, he must be pelted from the public stage. It's hard not to notice that many on the left seem to revile the "Taliban wing of the Republican Party" more than they revile the Taliban itself.[5]

There's even an offshoot of the phenomenon in the fields of robotics and computer animation called the "uncanny valley." Masahiro Mori, a Japanese pioneer in robotics, coined the term drawing on the writings of Freud and others. The theory of the uncanny valley holds that the more realistic a replica of a human being becomes, the creepier it gets. We don't mind looking at cute robots or the Man in the Yellow Hat in *Curious George.* But Tom Hanks in *The Polar Express,* Japanese sex robots, or the entire cast of *Mars Needs Moms* elicits feelings of revulsion in many people, and even in monkeys (though apparently not the typical Japanese sex robot connoisseur).[6] Personally, I've always suspected that the conventional wisdom about Al Gore had it backward. He didn't turn people off because he's so robotic; he turned them off because he's so lifelike.

Freud notes that the global phenomenon of anti-Semitism can be attributed in large part to the narcissism of small differences. Throughout history Jews have been the quintessential insider-outsiders. "In this respect the Jewish people, scattered everywhere, have rendered most useful services to the civilizations of the countries that have been their hosts; but unfortunately all the massacres of the Jews in the Middle Ages did not suffice to make that period more peaceful and secure for their Christian fellows."[7] Freud was hardly surprised that German nationalism rode to power on the back of anti-Semitism. Indeed, genocidal anti-Semitism emerged in a country where Jews were the most assimilated. Understanding between a non-Jewish majority and a Jewish minority was higher in Germany in the late 1920s and early 1930s than almost any place in the world, and we all know how that turned out.

If mutual ignorance were the author of war, then Mexico would be once again preparing for battle with the people of Moldova. And yet I'm sure you could waste the better part of a week trying to find a Mexican (or an American) with a strong opinion about Moldova one way or another.

Indeed, ignorance is often the source of love. Not real love, to be sure. But professed love. Who can forget the character of Mrs. Jellyby in Charles Dickens's *Bleak House*. Mrs. Jellyby is "a lady of very remarkable strength of character, who devotes herself entirely to the public." She is obsessed with the plight of the Borrioboola-Gha tribe on the banks of the Niger River. So concerned with their plight, she ignores the well-being of her own children. Mrs. Jellyby is one of those people who "had a curious habit of seeming to look a long way off. As if . . . they could see nothing nearer than Africa."[8] Who among us has not met a Mrs. Jellyby whose concern for people she doesn't know or truly understand overrides her or his concern for the people she actually loves—or is supposed to?

The confusion over understanding undoubtedly has ideological roots, but it is more directly fueled by the common mistake of misapplying the rules of people to the rules of *peoples*. On an individual level, it's quite common for a good conversation—perhaps even a "beer summit"—to clear the air of animosity. Though even here, the evidence is mixed. The most enduring hatreds are between former friends, members of the same family, or champions of lost causes. Consider, for example, Ishaq Levin and Zablon Simintov, the last two Jews of Kabul. Levin and Simontov were the last Jews living in Kabul after eight hundred years. They lived in the same run-down synagogue, but refused to speak to each other save to exchange insults and, more often, obscene gestures.

In modern times the most reliable—not foolproof, just reliable—engine of peace is not lofty dialogue or religion, or frilly exhortations but lowly, mercenary trade. The Austro-Hungarian Empire was a grab bag of different nationalities, religions, and ethnicities. What held it together more than anything else were common economic interests. From time immemorial the most bloodthirsty people in the world have been willing to put aside their differences in the cause of commerce. Mobsters tolerate those they find intolerable in the name of business. Modern democracies do not declare war on each other for numerous reasons, but near the top of the list is the fact that citizens recognize their interconnected economic interests. The cold peace between China and the United States may not be as strong and as healthy as anybody would like, but the sinews of the bond are surely our economic interdependence.

Marxist-Leninst doctrine holds that capitalism is based on war, but Montesquieu had it right: "Peace is the natural effect of trade. Two nations who traffic with each other become reciprocally dependent; for if one has an interest in buying, the other has an interest in selling; and thus their union is founded on their mutual necessities."[9] Daniel Griswold of the Cato Institute notes the global boom in trade has coincided with, and fueled, the decline in cross-border wars. Free trade agreements around the world expanded the incentives of nations to settle their conflicts peacefully.[10] University of California San Diego political scientist Erik Gartzke compiled data on economic freedom around the globe and gave each nation a ranking from 1 (most unfree) to 10 (most free). Examining military conflicts between 1816 and 2000, he found that nations ranking with a score of 2 or less were 14 times more likely to be engaged in hostilities than countries with a score of 8 or higher. Meanwhile, the annual death toll from war fell to its lowest point since World War II in 2005, thanks largely to the decline in interstate war. Between 2001 and 2010, only two of the twenty-nine major military conflicts in the world were interstate; the rest were wars between groups of people interested in killing people they understood most.[11] Meanwhile, wars between people who understood each other least continued to decline, in no small part because one of the only things they cared to know about each other was that they delivered goods and services on time or that their checks cleared. Commerce isn't as romantic as peace, love, and understanding. But that's what's so funny about peace, love, and understanding; sometimes they're beside the point.

24
DEMOCRACY AND UNITY

"An atavistic longing after the life of the noble savage is the main source of the collectivist tradition."

—FRIEDRICH HAYEK, *THE FATAL CONCEIT*

In 1928, then New York governor Al Smith famously said, "All the ills of democracy can be cured by more democracy."

This, of course, is high-proof nonsense. Where else do we talk this way? All the ills of gluttony can be cured by more eating? All the ills of pollution can be cured by more pollution? All the ills of disco can be cured with more disco? Aha, but that's not fair. Those are all bad things, and democracy is a good thing, a wonderful thing, a sacred thing. And, indeed, it is all that (though reasonable people might argue about the sacred part).

But there's a reason why we say you can have too much of a good thing. Love may be the only exception, and even there there are caveats. Too much unrequited love is an invitation to sorrow and, in certain instances, an excuse to pay through the nose for a telescope-lensed camera to spy on the subject of your affections. More seriously, while it's difficult to imagine a man could have too much love for his wife or a mother for her child, it is obvious that the phrase "love is all you need" is demonstrably wrong. You also need food, clothing, and shelter. You need marketable skills, a good work ethic, and a sense of responsibility. The tagline for the film *I Am Sam* was "Love is all you need." The story was about a severely mentally disabled man who insisted he could raise his daughter because, while he couldn't navigate daily life, he loved his daughter so very much. It was a saccharine but ultimately outrageous message to send. Many terrible fathers rotting in prison love their children very much. The reason they are in prison and are bad fathers is that they needed a good deal more than love to successfully honor their obligations as fathers and as citizens.

Anyway, something similar goes for democracy. It is a necessary but not sufficient ingredient of the good society. And let us remember that the perfect society—Heaven—is an absolute dictatorship where God rules absolutely. In fact, the best form of government is, in theory, enlightened dictatorship. Again theoretically, a dictatorship can protect freedom of speech, association, etc., better than any other institution. In practice, however, it doesn't work like that at all. Even if you could come up with a perfect dictator—what my ancestors called "the good czar"—there's no way to make sure such an institution would last beyond a single lifetime. This is true for many reasons, but one of the most overlooked is that the power we would be willing to bequeath to an infinitely just, wise, and kind ruler is precisely the power that would make it impossible to remove an evil, cruel, or dumb one. History shows that even halfway decent absolute rulers tend to be replaced by pretty crappy ones. The most decent dictators recognize the problem and set it up so that they are the last dictators. That's essentially what Franco and Pinochet did, yet they were still men whose sins and crimes make it quite unlikely that their souls will have an easy time of it in the hereafter.

A more accurate formulation of Smith's sentiment would be that more democracy is the cure to all the ills that come from a lack of democracy. Meanwhile, too much democracy makes all the ills of democracy worse. The same is true for all the ingredients of a healthy civilization. More order is a remedy for the ills of too much disorder. More freedom is a remedy for the ills of too little freedom. Food, after all, cures starvation. But food does not cure spontaneous human combustion or prevent meteor strikes. More democracy will not solve problems that are caused by either too much democracy or that simply have nothing to do with it. Simply put, there's such a thing as too much democracy.

A pure democracy, one unalloyed by republican institutions and virtues, is merely a populist dystopia where 51 percent of the people get to pee in the cornflakes of 49 percent of the people. A society without courts, codes, and laws is government by mob rule, the purest form of pure democracy. Even societies with laws and courts that put all authority and power in the hands of the elected can be despotic. As Thomas Jefferson put it in his *Notes on the State of Virginia* (quoted at length in *Federalist* 48), concentrating all of the powers of government in the hands of a legislature does not insulate against the dangers of tyranny. Rather, to do so "is precisely the definition of despotic government. It will be no alleviation, that these powers will be exercised by a plurality of hands, and not by a single one. One hundred and seventy-three despots would surely be as oppressive as one. Let those who doubt it, turn their eyes on the republic of Venice."[1]

All too often we throw the cheap paint of democracy over the edifice of despotism and think no one will notice the whitewash. The United Nations General Assembly is a mosh pit of "world leaders." Some so-called leaders represent decent and honest democratic regimes. Others are merely the bureaucratic lickspittles and yes-men of organized barbarisms and tin-pot tyrannies. "The world voted" to condemn Israel, they say, after the roll was called in the United Nations. The world did no such thing.

But even if it did, even if the UN really was the "parliament of man," so what? Voting isn't alchemy; it cannot transform the leaden dross of wrong into the gold of right. If the world votes on the issue of whether two plus two is four, the fact that the sum is four will not be changed if 51 percent say it is five. In America we have a Bill of Rights precisely to protect us from the tyranny of majorities. The simple fact is that the Southern slave-holding states were not merely tyrannies; they were *democratic* tyrannies.* Even if blacks enjoyed the vote in all likelihood they would have been outvoted on the issue of slavery in most of the slave states. The results of that vote would not have changed the moral equities of the issue one iota. That a certain despotism is democratic is as relevant as the color of a bullwhip lashing your back.

Madison likewise understood that the majority was no less apt to impose tyranny from below:

* The two obvious exceptions to this are South Carolina and Mississippi, where the slave population actually exceeded the nonslave population for most of the years preceding the Civil War.

> Since the general civilization of mankind, I believe there are more instances of the abridgment of freedom of the people by gradual and silent encroachments of those in power than by violent and sudden usurpations. On a candid examination of history we shall find that turbulence, violence, and abuse of power by the majority trampling on the rights of the minority, have produced factions and commotions, which in republics, have more frequently than any other cause produced despotism. If we go over the whole history of the ancient and modern republics, we shall find their destruction to have generally resulted from those causes.[2]

This is why Madison, Jefferson, and their colleagues established a system of government that pitted faction against faction, institution against institution. *The Federalist Papers*—the greatest instruction manual ever written for democratic, republican government—is one extended essay on this point. We have separation of powers, checks and balances, and divided government from the federal level down to the county seat so as to divide, dilute, and diminish power in any one place.

(Lost on many conservatives is the fact that the two core stanchions undergirding the American system are quite simply *unnatural.* Democracy is not natural. Capitalism is not natural. Both depend on and exploit natural phenomena—self-interest, the yearning for respect—just as a house depends on stone, wood, and metal. But you won't find a naturally occurring house in the woods, will you? Capitalism is the greatest system ever created for peacefully universalizing prosperity, but it doesn't feel like it because it is unnatural. Democracy is the noblest of experiments; you will be hard-pressed to find a tribe putting everything up for a vote as a matter of custom and ritual, never mind binding law.)

Very few people on the left or right disagree with this when their most treasured liberties are at risk. Progressives as a group do not believe that the majority can vote to deny gays the right to marry and conservatives as a group do not believe that the majority can vote to erase the right to bear arms.

Still, both left and right often fail to appreciate the scope of the Founders' wisdom. Anyone who's taken high school civics understands that the Constitution limits what the government can do. But too many do not recognize that by extension it necessarily limits what *the people* can do. We live in a representative system, but even a government that faithfully represents the wishes of the people cannot do what the people want if what the people want is unconstitutional.

At least in theory.

In practice the government has often done wrong because "the people" wanted to do wrong. The government did wrong and violated the Constitution (not always the same thing) repeatedly under Woodrow Wilson and FDR, in large part because the people either wanted it to or allowed it to. The Supreme Court overturned much of the early New Deal as unconstitutional and would have continued to had Franklin Roosevelt not scandalously bullied the Court into reversing itself in the famous "switch in time that saved nine."

There is a tendency in American politics to argue that the people cannot be wrong simply because the people are sovereign. But sovereigns—be they plural or singular—can always be wrong.

This is a point of considerable confusion. Power worship muddies the mind of democrats and autocrats alike. There's a vast swath of political discourse that begins and ends with the proposition that if the people are for it, it must be right. We usually call the extreme forms of this mind-set populism. "The people of Nebraska are for free silver and I am for free silver," announced William Jennings Bryan. "I will look up the arguments later." Or as Willie Stark says to the nurturing crowd in *All the King's Men*: "Your will is my strength. Your need is my justice."[3]

Populism is such a seductive intoxicant that it often infects mainstream political analysis. Liberal strategists have convinced themselves that if we just got everyone to vote, the people would force through policies held at bay by our antiquated and undemocratic system. Hence the various schemes to return the franchise to felons, lower the voting age, or let people vote online. Not surprisingly, these efforts are invariably aimed at constituencies they have good reason to believe will vote Democratic. What it says about the Democratic Party that boosting the number of ballots of the criminal, the less educated, and the lazy will deliver liberal policy victories is something to ponder. But the simple fact is that if everyone voted the results of elections would not change very much, if at all. This has been the record of past sweeping expansions of the franchise to women and eighteen- to twenty-one-year-olds (the record of giving the franchise to blacks is more mixed).

But at a broader level this obsession with expanding democracy by making it easier to vote is deeply unhealthy. Making voting easier is synonymous with making voting cheaper. Do we really think the level of democratic discourse would be greatly improved if people who could not otherwise be bothered to vote are afforded the opportunity to do so on their iPhones during a commercial break of *Jersey Shore*? In 2008 Arizona considered a proposal to turn your vote receipt into a lottery ticket on the assumption that what our politics desperately needs is more input from the crowds lining up to play Keno, or to buy Mega Millions tickets.

As discussed elsewhere in this book, the reason democratic capitalism has always been beset on all sides by movements eager to "move past" or "transcend" it is that, like water seeking its own level, humans have an innate desire to return to form. We hang rationalizations and extravagant theories on our natural human impulse to live tribally and call it a new idea. We reify our yearning for the security of family and tribe. All of the -isms opposed to democratic capitalism are in this sense reactionary, because they seek to restore the Old Order of Man written in our genes. Speaking outside the limiting jargon of political science, the only true revolution in the history of mankind is the Anglo-American revolution. And until we find a way to rewrite our programming at the genetic level, that revolution will remain a fragile one. We pedal forward, constantly, or we fall.

It is because of this elemental fact of the human condition that the most appealing clichés are the ones that cut through our reasoning minds and fire up our inner tribesman. The principle is easy enough to understand. If I shout "fire," your thinking mind is likely to put itself on pause and let the animal brain take over. Firefighters must be trained to suppress their natural fears. Soldiers must be trained not to let their natural instincts conquer them.

But not all appeals are quite so primal. Woodrow Wilson in his famous "Leaders of Men" essay explained that a "true leader" must play on men's passions, not their intellects. "[O]nly a very gross substance of concrete conception can make any impression on the minds of the masses," Wilson wrote.

"[T]hey must get their ideas very absolutely put, and are much readier to receive a half truth which they can understand than a whole truth which has too many sides to be seen all at once," Wilson explained. "The competent leader of men cares little for the internal niceties of other people's characters: he cares much-everything for the external uses to which they may be put. . . . He supplies the power; others supply only the materials upon which that power operates. . . . It is the power which dictates, dominates; the materials yield. Men are as clay in the hands of the consummate leader." Wilson, a craven lover of power for its own sake, is making the intellectual case for demagoguery.[4]

Cynical though it may be, Wilson was nonetheless onto a fundamental truth. What rouses the crowd is not dispassionate analysis and pertinent data. Appeals to our animal brain are what get people to rise to their feet and do the bidding of "leaders of men." And while my loathing of Wilson should be evident, it must be pointed out that this is in no way a uniquely evil insight. Martin Luther King, Jr.'s speeches spoke to our ideals, but also to our deepest selves. Football coaches do not explain in dry statistics why it would be good to win the game. When officers extract the last full measure of devotion from their troops, they don't do so with PowerPoint presentations alone. In short, it is what we do with these appeals that matters. This illuminates the great danger in the ubiquitous appeals to unity in our politics. How many speeches have we heard explaining that there's nothing we can't do if we all stick together? The problem with such appeals is that they tend to skip over the fact that people disagree, and that such dissent is valid. Like the No Labelers, unity worshippers want to ignore this inconvenient truth and hector the dissenter to drop his objections and fall in line. The upshot of countless liberal arguments is that unity is wonderful, so you should gladly open your wallets and give the government more money.

"Unity is how we shall overcome," Barack Obama proclaimed on Martin Luther King Day 2008, in arguably his best campaign speech. "Unity is the great need of the hour—the great need of this hour," he added, echoing King himself. "All too often when we talk about unity in this country, we've come to believe that it can be purchased on the cheap." Again and again, in ways subtle and overt, Obama returned to this theme of unity over the course of his campaign. "We are the ones we've been waiting for!" became a sort of spiritual mantra. Even his debut on the national stage in 2004 was all about unity—red and blue America coming together under a common god. One of the most brilliant props of his campaign was the crowd. The campaign used huge, massive, crowds electric with excitement not just to communicate enthusiasm for the candidate but to signal a kind of ethic. In *Crowds and Power*, Nobel laureate Elias Canetti writes that crowds are incredibly powerful psychological tools both for those in them and those looking at them. They speak a language all their own; "distinctions are thrown off and all feel *equal*. . . . It is for the sake of this blessed moment, when no one is greater or better than another, that people become a crowd."[5]

Roughly three years into his presidency, on December 6, 2011, President Obama was still at it. In Osawatomie, Kansas, the site where Theodore Roosevelt delivered his "New Nationalism" speech in 1910, President Obama cast himself as the heir to TR and his agenda the natural continuation of the New Nationalism of 1910. (Obama didn't say whether he favored allowing huge monopolies to conspire with the federal government as TR proposed.) He concluded his speech just as Roosevelt had, by declaring "The fundamental rule in our national life—the rule which underlies all others—is that, on the whole, and in the long run, we shall go up or down together."

His 2012 State of the Union address was dedicated to the theme of how much better America would be if it behaved like a military unit with a single mission. Obama is hardly alone. Scour the speeches of presidents, activists, community organizers, labor leaders, and virtually any leader of men and you will find appeals to unity. The cult of unity runs through every mass movement—how could they be *mass* movements otherwise? "The People! United! Cannot Be Defeated!" has been shouted into bullhorns since the invention of bullhorns (and they always seem to think it rhymes. It doesn't). The propaganda posters of World War I, the New Deal, and World War II are all variations on the same theme: "We're all in it together!"

Unity is great. Unity is wonderful. When a little girl falls down a well and the whole community drops what they are doing to save her, when civil rights activists marched, arm in arm, for their due share of the American dream, when you think of Todd Beamer's last words on Flight

93 that fateful day on September 11—"Are you guys ready? Let's roll!"—how can you not get a lump in your throat?

But you know where else you can find unity? Rape gangs. In fact, the Mafia, Crips, Bloods, MS-13, and the Yakuza, are nothing if not manifestations of man's yearning to belong to a "cause larger than themselves." Nazism would have remained the pathetic clubhouse of disgruntled losers if it wasn't for the cult of unity. Fascism got its start in Italy when returning veterans wanted to rekindle what Mussolini called the "socialism of the trenches." Hitler, Stalin, Mussolini, Mao—populists all—claimed they transcended the binding rules of law and tradition because they had the people on their side. Their authority derived directly from the unified might of the masses.[6] Indeed, the word fascism is derived from the ancient Roman symbol of the *fasces*, a bundle of sticks around an axe, symbolizing strength in numbers. Communism elevated unity, solidarity, and unwavering commitment to the cause above all things. As Bertolt Brecht put it in his 1930s play *The Decision*:

> Who fights for communism must be able to fight and not to fight, to speak the truth and not to speak the truth, to perform services and not to perform services, to keep promises and not to keep promises, to go into danger and to keep out of danger, to be recognizable and not to be recognizable. Who fights for communism has only one of all the virtues: that he fights for communism.[7]

In short, black hats and white hats alike can admire the principle of *unus pro omnibus, omnes pro uno* (all for one, one for all!). And yet, once you start paying attention you'll see how thoroughly the cult of unity infects our politics. On the right it generally gives its expression in the form of patriotism and is honest about it, though George W. Bush hammered the whole "I'm a uniter not a divider" refrain until it was wet mush. On the left and in the "center," overt appeals to patriotism are less common or more forced. What comes more naturally are appeals to unity and coming together. Unity is the secular humanist euphemism for patriotism.

Most of the time such appeals are as harmless as most of the pabulum in politics. Indeed, appeals to unity are unavoidable, because politics is ultimately about addition, about bringing sufficient numbers of people together. But taken to its rational conclusion, appeals to unity are troubling because they work on the assumption that strength in numbers is, on its own, a virtue. That is not the American political tradition or creed. In America the hero is not the mob. It is the man—or woman—who stands up to the mob and says: You will not lynch this man today.

AFTERWORD TO THE PAPERBACK EDITION

"Don't let this happen to you."

In the classic 1970s sitcom *The Odd Couple,* Felix Unger brags that he was the guy who came up with that slogan when he made training films for the army (he also wrote, starred in, and directed the film *How to Take a Shower*).

"Don't let this happen to you" took off like wildfire, according to Felix. Militaries around the world copied the slogan for their own training films. Except, he explained, for the Israeli Army. They changed "Don't let this happen to you" to "It serves you right!"

The episode came to mind for two reasons. First, I watched way too much TV as a kid. But, more relevantly, as I look back on the release of *The Tyranny of Clichés: How Liberals Cheat in the War of Ideas,* I'm torn between these two sentiments. You might even say I feel a bit like Buridan's ass—the hypothetical beast conjured by the 14th-century French philosopher Jean Buridan. He claimed that a donkey, equally thirsty and hungry, placed equidistant between a pail of water and a bale of hay will die before choosing one over the other (apparently Buridan ripped off Aristotle who'd claimed that "a man, being just as hungry as thirsty, and placed in between food and drink, must necessarily remain where he is and starve to death").

Buridan was making a (ridiculous) point about the limits of free will, but we'll come back to that later. For the moment it simply conjures my own torn feelings about the book's message, its reception, and my own inability to make up my mind about the experience.

Let's start with the personal. This was a very different experience than what I went through with my first book. *Liberal Fascism* was a big commercial success and—thanks in no small part to the actions of the Obama administration—seems to be enjoying a healthy life in paperback. Its impact on the right was substantial and, I think, lasting. It's been translated into a bunch of languages. But reviews from liberal publications were, to put it mildly, hostile. The reaction from scholars of fascism and historians generally—with a few notable exceptions—was downright hysterical and occasionally approached self-parody. Meanwhile, reviewers for conservative and libertarian outlets (including my own magazine, *National Review*) were often leery of the book. A few mavericks broke from the pack, but for the most part *Liberal Fascism* had few friends initially.

Fast forward to *The Tyranny of Clichés*. It had friends from day one, and I'm grateful to them for their support. Indeed, if it doesn't seem like too much of a humble brag (as the kids say on Twitter), I was stunned by how well-reviewed the book was on the right. But while it was an official bestseller, *The Tyranny of Clichés* never got the sort of lift we were hoping for. And when I say "we" I mean, for starters: me, my publisher, my family (particularly my dog), my creditors, my local liquor store, my bookie, and my chiropodist. Of course, I'm kidding. My chiropodist didn't care.

If not the biggest stumbling block, than certainly the most obvious, was the title itself, which was entirely my fault. First of all, you'd be shocked to discover how many educated Americans, including talk radio hosts, struggle to pronounce "clee-shays." Worse, *The Tyranny of Clichés* sounds like a really aggressive new edition of *The Elements of Style*.

The word *cliché* has become a cliché unto itself. People have an idea about what the word means, and it's not very elastic. This gave license to some liberal reviewers, such as the *Chicago Tribune's* Clarence Page and *The New Republic's* Tim Noah, to pontificate on "conservative clichés" as if such meditations amounted to some kind of rebuttal to my book.

These dull barbs of *tu quoque* logic missed the mark, not least because I never claimed that conservatives don't have their own clichés. Moreover, they and others missed the actual core argument of the book: that deeply progressive assumptions about the nature of politics, life, history, the role of government, etc., are firmly embedded in our language. These assumptions masquerade as non-ideological common sense, homespun truisms, or even "science." What is passed off as non-ideological discourse on college campuses, mainstream journalism, and everyday conversation is often in fact deeply ideological.

This is why hammering on the fact that conservatives have soundbites and buzzphrases misses the point utterly. When a Republican denounces the "death tax" or celebrates "job creators," no one is under the illusion that he is not coming from a conservative perspective, not least because Republicans tend to say things like "I'm a conservative." But when we say "hindsight is 20/20" or "get on the right side of history," the ideological algorithms are well camouflaged. This was a point made, in a more universal way, by George Orwell in his essay "Politics and the English Language." He didn't use the word *cliché*, but his point was the same. He argued that dead metaphors and stale idioms have the effect of trapping us in certain modes of thinking. "As soon as certain topics are raised, the concrete melts into the abstract and no one seems able to think of turns of speech that are not hackneyed: prose consists less and less of words chosen for the sake of their meaning, and more and more of phrases tacked together like the sections of a prefabricated henhouse." These phrases not only "will construct your sentences for you," Orwell added. They will "even think your thoughts for you."

The general problem Orwell pointed to is acute for liberals in particular because they tend to deny that they are liberals. Indeed, they deny that they're driven by an ideological agenda at all. They insist they are practical and just want to make sure that things work.

Or as President Obama told *Meet the Press* host David Gregory on December 30, 2012: "Generally, if you look at how I've tried to govern over the last four years and how I'll continue to try to govern, I'm not driven by some ideological agenda. I'm a pretty practical guy and I just want to make sure that things work."

This is the lynchpin argument of the whole book: Liberals (or progressives) have convinced themselves that their deep-seated ideological commitments are utterly non-ideological. Hence the first lie liberals tell is the one they tell themselves.

This brings me to the most amusing and frequent experience of the book tour: encountering liberals who believed that they could rebut my argument by confirming its thesis. Over and over again, liberal interviewers, radio show callers, and random audience members would insist that I simply don't understand a basic fact: Conservatives are obsessed with ideology while liberals just don't care about ideology. Their proof often amounted to the fact that I was talking about my ideology a lot while liberals don't talk about theirs at all.

They would glide past my point: that conservatives (and libertarians) are open and honest about their ideological commitments while liberals are blind to theirs. Instead they would insist that the proof liberals aren't blind to their ideological biases is that they can't see them!

This is what amounts to the fundamental dogma of liberalism—that it isn't really liberal except insofar as it is "not conservative." Conservatism is bad, ideological, racist, mean, or all of the above. Liberalism isn't conservatism and so therefore it isn't any of those nasty things. Rather, it's pragmatic, decent, tolerant, and nice. The upshot is that liberals are simply practical people who always do the smart and right thing. And what is the smart and right thing? Well, what liberals want to do, of course. It's a grotesque Manichaeism masquerading as self-adulation.

The most talked-about example of this from my book tour was my encounter with CNN host Piers Morgan (who as of this writing is facing a grassroots movement to have him deported back to the UK for grotesque asininity. Alas, there's a similar grassroots movement in the UK aimed at keeping him here). Like many hosts, he never bothered to read my book before interviewing me. And that's fine. A daily TV show doesn't give even literate hosts much time to read. But Morgan seemed particularly eager to demonstrate my point for me. Insisting he had no agenda, he proceeded to pursue an obviously biased agenda. If you missed the interview, feel free to type in my name and his into Google. The exchange went viral for the same reason videos of men getting hit in the groin go viral: they're fun to watch, particularly when you're not the person involved.

But I have a soft spot for Morgan, who comes from the British tradition of tabloid hackery which is so much more charming than the American version. Which brings me, naturally, to Joe Klein. In his review for *The New York Times Book Review*, Klein seemed determined to beclown himself to a degree he usually reserves solely for the topic of Israel. Hamming it up for the audience, Klein reveled in the fact that he didn't know what he was talking about. What was interesting, from my perspective, was the way in which Klein seemed truly threatened by the argument of the book. If you finish *The Tyranny of Clichés,* I invite you to read Klein's review and judge for yourself (you can also read my too-long response to it at the dormant *Tyranny of Clichés* blog. Once again, let Google be your guide).

So: The title invited lazy critiques and turned off potential readers. It didn't convey the core arguments of the book, nor did it convey that it's—I think—a fun book to read. To be indelicate, I was aiming for middle-to-high brow bathroom reading. I like books you can pick up and read little bits of. And as much as I believe in the thesis and themes of the book, I wanted as many of the chapters to stand alone and be fun to read, independent of the larger argument. As with any book, seeing what the author wants you to see requires a certain amount of good faith from the reader. It serves me right for expecting such good faith from some of the people threatened by its argument.

And then there's that "Don't let this happen to you" bit. Rather than steer toward anything like coherence in my invocation of either *The Odd Couple* or that Buridan's ass thing, I'll simply change gears. Rereading *The Tyranny of Clichés* in the aftermath of the terrible, horrible, no good, very bad presidential election, it seems to me the book was a pretty useful field guide to American politics. For starters, the mainstream media, liberal activists, and the Obama campaign—a meaningful distinction at least according to U.S. tax laws—asserted dominion over what constituted objective facts. The avant-garde of this effort: the legions of self-anointed "fact-checkers" who, often in good faith and in the name of the objective truth, sought to buttress and defend liberal assumptions about the role of government and the unreality of the conservative worldview. To be sure, Republicans deserve to be fact checked just as much as Democrats, because they, too, are politicians.

But that is beside the point. What were journalists *before* the outbreak of fact-checkers? Weren't they supposed to check the facts? The perniciousness of the fact-checking craze was that the authors were buying credibility by simply asserting it. We're fact-checkers, damn it.

If you spent even a few minutes reading into fact-checking features, you'd see that the authors were making claims about what they felt politicians should have said and what voters needed to hear. Sometimes these were narrow judgment calls. Other times, the partisanship was naked. When Rep. Paul Ryan delivered his acceptance speech at the Republican convention in Tampa, the effectiveness of his speech seemed to be proof of its dishonesty. "The verdict," reported *The Washington Post*, "rendered by a slew of media fact checkers, was immediate and unequivocal: In his first major speech before the American people, the Republican vice presidential nominee repeatedly left out key facts, ignored context and was blind to his own hypocrisy."

That's some trick for a fact-checker; diagnosing hypocrisy blindness. And while it's entirely true that Ryan made a one-sided case, it's also true that he was the vice presidential nominee! Was he supposed to say, "On the one hand, I prefer our position, but you know the Obama campaign makes a really good case, too." And, despite all the hysteria, virtually none of the "lies" cited by the chorus of fact-checkers, journalists, and Obama surrogates were actually, you know, *lies*. Everything he said was, in fact, true. His "lies" amounted to omitting the facts liberals wanted to hear.[1]

Or consider *The Washington Post's* fact-checking of Barack Obama's stance on abortion. After a lot of throat clearing, the fact-checker reluctantly conceded that, yes, it was true: Obama did oppose legislation that would have protected babies who survived botched abortions. Obama frequently denied this claim and accused anyone who repeated it of lying. But rather than give Obama a poor score, the fact-checker punted: "The evidence suggests we could have awarded Four Pinocchios [their worst score] to the former Illinois senator for his comments . . . but that interview is several years old now, and it's not the focus of this particular column." Ah. It's an old fact, so you know, never mind.

But more significantly, and more disturbingly, the place where *The Tyranny of Clichés* should have served as, if not exactly a cautionary tale than at least a helpful source of counter-arguments, was on the grand themes of the Democratic argument. As I discuss at considerable length in the chapter on "Community," we tend to talk about the government as if it is something it is not. Throughout the election, Barack Obama and his surrogates repeatedly talked about government as if was simply another institution of civil society like your family or your local community. "The most important question is, 'What kind of country do you want to live in?'" Bill Clinton asked during his speech at the Democratic Convention. "If you want a 'you're-on-your-own, winner-take-all' society, you should support the Republican ticket. If you want a country of shared prosperity and shared responsibility—a 'we're-all-in-this-together' society—you should vote for Barack Obama and Joe Biden."

Putting aside all the question begging about what creates prosperity (certainly not president Obama's policies to date), Clinton's formulation assumes that the government can provide that "we're all in it together" feeling. But it can't. Sure, during wars and natural disasters, the government can temporarily rally people to a singular cause (see the "Moral Equivalent of War" chapter) in the same way a movie or a song or a speech can temporarily lift people up. But the kind of enduring social solidarity the Democrats are appealing to cannot be delivered by a government program. The government cannot love you.

But it can lie to you. It can tell you it loves you. It can tell you all sorts of things. And one of the scariest things about the election returns is how susceptible people are to those lies.

Consider the "Obama electorate." President Obama's coalition was made up disproportionately of the unmarried, the un-churched, the young and (not unrelated) the un- and under-informed. Obama also won massively among urban and ethnically diverse communities (as discussed in the "Diversity" chapter, such diversity tends to be corrosive to civil society).

When you take a step back and look at who make up the core of the Obama electorate, you see a lot of single women, including unwed mothers. You see people from communities where Edmund Burke's little platoons have packed up and left. Communities without stable nuclear families, including engaged fathers, simply have less social capital. Mothers are more important than fathers, but that doesn't mean fathers are unimportant. As Charles Murray notes, single men rarely volunteer to coach soccer teams or little league.

The point is that when you live in communities where voluntary associations have dried up, where mothers are worked to the bone and fathers are absent, and where churches seem alien or unappealing, you will still find people with the natural human craving for community but few to no opportunities to satisfy that craving outside of a government program. This was the subtext of "The Life of Julia"—the Obama campaign's eerie slide show aimed at single women who find the idea of substituting government (or really, President Obama) for husbands, fathers, and family all too attractive. Julia's lifelong benefactor is the government ("Under President Obama, Julia decides to have a child . . ."). At the end of her subsidized single life (her apparently fatherless child leaves at age eighteen never to be heard from again) her reward is to work in a community garden. She doesn't even get her own garden. Chief among the creepy aspects of this appeal is that it was, in fact, appealing to many people.

We are hard wired to want to *belong* to something. Sweep away civil society and pare back the family, and that desire doesn't disappear—it seeks out its own fulfillment where it can. And that is what the politics of "we're all in it together" appeals to. This was the political and psychological point of the entire New Deal and, before that, Woodrow Wilson's progressivism. FDR looked at the millions of laborers uprooted from their homes and traditions, working in new factories in strange cities and promised a politics aimed at the "forgotten man." Woodrow Wilson insisted that the point of progressivism was to get the individual to "marry his interests to the state." President Obama wants the government to be the means by which we are our "brother's keeper."

The Democratic convention opened with the claim that the "Government is the one thing we all belong to." As the author of a book called *Liberal Fascism*, that sounds awful creepy to me. Indeed, it sounds like the overturning of the Founders' vision. Under our Constitution, we don't belong to the government, the government belongs to us. But my ear hears different notes than the typical Obama voter's. For people craving to belong to something, telling them the government is the *one thing* they belong to is reassuring.

And the perverse thing is the whole progressive project becomes self-perpetuating. As I discussed in the "Middle Class" chapter, the government supports policies and programs that undermine the need for and desirability of bourgeois values, and as those values erode people come to crave from government precisely the comforts traditionally supplied by bourgeois values.

I am a happy warrior by nature and conviction. But our problems are real. Politically, conservatives do not have a lot of experience appealing to an American electorate that has so little experience with religion, community, or traditional family. And for the same reason, America doesn't have a lot of experience with a citizenry so disconnected from the roots of our own success.

But as I say somewhere in this book, the only guarantee of failure is an unwillingness to pursue success. Buridan believed free will to be something of a canard. I don't. Decline is a choice. Failure is a choice. You can decide what the right side of history will be. For those with eyes to see, the world is full of examples of nations and peoples who've made the wrong choices. You can't say you weren't warned. You can't claim no one said "Don't let this happen to you." And, if America does choose the path of irrelevance, insolvency, and global chaos, God, or our grandchildren, or some other stand in for Felix Unger will say "It serves you right."

ACKNOWLEDGMENTS

At just about the moment I was starting to really hunker down to write this book, my only brother died in a terrible accident. Attempting to convey how terrible this tragedy was in this limited space—or any space, really—would be futile and inappropriate.

Save in one regard. After Josh died I didn't think I could ever get back to work on this, or any, book. But thanks to the support of family, friends, and colleagues, I did. In this my gratitude is multiplied beyond reckoning. So first off, let me thank The Committee to Buy Jonah Goldberg a Drink. You know who you are. Also I want to thank Ramesh and April Ponnuru, Jim and Kate O'Beirne, Shannen and Casey Coffin, Kathryn Lopez, Tevi Troy, John Podhoretz, Craig Turk, Vin Cannato, John Miller, Pam Friedman, and so many other friends and colleagues who helped me through probably the worst days of my life.

My agent, Jay Mandel, has revealed himself to be not just a frighteningly competent literary agent but a valued and trusted friend.

The folks at Fox News, particularly at *Special Report with Bret Baier*, have been kind and gracious beyond all need and expectation.

I am deeply indebted to Mitchell Boersma, my research assistant at the American Enterprise Institute (AEI), who went off to graduate school at precisely the moment I needed him most and yet stuck with the project to the bitter end anyway. (He was particularly helpful at navigating me through the rough terrain of social justice.) Mitch will go far. Joy Pavelski helped me in the early stages, only to leave too soon for entirely understandable reasons. Hiwa Alaghebandian joined the effort as the bitter end approached and helped make it much less bitter.

AEI, where I got my start in Washington, was supportive in every regard, and I'm grateful in particular to Arthur Brooks for inviting me back to my old stomping grounds. I should also single out my colleague

Nick Schulz, who is also one of my closest friends, and Eleanor Bartow, who has worked harder than necessary to make me feel welcome.

Other colleagues and friends who helped me in ways large and small include: Steven Hayward, Mark Perry, Kenneth Green and Andrew Rugg, Kevin Williamson, Donald Gooch, Doug Brosz, Bill Walsh, and Thomas Madden.

National Review has been my employer and home since 1998, and some of what I've written here was developed first in the gonzo twilight zone of the early Goldberg File, as well as in the more refined pages of the magazine. *NR*'s editor, Rich Lowry, has been unstinting in his generous support all of this time, both as a friend and a boss. But I'm particularly grateful to both Rich and Jack Fowler, *NR*'s devoted publisher, for their menschlike concern after Josh died.

I'd also like to thank my editors and friends at Tribune Media Services, particularly my always upbeat and insightful editor Patrick Fitzmaurice, as well as the respective gangs at the *Los Angeles Times* and *USA Today*. Writing a regular column can be a burden when things are going great. I'm fortunate to have people to lighten my load in good times and bad.

In the acknowledgments for *Liberal Fascism*, I thanked the readers of *National Review Online*. If it was appropriate then, it's downright mandatory now, because this book contains myriad conversations begun, and informed, by them. I cannot begin to say how lucky I have been by having you people to educate, correct, and encourage me. Thank you.

And then there's family. My mother, who's always been my biggest fan, had a worse year than I did but never flagged in her encouragement.

This year my wife, Jessica, had to juggle work and family in ways that leave me mute with awe and gratitude. Every day I think I couldn't love her and my daughter more. Every morning I discover I was wrong.

NOTES

Introduction

1. S. G. Tallentyre, *The Friends of Voltaire* (London: Smith Elder & Co., 1906).
2. Cyril Clemens, *Chesterton as Seen by His Contemporaries* (Webster Groves, Mo.: Mark Twain Society, 1939), p. 7.
3. Dennis Danielson, "That Copernicanism Demoted Humans from the Center of the Cosmos," *Galileo Goes to Jail and Other Myths About Science and Religion*, ed. Ronald L. Numbers, (Boston: Harvard University Press, 2009) pp. 50–59.
4. Ibid.
5. Ibid.
6. Robert Nisbet, *Prejudices* (Harvard University Press, 1983).
7. For a definitive account of these and other myths, I highly recommend *Galileo Goes to Jail and Other Myths About Science and Religion*, edited by Ronald L. Numbers, to which I am deeply indebted.
8. Jay Nordlinger, "The Right Side of History," *National Review*, April 16, 2011.
9. Jonathan Cohn, "Why Ryan's Medicare, Medicaid Plans Are Radical," *The New Republic*, April 4, 2011, accessed August 17, 2011, www.tnr.com/blog/jonathan-cohn/86189/ryan-republican-lbj-medicare-medicaid-covenant.
10. Paul Krugman, "Competitiveness: A Dangerous Obsession," *Foreign Affairs* (March/April 1994).
11. Kevin Phillips, *Staying on Top: The Business Case for a National Industrial Strategy* (New York: Random House, 1984)

1.: Ideology

1. Remarks of President-Elect Barack Obama as prepared for delivery on Inaugural Whistle Stop Tour Baltimore, Maryland. January 17, 2009; accessed June 17, 2011, www.cbsnews.com/8301-503544_162-4730806-503544.html.
2. Inaugural Address of President Barack Obama, January 20, 2009.
3. Transcript, Obama fund-raiser speech, April 6, 2008; accessed October 25, 2011, www.huffingtonpost.com/mayhill-fowler/obama-no-surprise-that-ha_b_96188.html.
4. Jonathan Chait, "Fact Finders: The Anti-Dogma Dogma," *The New Republic*, February 28, 2005; accessed August 17, 2011, www.tnr.com/article/politics/

fact-finders.

5. Scott W. Atlas, "The Worst Study Ever?" *Commentary* (April 2011).
6. See David Gratzer, "The Ugly Truth About Canadian Healthcare," *City Journal*; accessed April 10, 2011, www.city-journal.org/html/17_3_canadian_healthcare.html, and Gratzer "Socialism and Cancer," *New Atlantis* (Winter 2009); accessed April 10, 2011, www.thenewatlantis.com/publications/socialism-and-cancer.
7. See June E. O'Neill and Dave M. O'Neill, 2008. "Health Status, Health Care and Inequality: Canada vs. the U.S.," Forum for Health Economics & Policy, Berkeley Electronic Press, vol. 10(1).
8. Paul Krugman, "Ailing Health Care," *New York Times*, April 11, 2005.
9. Thomas Miller: "Debunking Richard Cohen: How Does the U.S. Health-Care System Stack Up?" *National Review Online*, November 15, 2010; accessed April 13, 2011, www.nationalreview.com/corner/253313/debunking-richard-cohen-how-does-us-health-care-system-stack-thomas-p-miller.
10. Christopher J. L. Murray, Kulkarni, Sandeep, and Ezzati, Majid. "Eight Americas: Investigating Mortality Disparities across Races, Counties, and Race-Counties in the United States," *American Journal of Preventative Medicine* 29-51 (2005).
11. Evelyn J. Patterson, "Incarcerating Death: Mortality in U.S. State Correctional Facilities, 1985–1998. *Democracy* 47, no. 3 (August 2010): 587–607:

    Using data from the U.S. Bureau of Justice Statistics and Census Bureau, I estimate death rates of working-age prisoners and nonprisoners by sex and race. Incarceration was more detrimental to females in comparison to their male counterparts in the period covered by this study. White male prisoners had higher death rates than white males who were not in prison. Black male prisoners, however, consistently exhibited lower death rates than black male nonprisoners did."

12. Erik von Kuehelt-Leddihn, "Is Ideology Useless?" *National Review*, June 10, 1983.
13. Ibid.
14. Russell Kirk, "Ten Conservative Principles," *The Politics of Prudence*, (ISI Books, 1993). The author of this formulation was actually H. Stuart Hughes, but it was popularized by Kirk.
15. Samuel Tanenhaus, *The Death of Conservatism* (New York: Random House, 2009), p. 2.
16. Andrew Sullivan, *The Conservative Soul* (New York: HarperCollins, 2006), p. 230.
17. Ibid. pp. 198–202.
18. Michael Oakeshott, "On Being Conservative," in *Rationalism in Politics and Other Essays*, expanded edition (Indianapolis: Liberty Fund, 2010), p. 194.
19. Edmund Burke, *Letter i. On a Regicide Peace.* vol. v., p. 331. Available in John

Bartlett, *Familiar Quotations* (10th ed., 1919); accessed November 2, 2011, www.bartleby.com/100/276.html.

2.: Pragmatism

1. "Réponse à l'adresse du Conseil d'Etat" in *Moniteur*, 21 décembre 1812. Cit and translated by Emmet Kennedy, "Ideology from Destutt De Tracy to Marx," *Journal of the History of Ideas* 40, no. 3 (July–September 1979), p. 360.
2. Timothy D. Terrell, "The Economics of Destutt de Tracy," *Mises Daily* (Ludwig von Mises Institute), November 28, 2008; accessed May 5, 2011, www.mises.org/daily/3222.
3. Murray Rothbard, *Classical Economics: An Austrian Perspective on the History of Economic Thought, Vol. 2*, (Auburn, Ala: Elgar Publishing, 1995), p. 8; accessed May 5, 2011, mises.org/books/histofthought2.pdf.
4. Ibid., p. 7.
5. Kennedy, p. 358.
6. John B. Thompson, *Ideology and Modern Culture: Critical Social Theory in the Era of Mass Communication* (Palo Alto, Calif.: Stanford University Press, 1991) p. 31.
7. Ibid.
8. Ibid.
9. Talleyrand, Me'maires, ed. Due de Broglie (Paris, 1891), Cit and translated by Emmet Kennedy, *A Philosophe in the Age of Revolution: Destutt de Tracy and the Origins of "Ideology," Vol. 1*, p. 452.
10. Ibid., p. 215.
11. *Napoleon: In His Own Words*, ed. by Jules Bertaut, trans. by Herbert Edward Law and Charles Lincoln Rhodes (Chicago: A. C. McClurg & Co., 1916), p. 112.
12. Steven Englund, *Napoleon: A Political Life* (Boston: Harvard University Press, 2005), p. 52.
13. "Hegel to Niethammer, October 13, 1806," *Hegel: The Letters*, trans. by Clark Butler and Christine Seiler (Bloomington: Indiana University Press, 1985); transcribed by Andy Blunden for marxists.org, (2005); accessed May 11, 2011, www.marxists.org/reference/archive/hegel/works/letters/1806-10-13.htm.
14. Friedrich Nietzsche, *The Genealogy of Morals* (New York: Random House, 1956), p. 187.
15. Bertrand Russell, "Pragmatism," *Edinburgh Review* 209 (April 1909), pp. 363–88. Reprinted in *The Collected Papers of Bertrand Russell. Vol. 6: Logical and Philosophical Papers 1909–13* (London: Routledge, 1992), pp. 260–84.
16. Karl Marx, *The German Ideology* (1845); accessed May 22, 2011, www.marxists.org/archive/marx/works/1845/german-ideology/ch01b.htm.
17. Richard Rorty, "Nietzsche and the Pragmatists," *The New Leader* 80, no. 9 (May 19, 1997).
18. The phrase comes from Thomas Hardy's poem "God's Funeral." It reads in

part:
XI
How sweet it was in years far hied
To start the wheels of day with trustful prayer,
To lie down liegely at the eventide
And feel a blest assurance he was there!
XII
And who or what shall fill his place?
Whither will wanderers turn distracted eyes
For some fixed star to stimulate their pace
Towards the goal of their enterprise?

See also A. N. Wilson, *God's Funeral: The Decline of Faith in Western Civilization* (New York: W. W. Norton, 1999).

19. William James, "The Dilemma of Determinism," in *Essays in Pragmatism* (New York: Meridian Books, 1955), pp. 37–64.
20. William James, "The Social Value of the College-Bred," in *Writings, 1902–1910* (William James Library of America, 1987), p. 1245.
21. William James, "Is Life Worth Living?" in *The Will to Believe and Other Essays in Popular Philosophy and Human Immorality* (New York: Dover, 1956), p. 42.
22. Daniel T. Rodgers, *Atlantic Crossings: Social Politics in a Progressive Age* (Cambridge, Mass.: Harvard University Press, 1998), p. 86.
23. Jane Addams, *Democracy and Social Ethics* (New York: Macmillan, 1902), p. 275.
24. Paul Krugman on *Fareed Zakaria GPS*, CNN, August 14, 2011; Transcript and video accessed September 1, 2011, www.huffingtonpost.com/2011/08/15/paul-krugman-fake-alien-invasion_n_926995.html.
25. Paul Krugman, "Reckonings: After the Horror," *New York Times*, September 14, 2001.
26. James T. Kloppenberg, *Reading Obama: Dreams, Hopes, and the American Political Condition* (Princeton University Press, 2010), p. 264.
27. See Thomas G. West and Douglas A. Jeffrey, "Essay Five: The Modern Rejection of the Principles of the American Founding," *The Rise and Decline of Constitutional Government in America* (Claremont Institute, 2000); accessed September 2, 2011, www.vindicatingthefounders.com/essay5.html.
28. See Henry T. Edmondson, "Deweyisms," (Claremont Institute, 2004); accessed September 2, 2011, www.claremont.org/publications/pubid.366/pub_detail.asp.
29. Tiffany Jones Miller, "John Dewey and the Philosophical Refounding of America," *National Review* (December 31, 2009).
30. "Liberalism vs. Fascism," editorial, *New Republic,* March 2, 1927, p. 35.
31. See Michael Tomasky, "Jackboots and Whole Foods," *The Guardian* (March 2, 2008); www.guardian.co.uk/commentisfree/2008/mar/02/jackbootsand

wholefoodsl; and see my response, Jonah Goldberg, "Clumsy Critique," *National Review Online* (March 13, 2008), www.nationalreview.com/articles/223903/clumsy-critique/jonah-goldberg.

3.: No Labels

1. William Galston and David Frum, "A No Labels Solution to Washington Gridlock?" *The Washington Post*, December 10, 2010.
2. Jon E. Dougherty, "Rosie's Armed Bodyguard," *World Net Daily*, May 26, 2000; accessed March 15, 2010, www.wnd.com/?pageId=1999; Jill Smolowe, "Mom on a Mission," *People* 23, no. 24.
3. Arianna Huffington on *Fareed Zakaria GPS*, CNN, June 27, 2010; transcript and video accessed November 25, 2011, www.huffingtonpost.com/huff-tv/arianna-fareed-zakaria-obama_b_627015.html.
4. John Dewey, "Who Might Make a New Party?" *New Republic* 66 (April 1, 1931), pp. 177–79.
5. Ronald Radosh, "Can Van Jones Create a 'Left-Wing Tea Party'? Don't Bet On It," *PJ Media*, August 17, 2011; accessed September 13, 2011, pjmedia.com/ronradosh/2011/08/17/van-jones-left-wing-tea-party/.

4.: Dogma

1. Fyodor Dostoyevsky, *The Possessed* (1872), part III, chapter II; see also James H. Billington, *Fire in the Minds of Men* (Transaction Publishers, 1980).
2. Norman Cameron and R. H. Stevens, trans. *Hitler's Table Talk 1941–1944: His Private Conversations* (London: Weidenfeld and Nicolson, 1953), p. 62.
3. Gilbert K. Chesterton, *Heretics* (New York: John Lane, 1905), p. 286.
4. Panama Publishing, *Jail: An Inmate's Survival Guide* (BookSurge Publishing, 2007), p. 27.
5. Franz Boas, "An Anthropologist's Credo," *The Nation* 147 (1938), pp. 201–4.
6. John Kenneth Galbraith, *The Great Crash, 1929* (New York: Mariner Books, 2009), p. 171.
7. Stephen Jay Gould, *Dinosaur in a Haystack: Reflections in Natural History* (New York: Harmony Books, 1995), p. 96.
8. "After 50 Years of Covering War, Looking for Peace, and Honoring Law: An Interview with Anthony Lewis," *New York Times* (December 16, 2001).
9. Horace Kallen, "Pragmatism," in Edwin Seligman, ed., *Encyclopaedia of the Social Sciences, Vol. 12* (New York: Macmillan, 1934), p. 310.
10. Scott Sumner, "The GMU Onslaught Continues . . . ," *The Money Illusion*, September 29, 2009; accessed November 9, 2011, www.themoneyillusion.com/?p=2427.
11. Nick Eberstadt, "Broken Yardstick," *New York Times*, September 9, 2005.

12. George Eliot, *Middlemarch* (New York: Penguin Classics, 1994), p. 739.
13. President Abraham Lincoln, "Annual Message to Congress—Concluding Remarks," (December 1, 1862), in Roy P. Basler, ed., *Collected Works of Abraham Lincoln, Vol. 5* (New Brunswick, N.J.: Rutgers University Press, 1953).
14. William F. Buckley, Jr., "Notes Toward an Empirical Definition of Conservatism," in Frank S. Meyer, ed., *What Is Conservatism?* (New York: Henry Holt, 1964), p. 217.
15. See P. J. Crutzen. "Albedo Enhancement by Stratospheric Sulfur Injections: A Contribution to Resolve a Policy Dilemma?" *Climatic Change* 77 (2006): 211–19. Also see Scott Barrett, "The Incredible Economics of Geoengineering," *Environmental and Resource Economics* 39 (January 2008), pp. 45–54: "Not all scientists welcomed the recent publication of a paper by Paul Crutzen, a Nobel Prize-winning chemist, on geoengineering. In the same issue of *Climatic Change,* Ralph Cicerone, the president of the National Academy of Sciences, wrote, 'I am aware that various individuals opposed the publication of Crutzen's paper, even after peer review and revisions, for various and sincere reasons that are not wholly scientific.' *Climatic Change* 77 (2006): 221."
16. Sister Mary Louise, . . . *Over the Bent World* (New York: Sheed & Ward, 1939), p. 590.
17. Manfred Henningsen, *Modernity without Restraint, The Collected Works of Eric Voegelin, Vol. 5* (Columbia: University of Missouri Press, 2000), p. 60.
18. Robert Nisbet, *Prejudices: A Philosophical Dictionary* (Cambridge, Mass.: Harvard University Press, 1983), p. 93.

5.: Separation of Church and State

1. Kim Hartman, "Atheists Sue Over Installation of 9/11 Cross at WTC Museum," *Digital Journal Online*, July 31, 2011; accessed August 3, 2011, digitaljournal.com/article/309760.
2. James Q. Wilson, "The Reform Islam Needs" *City Journal* (Autumn 2002), pp. 26–35 (28).
3. C. V. Wedgwood, *The Thirty Years War* (New York Review Books, 2005), p. 506.
4. Wilson, "Reform," p. 30.
5. Ibid., p. 31.
6. See Michael Novak, "The Truth About Religious Freedom," *First Things* (March 2006).
7. Ely scholar Benjamin Rader reports that "ministers across the country used Ely's writing as a basis for sermons." Ely's *Social Aspects of Christianity* was a definitive text. "For more than twenty years," writes Rader, "every minister entering the Conference of the Methodist Episcopal Church was required to read *Social Aspects* as well as Ely's *An Introduction to Political Economy.*" Benja-

min Rader, "Lay Spokesman for the Social Gospel," *The Journal of American History*, Vol. 53, No. 1 (June, 1966), pp. 61–74 (67–68).

8. Richard Ely, *Social Aspects of Christianity and Other Essays* (T. Y. Crowell & Company, 1880) p. 53; Cited in Rader, p. 72.
9. John Lukacs, *Remembered Past: John Lukacs on History, Historians, and Historical Knowledge* (Wilmington, Del.: ISI Books, 2005), p. 305.
10. *Social Aspects of Christianity*, p. 57.
11. Richard Ely, *The Social Law of Service* (New York, 1896), p. 167. Cited in Rader, p. 71.
12. Cathleen Falsani, *Barack Obama: The 2004 "God Factor" Interview* (April 30, 2008); Transcript accessed November 9, 2011, blog.beliefnet.com/stevenwaldman/2008/11/obamas-interview-with-cathleen.html.

6.: Power Corrupts

1. John Emerich Edward Dalberg-Acton (Lord Acton), "Letter to Bishop Mandell Creighton (1887)," in *Historical Essays and Studies* (1907).
2. Ibid.
3. James Fallows, "Edward M. Kennedy," *The Atlantic* (August 26, 2009); accessed March 22, 2011, www.theatlantic.com/technology/archive/2009/08/senator-edward-m-kennedy/23873/.
4. Melissa Lafsky, "The Footnote Speaks," The Huffington Post (August 27, 2009); accessed December 6 2011, www.huffingtonpost.com/melissa-lafsky/the-footnote-speaks-what_b_270298.html.

7.: Diversity

1. Unedited version of a letter to the *Los Angeles Times*, November 28, 2005; accessed December 10, 2010, www.barbrastreisand.com/us/statement/letter-la-times; published version: "Singing the Op-ed Blues," *Los Angeles Times*, November 23, 2005; accessed December 10, 2010, articles.latimes.com/2005/nov/23/opinion/le-wednesday23.3.
2. Stephanie Gaskell, "Statue Depicting Flag-Raising at Ground Zero Draws Criticism for 'Political Correctness,'" The Associated Press, January 12, 2002.
3. Alexis de Tocqueville, *Democracy in America*, trans. Bruce Frohnen (Washington, D.C.: Regnery Gateway, 2003), p. 128: "A proposition must be plain to be adopted by the understanding of a people. A false notion which is clear and precise will always meet with a greater number of adherents in the world than a true principle which is obscure or involved."
4. Irving Janis, one of the pioneers of Groupthink, explains the phenomenon thus: "The more amiability and esprit de corps there is among the members of a policy-making ingroup, the greater the danger that independent critical thinking will be replaced by groupthink, which is likely to result in irrational and

dehumanizing actions against outgroups." "Groupthink," *Psychology Today* (1971), pp. 43–46.

5. Lee Bollinger, "Pro: Diversity is Essential," *Newsweek*, January 26, 2003; accessed November 19, 2010, www.thedailybeast.com/newsweek/2003/01/26/pro-diversity-is-essential.html.
6. President Lyndon B. Johnson, "To Fulfill These Rights," commencement address at Howard University (June 4, 1965); LBJ Online Archives; accessed Nov 24, 2011, www.lbjlib.utexas.edu/johnson/archives.hom/speeches.hom/650604..asp.
7. Evan Thomas and Pat Wingert, "Minority Report," *Newsweek*, February 18, 2010; accessed November 19, 2010, www.newsweek.com/2010/02/18/minority-report.html.
8. See Kathryn Knight, "The Bizarre Truth about Life with Barbra Streisand," *The Daily Mail* (July 19, 2007), last accessed December 6, 2011; Peter Schweizer, *Do as I Say (Not as I Do): Profiles in Liberal Hypocrisy* (New York: Random House), pp. 173–91.

8.: Social Darwinism

1. Mario Cuomo, 1984 Democratic National Convention Keynote Address. Speech delivered at the 1984 Democratic National Convention, San Francisco, California, July 16, 1984.
2. Barack Obama, Commencement Address at Knox College, Galesburg, Illinois, June 4, 2005.
3. Edwin Black, *War Against the Weak: Eugenics and America's Campaign to Create a Master Race* (New York: Four Walls Eight Windows, 2003), p. 12.
4. See Geoffrey Hodgson's authoritative essay "Social Darwinism in Anglophone Academic Journals: A Contribution to the History of the Term," *Journal of Historical Sociology* 17, no. 4 (December 2004).
5. Hodgson writes: "The 1907 appearance of the term was in the *American Journal of Sociology* in an article by Collin Wells. Partly because the article itself is entitled 'Social Darwinism' it is worthy of more detailed discussion. This was the first use of the term in the title of an article in the JSTOR database. In addition, *it is the only article or review found in this entire database clearly and explicitly advocating 'Social Darwinism' in any sense whatsoever.* [Emphasis in original.] Wells insisted, however, that by 'Social Darwinism' he did 'not mean those propositions of the doctrine of evolution which Darwin chiefly emphasized'"! (1907): 695.
6. Charles Darwin, *Autobiography* (London), p. 120.
7. Charles Darwin, *The Origin of Species* (1859), p. 116. See also p. 67, where he telegraphed his intention to apply the doctrine of Malthus in this way:

   In the next chapter the Struggle for Existence amongst all organic beings throughout the world, which inevitably follows from their high geometrical powers of increase, will be treated of. This is the doctrine of Malthus, applied to the whole animal and vegetable kingdoms. As many more individuals of each species are born than can possibly survive; and as, consequently, there is a frequently recurring struggle for existence, it follows that any being, if it vary however slightly in any manner profitable to itself, under the complex and sometimes varying conditions of life, will have a better chance of surviving, and thus be naturally selected. From the strong principle of inheritance, any selected variety will tend to propagate its new and modified form.

8. Charles Richard Van Hise, *The Conservatism of Natural Resources in the United States* (New York: Macmillan, 1910), p.378.
9. Scott Gordon, *The History and Philosophy of Social Science* (New York: Routledge, 1993), p. 521; Daniel Kelves, *In the Name of Eugenics: Genetics and the Uses of Human Heredity* (Cambridge, Mass.: Harvard University Press, 1986), p. 68.
10. Edward Alsworth Ross, "Social Darwinism," *American Journal of Sociology* 12 (1907): 715.
11. E. A. Ross, *Seventy Years of It* (New York: Appleton-Century, 1936), p. 70, cit. in Thomas Leonard, "'More Merciful and Not Less Effective': Eugenics and American Economics in the Progressive Era," *History of Political Economy* 35, no. 4 (Winter 2003), p. 699.
12. Sydney Webb, "Eugenics and the Poor Law: The Minority Report," *The Eugenics Review*, 237; accessed November 10, 2011, www.ncbi.nlm.nih.gov/pmc/articles/PMC2986721/pdf/eugenrev00382-0077.pdf.
13. Unsigned editorial, *The New Republic*, March 18, 1916.
14. Richard Hofstadter, *Social Darwinism in American Thought* (Philadelphia: University of Pennsylvania Press, 1944), p. 44.
15. Robert B. Reich, "Having It Both ways," *The American Prospect*, November 28, 2005; www.prospect.org/cs/articles?articleId=10666; accessed July 28, 2011.
16. Burt Folsom, *The Myth of Robber Barons: New Look at the Rise of Big Business in America* (Herndon, Va.: Young America's Foundation, 1991).
17. Ibid.
18. Henry Hazlitt, "Capitalism Without Horns," *National Review*, March 12, 1963.
19. Timothy P. Carney, *The Big Ripoff: How Big Business and Big Government Steal Your Money* (Hoboken, N.J.: Wiley & Sons, 2006), p. 40.
20. Irwin G. Wyllie, "Social Darwinism and the Businessmen," *Proceedings of the American Philosophical Society* 103 (1959): 629–35; Robert C. Bannister, *Social Darwinism: Science and Myth in Anglo-American Social Thought* (Philadelphia: Temple University Press, 1988).
21. Wyllie, p. 633.
22. Ibid.

23. Edwin Palmer Hoyt, *The Vanderbilts and Their Fortunes* (Garden City, N.Y.: Doubleday, 1962), p. 266.
24. Wyllie, 634.
25. Andrew Carnegie, "Memo to Self" (December 1868), accessed November 23, 2011, www.carnegiebirthplace.com/images/Memo_sheet.pdf.
26. Hofstadter, p. 5.

9.: Slippery Slope

1. See Eugene Volokh's typically exhaustive and insightful "The Mechanism of the Slippery Slope," *Harvard Law Review* (2003); David Enoch, "Once You Start Using Slippery Slope Arguments, You're on a Very Slippery Slope," *Oxford Journal of Legal Studies* (Winter 2001).
2. Eugene Volokh, "The Mechanism of the Slippery Slope," *Harvard Law Review* 116, no. 4 (Feb. 2003), pp. 1026–37.

10.: Dissent

1. See Mark Steyn, "Liberal Fabrications about Thomas Jefferson," *Insight*, May 1, 2006.
2. Ibid.
3. *The Use of Force in International Affairs* (Philadelphia: Friends Peace Committee, 1961), p. 6.
4. Peter Beinart, "Election Night's Big Loser," *The Daily Beast*, November 2, 2010.
5. Michael Kinsley, "U.S. Is Not Greatest Country Ever," *Politico*, November 2, 2010.
6. Hayley Tsukayama and Liz Lucas, "Thousands Cheer Obama at Rally for Change," *Missourian*, October 30, 2008. Video of speech accessed November 23, 2011, www.youtube.com/watch?v=_cqN4NIEtOY.
7. "Charges Traitors in America Are Disrupting Russia," *New York Times*, September 16, 1917, p. 3.
8. Walter Winchell, "Americans We Can Do Without," *Liberty*, August 1, 1942, p. 10.
9. Video accessed October 20, 2011; newsbusters.org/blogs/noel-sheppard/2009/04/16/garofalo-tea-partiers-are-all-racists-who-hate-black-president.

11.: Social Justice

1. Jalees Rehman, "Why We Were Attacked in Norway," *The Huffington Post*, July 23, 2011; accessed July 27, 2011, www.huffingtonpost.com/jalees-rehman/why-we-were-attacked-in-n_b_907567.html.
2. AFL-CIO Mission Statement, accessed February 2, 2011, www.aflcio.org/

aboutus/thisistheaflcio/mission/.

3. SEIU 2008 Constitution and Bylaws, accessed August 10, 2011, www.seiu.org/images/pdfs/Con.BylawsFinal3.4.9.pdf.
4. Editorial, "$10 for Harvard," *The Harvard Crimson*, May 23, 2011.
5. Accessed August 11, 2011, www.fordfoundation.org/grants/grantdetails?grantid=8108.
6. Accessed August 11, 2011, www.ethicshare.org/node/714181.
7. Accessed September 5, 2011, www.masnet.org/main/content/mas-freedom.
8. Accessed September 7, 2011, www.americannaziparty.com/about/index.php.
9. Accessed August 22, 2011, www.yale.edu/sjn/.
10. GLADD and NGLCC, "Re: Proceeding 11-65 involving the AT&T merger with T-Mobile." An open letter to the FCC. May 31, 2011; accessed November 26, 2011, www.scribd.com/doc/57008791/GLAAD-ATT-letter.
11. K. C. Johnson, "Disposition for Bias," *Inside Higher Ed*, May 23, 2005; accessed June 10, 2011, www.insidehighered.com/views/2005/05/23/johnson; "Dispositions, Education Programs, and the Social Justice Requirement," accessed June 10, 2011, academic.brooklyn.cuny.edu/history/johnson/dispositions.html.
12. For a complete account of the history, development, and nuanced role of social justice within Catholic Social Doctrine, see Russell Hittinger, "The Coherence of the Four Basic Principles of Catholic Social Doctrine: An Interpretation," a paper delivered to the Pontifical Academy of Social Sciences, May 2, 2008.
13. Luigi Taparelli D' Azeglio, *Saggio Teoretico*, "Ogni consorizio dee conservare la propria unità in modo da non perdere la unità del tutto; ed ogni società maggiore provvede alla unità del tutto senza distruggere la unità dei consorzii"; in Thomas C. Behr, "Luigi Taparelli D'Azeglio, S.J. (1793–1862) and the Development of Scholastic Natural-Law Thought as a Science of Society," *Journal of Markets & Morality* 6, no 1 (Spring 2003): 99–115.
14. Used by Mussolini in a speech before the Chamber of Deputies on May 26, 1927, *Discorsi del 1927*, Milano, Alpes, 1928, p. 157.
15. See Ryan Messmore, "Real Social Justice," *First Things Online*, November 26, 2010; accessed June 11, 2011, www.firstthings.com/onthesquare/2010/11/real-social-justice.
16. Pope Leo XIII, *Rerum Novarum*, May 15, 1891.
17. Reverend John A. Ryan, "Roosevelt Safeguards America," a radio address made to the faculty of Catholic University of America, October 8, 1936.
18. Principles of the National Union for Social Justice, quoted in Alan Brinkley, *Voices of Protest: Huey Long, Father Coughlin, and the Great Depression* (New York: Vintage, 1983), pp. 287–88.

19. Charles A. Beard and George H. E. Smith, eds., *Current Problems of Public Policy: A Collection of Materials* (New York: Macmillan, 1936), p. 54.
20. "Attack on AFL by Coughlin Backed; Radio Priest Right, J.L. Ryan, Union President, Tells Protesting Clergymen." *New York Times* (December 3, 1933).
21. Accessed April 10, 2011, www.ssa.gov/history/cough.html.
22. F. A. Hayek, *Law, Legislation, and Liberty, Vol. 2: The Mirage of Social Justice* (Chicago: University of Chicago Press, 1978), p. 97.
23. Herbert Croly, *Progressive Democracy*, vol. 3 (New York: Macmillan, 1915) pp. 148–49. True, Croly says here that the moral ideal of society must be pursued "supplementary" to the individual. But should the interest of the State and the individual collide, there is little doubt with whom Croly would side: "The individual has the best chance of giving integrity to his life in a society which is being informed by the social ideal. . . . Although an advance towards social salvation will be accelerated by increasing individual integrity, society will never be saved as a consequence of the regeneration of individualism." p. 199. In other words, Croly understood the language of social justice as the language giving credence to his ideological project of enabling the State to take the reins.
24. "Social Justice in an Open World: The Role of the United Nations," United Nations Division for Social Policy and Development (2006), pp. 2–3.

12.: Community

1. Ricardo Alonso-Zaldivar, "Average Medicare Benefits By Far Top Lifetime Costs," *Associated Press*, December 31, 2010.
2. The Hoover Dam contains 4.36 million cubic yards of concrete and created Lake Mead, a massive reservoir that flooded nearly three hundred square miles of desert, diverted a river, and endangered the existence of numerous species of plants and animals, including the Bonytail, Colorado pikeminnow, Humpback chub, and razorback sucker. It was an astounding human accomplishment, but it was also a devastating blow not just to the surrounding ecosystem, but to the entire West Coast: Los Angeles, Las Vegas, and much of the Southwest would be inhospitable to large communities of human beings were it not for the electricity it provided. The idea that the same people who shudder at the mere suggestion of drilling in the unoccupied arctic wastelands of Alaska would today countenance such a wholesale rape of Mother Nature is laughable.
3. Murray N. Rothbard, "Richard T. Ely: Paladin of the Welfare-Welfare State," *Independent Review* 6, no. 4 (Spring 2002), p. 586, citing Sidney Fine, *Laissez Faire and the General-Welfare State: A Study of Conflict in American Thought, 1865–1901* (Ann Arbor: University of Michigan Press, 1956), pp. 180-81.

13.. Ten Guilty Men

1. "Mallen reuera vigita facino rosos mortem pietate euadere, quã iustu vnu condempari." John Fortescue, *De Laudibus Legum Angliæ [A Learned Commendation of the Politique Lawes of England]*, ch. 27, at 63 trans. Robert Mulcaster 1567, Da Capo Press, 1969.
2. Alexander Volokh, "Ten Guilty Men," *University of Pennsylvania Law Review* (1997), pp.146–73, www2.law.ucla.edu/volokh/guilty.htm#53.
3. Hoover Institution, "Mugged by Reality," *Policy Review* no. 84 (July 1, 1997); accessed February 21, 2010, www.hoover.org/publications/policy-review/article/7500.
4. Ibid.: In Miami, sociologist James A. Inciardi used a "snowballing" interview technique to find them. He sent researchers into high-crime neighborhoods to talk to youngsters about "who's doing drugs" and "who's into crime." They found 611 youngsters ages 12 to 17 who admitted to multiple crimes and repeated drug use. Ninety percent of them had been arrested, an equal proportion had been thrown out of school, and almost half had been incarcerated. Typically they began to use alcohol at age seven and turned to crime and drugs at 11; almost two-thirds had participated in a robbery by the age of 13. The interviewees confessed to a total of 429,136 criminal acts during the year prior to their interviews—more than 700 each, or nearly two a day. Of these acts, 18,477, or 30 apiece, were major felonies, including 6,269 robberies and 721 assaults. Nearly 18 percent had committed armed robberies, as young as 14, and 90 percent carried weapons most of the time. Among this violent crowd, 361 committed the 6,269 robberies—an average of 17 each—and two-thirds of them robbed before the age of 13.
5. Jeremy Bentham, *A Treatise on Judicial Evidence* (London: Baldwin, Cradock, and Joy, 1825).
6. "That is an old saying, and true, *Prestat reum nocentem absolvi, quam ex prohibitis Indiciis & illegitima probatione condemnari.* It is better that a Guilty Person should be Absolved, than that he should without sufficient ground of Conviction be condemned." Volokh citing David Levin, *What Happened in Salem?* 125-126 (1960), citing Increase Mather, *Cases of Conscience Concerning Evil Spirits Personating Men* (1693).

14.: Living Constitution

1. William Watson, *Ten Quodlibetical Questions Concerning Religion and State*, 1601.
2. Herbert David Croly and Sidney A. Pearson, *Progressive Democracy* (New Brunswick, N.J.: Transaction Publishers, 1998), p. 369.
3. Bert J. Loewenberg, "Darwinism Comes to America, 1865–1900," *Mississippi Valley Historical Review* 28, (1941).

4. Richard Ely, *Ground Under Our Feet: An Autobiography* (New York: Macmillan, 1938), p. 154.
5. John Dewey, "Darwin's Influence Upon Philosophy," *Popular Science* (July 1909), p. 90.
6. Woodrow Wilson, *The New Freedom: A Call for the Emancipation of the Generous Energies of a People* (New York: Doubleday, Page & Company, 1913).
7. Ronald J. Pestritto, *Woodrow Wilson and the Roots of Modern Liberalism* (Lanham, Md.: Rowman & Littlefield, 2005), p. 122.
8. See Robert Livingston Schuyler, "Forrest McDonald's Critique of the Beard Thesis," *Journal of Southern History* 27, no. 1 (1961): 73–80; Peter J. Coleman, "Beard, McDonald, and Economic Determinism in American Historiography," *Business History Review* 34, no. 1 (1960): 113–21.
9. John Dewey and James Tufts, *Ethics* (New York: Henry Holt and Company, 1913), p. 479.
10. See Leonard Frank James, *The Supreme Court in American Life* (Chicago: Scott, Foresman. 1964), p. 159.
11. Supreme Court Justice Felix Frankfurter, concurring statement, *Joseph Burstyn, Inc. v. Wilson* (1952).
12. George Will, *This Week*, ABC, July 3, 2011. Video and transcript accessed July 12, 2011, www.newsbusters.org/blogs/noel-sheppard/2011/07/03/will-asks-week-panel-does-congress-have-constitutional-power-require-.
13. Al Gore interview, *NewsHour with Jim Lehrer*, PBS, March 14, 2000; accessed July 12, 2011, www.pbs.org/newshour/election2000/candidates/gore_3-14c.html.
14. David Finnigan, *Community Briefs* (June 23, 2005); accessed July 14, 2011, www.jewishjournal.com/community_briefs/article/community_briefs_20050624./.
15. Sonia Sotomayor, Judge Mario G. Olmos Memorial Lecture, 2001, delivered at the University of California, Berkeley, School of Law.
16. Senator Barack Obama speaking before Planned Parenthood Action Fund, July 17, 2007.
17. Remarks of Senator Barack Obama at confirmation of Justice John Roberts; accessed July 14, 2011, www.obamaspeeches.com/031-Confirmation-of-Judge-John-Roberts-Obama-Speech.htm.
18. Michael Dorf, "Who Killed the 'Living Constitution'?" *FindLaw*, March 10, 2008; accessed July 14. 2011, www.writ.news.findlaw.com/dorf/20080310.html.
19. William Leuchtenburg, *Supreme Court Reborn* (New York: Oxford University Press, 1996), pp. 15–22.
20. Mark DeWolfe Howe, *Holmes-Laski Letters: The Correspondence of Mr. Justice*

Holmes and Harold J. Laski 1916–1935 (Cambridge, Mass.: Harvard University Press, 1953).

21. Dorf, "Who Killed the 'Living Constitution'?"
22. Ibid.
23. Dahlia Lithwick, "It's a-Living," *Slate*, August 25, 2005; www.slate.com/id/2125095/; accessed September 12, 2011.
24. Laurence H. Tribe, "On Health Care, Justice Will Prevail," *New York Times*, February 7, 2011.
25. Representative Raul Grijalva, interview on *Hardball with Chris Matthews*, MSNBC, January 7, 2011.
26. Miriam Jordan, "U.S. Immigration Fight Widens to Native-Born," *Wall Street Journal*, July 20, 2010.
27. Senate Judiciary Committee, Justice Elana Kagan confirmation hearing, 111th Cong., June 29, 2010.
28. Ibid.
29. Senate Judiciary Committee, statement of chairman, Senator Patrick Leahy (D-Vt.), on the proposal requiring an amendment to the Constitution, H.R. 2560, 112th Cong., July 22, 2011.

15.: Let Them Eat Cake

1. Speech published by the WPA a year later: Harry Hopkins, "The Realities of Unemployment," PDF available online; accessed November 28, 2011, http://fraser.stlouisfed.org/publications/roune/issue/5315/download/89358./1937_rounemp.pdf; Franklin D. Roosevelt, "Address at the Democratic State Convention," Syracuse, N.Y., September 29, 1936.
2. Mario Puzo, "Like Marie Antoinette," *New York Times*, September 15, 1968.
3. William Safire, *Safire's Political Dictionary* (New York: Oxford University Press, 2008), p.396; Patrick Buchanan, "The Toyota Republicans," *Human Events*, December 16, 2008.
4. Myron Magnet, *The Dream and the Nightmare: The Sixties Legacy to the Underclass* (San Francisco: Encounter Books, 2000), p 116.
5. Penelope Wang, "Is College Still Worth the Price?" *Money*, April 13, 2009.
6. Mark Perry, "Chart of the Day: The Higher Education Bubble," *The Enterprise Blog* July 25, 2011; accessed August 3, 2011, blog.american.com/2011/07/chart-of-the-day-the-higher-education-bubble/.
7. David Holwick, "Demanding Divas," *America Online, Inc.* August 5, 2001; accessed November 25, 2011, www.findthepower.net/CP/IL/PostNewABC2_I.php?IL=ON&SeeAlso=DIVA.
8. See Kathryn Petras Holwick and Ross Petras, *Unusually Stupid Celebrities: A*

Compendium of All-Star Stupidity (New York: Villard, 2007), p. 72.

9. See Holwick; Tom Whipple, "Keeping up Appearances," *The Guardian*, May 28, 2005.
10. See Holwick; Jane Bell, "Do We Really Want to Live to 130?" *Belfast Telegraph*, February 17, 1999; "Studios Say No to Stars' Pet Perks," *The Sunday Telegraph*, February 21, 1999.
11. See Holwick; Karen Heller, "Conspicuous Stardom to John Travolta," *Philadelphia Inquirer*, January 12, 1999; Dan Cox, "Star Treatment; Chefs, Jets, Pets Inflate Pic Tabs," *Variety*, June 23–29, 1997; Avashti, "Lulu's from LA-LA Land," the *New York Post*, February 14, 1999.
12. See Holwick; Petras, p. 113.
13. See Holwick; "Zane's Titanic Ego, Myers' Margarine Mania," *ABC NEWS*, September 11, 2000.
14. See Holwick; Petras p. 115; Leah Garchik, "Personals," *San Francisco Gate*, March 8, 1995.
15. See: "Give global warming the bum's rush: Sheryl Crow," Agence France Presse, April 23, 2007.
16. Joseph Farah, "Oliver Stone, Far from the Malibu Crowd," *Los Angeles Times*, March 7, 1993.
17. Daniel Radosh, "Moore Is Less," *Salon* (June 1997); accessed November 26, 2011, www1.salon.com/june97/media/media970606.html.
18. Iris Nowell; *Generation Deluxe: Consumerism and Philanthropy of the New Super-rich* (Dundurn, 2004), p. 62.
19. Dominic Turnbull, "Madonna: I Have Never Changed a Single Nappy," *Sunday Mirror*, July 29, 2001.

16.: Violence Never Solves Anything

1. George Orwell, "Notes on Nationalism," *Polemic* (London, May 1945), Reprinted in *England, Your England, and Other Essays* (London: Secker and Warburg, 1953).
2. Leviathan, chapter xvii.
3. *New York Times*, September 17, 2011.
4. George Orwell, "No Not One: A Review of *No Such Liberty* by Alex Comfort," *The Adelphi* (October 1941).
5. Paul Johnson, *Modern Times: The World from the Twenties to the Nineties* (New York: Harper Collins, 2001), p. 471.
6. George Orwell, "Reflections on Gandhi," *Partisan Review* (January 1949).
7. Mohandas Gandhi, "To Every Briton," Radio Address, New Delhi (July 2, 1940).
8. Orwell, "Reflections on Gandhi."

17.: Middle Class

1. William Voegeli, "Reforming Big Government," *Claremont Review of Books* (Fall 2008); accessed May 2, 2010, www.claremont.org/publications/crb/id.1570/article_detail.asp.
2. In *Words That Changed a Nation: The Most Celebrated and Influential Speeches of Barack Obama*, the word "poor" barely appears. In the seven instances where it does and is used to describe impoverished Americans (as opposed to, say, "poor nations"—the only time the word appears in his inaugural), not once does the former community organizer ever speak about doing things *for* poor people. Rather, in most cases he uses it in the context of elevating himself. Most commonly, he cites the group as a significant member of the coalition of people who think he's great. As in his famous "yes we can" speech in South Carolina: "You can see it in the faces here tonight. There are young and old, rich and poor. They are black and white, Latino and Asian and Native American." In fairness, Obama has of course talked about alleviating poverty, occasionally in speeches and more often when asked specifically about it in interviews. Most often, however, his explanations are often retrospective, and the intent is to illustrate that government can do great things, even if alleviating the plight of the poor isn't one of them anymore.
3. Peter Gay, *Pleasure Wars: The Bourgeois Experience: Victoria to Freud* (New York: W. W. Norton, 1998), p. 26.
4. Harold Stearns, *America Now: An Inquiry into Civilization in the United States* (New York: Literary Guild of America, 1938).
5. Sinclair Lewis, "Minnesota, the Norse State," *The Nation*, May 30, 1923.
6. "Port Huron Statement of the Students for a Democratic Society, 1962." Courtesy of the office of Senator Tom Hayden; PDF accessed November 12, 2011, www.coursesa.matrix.msu.edu/~hst306/documents/huron.html.
7. Betty Friedan, *The Feminine Mystique* (New York: W. W. Norton, 2001), p. 425.
8. Karl Marx, *The Communist Manifesto* (London: Verso, 1998), p. 34.
9. See Bertell Ollman, "Marx's Use of 'Class,'" *American Journal of Sociology*, 73, no. 5 (March 1968): 573–80.
10. Marx, *The Communist Manifesto*, p. 48.
11. Karl Marx, *The Eighteenth Brumaire of Louis Bonaparte* (New York: International Publishers, 1994).
12. David Brooks, *Bobos in Paradise: The New Upperclass and How They Got There* (New York: Simon & Schuster, 2000), p. 43.
13. See Max Weber, *The Protestant Ethic and the Spirit of Capitalism* (New York: Scribner, 1958).
14. Megan McArdle, "Should We Raise Tax Rates on the Rich?" *The Atlantic*, August 9, 2010.

15. William Voegeli, *Never Enough: America's Limitless Welfare State* (New York: Encounter Books, 2010), p. 133.
16. Adam Smith, *The Theory of Moral Sentiments* (New York: Prometheus Books, 2000), p. 380.
17. For a further discussion of Smith's fundamentally moral case for capitalism, see Yuval Levin, "Recovering the Case for Capitalism," Bradley Lecture at the American Enterprise Institute (January 11, 2011).

18.: Science

1. James H. Fowler and Christopher T. Dawes, "Two Genes Predict Voter Turnout," *Journal of Politics* 70, no. 3 (July 2008): 579–94.
2. David M Amodio et al., "Neurocognitive Correlates of Liberalism and Conservatism," *Nature Neuroscience;* published online, September 9, 2007; accessed October 17, 2011, doi:10.1038/nn1979.
3. Alok Jha, "Brain Type May Dictate Politics," *The Guardian*, September 10, 2007.
4. Editorial, "Left Brain, Right Brain," *Los Angeles Times*, September 12, 2007.
5. Douglas R. Oxley et al., "Political Attitudes Vary with Physiological Traits," *Science* 321, no. 5896 (September 19, 2008): pp. 1667–70.
6. Ibid.
7. Zeev Sternhell, *The Birth of Fascist Ideology*, trans. David Maisel (Princeton: Princeton University Press, 1994), p. 56.
8. Kathleen Maclay, "Researchers Help Define What Makes a Political Conservative," University of California–Berkeley press release, July 22, 2003; www.berkeley.edu/news/media/releases/2003/07/22_politics.shtml.
9. John T. Jost et al., "Political Conservatism as Motivated Social Cognition," *Psychological Bulletin* 129, no. 3 (2003): pp. 339–75.
10. www.criticalreview.com/2004/pdfs/cardiff_klein.pdf.
11. www.psychologytoday.com/blog/ironshrink/201004/conservatism-thought-disorder-in-need-cure.
12. www.latimes.com/news/science/la-sci-politics10sep10,1,5376455.story?ctrack=1&cset=true.
13. www.slate.com/articles/health_and_science/human_nature/2007/09/liberal_interpretation.html.
14. See the excellent reporting by Daniel Engber of *Slate* magazine on the burgeoning field of neuropunditry. For example, Daniel Engber, "Jeffery Goldberg, Neuropundit?" *Slate* (June 18, 2008).

19.: Youth

1. Jean Twenge et al. "Egos Inflating Over Time: A Cross-Temporal Meta-Analysis of the Narcissistic Personality Inventory," *Journal of Personality* 76, no. 4 (August 2008).
2. I discuss this extensively in *Liberal Fascism.*
3. Paul Farhi, "Dean Tries to Summon Spirit of the 1960s," *Washington Post*, December 28, 2003, p. A05.

20.: Ounce of Prevention

1. In fairness, many of Franklin's famous aphorisms for his *Poor Richard's Almanack* were simply deliberate rewrites of ancient expressions. The phrase "an ounce of prevention is worth a pound of cure" is often attributed to Franklin but in fact is traceable back to Henry de Bracton's 1240 classic *De legibus et consuetudinibus Angliae* (On the Laws and Customs of England). That in itself was an updating of what must be a prehistoric concept of nipping a problem in the bud, or "meeting the malady on its way," as the Roman poet Persius (A.D. ca. 58) put it.
2. See Russell's more recent paper "Preventing Chronic Disease: An Important Investment, but Don't Count on Cost Savings" in *Health Affairs* 28 no. 1 (January/February 2009): 42–45. From the abstract:

   > Over the four decades since cost-effectiveness analysis was first applied to health and medicine, hundreds of studies have shown that prevention usually adds to medical costs instead of reducing them. Medications for hypertension and elevated cholesterol, diet and exercise to prevent diabetes, and screening and early treatment for cancer all add more to medical costs than they save. Careful choices about frequency, groups to target, and component costs can increase the likelihood that interventions will be highly cost-effective or even cost-saving.

   Also see David Brown, "In the Balance," *Washington Post*, April 8, 2008.
3. Ibid.
4. Ryan Tracy and Stephanie Gleason, "New Flare-up in Light-Bulb Wars," *Wall Street Journal*, July 9, 2011.
5. Michael McGerr, *A Fierce Discontent: The Rise and Fall of the Progressive Movement in America, 1870–1920* (New York: Free Press, 2003), p. 196.
6. Tocqueville, *Democracy in America.*

21.: The Catholic Church

1. Martin Kramer, *Ivory Towers on Sand: The Failure of Middle Eastern Studies in America*, (The Washington Institute for Near East Policy Publications, 2001), p 52.:

> The idea of "Islamic reformation" perfectly fit the agenda of presenting Islam in Western categories. It first surfaced in journalistic usage. "Islam is now at a pivotal and profound moment of evolution," wrote the journalist Robin Wright in 1992, "a juncture increasingly equated with the Protestant Reformation." Islam was experiencing a "new spirit of reform," she wrote in 1993, addressing some of the same issues—such as the relationship between church and state—central to the 16th-century Christian Reformation. "The reformers' impact is not mere academic," she wrote in 1996. "By stimulating some of the most profound debate since Islam's emergence in the seventh century, they are laying the foundations for an Islamic Reformation"

Kramer adds that the "Reformation trope" soon became a staple of academic discussion of the Middle East, as one academic or another waited for the Muslim Reformation as if it would coincide with a Times Square ball drop. As Kramer notes, this Reformation trope was not new in the field of Orientalism; it was simply making a comeback. Earlier generations of academics had assumed the "inevitability of the Reformation" without considering the possibility that they were imposing their own parochial assumptions on a very different culture at a very different time with—importantly—a very different theology.

2. See Erik von Kuehnelt-Leddihn, "Martin Luther's Conservatism," *National Review*, November 25, 1983.
3. Deborah Sontag, "The Holy Land, in an Edgy Mood, Awaits the Pope's Visit," *New York Times*, March 19, 2000; www.nytimes.com/2000/03/19/world/the-holy-land-in-an-edgy-mood-awaits-the-pope-s-visit.html; accessed July 29, 2011.
4. Sarah Pulliam Bailey, "Campus Crusade Changes Name to Cru," *Christianity Today*, July 19, 2011; www.christianitytoday.com/ct/2011/julyweb-only/campus-crusade-name-change.html; accessed July 29, 2011.
5. Bernard Lewis, "Jihad vs. Crusade: Learning the Lingo," *Wall Street Journal*, September 27, 2001.
6. Thomas F. Madden, "Crusade Propaganda: The Abuse of Christianity's Holy Wars," *National Review Online*, November 2, 2001.
7. Lewis, "Jihad vs. Crusade."
8. Madden, "Crusade Propaganda."
9. Robert Lerner, Standish Meacham, and Edward Burns, *Western Civilizations: Their History and Their Culture* (New York: W. W. Norton, 1998), pp. 322–23, 329.
10. Maureen Dowd, *Bushworld: Enter at Your Own Risk* (New York: Berkley Books, 2005), p. 388.
11. Adam LeBor and Roger Boyes, *Seduced by Hitler: The Choices of a Nation and the Ethics of Survival* (Naperville, IL: Sourcebooks, 2001), p. 119.

12. From Norman Cameron and R. H. Stevens, trans., *Hitler's Table Talk 1941–1944: His Private Conversations* (London: Weidenfeld and Nicolson, 1953):

> There are towns in Germany from which all joy is lacking. I'm told that it's the same thing in certain Calvinistic regions of Switzerland. In Trier and Freiburg, women have addressed me in so ignoble a fashion that I cannot make up my mind to repeat their words. It's on such occasions that I become aware of the depth of human baseness. Clearly, one must not forget that these areas are still feeling the weight of several centuries of religious oppression. Near Wurzburg, there are villages where literally all the women were burned. We know of judges of the Court of the Inquisition who gloried in having had twenty to thirty thousand "witches" burned. Long experience of such horrors cannot but leave indelible traces upon a population. In Madrid, the sickening odour of the heretic's pyre remained for more than two centuries mingled with the air one breathed. If a revolution breaks out again in Spain, one must see in it the natural reaction to an interminable series of atrocities. One cannot succeed in conceiving how much cruelty, ignominy and falsehood the intrusion of Christianity has spelt for this world of ours. If the misdeeds of Christianity were less serious in Italy, that's because the people of Rome, having seen them at work, always knew exactly the worth of the Popes before whom Christendom prostrated itself. For centuries, no Pope died except by the dagger, poison or the pox.

13. Gloria Steinem, *The Revolution Within: A Book of Self-Esteem* (Boston: Little, Brown, 1992), p. 133.
14. Dan Brown, *The Da Vinci Code* (New York: Anchor Books, 2003), p. 134.
15. Jenny Gibbons, "Recent Developments in the Study of the Great European Witch Hunt" *The Pomegranate* 5 (Lammas, 1998).
16. Brian Levack, *The Witch Hunt in Early Modern Europe* (Longman, 2006), p. 23.
17. Laura Miller, "Who Burned the Witches?" *Salon*, February 1, 2005; www.salon.com/books/review/2005/02/01/witch_craze; accessed July 29, 2011.
18. Joseph Klaits, *Servants of Satan: The Age of the Witch Hunts* (Bloomington: Indiana University Press, 1985), p. 85.
19. Thomas F. Madden, "The Real Inquisition: Investigating the Popular Myth," *National Review*, June 18, 2004; old.nationalreview.com/comment/madden200406181026.asp; accessed July 29, 2011.
20. Jenny Gibbons, "Recent Developments in the Study of the Great European Witch Hunt," *The Pomegranate* 5 (Lammas, 1998).
21. *Suprema Congregatio Sanctæ Romanæ et Univeralis Inquisitionis.* The name went through several formulations before this one. According to the "Roman Congregations" entry in the *Catholic Encyclopedia* (available online at www.

newadvent.org/cathen/13136a.htm): "From its first title of *Romana Inquisitio* was derived the usage of calling this body Congregation of the Holy Roman Universal Inquisition. Sixtus V, in the Bull 'Immensa', calls it *Congregatio pro S. inquisitione* and also *Congregatio sanct inquisitionis hæreticæ pravitatis.* Benedict XIV calls it *Romanæ Universalis Inquisitionis Congregatio* (Const. 'Sollicita')".

22. Thomas F. Madden, "The Truth about the Spanish Inquisition," *Crisis* (September 2003); accessed June 20, 2011, www.crisismagazine.com/2011/the-truth-about-the-sp.
23. Ibid.
24. Ibid.
25. Henry Kamen, *The Spanish Inquisition: A Historical Revision* (New Haven, Conn.: Yale University Press, 1997), p. 49.
26. Friedrich Nietzsche, *The Antichrist* (1888). Republished by See Sharp Press (January 1999), p. 91.
27. For instance, Steven Pinker writes in "A History of Violence," *The New Republic Online*, March 20, 2007:

    > [Q]uantitative body-counts—such as the proportion of prehistoric skeletons with axe marks and embedded arrowheads or the proportion of men in a contemporary foraging tribe who die at the hands of other men—suggest that pre-state societies were far more violent than our own. . . . If the wars of the 20th century had killed the same proportion of the population that died in the wars of a typical tribal society, there would have been two billion deaths, not 100 million.

    For more on the subject, see Lawrence Keeley's seminal *War Before Civilization: The Myth of the Peaceful Savage* (New York: Oxford University Press, 1997) and Matt Ridley's brilliant *The Rational Optimist* (New York: Harper, 2010).
28. John Reed, *Ten Days That Shook the World* (New York: Boni and Liveright, 1919), p. 144.
29. John D. Sutter "Philosopher: Why we should ditch religion," *CNN Opinion*, March 25, 2010.

22.: Spiritual but Not Religious

1. Michael Valpy, "International Man of Mystery," *The Globe and Mail*, April 10, 2004.
2. Chris Colin, "The Bodhisattva of PR," *Salon*, December 6, 2000.
3. Rod Dreher, "Disney's Curious Aversion to Catholicism," *Dallas Morning News*, December 23, 2009.
4. Charles Krauthammer, "Home Alone 3: The White House," *Washington Post*, May 14, 1993, p. A31.

5. Norman Lear, "A Call for Spiritual Renewal," *Washington Post*, May 30, 1993, p. C7.

23.: Understanding

1. See Gil Hoffman, "6 in 10 Palestinians Reject 2-State Solution, Survey Finds," *Jerusalem Post*, July 15, 2011; accessed August 11, 2011, www.jpost.com/DiplomacyAndPolitics/Article.aspx?id=229493.
2. Russell Jacoby, *Bloodlust: On the Roots of Violence from Cain and Abel to the Present* (New York: Free Press, 2011).
3. Ibid., p. 42.
4. Sigmund Freud, *Civilization and its Discontents* (1930), trans., James Strachey (London: W.W. Norton, 1961).
5. For example, see Maureen Dowd, "Not O.K. at the O.K. Corral," *New York Times*, July 26, 2011.
6. Masahiro Mori, "The Uncanny Valley," trans., Karl F. MacDorman and Takashi Minato, *Energy*, 7 no. 4 (1970) pp. 33–35.
7. Freud, *Civilization and its Discontents*.
8. Charles Dickens, *Bleak House* (London: Bradbury and Evans, 1853), p. 26.
9. Montesquieu, "Book XX: Of Laws in Relation to Commerce, Considered in its Nature and Distinctions," *The Spirit of the Laws* (Cambridge University Press, 1989).
10. Daniel Griswold, "Peace on Earth? Try Free Trade among Men," *Cato Online* (December 28, 2005); accessed May 22, 2010, www.cato.org/pub_display.php?pub_id=5344.
11. Erik Gartzke, "Future Depends on Capitalizing on Capitalist Peace," October 1, 2005; accessed May 22, 2010, www.cato.org/pub_display.php?pub_id=5133. See also Donald J. Bordeaux, "Want World Peace? Support Free Trade," *Christian Science Monitor*, November 20, 2006; accessed May 22, 2010, www.csmonitor.com/2006/1120/p09s02-coop.html.

24.: Democracy and Unity

1. Thomas Jefferson, "Notes on the State of Virginia, Query 13, 120–21," *The Founders Constitution* (A web project of the University of Chicago); accessed August 17, 2011, press-pubs.uchicago.edu/founders/documents/v1ch10s9.html.
2. James Madison, "Speech at the Virginia Convention to Ratify the Federal Constitution," June 6, 1788.
3. William Jennings Bryan, *Omaha World-Herald*, September 23, 1892, quoted in Paolo E. Coletta, *William Jennings Bryan: Volume 1* (Lincoln: University of Nebraska Press, 1964), p. 75; H. Wayne Morgan, *From Hayes to McKinley: National*

Party Politics, 1877–1896 (Syracuse, N.Y.: Syracuse University Press, 1969), p. 496.

4. Woodrow Wilson, *Leaders of Men*, ed. T. H. Vail Motter (Princeton, N.J.: Princeton University Press, 1952), pp. 20, 25.
5. Elias Canetti, *Crowds and Power* (New York: Farrar, Straus & Giroux, 1984), p. 18.
6. In this they were all Rousseau's children. It was his idea of the general will that empowered secular despots to find legitimacy in "the people" without paying heed to actual persons: "For the rulers well know that the general will is always on the side which is most favorable to the public interest, that is to say, the most equitable; so that it is needful only to act justly to be certain of following the general will." *A Discourse on Political Economy*, 1755.
7. Bertolt Brecht, "The Decision," in John Willett, *The Theatre of Bertolt Brecht: A Study from Eight Aspects* (London: Methuen, 1959).

Afterword to the Paperback Edition

1. Nearly every charge of lying boiled down to Ryan's not raising counterarguments favorable to Obama—a standard not normally applied to politicians, and certainly never considered the litmus test for truth-telling. Notoriously, Ryan noted that in 2008 Obama suggested that an auto plant in Ryan's district that was scheduled for closure would stay open for 100 years if he was elected. The fact-checkers and Obama campaign surrogates immediately cried foul: The plant, they said, actually closed under Bush! But the AP ignored its own (accurate) reporting on the plant's closing in 2009 in order to make its "fact-check" as damning as possible. The second problem: Ryan's point was not that Obama's prediction was factually wrong, but that Obama over promised. The fact-checkers opted to twist Ryan's point into something he wasn't saying, and then charged him with lying for saying it.

INDEX

abortion, 29, 72, 80, 81, 232, 258–59
ACLU, 76, 123
Acton, Lord, Axiom of, 84–86, 178
Adams, John, 41
Addams, Jane, 49, 107
Adorno, Theodore, 34, 212–13, 214
affirmative action, 96–98, 187
Affluent Society, The (Galbraith), 57, 201
Affordable Care Act, 129, 203
AFL-CIO, 133
African Americans, 95–96, 106, 164, 166, 168, 202, 205, 217, 225, 226, 227, 270, 273, 282*n*
  life expectancy rates of, 29, 30
  9/11 commemorating statue and, 91–92
  racial quotas and, 96–98
Albom, Mitch, 122–23
All the King's Men (Warren), 272
American Atheists, 76
American Civilization, 193
American Communists, 124, 129
American Economic Association, 49, 82, 83
"American exceptionalism," 126–27
American Indians, 29, 96, 252
American Journal of Sociology, 288*n*–89*n*
American Mind, The (Commager), 108
American Nazi Party, 133
American Political Science Review, 213
American Pragmatism, 44, 45, 46–58
  Dewey's contributions to, 54–56, 69
  ideology as supposedly absent in, 14, 22, 24–25, 52, 55–56, 57–58
  James's optimistic approach to, 46–50, 53
  "moral equivalent of war" idea in, 48, 49–52
  Obama and, 22, 52–53, 69
  see also pragmatism
American Society of Newspaper Editors, 93
Angelou, Maya, 190, 202
Animal House, 90, 234–35
anti-Semitism, 250, 251, 264–65
Architectural Digest, 177
Aristotle, 9, 96, 221
Arizona, 273
Ashcroft, John, 68, 69
Asian Americans, 29, 95, 97
atheists, atheism, 76–77, 204, 211, 214, 244, 252, 254
Atlas, Scott W., 26–27
Audacity of Hope, The (Obama), 22
Austro-Hungarian Empire, 266
Authoritarian Personality, The (Adorno), 212–13
Autobiography (Darwin), 104
Avatar, 259

Bannister, Robert C., 110, 112
Barrett, Scott, 286*n*
BBC World Service, 5
Beamer, Todd, 275–76
Beard, Charles, 58, 110, 124, 163, 213
Bentham, Jeremy, 156–57
Better Angels of Our Nature, The (Pinker), 182
Bill of Rights, 142, 148, 162, 270
bin Laden, Osama, 5, 68–69, 235, 240, 242
Bismarck, Otto Von, 45, 49
"Blackstone ratio," 153–58
Blazing Saddles, 196
Bleak House (Dickens), 265
Bloodlust (Jacoby), 262–63
Bloomberg, Michael, 59, 60, 64, 230, 231
"boiling frog" parable, 115, 118–19
Bollinger, Lee, 95, 96
Bolsheviks, 36, 253–54
bourgeoisie, 192, 195, 196, 198, 199, 200, 201, 203
Boutelle, Paul (Kwame Montsho Ajamu Somburu), 123

Bracton, Henry de, 228, 299*n*
Britannica Concise Encyclopedia, 8
British Empire, 33, 187, 188
Brooklyn College School of Education, 136, 137
Brooks, David, 8, 192, 198
Browder, Earl, 63
Buchanan, Pat, 172, 199
Buckley, William F., Jr., 1, 5, 71, 172
Buck v. Bell, 107, 165–66
Buddhism, 239, 256, 257–59
Burke, Edmund, 33, 37, 40, 116, 117, 121
Bush, George W., 26, 34, 81, 120, 121, 122, 168, 183–84, 240, 242, 276

Caddyshack, 131–32
California, 97, 155, 217, 223
California, University of, Berkeley, 204, 205, 214, 217
Calvinists, 77, 237, 238, 301*n*
Campus Crusade for Christ, 240
Canada, 28, 73, 161, 231
capitalism, 40, 54, 83, 116, 141, 143, 177, 195, 196, 201–2, 266, 271, 273
  Social Darwinism and, 100, 103, 107–9, 110–12
Capital Times, 123
Carnegie, Andrew, 109, 110, 111, 112
Cartagena, Alonso de, bishop of Burgos, 250
Carter, Jimmy, 51, 260
Castile Inquisition, 251
Castro, Fidel, 84, 214, 215
Catholic Church, 44, 74, 77, 78, 106, 119, 234, 235, 254–55
  conversos of, 250–51
  criticisms and hatred of, 252, 253, 254
  Crusades and, 240–43
  doctrine of infallibility in, 86
  Galileo controversy and, 8, 10–11, 78, 247
  as hindrance to science and progress, 8–9, 10–11, 254
  Inquisitions and, *see* Inquisitions
  JFK and, 79–80
  Protestant Reformation and, 77, 85, 235, 236–38, 239, 246, 247, 300
  "social justice" concept in, 137–41
  "tradition of existence" in, 235, 239
  witch hunts and, 243–47, 301*n*
Catholic Encyclopedia, 302*n*
censorship, 37, 50, 120, 135
"center," false notion of, 6–11, 23
Chait, Jonathan, 25–26, 28, 30
Chappaquiddick scandal, 86–88
Chase, Stuart, 16, 53
Chesterton, G. K., 5, 66, 68, 106, 127
China, 15, 16, 51, 86, 149, 266
"China Syndrome" pragmatism, 58
Christian Coalition, 76
Christianity, 9, 44, 46, 67, 76, 77, 81, 82, 111, 180, 185, 214, 215, 217, 235, 236, 240, 247, 248, 250, 256, 258, 260, 265
  businessmen influenced by, 111–12
  criticisms and hatred of, 252, 253, 254, 301*n*–2*n*
  geocentrism myth of, 8–11
  heretical movements in, 247–48, 249, 251, 53, 301*n*
  Islam vs., 238
  in Progressive movement, 82–83
  see also Catholic Church; religion
Christianizing the Social Crisis (Rauschenbusch), 83
"Christian socialism," 82–83
Chu, Steven, 231–32
Civilization and Its Discontents (Freud), 264
civil liberties, 253
  slippery slope arguments and, 116, 119–21
civil society, 138, 151
Civil War, U.S., 114, 119, 181
  and postwar prosperity, 109–10
class systems, 45–46, 195–99, 211
  see also middle class
clichés, 2–17
  in advancing of ideological agendas, 14–17
  "center" concept and, 6–11
  cowardice of, 2–4
  misquoted phrases as, 2–3, 4
  as political buzzwords, 6, 15
climate change, 72–74, 205, 206
Climate Change, 286*n*
Clinton, Bill, 95, 129, 190–91, 200, 230, 264
  appeal to "middle class" by, 191, 199–200, 202
Clinton, Hillary, 22, 129–30, 151, 191, 199, 200, 260
Cohn, Jonathan, 13–14
Collected Essays, Journalism and Letters of George Orwell (Orwell), 1
collectivism, 11, 49, 54
colonial America, 33, 116, 188
  religious pluralism in, 78–79
Colorado, University of (Boulder), 137
Colorado, University of Northern, 92
Columbia University, 95, 97, 123, 125
Columbus, Christopher, 10, 70, 124
Communist Manifesto, The (Marx), 195, 196
Communists, communism, 21, 46, 63, 103, 116, 124, 129, 140, 150, 152, 194, 211, 212, 213, 215, 243, 248, 253, 276

"Competitiveness: A Dangerous Obsession" (Krugman), 15
Conference of the Methodist Episcopal Church, 287*n*
Confessions (Rousseau), 172
Congress, U.S., 30–31, 51, 69, 79, 120, 129, 168, 228
"Conservatism and Personality" study (McClosky), 213
conservatives, conservatism, 40, 63, 64, 69, 84, 86, 92, 93, 95, 103, 127, 149, 211, 215, 235, 252, 259, 271
  alleged "antiscience" stance of, 204, 205–7
  and amending of Constitution, 168–70
  as first opponents of ideology, 31, 32–34
  health care and, 26, 117
  as "inflexible ideologues," 23–26, 30, 34–35
  institutional biases against, 216–17
  "Let-them-eat-cake" indictment of, 171–72, 174, 175
  liberal eugenicists vs. eugenicists in, 106–7
  living constitution opposed by, 165, 167
  pseudoscientific studies on causes of, 34, 46, 207–10, 212–16, 217–19
  slippery slope arguments of, 116, 117
  Social Darwinism unfairly linked to, 100, 101, 102, 108–9, 112
Conservative Soul, The (Sullivan), 34–35
Constitution, U.S., 151, 153, 159, 160, 271–72
  amending of, 168–70
  Article II of, 166–67
  call for reinterpretation of, 14, 162–70
  liberals on "original intent" of, 168–70
  Progressive criticisms of, 162–63
Constitution of Social Justice (Rosmini-Serbati), 138
conversos, 250–51
Cooper, Alice, 220, 222
Copernicus, Nicolaus, 8, 9, 10
Coughlin, Charles, 55, 139, 140–41
Crawley, Ernest, 263–64
criminals, 153–58, 184, 293*n*–94*n*
Croly, Herbert, 57, 82, 106–7, 143–44, 160–61, 292*n*
Crowds and Power (Canetti), 275
Crusades, 240–43
Crutzen, Paul, 286*n*
Cuba, 86, 177
Cuomo, Mario, 80, 101

Dalai Lama, 257, 258–59
Danielson, Dennis R., 9, 10
Darwin, Charles, 103–5, 107, 108, 110, 111, 112–13, 160, 162, 289*n*
Darwinism, 46, 100, 102, 103–5, 107, 108, 111
  Progressives influenced by, 112–13, 161–62, 168
  see also Social Darwinism
"Darwin's Influence Upon Philosophy" (Dewey), 162
Das Kapital (Marx), 105, 195, 211
Da Vinci Code, The (Brown), 244–45
Dawes, Christopher T., 207–8
Dean, Howard, 226–27
"Death of Conservatism, The" (Tanenhaus), 34
Décade philosophique, littéraire, et politique, La, 40, 41
Defendant, The (Chesterton), 127
De l'Espirit (Helvétius), 3
Delisi, Matt, 155–56
democracy, 48, 268–73, 304*n*
  purest form of, 269–70
  tyrannies imposed by, 270–71
  voting rights and expansion of, 272–73
Democracy in America (de Tocqueville), 232, 33, 288*n*
Democratic Party, Democrats, 6, 31, 59, 64, 80, 84, 101, 120, 128, 129, 141, 172, 190–91, 199, 207, 217, 227, 272
  identity politics of, 190, 191, 199
  "interest-group liberalism" of, 191, 202
  "middle class" agenda of, 191–92, 199–200, 202–3
  National Conventions of, 82, 101, 191, 200
Descartes, René, 66, 220
despotism, 270–71, 304*n*
Destutt de Tracy, Comte Claude, 40–41
Detroit Free Press, 122–23
Dewey, John, 50, 54–56, 62, 63, 64, 69, 160, 162, 163, 203
dictators, 86, 151, 269
Disney, 260
dissent, 122–25
  as "highest form of patriotism," 122–23, 124, 126
  liberal persecution of, 128–30
diversity, 4, 89–99, 137
  affirmative action and, 96–98
  in educational environments, 95–98
  Progressives' view of, 91, 95, 99
  social fraying as result of, 98–99
  Streisand-*LA Times* controversy and, 89–91
  in weakening of groups and communities, 93, 94–95, 98–99
Do as I Say (Not as I Do) (Schweizer), 99
dogma, 66–75, 80, 117, 154, 157, 174
  Buddhism as form of, 257–59
  of climate change, 72–74

enemies of, 66, 67–69
karma vs., 256
pragmatism and dissolution of, 46, 48, 53, 56, 58, 69
as source of progress, 70–71
Dorf, Michael C., 165, 166–67

Eastern Orthodox Church, 77
Eastern philosophy, 256–59
Economic Freedom and Representative Government (Hayek), 131
Economic Interpretation of the Constitution of the United States, An (Beard), 163
economics, 14–16, 25–26, 30, 41, 54–55, 82, 100, 116–17, 201
laissez-faire, 16, 40, 83, 105, 106–7
"Let-them-eat-cake" mentality and, 171, 172, 173–75
Marxist theory of, 195–97, 198, 266
Progressive thought on, 16, 30, 53–54, 57, 105–7, 139
Social Darwinism and, 105–12
socialist, 53, 54–56, 109
war as boon in, 51–52
see also capitalism
education, 135, 202, 205, 223, 259
anti-conservative bias in, 217
"disposition for social justice" in, 136–37
in diverse environments, 95–98
religious schools and, 119
tuition increases in, 174–75
Eight Americans (2006 study), 29
Einstein, Albert, 95, 161
elections, U.S., 8, 34, 120, 141, 208, 272
of 1932, 50, 140
of 1964, 129
of 1992, 190–91, 199–200
of 2000, 164
Ely, Richard, 82–83, 152, 161–62, 287*n*
Emerson, Ralph Waldo, 44, 261
"Emperor's New Clothes, The" (Anderson), 224
empiricism, 36–37, 55, 56, 116, 154, 207
ideologies disguised with, 14, 24–27, 28–31, 35, 69
see also pragmatism; science
Enlightenment, 39, 40, 66, 175, 181, 237
environmentalism, 51, 81, 104, 135, 137, 147, 50, 177
dogma of, 72–74
Ethics (Dewey and Hayden-Tufts), 163
eugenics, 212, 218
conservative vs. liberal, 106–7
in Progressive economics, 105–7
Social Darwinism and, 101, 103, 105–7, 113
evolutionary theory, 100, 103, 104, 111, 115, 204, 289*n*
Progressives influenced by, 112–13, 161–62
extremists, 6–7, 21

"Fact Finders: The Anti-Dogma Dogma" (Chait), 25–26
Fallows, James, 16, 86
fascism, 21, 46, 49, 100, 103, 138, 147, 152, 168, 183, 184, 197, 211, 212, 215, 224, 276
Fast Company, 119
Federal Communications Commission (FCC), 134
Federalist Papers, 270, 271
Feminine Mystique, The (Friedan), 194–95
feminism, 31, 191, 194–95, 200, 205, 244, 259
Ford Foundation, 133
Foreign Affairs, 15
Founding Fathers, 40, 152, 159, 163, 164, 213, 271
Hamiltonian vs. Jeffersonian, 192
"original intent" of, 168–70
religious pluralism and, 79
Fourteenth Amendment, 107, 169
Fowler, James H., 207–8
France, 29, 31, 39, 172, 175, 198
bakery regulation in, 173–74
"ideology" in, 40–45
Reign of Terror in, 40, 42, 253
"Francis Herbert Bradley" (Eliot), 114
Frank, Barney, 147, 149, 150
Franklin, Benjamin, 168, 228, 229, 299*n*
freedom fighters, 4–6
free markets, 16, 21, 40, 100, 103, 143, 202
French Revolution, 32, 33, 34, 40–41
Freud, Sigmund, 263–65
Friedan, Betty, 194–95
Friedman, Milton, 30, 109
Friedman, Thomas, 14–15, 16, 51
Friends of Voltaire, The (Tallentyre), 2–3
"F-scale" test, 212, 218

Galbraith, John Kenneth, 39, 56–57, 68, 201
Galileo Galilei, 8, 10–11, 78, 95, 247
Galston, William, 60–61
Gandhi, Mohandas K., 5, 185–89, 259, 263
nonviolent stance of, 180, 185, 187–89
Gandhi (film), 187
gay rights, 119, 134, 200, 201, 271
gender quotas, 96–98
Genesis, book of, 153–54
geocentrism, 9, 10
geoengineering, 73, 206, 286*n*

Germany, 49, 109, 128, 129, 151, 183, 188, 212, 214, 244, 246, 251, 265, 301*n*
Gilded Age, 107, 108, 109, 111
global warming, 51, 72–74, 219
"God's Funeral" (Hardy), 284*n*
Goldman, Eric, 49, 53, 107
Goldwater, Barry, 129, 213
Gore, Al, 73, 159, 164, 191, 264
government, 147–52
  constitutional limits on, 271–72
  democracy and, 268–73
  "living constitution" and, *see* "living constitution"
  in obligation to protect citizens, 157–58
  prevention principle as crusade of, 229–33
  progressive support for expansion of, 13, 14–17, 26, 30–31, 50–51, 152, 163, 165–66, 230–33
  social justice and intervention of, 142–43
  universal health care and, 230–31
  "war socialism" and, 50–51, 232
Great Britain, 33, 78, 109, 110, 116, 161, 183, 187, 188, 196, 248, 259
  abolition of slavery in, 180, 185
Great Depression, 50, 52
Great Society programs, 51, 201
Greece, ancient, 159, 160, 236
Greenberg, Stanley, 199, 262
Green Party, 135–36, 137
groupthink, 93–94, 216, 218, 288*n*
Growth of American Thought, The (Curti), 108
Guardian, 209
Gulf oil spill (2010), 52, 206

Harvard Crimson, 133
Harvard University, 27, 98, 119, 168, 206
Hawaii, 135
Hayek, Friedrich A., 32, 33, 54, 131, 142, 143, 211
Hazlitt, Henry, 109–10
Head Start, 69–70, 149, 226
health care, 13–14, 26–30, 71, 86, 117, 129, 135, 202–3, 230
  prevention principle in, 228, 229–31, 299*n*–300*n*
  WHO study on, 26–27, 28
Hegel, F. W., 45, 113, 152, 160
Helvétius, Claude Adrien, 3
Henry IV, Holy Roman Emperor, 77
Henry VIII, King of England, 176, 248
Hillel, Rabbi, 257, 258
"hindsight is 20/20," 12–14
Hinduism, 187, 256, 263
Hippocratic Oath, 72
Hispanics, 92, 96
history:
  Progressive pragmatist disregard for, 12–14, 53–54, 66, 69, 162, 166, 167–68
  "right side"/"wrong side" of, 11–12
  as science, 85, 86
History of the Conflict Between Religion and Science (Draper), 234
History of the World Part I, 249
"History of Violence, A" (Pinker), 302*n*–3*n*
Hitler, Adolf, 32, 61, 67, 103, 105, 124, 129, 188, 189, 204, 214, 244, 246, 276, 301*n*–2*n*
Hitlerism, 100, 107, 129
Hitler's Table Talk 1941–1944 (Cameron and Stevens, trans.), 301*n*–2*n*
Hofstadter, Richard, 107–8, 110–11, 112, 213
Hollywood culture, 175–79
  spirituality over religion promoted in, 256, 257, 258, 259
Holmes, Oliver Wendell, Jr., 161, 162, 163
  Buck v. Bell decision and, 107, 165–66
Holocaust, 188, 189, 239, 240, 253
homosexuality, 205, 258–59, 264
  see also gay rights
Hoover, Herbert, 232
Hoover Dam, 149, 292*n*–93*n*
House of Representatives, U.S.:
  Select Committee on Intelligence of, 73
  Un-American Activities Committee of, 128
housing laws, 174
Huffington Post, 88, 132
Hurricane Katrina, 91
Hussein, Saddam, 183, 257

I Am Sam, 268
Ibn Saud of Saudi Arabia, 238
identity politics, 190, 191, 199, 201, 225, 226
idéologistes, 40–42
ideologues, 21, 22, 25, 27, 35, 42, 43, 44, 45, 53, 57, 61, 62, 214–15
  conservatives perceived as, 23–26, 34–35
ideology, 19, 21–38, 53, 91, 185, 207–19
  American pragmatism seen as lacking in, 22, 24–25, 52, 55–56, 57–58
  bipartisan antipathy to, 3, 31–32, 39
  coining of term, 40, 41
  conservatives as first opponents of, 31, 32–34
  definitions of, 31, 32, 33–34, 37–38
  in delegitimizing political opponents, 22–25, 30, 35, 39, 43–44, 46, 64
  empiricism in disguising of, 14, 24–27, 28–31, 35, 69
  "false consciousness" and, 45–46

French Revolution and birth of, 40–41
liberal/Progressive platform and, 14, 19, 21–26, 27, 30–31, 34, 56, 57–58, 69
Napoleon's role in shaping connotations of, 39, 42–45
No Labels movement and, 61–62, 64–65
political "center" vs., 7–8
scientific rhetoric and, 72–74, 205, 207, 211–12, 215, 219
separation of church and state as, 76–77, 79
"social justice" as, 143–44
imperialism, 146, 185, 189
Crusades myth and, 241–43
India, 185, 186–87, 188, 263
individualism, 49, 82, 106
infant mortality, 28–29
Inferno (Dante), 9
Inquisitions, 234, 247–53
Medieval, 247–48
Spanish, 248–52, 253, 301*n*
torture in, 249
"witch hunts" myth of, 243–47, 301*n*
Institut National, 41
International Herald Tribune, 184
Introduction to Political Economy, An (Ely), 287*n*
Iran, 76, 239
Iranian Revolution (1979), 239
Iraq war, 122, 129, 184, 209, 210
Islam, 235, 241, 242, 263, 264
Christianity vs., 238
fanatical reformation of, 238–39, 240
need for central authority in, 239
search for "Protestant Reformation" of, 235–36, 238, 239, 300*n*
see also Muslims
"Is Prevention Better Than Cure?" (Russell), 229
Israel, 6, 189, 205, 262, 270
Italian Fascism, 49, 211, 224, 276
Italian Socialist Party, 214
Italy, 51, 197, 211, 246
It Takes a Village (Clinton), 151
Ivory Towers on Sand (Kramer), 235–36

Jackson, Jesse, Jr., 91, 191
Jacobins, 33, 36, 42, 67, 253
Jacoby, Russell, 262–63
James, William, 44, 46–49, 50, 53
Japan, 16, 29
Japanese Americans, 120
Jefferson, Thomas, 40, 41, 79, 122, 123, 144, 270, 271
Jerusalem, 240, 241
Jesus Christ, 11, 32, 69, 77, 82, 185, 211, 212, 242, 250, 257
Jeweler's Eye, The (Buckley), 172
Jews, Judaism, 78, 81, 95, 194, 205, 240, 241, 243, 254, 256, 257, 258, 262, 263, 265–66
anti-Semitism and, 250, 251, 264–65
educational quotas and, 97
Gandhi's peculiar advice to, 188–89
in Spanish Inquisition, 249–52
jihadists, 21, 69, 240, 241
Johnson, KC, 136–37
Johnson, Lyndon B., 13–14, 51, 59, 96, 209
Johnson, Paul, 185–86, 187
Journal of Criminology, 155
Journal of Forensic Psychiatry & Psychology, 155–56
justice, 159–61
"ten guilty men" principle and, 153–58

Kaballah, 258
Kabul, 265–66
Kagan, Elena, 167, 169
Kallen, Horace, 53, 69
Kanaka Maoli, 135
Kanazawa, Satoshi, 204, 216–17
Kansas, 193
Kansas, University of, 137
karma, 256–57
Kennedy, Edward Moore "Ted," 86–88, 122
Kennedy, John F., 51, 209
Catholicism of, 79–80
"cool pragmatism" of, 56–57
Kerry, John, 77, 80–81, 122, 191
Kevorkian, Jack, 68, 124
Keynes, John Maynard, 51, 54
King, Martin Luther, Jr., 4, 5, 236, 274
Kloppenberg, James, 52–53
Kopechne, Mary Jo, 87–88
Korean Demilitarized Zone (DMZ), 59–60
Kosovo, 129
Kramer, Martin, 235–36, 300*n*
Krugman, Paul, 15, 28, 51–52, 204
Kuehnelt-Leddihn, Erik von, 31, 32, 236

labels, 38, 44, 59–65, 231
movements to get rid of, 59–62, 64–65
rebranding of, 62–64
Lady Justice, 159–61, 168
laissez-faire economics, 16, 40, 83, 105, 106–7
Lakoff, George, 6
Lasch, Christopher, 193*n*, 194
Leahy, Patrick, 169–70
"Lean Forward" ad campaign, 149–50
Leninism, 63, 211, 266

lesbian, gay, bisexual, and transgender (LGBT) movement, 134
"Let them eat cake," 171–79
alleged conservative mentality of, 171–72, 174, 175
authorship of, 171–73
French bakery regulations and, 173–74
Hollywood celebrities as embodiment of, 175–79
Levin, Ishaq, 265–66
Lewis, Anthony, 68–69, 129
Lewis, Bernard, 240–41
Lewis, Sinclair, 193, 194, 264
Liberal Fascism (Goldberg), 50
liberals, liberalism, 11, 63, 83, 86, 103, 112, 115, 152, 164, 165, 168, 175, 182, 187, 200, 204, 212, 215, 240
"American exceptionalism" deplored by, 126–27
anti-ideological/non-ideological stance claimed by, 14, 19, 21–26, 27, 30–31, 34, 56, 57–58, 61, 62, 64, 69
anti-label movement of, 62, 63–65
confusing patriotic stance of, 126–28, 130
conservative eugenicists vs. eugenicists in, 106–7
"conservative phrenology" studies and, 34, 207–10, 212–16, 217–19
Constitutional amendments opposed by, 169–70
damaging "compassionate" schemes endorsed by, 174–75
definitions of, 216, 242
dissent and, 122–23, 128–30
empirical reasoning claimed in, 24–27, 28, 69, 207
expansion of voting rights and, 226, 272–73
"factual correctness" and, 92
Founders' "original intent" invoked by, 168–70
health care and, 13–14, 26–30, 202–3, 228, 230, 231
limiting principle lacking in, 38, 58, 144, 232–33
McCarthyite tactics employed by, 128–29
middle class denigrated by, 192–94, 200
1950s prosperity and threat to, 200–201
patriotism questioned by, 125–26, 130
political fetishization of youth by, 224, 225, 226–27
pragmatism's lasting impact on, 22, 23, 24–25, 48, 50–53, 56–58, 69
prevention principle of, 230, 231–33
Progressives rebranded as, 103
"proscience" stance maintained by, 205–7, 218–19
public-work projects and, 149–51
scientific bias in favor of, 210, 215–18
Social Darwinism villified by, 101, 103, 105, 107, 109, 112, 113
social justice as hallmark of, 132, 135, 139–42, 143–44
spirituality endorsed by, 259–60
"Understanding brings peace" belief of, 261–62
see also Democratic Party, Democrats; Progressives, progressivism
libertarianism, 40, 69, 71, 81, 181, 182, 203, 215
flexible ideologies of, 23–24
Social Darwinism and, 103, 105, 107
life expectancy, 28, 29–30, 230
Life of Brian, 145, 261
Limbaugh, Rush, 204, 214
Lincoln, Abraham, 71, 114, 185
"living constitution," 14, 159, 161, 162–70
intellectual roots of, 161, 162, 163–64, 167–68
State expansions in, 13, 163, 165–66
Supreme Court appointments and, 164–65
Living Constitution, Dying Faith (Watson), 164*n*
Living Wage, A (Ryan), 140
Lochner decision, 107
Lopez, Jennifer, 175, 176
Los Angeles, Calif., 98, 99
Los Angeles Times, 89–91, 209, 218
Louis XVI, King of France, 171
Luther, Martin, 235–38, 239
Lutherans, 77, 237, 238

McCarthy, Joseph, 128, 243
McCarthyism, 120, 125, 128, 243
McClosky, Herbert, 213, 214
McGovern, George, 199, 226
Madden, Thomas, 241–42, 246, 248, 250
Maddow, Rachel, 149–50
Madison, James, 270–71
Madonna, 178, 258
Maimonides, Moses, 9, 154
Malleus Maleficarum (*This Witches' Hammer*) (Kraimer), 244, 245
Malthus, Thomas, 104, 289*n*
Marie Antoinette, Queen of France, 171–72, 173–74
Marie-Thérèse, Queen of Spain, 172
Marx, Karl, 45–46, 105, 195–97, 198
Marxism, 12, 32, 34, 47, 55, 63, 67, 140, 197, 198, 253, 266

class system in, 45–46, 195–97, 198, 211
"false consciousness" theory of, 45–46, 202, 211
scientific gospel of, 46, 211–12
Maryland, University of (Baltimore County), 137
"Mechanisms of the Slippery Slope, The" (Volokh), 118
Medicare, 13–14, 25, 149, 215, 226, 229
Medieval Inquisition, 247–48
Michigan, University of, 96–97
Middle Ages, 183, 265
"Middle America," 192–94
middle class, 191–95, 199–203
cultural elite's denigration of, 192–95, 199
Democratic strategic appeal to, 191–92, 199–200, 202–3
meaning of, 191–92
Middle East, 185, 236, 238–39, 240, 241, 242, 300*n*
Middlemarch (Eliot), 70
military, U.S., 52, 148, 181, 200, 216, 222
Miller, Laura, 245
minimum wage, 106
Ministry of International, Trade and Industry (MITI), 16
Mirage of Social Justice (Hayek), 142
Mr. Rogers Neighborhood, 223
Money, 174
Monty Python, 55, 249, 261
Monty Python and the Holy Grail, 246
Moore, Michael, 149, 177
moral equivalence, 48–52
More, Thomas, 124, 248
Morehouse College, 96
MSNBC, 149–50
Muhammed, 238, 242
Muslim American Society, 133
Muslims, 180, 189, 235, 239, 249, 250, 263
Crusades myth and, 240–43
see also Islam
Mussolini, Benito, 51, 57, 138, 197, 204, 214, 276

Napoleon I, Emperor of France, 39, 41–45, 59, 64, 196
Nation, 193
National Council for Accreditation of Teacher Education (NCATE), 136
National Gay & Lesbian Chamber of Commerce (NGLCC), 134
National Intelligence Council, 73
National Recovery Administration (NRA), 50–51
National Review, 1, 11, 30, 89
National September 11 Memorial and Museum, 76
National Union of Social Justice (NUSJ), 141
Nazis, Nazism, 21, 32, 61, 69, 128, 129, 133, 151, 183, 187, 188–89, 212, 213, 244, 251, 253, 276
Never Enough (Voegeli), 58
New Deal, 16, 24, 50–51, 53, 54, 58, 128, 140–41, 168, 201, 272, 275
New England Primer, 234
New Orleans, La., 260
New Republic, 13, 25, 34, 57, 106–7, 160–61, 183
Newseum, 133
New Yorker, 192
New York Times, 28, 38, 68, 89, 118, 129, 168, 182, 204, 213, 240, 242
"*n* Guilty Men" study (Volokh), 153–54
Nietzsche, Friedrich, 45, 46–47, 48, 49, 103
Nixon, Richard, 120, 199, 226
No Labels movement, 59–61, 64, 274
Nordlinger, Jay, 11, 12
North Korea, 60, 143, 183
Norwegian massacre (2011), 132
Notes on the State of Virginia (Jefferson), 270

Oakeshott, Michael, 33, 34, 35–37
Obama, Barack, 14, 15, 31, 63, 70, 101, 121, 126, 128, 133, 134, 147, 149, 150, 171, 182, 191, 206, 230, 231, 232, 297*n*
alleged racism in opponents of, 129–30
anti-ideology stance of, 19, 21, 22–23
health care policies of, 30, 117, 129, 168, 203, 228
"new declaration of independence" speech of, 19–21, 22
pragmatism of, 22, 52–53, 69
religion and, 81–82, 83
Supreme Court nominations and, 164–65
"unity" as campaign theme of, 274–75
Obama, Michelle, 125
ObamaCare, 30, 117, 129, 168, 203
Occupy Wall Street, 124–25
Of the Liberty of the Press (Hume), 114
Ohio, 193–94
"On the Pulse of Morning" (Angelou), 190
Oration on the Dignity of Man (Pico), 9
Origins of Species, The (Darwin), 104, 289*n*
Orwell, George, 1, 127, 181, 183, 184, 187–88
Ottoman Empire, 238, 239
Oxford English Dictionary, 102, 137

pacifism, 183, 185, 210
Pakistan, 263
Palestinians, 189, 262
Partisan Review, 183
Patriot Act, 121, 168
patriotism, 125–30, 276
 dissent as "highest form" of, 122–23, 124, 126
 liberal indignation over questioning of, 125–26, 130
Peace of Augsburg, 78
Peace of Westphalia, 78
Peirce, Charles S., 44, 47–48
Peloponnesian War, 262–63
Pelosi, Nancy, 129, 147, 203
Perry, Mark, 174–75
Philosophy of History, The (Hegel), 152
Pinker, Steven, 182, 302*n*–3*n*
pluralism, 78–79, 92, 236, 237, 238
Polanski, Roman, 178–79
"Political Conservatism as Motivated Social Cognition" (Jost et al.), 204–5, 214–15, 218
Politico, 19, 126
Politics as a Vocation (Weber), 181
Poor Richard's Almanack (Franklin), 299*n*
Popular Science, 162
Port Huron Statement, 194
"positive liberty" doctrines, 116, 203
poverty rates, 70
"power corrupts," 84–88, 178
pragmatism, 14, 23, 39, 44–45, 50, 56–58, 92, 162, 212
 demonization of ideologies by, 24–25, 35
 dissolving of dogmas in, 46, 48, 53, 56, 58, 69
 empirical reasoning of, *see* empiricism
 historical precedent disregarded in, 47, 53–54, 66, 69
 and modern liberalism, 22, 23, 24–25, 48, 50–53, 56–58, 69
 Nietzschean, 46–47, 48, 49
 see also American Pragmatism
Prejudices: A Philosophical Dictionary (Nisbet), 11
prevention principle, 228–33
 in health care policies, 228, 229–31, 299*n*–300*n*
Princess and the Frog, The, 260
Princeton Regional Health Commission, 118
Progressive Democracy, 292*n*
progressives, progressivism, 30, 36, 45, 103, 104, 115, 116, 132, 143, 150, 192, 201, 203, 211, 212, 231, 236, 271
 contemporary liberalism as descendant of, 57–58, 103
 Dewey's philosophical impact on, 54–56, 69, 160, 203
 "diversity" as viewed by, 91, 95, 99
 economic ideas of, 16, 30, 53–54, 57, 105–7
 evolution's influence on philosophy of, 112–13, 161–62
 as fundamentally Christian movement, 82–83
 German academic background of, 49
 governmental expansion endorsed by, 13, 14–17, 26, 30–31, 50–51, 152, 163, 165–66, 230–33
 historical precedent dismissed by, 12–14, 47, 69, 162–63, 166, 167–68
 "living constitution" concept of, 13, 14, 161, 162–70
 McCarthyite tactics employed by, 128
 Middle America denigrated by, 193–94
 "moral equivalent of war" and, 48, 49–52
 in New Deal era, 16, 50–51, 53, 54, 58, 128, 140–42, 201
 pragmatism's influence on, 24–25, 47, 48, 49–58, 69, 116
 rebuilding of Lady Justice proposed by, 160–61, 168
 Social Darwinism as basic to, 105–7, 112–13
 State-centric philosophy of, 151–52
 war socialism endorsed by, 50–51, 232
 in Wilson era, 16, 49–50, 58, 82, 120, 128, 162–63, 167, 193–94
 see also liberals, liberalism
proletariat, 195, 197–98, 211–12
Promise of American Life, The (Croly), 57, 82
Protestantism, 10, 78, 237, 238
Protestant Reformation, 32, 77, 85, 235, 236–38, 239, 246, 247, 300*n*
Prussia, 43, 49
Psychological Bulletin, 205, 214–15
Psychology Today, 216, 288*n*
public-works projects, 149–51

racial quotas, 96–98
racism, 98, 100, 125, 137, 185, 205
 Obama's opponents and, 129–30
 in Progressive economics, 105–7
 Social Darwinism and, 103, 105–7
"Rationalism in Politics" (Oakeshott), 35–37
Rauschenbusch, Walter, 49, 82, 83
Reading Obama (Kloppenberg), 52–53
Reagan, Ronald, 4, 22, 23, 101, 202, 204, 209, 214, 223, 227
Real Majority, The (Scammon and Wattenberg), 199
"Recent Developments in the Study of the

Great European Witch Hunt" (Gibbons), 247
Record, The (Bergen County), 118
Red Scare, 243
Reed, John, 212, 253–54
Reformation, 32, 77, 85, 235, 236–38, 239, 246, 247, 300*n*
Reform Darwinism, 107
Reich, Robert, 100, 108–9, 111
religion, 44, 48, 76, 215, 234, 252
  American pluralism and, 78–79
  businessmen influenced by, 111–12
  criticisms and hatred of, 252, 253, 254, 259, 301*n*–2*n*
  dogmas of, *see* dogma
  in guiding of politics, 79–82
  Obama and, 81–82, 83
  spirituality vs., 256–60
  theology of the State and, 152
  wars fought over, 77–78, 237–38, 240–42
  see also separation of church and state; *specific religions*
religious schools, 119
Rendezvous with Destiny (Goldman), 53
rent control laws, 174
Republican National Committee, 169
Republicans, 6, 13, 22, 34, 50, 59, 64–65, 72, 84, 89, 92, 120, 127, 128, 129, 171, 172, 176, 200, 207, 215, 217, 227, 264
  see also conservatives, conservatism
"Republicans Against Science" (Krugman), 204
Rerum Novarum (Pope Leo XIII), 139, 140
Reuters, 5
Revolution from Within (Steinem), 244
Right Is Wrong (Huffington), 62
"robber barons," 107–9, 110–12, 171, 176
Robber Barons, The (Josephson), 109
Robespierre, Maximilien, 40, 41, 42
Rockefeller, John D., Jr., 111
Rockefeller, John D., Sr., 108, 111
Roman Empire, 77, 145–46, 150, 154, 236, 254, 255
Roman mythology, 159, 160
Roosevelt, Franklin D., 22, 23, 55, 120, 131, 172, 202, 203
  New Deal of, 50–51, 128, 140–41, 272
  opponents persecuted by, 128–29
  Supreme Court and, 162, 272
Roosevelt, Theodore, 105, 128, 152, 193, 275
Ross, E. A., 105–6
Rousseau, Jean-Jacques, 33, 138, 172, 252, 304*n*
"ruling classes," 45–46, 196, 198
Russell, Louise B., 229, 230, 299*n*–300*n*
Russia, 124, 211, 212
Russian Revolution, 67, 212, 253–54
Ryan, John, 139–40, 141

Saletan, William, 210, 218
Salon, 245, 259
same-sex marriage, 119, 134, 201, 271
Say, Jean-Baptiste, 40, 41
Scheer, Robert, 90–91
science, 34, 207–19
  camouflaging ideologies with, 72–74, 205, 207, 211–12, 215, 219
  Church seen as hindrance to, 8–11, 254
  conservatives viewed as foes of, 204, 205–7
  dogma vs., 70–75
  history as, 85, 86
  of human brain development, 220–21
  Marxist gospel of, 46, 211–12
  pro-liberal bias in, 210, 215–18
  "scientism" vs., 211
Senate, U.S., 168, 169
separation of church and state, 76–83, 260
  in colonial America, 78–79
  religious bias of politicians and, 79–82
  roots of, 77–79
September 11, 2001, terrorist attacks, 52, 132, 235, 276
  commemoration controversies and, 76, 91–92
Service Employees International Union (SEIU), 133
60 Minutes, 22, 23, 223
Slate, 167, 210
slavery, 71, 105, 114, 119, 150, 166, 168, 185, 198, 270
  abolition of, 180–81, 185
slippery slope arguments (SSAs), 4, 115–21
  "boiling frog" parable and, 118–19
  civil liberties and, 116, 119–21
  examples in validation of, 117–18
  political circuit breakers and, 120–21
  weaknesses of, 117, 118, 119
Smith, Adam, 40, 41, 142, 202, 203
Smith, Al, 268, 269
Smith, Shawn, 217–18
Smithsonian, 133
Social Animal, The (Brooks), 8
Social Aspects of Christianity (Ely), 82, 287*n*
Social Catholicism, 139
Social Darwinism, 100–113
  conservatism unfairly linked to, 100, 101, 102, 108–9, 112
  eugenic connotations of, 101, 103, 105–7, 113

liberal villification of, 101, 103, 105, 107, 109, 112, 113
in progressive economic thought, 105–7
"robber barons" and, 107–9, 110–12
Spencer as "founder" of, 101–2, 103–4, 105
"survival of the fittest" and, 103–5, 108, 112
Social Darwinism in American Thought, 1860–1915 (Hofstadter), 107–8, 110
socialism, 11, 21, 24, 40, 47, 49, 53, 67, 104, 106, 109, 139, 177, 212, 224, 252, 276
"Christian," 82–83
Dewey's philosophy and, 54–56
Marxist, 195–98, 211–12
rebranding of, 63–64
war, 50–51
Socialist Party, 55, 63
social justice, 69–70, 81, 131–46, 160–61, 292*n*
"disposition standards" of, 136–37
as euphemism for "goodness," 132, 134, 143, 144–45
evolving meaning of, 137–42
in Green Party platform, 135–36, 137
as ideological concept, 143–44
ill-defined sentiment of, 132, 133–36, 137, 144, 145–46
in mission statements, 132–34
as "redistribution of wealth," 137, 138, 141–42, 144
Social Psychology Quarterly, 204
Social Security, 25, 215, 229
Social Statics, or The Conditions essential to Happiness specified, and the First of them Developed (Spencer), 102
Socrates, 96, 210, 220
South Carolina, University of, 137
Soviet Union, 14, 16, 55, 151, 183, 215
Sowell, Thomas, 89, 185
Spanish Inquisition, 248–52, 253, 301*n*
Spencer, Herbert, 101–2, 103–4, 105, 106, 107, 108, 111
spirituality, religion vs., 256–60
Stalin, Joseph, 64, 84, 124, 150, 212, 214, 215, 276
Stanford University, 27, 217
Starry Messenger (Galileo), 11
Star Wars, 40, 134–35
State, 17, 67, 143, 292*n*
"competitiveness" argument for interference by, 14–16
government vs., 151–52
"living constitution" and, 13, 163, 165–66
regulation of violence by, 181, 182–83
social ecosystems within, 138
see also government
Staying on Top (Phillips), 16
Stearns, Harold, 193, 194
Steffens, Lincoln, 14–15
Steinem, Gloria, 244, 246
stem cell research, 205, 206
sterilization, 107, 165–66, 218
Streisand, Barbra, 89–91, 92, 98–99, 176
Students for a Democratic Society, 194
Sullivan, Andrew, 34–36, 37, 65
Summers, Lawrence, 51, 206
Sumner, William Graham, 102, 103
Suprema Congregatio Sanctæ Romanæ et Univeralis Inquisitionis, 247, 302*n*
Supreme Court, U.S., 148, 160, 162, 226, 272
Buck v. Bell decision of, 107, 165–66
"living constitution" and, 162, 163, 164–66
nominations to, 164–65
"survival of the fittest," 103–5, 108, 112
Switzerland, 237, 301*n*

"Taboo of Virginity, The" (Freud), 264
Taliban, 238, 239, 264
Tallentyre, S. G., 2–3
Taparelli d'Azeglio, Luigi, 137–38, 139, 291*n*–92*n*
Tea Party, 129
Ten Days That Shook the World (Reed), 212
"ten guilty men" principle, 3, 153–58, 294*n*
terrorists, 52, 76, 121, 168, 184, 189, 232, 238, 239, 242, 243
freedom fighters vs., 4–6
Theodosius, Emperor of Rome, 77
Theory of Moral Sentiments, The (Smith), 202
Thomas Aquinas, 9, 74
Thompson, John B., 43
Thoughts on the Cause of the Present Discontents (Burke), 121
Thucydides, 262–63
Tibetan Book of the Great Liberation, The (Jung), 19
Tocqueville, Alexis de, 93, 232, 233, 288*n*
Toleration Act (England), 78
trade, peace sustained by, 183, 266–67
"tradition of existence," 235, 239
Travolta, John, 175–76
Treatise on Judicial Evidence, A (Bentham), 156–57
Treatise on Political Economy (Tracy), 41
True and Only Heaven, The (Lasch), 193*n*
"Two Genes Predict Voter Turnout" (Fowler and Dawes), 207–8

"uncanny valley" phenomenon, 264
understanding, as bringing peace myth, 261–67

"narcissism of minor differences" as rebuttal to, 263–65
unemployment, 140, 142, 201
unions, 133, 177, 191, 202
United Nations, 144–45, 184, 270
United States:
class system in, 197–99
current health-care system in, 26–30
political circuit breakers of, 120–21
post-Civil War prosperity in, 109–10
system of government in, 271–72
see also colonial America; government
unity, appeals to, 274–77
Use of Force in International Affairs, The, 123

Victorian Studies, 101
violence, 180–89, 261, 262, 294*n*
of early humans, 252–53, 303*n*
enforcement of law with, 181–83
Gandhi's opposition to, 180, 185, 187–89
and "might makes right" debate, 184–85
as "never solving anything," 4, 180–85, 187–89
pacifism vs., in war efforts, 183–84
as sometimes necessary, 180–81, 182, 183, 185, 188
Voegeli, William, 58, 200–201
Voegelin, Eric, 33, 75
Volokh, Eugene, 117–18, 153–54, 294*n*
Voltaire, 2–3, 253
voting rights, 168, 222, 226, 270, 272–73

War Against the Weak (Black), 101
War on Poverty, 51, 70
war socialism, 50–51, 232
Washington, D.C., 61, 174
Washington Post, 61, 226, 230
Weber, Max, 181, 198
welfare state, 24, 82, 107, 135, 169, 191, 200, 201
Western Civilizations: Their History and Their Culture (Lerner et al.), 242
What's Wrong with the World (Chesterton), 66
Wheaton College, 240
Who's Who in America, 111
Why Is There No Socialism in the United States? (Sombart), 198
"Why Liberals and Atheists Are More Intelligent" (Kanazawa), 204
Wikipedia, 8–9
Will, George, 1, 164
Wilson, Woodrow, 16, 49, 51, 58, 82, 120, 128, 152, 161, 167, 193, 272
"Leaders of Men" essay of, 273–74
on "living constitution," 162–63
war socialism of, 50, 232
witch hunts, 157, 243–47, 252, 301*n*
Without Feathers (Allen), 147
women, 95, 133, 166, 205, 206, 264
forced sterilization of, 107, 165–66
gender quotas and, 96–98
witch hunts and, 244–45, 246, 301*n*
women's rights, 135, 168, 273
see also feminism
Words That Changed a Nation (Obama), 297*n*
working classes, 46, 195, 197–98
World Day of Social Justice, 144
World Health Organization (WHO), 26–27, 28
World War I, 50
World War II, 51, 52, 124
Japanese-American internment in, 120
"Worst Study Ever?, The" (Atlas), 26–27
Worst Years of Our Lives, The (Ehrenreich), 122
Wylie, Irwin, 110, 111, 112

Yale University, 8, 27, 49, 57, 102, 133–34
Young Americans Foundation, 225
youth, 220–27
as "inherently" liberal, 225–27
political fetishization of, 224, 225, 226–27
voting rights of, 222, 226

Zwinglians, 78, 237, 238